MAN AND SOCIETY

A NEW EDITION

VOLUME ONE

John Plamenatz

MAN AND SOCIETY

POLITICAL AND SOCIAL THEORIES FROM MACHIAVELLI TO MARX

VOLUME ONE

From the Middle Ages to Locke

A New Edition
Revised by M. E. Plamenatz and Robert Wokler

Longman
London and New York

Longman Group UK Limited,
Longman House, Burnt Mill, Harlow,
Essex CM20 2JE, England
and *Associated Companies throughout the world.*

Published in the United States of America
by Longman Publishing Group, New York

First published 1963
Second edition 1992

British Library Cataloguing in Publication Data
Plamenatz, John
  Man and society: political and social theories
  from Machiavelli to Marx: Vol 1. From the Middle
  Ages to Locke. – New ed.
  I. Title II. Plamenatz, M. E.   III. Wokler, Robert
  320.509

  ISBN 0–582–05540–7

Library of Congress Cataloging in Publication Data
Plamenatz, John Petrov.
  Man and society: political and social theories from Machiavelli
  to Marx/John Plamenatz. — A new ed./revised by M. E. Plamenatz
  and Robert Wokler.
    p.   cm.
    Includes indexes.
    Contents: v. 1. From the Middle Ages to Locke — v. 2. From
  Montesquieu to the early socialists — v. 3. Hegel, Marx and Engels,
  and the idea of progress.
    ISBN 0–582–05540–7(v. 1): — ISBN 0–582–05546–6 (v. 2):
  — ISBN 0–582–05541–5 (v. 3):
    1. Political science—History.   2. Social sciences—History.
  I.   Plamenatz, M. E.   II. Wokler Robert   III. Title.
  JA83.P53   1991
  306.2'09—dc20
                                                                    91-19404
                                                                        CIP

Set by 5 in 10/12pt Bembo Roman.
Printed in Malaysia by VP

To My Father

Contents

Contents

Editors' Preface

John Plamenatz first conceived this work in the 1950s, as a set of twenty-eight lectures which he gave at Oxford and then at other universities. Substantially revised and extended over a number of years, these lectures were then recast once again, for publication in two volumes, in 1963. Subject only to occasional minor alteration, *Man and Society* has remained in print, in that form, ever since.

In his original preface Plamenatz observed that his text was 'not a history of political thought', but rather, as his subtitle made clear, a critical examination of some important social and political theories from Machiavelli to Marx. His interpretation of the ideas and assumptions of past thinkers was mainly designed to elucidate significant treatments of central problems in political and social thought which are still pertinent today. It was intended not only as a commentary on the doctrines of important thinkers but equally as a contribution to political theory by way of commentary – that is, through an assessment of the profound insights and fundamental errors of influential thinkers of the past whose ideas have continued to inform the beliefs of persons who reflect upon the nature of society and government. That critical approach was and remains the chief focus of *Man and Society*. In examining the views of others, Plamenatz sought to show why they still matter to us, why propositions put forward at times very different from our own may be judged in the light of their universal application, as their authors themselves so frequently imagined, and often postulated, was the case. Plamenatz believed that while the idiom of discourse of political and social thinkers is always particular and unique, the substance of their arguments, and the truth or falsity of their contentions, do not depend on the local and specific circumstances which give rise to them. Great political thinkers are themselves characteristically critical and innovative. In flouting the political assumptions or linguistic conventions of their age, they aspire to free themselves and their readers from dead dogma. They develop or cross-examine the ideas of pre-eminent thinkers of previous ages and thereby add to or break from traditions of discourse not circumscribed by the lifetime of any single figure. That wider context – indeed the whole of the discipline of political and social theory – is the main subject of Plamenatz's work, to which his critical interpretation of other doctrines itself forms a major contribution.

It would, however, be misleading to read his commentary only in that light. Plamenatz wished to show, to historians, that the meaning of theories was not determined solely by the circumstances that occasioned their production, and, to political scientists, that old theories are often deeper, richer and more lucid than new theories which ignore them. But crucial to both endeavours was the need for accuracy in the interpretation of past thinkers, for familiarity with the varieties of language they employed, for a proper grasp of the meaning they intended to convey through their writings, in so far as it remains accessible. In distinguishing a critical examination of past doctrines from an historical investigation of their origins, Plamenatz was anxious to ensure that he conveyed their sense, as well as their significance, correctly. He was convinced that anachronistic interpretations of ideas were no less discreditable to the political theorist than to the historian, and he went to great lengths to ensure the contextual reliability of his readings. His views on Marx came to be progressively refined by the historical research of other scholars, particularly that which was devoted to Marx's earlier writings, in the years prior to the publication of *Man and Society;* his interpretation of Hobbes, by contrast, was strengthened and reaffirmed in reply to recent scholarship which he regarded as more ingenious than plausible; the best-informed contextual readings of Locke prompted significant revisions of his lecture notes on the subject, especially with regard to the dating of the *Two Treatises of Government* and Locke's connection with the Glorious Revolution.

Over the past twenty-six years or so, readers of *Man and Society* may not have been sufficiently aware of the importance Plamenatz attached to the contextual interpretation of political doctrines, particularly with regard to relatively minor writers who helped more to shape than to transform the conventions and discourse of their age. In his lectures Plamenatz recognized, and indeed emphasized, the historical significance of thinkers who were not so much innovatory as re-presentative, who articulated the widely shared assumptions of their contemporaries but did not seek to undermine them, or whose contributions to political disputations were more polemical than philosophical, more apposite and influential within a particular context, because less abstract. For no other reason than that of sheer lack of space in a work already too long for a two-volume format, Plamenatz was obliged to compress his material, truncating certain chapters and deleting others. Because doctrines most circumscribed by local and contingent interests have less bearing on the aspirations of other thinkers in different cultures, he elected, when required to be more brief, to remove sections which were of more restricted, more exclusively historical, concern. This foreshortening of particular topics, including even the excision of whole periods of debate and controversy, somewhat reduced the breadth and scope of the original lectures. In restoring mainly that material – devoted above all to doctrinal disputes and to the cut and thrust of battles fought in pursuit of power as well as the truth – we have, now in three volumes, sought to rectify this abridgement. More than was possible in the two-volume edition of *Man and Society,* we have followed Plamenatz's initial scheme in joining the peaks of political argument, as he perceived them, not only to each other, but also to the foothills from which they separately rise.

To the original introduction of 1963 we have added a number of lines drawn from his preface to the lectures, which address what Plamenatz took to be the contribution to political theory of minor authors and their polemical writings. We have assembled two lectures on ancient and mediaeval thought, together with fragments of some earlier drafts, to form the new opening chapter in volume I of this edition, including some of the most historically discursive additional material, under the title, 'The Political Thought of the Middle Ages'. Chapter three of volume I, here entitled 'The Reformation and Liberty of Conscience', has been expanded in length by about one-third, embracing fuller discussions of the mediaeval church, the doctrines of Luther and Calvin, and the ideas of their disciples and critics, especially Knox and Castellion. Chapter six of volume I, now bearing the title 'Divine Right, Absolute Monarchy and Early Theories of the Social Contract', has been enlarged by a similar amount, incorporating material from one lecture which Plamenatz offered on contract theory before Hobbes and Locke. In this chapter will be found extended commentaries on Hotman, Mornay, Mariana and Suárez, previously eliminated; the sections on Hotman and Mornay, in particular, initially presented in the form of two much compressed footnotes uncharacteristic of Plamenatz's style, are hereby restored to their originally intended place in this work, more conspicuously, perhaps, than any of our other revisions; we have, moreover, followed the practice of most recent scholarship in attributing the *Vindiciae contra tyrannos* to Mornay rather than Languet. Volume I, chapter seven, entitled 'English Political Theory from the Breach with Rome to the Restoration', comprises material entirely unpublished before, distilled from two lectures in different formats devoted to Elizabethan and Jacobean political thought and to the English Civil War, to which we have appended another lecture on Harrington. In volume II, chapter five, we have incorporated sections from two lectures on Bentham and Philosophical Radicalism and a third on John Stuart Mill, clearly a centrally important figure in modern political thought, whose ideas had already engaged the attention of Plamenatz in his study of *The English Utilitarians,* but who, again on account of lack of space, received only passing mention before in *Man and Society*. In volume II, moreover, we have divided what was originally the longest chapter, on 'The Early Socialists, French and English', into two, now chapters six and seven, adding to each a few pages, where appropriate, drawn from a lecture devoted to the ideas of Saint-Simon. Volume III, embracing the last five chapters of what was volume II, remains largely unaltered, although we have made a number of slight changes to accord with our corrections to the other volumes and have amended the titles of three chapters.

In each case we have tried to shape the new material in a style and order closely approximating the initial format of the published work. Although the lecture variants of several other chapters contain substantial additional and striking differences as well, we have decided not to include any extracts which would have required major alteration to the text of the already printed volumes. In many instances, however, we have changed a term or phrase of the original version, sometimes to accommodate the intercalations, occasionally for the sake of fluency or coherence. We have corrected several passages in the light of evidence of which Plamenatz himself could not have been aware. We have also corrected or identified quotations – in a few cases thanks to the assistance of Dr Terrell Carver, Mr Alistair Edwards or Mr Michael Evans – whose previous citation was inaccurate or incomplete. Since particular themes are raised in the more historically contextual chapters that have great bearing upon the argument of the work as a whole, we have not attempted to reassemble those chapters so that they might incorporate the findings of recent scholarship or the most up-to-date interpretations of old issues and debates. In revising a text originally prepared several decades ago, we felt no duty to speculate on what

Plamenatz might choose to say if he were able to embark upon it now. It is therefore unavoidable that at least some of the material which is published here for the first time must reveal its age. For each chapter, we have, accordingly, appended a list of the most salient contemporary writings on the subject.

We have thus tried to remain faithful both to the published tomes and to the work originally projected, which was of markedly broader conception and more historical in focus. No opportunity arose before his death in 1975 for Plamenatz to make these revisions himself. In attempting to enhance and lend fresh impetus to the most durable and popular of all his writings, our aim has been, not so much to append additional material to an established text, as to impart new breath into old bones and therefore restore the full vigour and vision of *Man and Society*'s original design. We are grateful to Dr Chris Harrison and Mrs Joy Cash of Longmans for all their encouragement and patience; to the British Academy for enabling us, intermittently over a number of years, to meet and sort out the papers we required from a substantial corpus of other unpublished texts; to Dr Janet Coleman and Dr Mark Goldie for their invaluable comments on the new and revised chapters, for which, however, they bear no responsibility and with whose conclusions they do not always concur; and to Mrs Jean Ashton and to Miss Karen Hall for typing them and for their forbearance, in deciphering densely written passages, on demand.

April 1990

Preface

This book is not a history of political thought; it is, as its title implies, a critical examination of a number of important theories. It is not concerned to argue for some interpretations of these theories against others but to examine assumptions, ideas and attitudes.

The book is an expansion of lectures given at various times at three universities, Columbia, Harvard and Oxford. It is hoped that it will prove useful to students of social and political theory whose interest in the subject is more philosophical than historical; and the author has had in mind students in the United States as much as in Britain. He has aimed at lucidity but is aware that some parts of the book make difficult reading.

The most difficult part of all, which treats of Hegel, has been read by Professor H. L. A. Hart and Sir Isaiah Berlin, by Professor Herbert Deane of Columbia University, and by Mr William Weinstein and Mr John Torrance of Nuffield College, and the author is grateful to them for valuable comments and criticisms. He thanks Mr Alan Ryan of Balliol College for making the index. He also thanks his wife for reading the book in manuscript and suggesting improvements of grammar and style.

July 1961

J. P.

Introduction

The artist ploughs his own furrow; the scholar, even in the privacy of his study, cultivates a common field. He is responsible to others for what he does; he feels the need to explain his purpose, to justify his efforts.

There are many things well worth doing not attempted in this book. It is not, for the most part, a history of social and political thought; it does not enquire how one thinker influenced another, and compares them only to make clearer what they said. It scarcely looks at the circumstances in which this or that theory was produced. And it quite neglects several important thinkers. Althusius will get into the index only because he is mentioned on this page, and so too will Vico, who has been greatly and rightly admired. Grotius and Kant are mentioned only in passing. If my purpose had been to produce a history, however brief, of political thought from Machiavelli to Marx, this neglect or scanty treatment would have been without excuse.

Every thinker, even the most abstract, is deeply influenced by the circumstances of his day. To understand why Machiavelli or Hobbes or Rousseau wrote as he did, we must know something of social and political conditions in their day and country and of the controversies then to the fore. But this does not, I hope, mean that whoever discusses their theories must also discuss these conditions and controversies. Is there to be no division of labour? Those conditions and controversies have often been described, and the writer who is primarily concerned with arguments and ideas need not discuss them except to make something clear which might otherwise be misunderstood. He must use his judgement: at times he may need to make a considerable digression, and at other times a passing reference or mere hint will be enough.

Those who say that to understand a theory we must understand the conditions in which it was produced sometimes put their case too strongly. They speak as if, to understand what a man is saying, we must know why he is saying it. But this is not true. We need understand only the sense in which he is using words. To understand Hobbes, we need not know what his purpose was in writing *Leviathan* or how he felt about the rival claims of Royalists and Parliamentarians; but we do need to know what he understood by such words as *law, right, liberty, covenant* and *obligation.* And though it is true that even Hobbes, so 'rare' at definitions, does not always use a word in the sense which he defines, we are more likely to get the sense in which he does use it by a close study of his argument than by looking at the condition of England or at political controversies in his day. These are, of course, well worth looking at on their own account. Nevertheless, we can go a long way in understanding Hobbes's argument and yet know very little about them.

No doubt, Hobbes is a special case. We can get more of his meaning by merely reading what he wrote than we can, say, of Machiavelli's or Montesquieu's or Burke's. It is a matter of degree. But, even in their case, we learn more about their arguments by weighing them over and over again than by extending our knowledge of the circumstances in which they wrote. Hobbes was not less a child of his times than they were. If we want to know why he wrote as he did, or why an argument such as his was produced and found exciting, we have to look at what was happening when he wrote; he was no more independent of his age than was Machiavelli or Burke. Of every really great thinker we can say that, compared with lesser men, he is idiosyncratic; he is, for a time, more liable than they are to be misunderstood because he has more to say that is unfamiliar. He uses the common language but uses it differently. But this is not more true of Hobbes than of Machiavelli. Hobbes belongs as completely to his period as Machiavelli does to his; and if, in order to understand him, we need take less notice of the circumstances in which he wrote, this is because his style and method are different. To understand the argument of *Leviathan* is one thing; to understand the age in which alone it could have been written is another. I do not deny that the second understanding may contribute to the first; I merely doubt whether the contribution is anything like as great as it is sometimes made out to be. Of course, it is of absorbing interest to see a great thinker in the setting of his age. How society and politics are related to political and social theory is as well worth studying as theory itself. Who would deny it? But that is another matter.

Students of society and government make use of ideas and assumptions inherited from the past. In this book I have not been concerned to trace the origins and evolution of these ideas, but rather to examine them critically by considering some of the most familiar and most famous theories which contain them. I have chosen these theories, rather than others, precisely because they are familiar, and because, between them, they contain most of the important ideas and assumptions still used or made, whether by students of society and politics or by persons engaged in political controversies. All these theories, in one way or another, are inadequate; they fail to explain satisfactorily what they set out to explain. They are also – though this is less important – 'out-of-fashion': by which, I am sorry to say, I mean no more than this, that sociologists and political scientists in many places (though not in all) now believe that they have less to learn from them than from one another.

These ideas and assumptions ought to be examined critically; and where can they be so examined to better advantage than in the context of well-known, long discussed and, in some cases, still influential theories? It is sometimes objected that the questions raised by, say, Hobbes or Locke are no longer relevant. But if we discuss social and political matters, we must still speak, as they did, of *law*, of *rights*, of *obligation* and of *consent*. By seeing how they used these words and what arguments they constructed, we learn to use them ourselves. By seeing where their explanations are inadequate, we learn something about what they sought to explain. To treat *right* as absence of obligation (which is what Hobbes did) may do for some purposes, but not for others. By examining critically the argument of *Leviathan* and *De cive,* we learn why this is so. It may be true, as Locke said, that the authority of governments rests in some sense on the consent of the governed; but perhaps it cannot do so unless consent is understood in a sense different from his. By seeing where his argument goes wrong, we are better able to construct another to take its place. If we do not get from Hobbes or Locke answers to the questions we now put, we do, by examining their theories, learn to put our own questions more clearly. And I take Hobbes and Locke for examples deliberately because they are among the most abstract of political theorists. Machiavelli, Bodin, Montesquieu, Hume, Burke, Hegel and Marx all take larger account than they do of history and of the machinery of government.

It is, of course, not only the great thinkers who produce the thought of their age; indeed, they are not even the largest contributors to it. No doubt, they are often the most original, but they are not so always, for they are sometimes only more lively and more vigorous than the rest. The others, the lesser thinkers, enormously outnumber them; and though, as individuals, they may give much less, what they give collectively is much more. What any thinker, however remarkable, has to give is incomparably less than what he takes from others; and the greater part of what he takes does not come from other great thinkers, but from many relatively minor figures, of which most are soon forgotten by posterity. Even in the period of their predominance, the great works do not cover all that is worth noticing. There are important shifts of opinion and outlook not mediated by genius; there are new ideas that find currency and endure, though no Hobbes or Hume has given them a memorable place in his theory.

Much of the political thought of the sixteenth century is to be found in treatises and pamphlets of real interest only to specialists; and yet that thought, taken as a whole, is historically of immense importance. The religious minorities, by pressing their claims against their governments, were not fighting for liberty of conscience but to secure privileges for themselves. Yet, as a result of their struggle, liberty of conscience – perhaps the most precious of all liberties – was eventually established. These minorities made it impossible for the governments of Europe to achieve domestic peace except by conceding religious liberty; and when this concession was eventually made, the greatest moral revolution in modern history was completed. In attempting to follow that revolution in thought and feeling, we must consider such writers not individually but in schools, examining the types of arguments they use and the general conclusions they reach. Our approach in addressing their doctrines must therefore be more historical than may be the case with regard to the pre-eminent thinkers.

The great advantage of these old theories is that they are both rich in content and familiar. If our purpose is to examine ideas used to explain society and government, these theories provide them abundantly, vigorously and attractively. They are a fertile field for the exercise we have in mind. Everyone agrees that students of society and government need to look carefully at the assumptions they make and the ideas they use; that – owing to the nature of their subject – they are especially liable to be the dupes of words. Yet there are now many who question the use of a close study of theories produced long ago in circumstances widely different from our own. It is therefore a point worth making, that such ideas are nowhere better or more economically studied than in these old theories. Nowhere *better* because of the richness and variety they present, and nowhere *more economically* because they have been sifted again and again, so that we can get down quickly to essentials.

The predominant figures in the history of political thought are not great for nothing, or just by chance. They are more original, more profound, than the forgotten or almost forgotten men, who are remembered only by scholars. Their theories are often better constructed; there is usually a greater weight of thought and feeling in their works, and they make a deeper and more lasting impression. Though most of what they offer their readers is taken from others, their powers of selection are unusually fine; they have perception and imagination and an eye for the important, and so their ideas, original to a much smaller extent than appears to the reader who knows little or nothing of their contemporaries, do none the less contain a large part of what is best worth preserving in their age. Most of their contributions to political thought, moreover, are far from dead; they are either still with us – though sometimes in forms we do not immediately recognize – or they are revived among us from time to time when occasion serves. The world is full, not only of Marxists and democrats, but of people who, though they mostly do not know it, are still using the ideas and arguments of Hobbes, or Machiavelli, or Montesquieu, or Hegel or Burke. These thinkers may have originated only a small part of our stock of ideas about human nature and politics, but they gave it the appearance still familiar to us. They mixed only a fraction of the ore, but they refined much of it, put their stamp on it, made it profitable and good currency for our use.

In some circles where the study of these theories is depreciated, there is nevertheless a keen interest taken in the ideas and assumptions used or made by the sociologist or the political scientist. There are sociologists and political scientists who put themselves to great trouble to define the terms they employ and to state their assumptions. They do not always do it well. They wish to be lucid, precise and realistic; they aim at explaining the facts and are in search of a vocabulary adequate to their purpose. It is impossible not to sympathize with them. Yet, for all their efforts, they are often more obscure, or looser in their arguments, or more incoherent, than the makers of the old theories which they neglect on the ground that they are irrelevant. A close study of these theories might be a good discipline for them. Or the social scientist, though he does not know it, repeats what has been said as well, or better, long ago. Ideas very like his own have been used long before his time, and yet he thinks them new because he has coined new words to express them. It is sad to read a book for which it is claimed that it breaks new ground, and to find it thin and stale.

Not for a moment do I suggest that these old theories provide the social scientist with all that he is looking for. They are not a stock of ideas sufficient for his purposes. They are inadequate for all kinds of reasons, some of which are discussed in this book. I suggest only that the study of them is still amply rewarding, and to no one more so than to the student of society who feels that he lacks the ideas needed to explain what he studies. Of course, he will not find the ideas he wants ready-made in these theories, but he will become more adept in the handling of ideas and a better judge of their uses. He will be more discriminating, more scrupulous, and perhaps also more severe with himself and his contemporaries. Bentham said that his purpose in writing *A Fragment on Government* was to teach the student 'to place more confidence in his own strength, and less in the infallibility of great names: – to help him to emancipate his judgement from the shackles of authority'. An admirable purpose. But today, in some intellectual circles, the authority of great names is less oppressive than is fashion, which is an even worse guide. If we neither neglect great names nor defer to them, but seek, to the best of our ability, to take their measure, we are then better placed to take our own.

It is said that, in the past, it was difficult, if not impossible, to study the facts, social and political, whereas now it is much less difficult. There are vastly greater records than there were, more easily accessible; there are methods now used to get at the facts which could not have been used in earlier periods; it is easier than it was to test hypotheses, and we are more sophisticated in making and testing them. The social sciences may have no spectacular achievements to their credit, but then it is not to be expected that they should. It is admitted that they differ greatly from the natural sciences, that there are difficulties peculiar to them, that their conclusions are less precise and more open to question. Such is their nature that – though they call for no less imagination, no less intelligence, no smaller talents from their devotees than other sciences – they afford lesser opportunities; and we are not to expect from them hypotheses as precise, as impressive, as revolutionary and as widely acclaimed as those of, say, Copernicus or Newton or Darwin or Pasteur. And yet it is claimed for them that they do now deserve to be called *sciences*, because those who practise them are seriously concerned to construct theories to explain the facts, and are self-critical and open-minded. As much as the natural scientists, they are imbued with the scientific spirit, even though their methods are more uncertain and their results looser and less well-established. The social scientist is much more apt than the natural scientist to talk nonsense and to make a fool of himself. This is one of the hazards of his occupation. Yet his occupation is science.

But the occupation of the great social and political theorists of the past was not science. They did not study the facts or did so only at random; they did not construct hypotheses and test them. They deduced their conclusions from axioms *a priori* and from definitions, or they relied on what they chose to consider the common sense of mankind. They were not scientific but speculative. What is more, their aim was often less to explain than to justify or to condemn. That they seldom distinguished between their aims is only one further proof that they were not scientists. And so it is sometimes held that their theories are much more impediments than helps to the social scientist, who need not rate his own achievements high to feel that, as compared with them, he is moving in the right direction, given that the object of the journey is to extend knowledge. Hence the need often felt by the social scientist to turn his back on these old and famous theories.

There is nothing arrogant about this attitude, with which it is easy to sympathize.[1] But there can be no real turning of the back on these old theories, whose ideas and assumptions still permeate our thinking about society and government, whether we know it or not. We are not free of them as the natural scientists are of the essences and entelechies of mediaeval and Aristotelian philosophy. We have still to come to terms with these thinkers of the past, to make up our minds about them, if we are to learn to think more clearly than they did.

These theories, moreover, were by no means entirely speculative, nor was their function always primarily to justify or to condemn. They were also, to a greater or a lesser extent, attempts to explain the facts – to explain what the social scientist aims at explaining. To examine them, as is still sometimes done, merely in order to establish how far they are internally consistent, is not an exercise of much use to the social scientist. Nor does it matter to him just which, among several different interpretations of a well-known doctrine, is the nearest to being correct. The enquiry perhaps most useful to him is an enquiry into the adequacy and relevance of these theories. How far do they provide a satisfactory explanation of what they seek to explain? How far are their assumptions and ideas useful for purposes

---

[1] There is more that is arrogant about the disparagement of the social sciences still common in England than about the claims made for them in the United States.

of explanation? Granted that the theories are in many ways inadequate or irrelevant, just why are they so? This book attempts, among other things, to answer these questions – and never more so than when it treats, sometimes at considerable length, of three among the more recent and still widely influential theories, those of Rousseau, Hegel and Marx.

The expositor and critic is bound to give what he honestly believes to be a fair interpretation of the doctrines he discusses. But, if his purpose is not to offer an interpretation which he believes to be an improvement on others, or to pronounce in favour of one among several current versions, he is not bound to argue the case for his interpretation. Since I have been concerned much more to examine the adequacy and relevance of assumptions, ideas and arguments than to establish that Machiavelli or Hume or Marx meant this rather than that, I have refrained from defending my interpretations, except where it has seemed to me that they might strike the reader as unusual or implausible.

Again, I have not considered every aspect of the most important theories; I have considered only those aspects which raised most sharply the issues I wanted to discuss. I have not considered, for example, what Montesquieu has to say about religion and its social functions, though in fact he has a great deal to say about it and says it in the most interesting way. The points I wished to make about religion, and its place in society, I have tried to make in discussing certain beliefs of Machiavelli and of Marx. It may well be that to someone whose field of study is the sociology of religion, Montesquieu has more to offer than either Machiavelli or Marx. Certainly, he treats of religion more elaborately and with greater subtlety than they do. But it seemed to me that their simpler and perhaps cruder treatment served my purposes better.

These theories are more than attempts to explain society and government, and more also than apologies for or attacks upon the established order. They are philosophies of life; and philosophies of this kind are often dismissed as useless or pernicious on the ground that they claim to be more than they really are.

They flourished, it is said, before the scientific study of man, of society and of government had properly begun; they pretended to a knowledge they did not possess. But now that men are beginning to see how to get this knowledge – how to study themselves and society to good purpose – they can do without these pretentious theories. When these theories are not, in the Marxian sense, *ideologies* (when their function is not to defend or challenge the interests of some class or group), they are merely personal statements. They express what somebody feels about man and man's condition in the world. Taken for what they are they may be interesting, but they must not be taken for more.

Certainly, the makers of these theories had illusions about them, and often claimed a knowledge they did not possess. I have already said in their defence that they took some account of the facts and made some attempt to explain them, and I do not suppose that the persons who call their theories 'ideologies' or 'fantasies' or 'mere personal statements' mean to deny this. I believe that these theorists took larger account of the facts and were more seriously concerned to explain them than their critics imply, but that is not what I now want to argue. Nor do I want to argue that the element of class or group *ideology* in these theories is smaller than Marxists have supposed. I want rather to insist that these theories – even when they are not attempts to explain the facts and do not serve to defend or challenge class or group interests – are more than mere personal statements, and that to call them so is grossly misleading. They do more than express personal preferences, even when those are preferences which many share.

Some of these theories are integral parts of a cosmology, of a sometimes elaborate theory about the universe and man's place in it; others are not. Hegel affirms that reality is an infinite Mind or Spirit seeking self-realization, an activity or process passing from level to level, and which is manifest, at its highest levels, in communities of finite selves – that is to say, in communities of men. His social and political theory is rooted in a philosophy which purports to explain everything; or alternatively (and this alternative is perhaps nearer the truth) his philosophy is an attempt to apply to all things ideas which make sense only when applied to human activities and social institutions. Others, as for example the Utilitarians, are more modest. The Utilitarians, for the most part, do not seek to improve upon or to add to the explanations of the physical and biological world offered by science; with rare exceptions they say nothing about divine or immanent purposes. They confine themselves to explaining man and his social behaviour. They take man as they think he is, as a creature of desires who seeks to satisfy them as abundantly as he can at the least cost to himself. They seek to explain his behaviour and all social institutions on this and a few other assumptions about man and his environment; and in support of their assumptions they appeal above all to what they take to be the common sense of mankind. Yet they, too, are concerned to do much more than explain the facts; they too seek to criticize and to persuade. They too have a philosophy of life which is something more than an explanation (however inadequate) of how men actually live.

All these theories, no matter how 'pretentious' or 'modest' they may be, are elaborate philosophies which contain a large element that is not science or conceptual analysis or ideology in the Marxian sense. They are what I venture to call, for want of a better word, practical philosophies or philosophies of man; they are forms of self-expression of which it is lamentably inadequate to say that they are mere personal statements. They are neither mere exercises in psychology – statements about how men feel and think and behave – nor mere excursions into morals. They involve much more than the laying down of ultimate rules (as, for example, the 'greatest happiness' principle or the principle of 'self-realization') or even the construction of elaborate hierarchies of rules.

There is always a close connection between a philosopher's conception of what man is – what is peculiar to him, how he is placed in the world – and his doctrines about how man should behave – what he should strive for, and how society should be constituted. The connection is there, multiple and close, whether the philosopher is a Rousseau or a Hegel, who does not agree with Hume that there is no deriving an *ought* from an *is*, or whether he is Hume himself. For Hume – though he believes that no rule of conduct follows logically from any description of man and his condition in the world – offers to show how man, being the sort of creature he is, comes to accept certain rules. Man and the human condition are, in some respects, everywhere the same, and therefore there are some rules which are everywhere accepted. They are not the only rules which men accept, and are not always in keeping with the other rules. Indeed, these other rules are sometimes preferred to them. Nevertheless, there are some rules which men everywhere accept, or would accept if they understood themselves and their condition; we have, therefore, only to understand what man is and how he is placed in the world to know what those rules are. This way of thinking is not confined to the natural law philosophers and Idealists; it is common to them and to the Utilitarians, and (as we shall see) there is a large dose of it even in Marxism.

In this book I am as much concerned to discuss these theories as *philosophies of life* as I am to examine critically the assumptions they make and the ideas they use in the attempt to explain the facts. And, here again, I confine myself almost entirely to what my authors have to say, attending hardly at all to the origins of their theories or the circumstances in which they were produced. I have already said enough, I hope, to show that this neglect does not come of a failure to appreciate the importance of what I have not tried to do. I have learnt much from many scholars, but the attempt to tread in all their footsteps would be absurd.

Man, as Machiavelli sees him, is self-assertive. He lives, not to seek God's favour or to serve some larger than human purpose, but to satisfy himself; he seeks security and something more; he seeks to make himself felt. He seeks reputation, to make his mark, to create some image of himself which is impressive to others. The stronger he is, the more he is willing to risk security for reputation. Man is both self-preserving and self-assertive; but Machiavelli sympathizes more with the second than the first of these needs. He values above all the two qualities which enable a man to assert himself: courage and intelligence. These are not just preferences which Machiavelli happens to have; they are rooted in his conception of what it is to be a man. Hobbes also sees man as self-assertive but sees him even more as in search of security in a world of self-seeking men; and he puts a high value on prudence and consistency of purpose. Organized society is a discipline which the prudent accept and to which the imprudent must be forced to submit. Rousseau sees man as the victim of society, as a creature who has lost his integrity. Society derives from his needs, develops his faculties, and yet is oppressive to him. As a rational and moral being, man is at once the creature and the victim of society, and can be cured of the ills it produces in him only in a reformed society. Bentham sees man as a subject of desires who, unlike other animals, can compare and foresee; he sees him as a competitor and collaborator with other men in the procuring of what satisfies desires. The proper function of rules and institutions is to ensure that competition and collaboration are as effective as possible – that they help and do not impede men in their efforts to satisfy their desires. Hegel sees man as a creature who becomes rational and moral in the process of coming to understand and master an environment; he sees him transformed and elevated by his own activities. He sees him as changing from age to age, and the course of this change as 'implicit' in his nature, in his capacity to reason and to will. Marx sees man as a creature whose image of himself and the world is a product of what he does to satisfy his basic needs; and yet he also sees him as a creature who comes in the end to know himself and the world, understanding his condition and accepting it, and who thereby attains freedom.

We have here six very different philosophies, even though there are elements common to several of them. And, though we can say of each of them that it was 'the product of its age' – though we can give reasons for its appearing when and where it did – we cannot say of any one of them that it is obsolete or irrelevant. They are ways of looking at man and society which are of perennial interest; we can find traces of them in philosophies much older than the ones which now seem to us to give fullest expression to them. Man and his social condition do change from age to age, but they also remain the same; and the different philosophies which men have produced reflect, not only how they and their condition have changed, but also the diversity of their reactions to what has not changed. Alfred North Whitehead once said that all later philosophies are footnotes to Plato. This may be extravagant but is not absurd, and is least extravagant when applied to Plato's views about man and society. Plato's theory of knowledge and Aristotle's logic have been superseded in a sense in which their political philosophies have not. That is not because epistemology and logic have made progress since their time as the study of man and society has not; it is because political philosophy has always aimed at something more than explanation. One explanation of what is involved in having knowledge or in reasoning may be an improvement on another. But with philosophy, in the sense in which I am now using the word, it is a different matter.

Today, in the social as in other studies, two kinds of enquiry find favour: the aim of one is to explain the facts, and when its methods are (or are held to be) adequate to its aim, it is called science; the aim of the other is to examine the ideas and methods used in explanation and in other forms of discourse, and when those ideas and methods are of wide application, it is sometimes called analytical philosophy. The theories expounded and criticized in this book, though by no means unscientific and unphilosophical in these two senses, are also more than science and analytical philosophy. Moreover (as I have said already, though in different words), as science and analytical philosophy they are often grossly inadequate. Therefore, since science and this kind of philosophy are in favour, these theories, which are often indifferent specimens of both, are in disfavour. And even when it is conceded that there is a large element in them which is neither the one nor the other, this element is written off as an aberration, due to a failure to understand what is the proper business of science or philosophy.

The suggestion is that these theories aim at extending knowledge but do not know how it is to be extended, or that they confuse other things with the extension of knowledge. They have several purposes but fail to distinguish between them, or have purposes so vague that they are not really purposes at all. They aim at explaining the facts or at elucidating ideas or at defining rights and obligations or at persuasion, and move from one aim to the next without knowing that they have done so. They are uncertain of purpose. The present-day critic, coming upon this confusion and trained to make the distinctions these theories too often fail to make, easily concludes that, if they have some purpose beyond explanation, elucidation, definition or persuasion – beyond the purposes familiar to him (and which he does not quarrel with, provided the man who has them knows what he is doing) – that purpose is illusory, rooted in misunderstanding. By all means let a political writer explain or analyse or persuade, but let him know what he is doing. For, if he does not know what he is doing, he will aim at the impossible, or will delude himself into believing he is contributing to knowledge when he is not, or will unconsciously seek to pass off his peculiar preferences as eternal truths.

I have already conceded that most of the great political and social thinkers of the past failed to make certain distinctions now commonly made, and that they were under illusions about their theories. Yet it is a mistake to conclude that, to the extent that they aimed at more than explanation, analysis or persuasion, their efforts were pointless or useless. Their theories have another function besides these, and a function which is not less important than they are.

Sophisticated man has a need to 'place' himself in the world, to come to terms intellectually and emotionally with himself and his environment, to take his own and the world's measure. This need is not met by science. It is not enough for him to have only the knowledge which the sciences and ordinary experience provide. Or perhaps I should say – to avoid misunderstanding – it is not enough for him to have only knowledge; for I do not wish to suggest that what he needs, and science and ordinary experience cannot provide, is knowledge in the same sense as they supply, merely coming to him from another source. Nor is it enough for him to have this knowledge together with a moral code and a set of preferences. He needs a conception of the world and of man's place in it which is not merely scientific – a conception to which his moral code and preferences are closely related. I have here in mind something more than the assumptions on which science and everyday experience themselves rest, assumptions which cannot be verified because they must first be accepted before it makes sense to speak of verification. This need is not felt by all men; and it is felt by some much more strongly than by others; but it is a persistent need. It is a need which can be met for some only by religion, but which for others can be met in other ways

(unless any system of beliefs which meets it is to be called a religion).
The theories examined in this book are systems of belief of this kind;
or, rather, that is one aspect of them, and a very important aspect of
some of them.

It would be profoundly misleading to speak of this aspect as if it
were no more than a statement of preferences or a laying down of
rules or a defining of goals. If it were only that, it would be possible
to reduce it to a list, which is not in fact the case. A hostile or perverse
critic may say that, as far as he can see, there is nothing more to it than
that and a whole lot of verbiage besides, which to him means nothing.
If he says this, there may be no arguing with him, beyond pointing
out that it is perhaps a kind of verbiage in which he himself indulges
when, momentarily, he forgets his opinions about it. When Rousseau
or Hegel or Marx tells us what is involved in being a man, he is not –
when what he says cannot be verified – either expressing preferences
or laying down rules; he is not putting 'imperatives' in the indicative
mood; he is not prescribing or persuading under the illusion that he
is describing. He is not doing that or else talking nonsense. It might
be said that he is telling his reader how he feels about man and the
human predicament – or, more adequately and more fairly, that he
is expressing some of the feelings that man has about himself and his
condition. But he is not describing those feelings or just giving vent
to them; he is *expressing* them, and the point to notice is that this
expression takes the form of a theory about man and his condition.
It could not take any other form. Thus, if it is an expression of
feeling, the feeling requires systematic and conceptual expression.
Only a self-conscious and rational creature could have such feelings
about itself and its condition; and the theories which express these
feelings, far from being statements of preference or rules of conduct
passed off as if they were something different from what they really
are, serve only to give 'meaning' to these statements and rules. Not
that they are needed to make the statements and rules intelligible,
to make it clear what the preferences are or what is involved in
conforming to the rules; nor yet to justify the preferences or rules
by pointing to their consequences. They give 'meaning' to them, not
by explaining or justifying them, but by expressing an attitude to man
and the human condition to which they are 'appropriate'; so that, even
when we do not share the attitude, we understand how it is that those
who do share it have those preferences and accept those rules. We
do not infer the rules from the attitude, nor do we establish, in the
manner of the scientist, a constant connection between the attitude
and the rules and preferences; our understanding is different in kind

from that of the scientist or the logician. It is neither an understanding of how things happen nor that some things follow from others; and yet it is an intellectual enterprise, a rational experience.

Man, being self-conscious and rational, has theories about himself and his social condition which profoundly affect his behaviour: theories which have not been, are not and never will be merely scientific. They will always be more than explanations of how he behaves and how institutions (which are conventional modes of behaviour) function. And they will always be more than statements of preference or assertions of principle and attempts to justify them; they will be more than 'personal statements' and more than exercises in persuasion. I do not say that there cannot be theories about man and society which are merely scientific, nor yet that any social theory which is more than merely scientific must have this particular more to it; I say only that the need for this more is enduring, and is in no way weakened by the spread of the scientific spirit.

But, it may be asked, granted that this is so, is not the study of these old theories, in so far as they do not attempt to explain the facts or do not examine the ideas used in explanation, of merely historical interest? They may once have been persuasive but are not so today, when the issues which inspired them are dead; and, to the extent that they do not seek to persuade but express what you have called attitudes to man and the human condition, our attitudes are no longer what they were. These theories, in this aspect of them, speak for their contemporaries and not for us; they belong to the past, and the study of them is mere history.

To this there are two answers. Issues and attitudes change less than they seem to, for the language used to express them changes more than they do. These theories are products of their age but are also ageless; their diversity shows not only how epochs and countries differ from one another but also the variety of man's attitudes to himself and his condition. It has been said that all men (or is it all thinking men?) are either Platonists or Aristotelians – which, though not literally true, makes a point worth making. So too, in similar style, we can say that in all ages there are Machiavellians and Marxists and Utilitarians, and even men who, like poor Rousseau, despair of the future of mankind while protesting that man is naturally good.

Secondly, man is an object of thought to himself and would not have the capacities peculiar to his kind unless he were such an object. His being a person, his sense of his own identity, his feeling that he has a place in the world, depend on memory – his own and other men's – for he has rational intercourse with them and belongs to enduring communities. Man is more than just the product of his past; he is the product of memory. The past 'lives on' in him, and he would not be what he is unless it did so. Thus, for him, as for no other creature, to lose his past, to lose his memory, is to lose himself, to lose his identity. History is more than the record of how man became what he is; it is involved in man's present conception of what he is; it is the largest element in his self-knowledge.

Man, being rational and capable of self-knowledge, puts to himself two sorts of questions, and science answers only one of them. The sort of question which science answers he puts both of himself and of what is external to him; but the sort which science does not answer he puts only of himself or of creatures whom he believes to be in his own condition. And these questions which science does not answer are also not answered by analytical philosophy. They are questions which have no final answers; for the answers to them differ from age to age and, perhaps even more, from person to person. These questions which science cannot answer are often put in the same form as the questions which science can answer. We may ask, 'What is man?', meaning 'What sort of creature is man?', and look for answers to the biologist, the psychologist and the social scientist. Or we can put the question which Pascal tried to answer in his *Pensées,* which is a different question altogether, though put in the same words. Pascal believed in God; but the need to put that question does not arise from this belief. An atheist may put it and find an answer which satisfies him, and yet remain an atheist. But the answer, whatever it is, is not a mere set of rules. The question, 'What is man?', as Pascal put it – a question which science cannot answer – is not to be reduced to the question, 'How ought man to behave?'.

Political and social theories of the kind discussed in this book are not the only theories, nor even the most important, which attempt answers to that sort of question; and of course they also put questions of other sorts. But this is an important element in them, and still as much worth studying as any other. The putting and answering of questions of this sort is an activity not less rational and not less difficult than scientific enquiry, and neither more nor less useful. These theories have helped to form sophisticated man's image of himself. No doubt, in primitive and illiterate communities men make do without them; but then they also make do without science. To ask, as some have done, 'What is the use of these theories?', is as pointless as to put the same question of science.

CHAPTER 1
The Political Thought of the Middle Ages

I. ANCIENT GREEK AND ROMAN SOURCES

The political philosophy of the Middle Ages, like everything else belonging to the intellectual life of Europe, was Greek in origin. By the thirteenth century some of its Platonic sources may have been supplanted by principles of an Aristotelian character, but it was, above all, Stoic in inspiration. For two or three centuries before the Christian era, and then, for some seventeen hundred years after Christ's death, most Europeans who had any kind of sophisticated ideas about political society – that is to say, who had any kind of political philosophy – thought of that society as something conventional, wilfully established to satisfy men's earthly needs, rather than to fulfil the sublime essence of their nature. In Platonic and Aristotelian philosophy the State was regarded as natural, not so much in the superficial sense, as not having been made by men deliberately, but, more notably, as the social environment necessary for their complete development, moral and intellectual. Man, for Aristotle, is a political animal because, outside the *polis*, he is not yet fully a man, because only inside it is there thorough scope for his highest faculties. For the Stoics, for the Roman lawyers who tried to define law and its place in society, for the Christian Fathers who sought to explain man's passage through this world as a preparation for a better one, man was not, in the same sense, a political animal. No doubt, Aristotle's dictum was sometimes repeated, since in the later Middle Ages he became *the* philosopher, but it was seldom understood in the way he had meant. In a quite obvious sense – a sense that leaves us still a long way from the profounder conceptions of the Platonic and Aristotelian philosophies – man is a political animal, for he lives under and needs

1

government, while other animals do not. But this fact and that need may be recognized, and yet political society be thought of as merely conventional.

Two important mediaeval political thinkers have often been treated as more Aristotelian than the rest: St Thomas Aquinas in the thirteenth century and Marsilio of Padua in the fourteenth. St Thomas admitted that the State, the Temporal Power, not only maintains security but is also a moral agency, providing an environment and a discipline that man needs to attain his full moral personality. Marsilio thought of the State as having a life of its own and as composed of parts performing functions necessary to that life, and he also believed that it supplies all the conditions of the good life here on earth. Though these are truly Aristotelian ideas, we must not exaggerate their significance. Aquinas considered the State a condition of the good life, but he held the Church responsible for the far more important matter of man's salvation. His conception of justice differed from Aristotle's, and his idea of natural law was essentially Ciceronian and Stoic. Marsilio was more eager to attack the pretensions of the Church than to revive the Aristotelian political philosophy; so much so that it may even be said that he extolled the State because he wished to berate the Church. Whatever is fresh and untypical of the Middle Ages about his theory of law savours more of Hobbes than of Aristotle. He was certainly more worldly than most mediaeval thinkers before the fourteenth century, more willing to confine the Church within narrow limits and to let the hereafter look after itself; but he did not possess, in its Aristotelian fullness, the conception of the State as the indispensable and sufficient condition of the good life. The generalization is therefore broadly true – though it needs qualification – that in the Middle Ages men who thought at all about such things thought of political society as something conventional – necessary, no doubt, to man's security and well-being, but not sufficient to enable him to attain his 'true' nature. Coming from the Stoics, this conception of the State was passed on eventually, though with something new added to it, to Hobbes and Locke.

The Platonic and Aristotelian theory assumed that the city-state was, or should be, self-sufficient. Their ideal was a political society whose every member occupied the place in it for which he was fitted by his natural abilities, and in which only a minority of the whole population took an active part in political life. In that society, provided it was properly constituted, every member, merely by occupying the place he was fitted for, became most fully himself. Aristotle was less austere than Plato, more tolerant of variety, more respectful of custom, more inclined to find his ideal in something not too unlike what existed – but at bottom their conception of the good society was much the same. They thought of it as a harmonious community of men of unequal abilities and merit who could attain the best that life had to offer them only by keeping to their respective places. They believed neither in equality nor in democracy, as we today conceive them; and they had no notion at all of the rights of the individual. Their ideas about society were not perhaps more typically Greek than many others, though they nowadays – in spite of all the warnings of scholars – give that appearance; so much greater are their reputations than any others that have come down to us. Plato – as the very form of his writings, the dialogue, attests – was continually engaged in combating theories unlike his own; and so, too, was Aristotle. To the extent that democratic principles and beliefs were widely embraced by their contemporaries, they may, indeed, have been largely unrepresentative exponents of ancient Greek political thought. But they were the two greatest apologists of the *polis*, the city-state; and while Greeks retained their faith in that institution and were still strongly loyal to it, their theories were bound to be influential.

Of course, the city-state was not self-sufficient, even in their day, and still less afterwards. A very considerable foreign trade was needed to maintain the level of civilization achieved by Athens and several other Greek states, and any attempt to make them self-sufficient, in the manner that Plato and Aristotle thought they should be, would have deeply impoverished them and would therefore have seemed to many citizens retrograde. At the same time, this greatly extended trade had disrupted the old social order, creating for all the larger or economically more developed Greek states very similar social and political problems. It was only natural, therefore, when these states went to war, that the wars between them should take on an 'ideological' character. What is happening at present the world over was happening on a much smaller scale in the Greece of the fourth and third centuries before Christ. A form of political organization that had long existed was felt to be inadequate, and there seemed to be nothing generally acceptable that could be put in its place. The Platonic and Aristotelian philosophy idealized what was no longer sufficiently large or strong to give men security and well-being whilst they declined to forgo the advantages that a more extensive trade had brought them. There was nothing particularly wrong with the Platonic and Aristotelian ideal; it was only that it could not be attained except at the cost of sacrifices which few were willing to make.

On the other hand, there was no alternative to the *polis* to excite men to new loyalties. The alliances and leagues that the Greek states formed among themselves were weak and ephemeral; the Macedonian Empire offered nothing that could compensate the Greeks for the failure of the *polis*; and the same is true of the Roman Empire. The only political organization in antiquity capable of inspiring real devotion was the city-state. The Roman Empire itself was at bottom no more than a vast mass of municipalities held together under one law by an imperial bureaucracy and protected from the barbarian by imperial armies. Its only important function was to preserve peace. A man, under the Empire, might feel affection for the place of his birth; he might, if he were a Roman citizen, feel proud of his status; and he might also feel a personal loyalty and reverence for the divine Emperor and respect for his local representatives. But he was not a citizen in the older Greek and Roman sense, a member of a closely knit political community taking an active part in its communal life.

With the failure of the *polis* – or, rather, the *polis* reduced to the level of a municipality inside empires incapable of imposing the moral discipline and inspiring the loyalties which it had once imposed and inspired – the social philosophies of the Greeks treated the political community with much greater coldness. The Epicureans taught that laws, both moral and positive, are designed merely to enable men to obtain happiness more efficiently, by protecting them against the harmful effects of each other's and their own passions. States exist only to promote security by maintaining law, and there is otherwise no special virtue in them. There is no proper end for man except the pursuit of happiness, though the wise man will know that moderation, concern for the feelings of others, and respect for institutions maintained for the general convenience, are the surest means to happiness. The Epicureans were above all enemies of religion, wishing to free men from all fears that they thought unnecessary to happiness; but they also sought to diminish the State, to undermine its prestige, by treating it as a mere contrivance for limited ends.

Stoicism, the other great post-Aristotelian Greek philosophy, was also, in the beginning, much more moral than political. It developed out of the theories of the Cynics, who were anarchists and ascetics, despising governments and the comforts of life about equally. Diogenes, the most notorious of them, preferred – as we recall – life in a tub to life in a *polis*, and had no other favour to ask of Alexander the Great except that he should get out of his light. Contemptuous of all conventions and without worldly ambitions, the Cynics felt no attachment to any state. In this negative sense, they were cosmopolitan. But in fact they were not true citizens of the world; they acknowledged no duties to their fellow-men, trying rather to make themselves completely independent of them. It was upon this independence that they placed the highest value, and they thought themselves, for having attained it, to possess greater merit than all the imbeciles who still huddled together in communities for comfort and happiness. They taught that men are all equal, but in practice they meant by this little more than that distinctions of birth and wealth, in virtue of which other people might fancy themselves more creditable, are insignificant. They believed that they themselves were really far better than the great mass of law-abiding and reverential fools. They were the first and much the most complete isolationists, and therefore, as one might expect, really very superior persons.

Zeno, the founder of the Stoic school of philosophy, was a disciple of one of the Cynics; but his philosophy was something altogether more generous and humane. It taught that, though man's nature is not fulfilled in the State, though he has a private and independent life of his own which is better than his life as a citizen, he has duties to other men and rights against them; and has them, whether he and they are members of the same or of different states. For there is a law to which all men are subject in virtue of their humanity, whatever the state they belong to; and as subject to that law, they are equals. This is cosmopolitanism and equality conceived in an altogether different manner from the Cynics. It is also the foundation of the morality which we sometimes like to think of as specifically Christian, the morality that teaches that there are rules of behaviour more fundamental than any imposed by human authority, rules bearing equally on all men for their common welfare, and indeed known to them prior to the establishment of government. Aristotle, no doubt, had wanted for the citizens a certain equality before the law, but he had confined that equality exclusively to citizens. Both he and Plato had distinguished between the just and the merely legal, but their idea of justice had been political, that is, proper only to men living in a *polis*; and it had also been designed to accord with what they considered fundamental inequalities of merit, if not of wealth or birth.

The older Stoicism of the third century B.C., the Stoicism of Zeno and Chrysippus, had been, on the whole, unpolitical; it had preached the supremacy of the law of nature and of reason, to which both gods and men are subject; and had distinguished between the wise and the unwise, of whom the former obey the law because they fully understand and accept it, whereas the latter need to be compelled to obedience. If all men were wise, there would be no need for compulsion or indeed for the State, which exists, not that human nature might be fulfilled in it, but as a consequence of human folly. The older Stoics sought to improve human nature by training men's minds towards fortitude, devotion to duty, and indifference to pleasure. Theirs was a kind of education not unlike what Plato advocated in the *Republic*, but with this great difference, that for Plato it had been the means of supplying his ideal state with working rulers, whereas for the Stoics it was the means to individual self-sufficiency. Not economic, of course, nor even social – for the Stoic wanted men to be of service to one another – but moral. The well-educated man is fortified against all disasters, which leave his soul intact; and with it his self-respect, his integrity and his intelligence, the qualities in virtue of which he is most human.

The Stoic philosophy came to Rome in the second century B.C., to the circle of Scipio Aemilianus; and there its character was modified. It became less unpolitical and also less hostile to the passions. The Roman Stoic praised the emotions that make men useful to one another – generosity, sympathy and the nobler kinds of ambition. Service to the State he thought of as a duty that every well-born and well-educated Roman owed to his country. The Greek historian Polybius, who was a friend of Scipio, elaborated the first rational theory of the Roman state, ascribing its endurance and astonishing victories to its mixed character, monarchic, aristocratic and democratic at the same time. In the next century, Cicero, whose ideas came mostly from Polybius, gave to the theory of natural law the form it retained for centuries, and in which it was passed on, first to the Roman lawyers, then to the Christian Fathers, and at last to mediaeval philosophers. According to Cicero, there is a law, coming from God, which all men can discover by the proper exercise of their reason, a law teaching them how they should behave to one another. This law is eternal and universal, the same for all men at all times. In his dialogue on the *Republic*, Cicero makes one of the interlocutors say: 'True law is right reason in agreement with nature; it is of universal application, unchanging and everlasting. . . . It is a sin to try to alter this law, nor is it allowable to attempt to repeal any part of it. . . . We cannot be freed from its obligations by senate or people, and we need not look outside ourselves for an expounder or interpreter of it.'[1] Mediaeval thinkers might choose different words to describe this law, but they added nothing of importance to the Stoic conception. What it was

[1] *De re publica*, III.xxi.32, in Cicero, *De re publica, De legibus*, ed. C. W. Keyes, Loeb Classical Library (London 1928), p. 211.

already for Cicero in the first century B.C., it was in all essentials for Aquinas in the thirteenth century of our era, and even for Locke in the seventeenth.

Cicero also believed, as all the Stoics did, in the moral equality of men, by which he meant, not that their circumstances were the same or that their talents or aptitudes were identical, but that they were all subject to the same rules of conduct. 'There is', he remarked in the *Laws*, 'no difference in kind between man and man'; and 'no human being of any race who. . .cannot attain to virtue. . . . We are so constituted by Nature as to share the sense of justice with one another and to pass it on to all men'.[1] For Cicero, as for the Christian philosophers, social inequalities are merely conventional; they do not rest on differences that inhere in men as men. In Cicero, too, we find much the same conception of the nature of civil society as we do in mediaeval thinkers. In the *Republic* he defined the *res publica*, the commonwealth, as 'the affair of the people', with the people conceived not as a mere collection of men, but as a 'gathering of the multitude united in agreement about law and in partnership for the good of all'.[2] Cicero thought of the body politic as resting ultimately on the wills of its members, and of magistrates as subject to law; and he said that positive laws are not properly laws unless they conform to the laws of nature. These sentiments are not merely pious generalizations; they express a lively sense that all authority rests on opinion, that where there are no commonly received conceptions of justice which express, in reason, rules that are inscribed in men's hearts, there can be neither command nor obedience. On the other hand, there is nothing specifically democratic about them. Cicero did not believe that those who actually govern must derive their authority from the very people subject to them or be answerable to them for the way they govern. He was a constitutionalist, desiring that Rome should be governed in what he thought the traditional manner, but free of the corruptions recently introduced. There was, no doubt, a certain popular element in the government of the Roman Republic, but Cicero, like many aristocratic defenders of the republican constitution, exaggerated its importance. He was what we should nowadays call a Whig, like the men who ruled England throughout much of the eighteenth century and like those who founded the United States. He had the same respect for law, the same love of freedom, the same conviction that authority comes somehow ultimately from the people, and the same distrust of democracy.

[1] *De legibus*, I.x.30 and I.xii.33, ibid., pp. 329–33.
[2] *De re publica*, I.xxv.39.

II. EARLY CHRISTIANITY AND ITS DOCTRINES

Christianity added little to the moral philosophy of the Stoics except the virtues, uncharacteristic of either Greeks or Romans, of humility and other-worldliness, admirable in themselves but not useful to the State. To the Stoic philosophy of government it added almost nothing at all. Though Cicero had said that positive law, if contrary to the law of nature, is not properly law, he had avoided the conclusion that men must not obey it. His political philosophy embraced no account of the limits of political obligation. The question that Cicero avoided was answered by St Paul in the thirteenth chapter of his Epistle to the Romans: 'Let every soul be subject unto the higher powers', he said. 'For there is no power but of God: the powers that be are ordained of God. Whosoever therefore resisteth the power, resisteth the ordinance of God. . . . For rulers are not a terror to good works but to the evil.' The plain meaning of these words is that all rulers, whatever their origins, fall under God's order; and that to resist them is to sin, that is to say, to disobey God. St Paul did not consider the position of the Christian who is commanded by his ruler to do what God forbids. Is his dilemma insoluble? Must he sin whether he obeys or disobeys? Later Christian writers, noticing that St Paul had condemned all resistance but had not required perpetual obedience, resolved the dilemma by saying that, though the Christian must never resist his ruler, he must disobey him when what he orders is against God's law. Tertullian and St Augustine, for instance, both claimed that in defiance of human laws which contravene the will of God and command sin, devout Christians must suffer the consequences of martyrdom. St Paul's doctrine of non-resistance, nevertheless, weighed heavily on Christian political theory right up to the eighteenth century, and was not effectively challenged by professing Christians before the latter part of the sixteenth century.

The early Christians did not believe that the authority of rulers is derived from the people; it comes, they thought, only from God. They did not, of course, explain more particularly how this authority is derived from God, any more than the Stoics and the Roman lawyers explained how it was derived from the people. Just as the Stoics and lawyers thought it enough to say that the people had, sometime in the past, granted this authority to the Emperor, who now exercised it on their behalf, so the Christian Fathers were content to assume that, since God is omnipotent and government necessary, whoever has authority must have got it from God and for the people's good. It was not until much later, long after Christianity had become the established religion, that Aquinas and other Christian theorists began to argue that the authority of rulers comes both from God and from the people: from God primarily and from the people secondarily, in the sense that God grants authority (for He alone can grant it) to persons chosen by the people or who acquire office in the customary, that is to say, generally accepted, manner.

Neither the Stoics nor the Christian Fathers, though they believed in the essential equality of men, protested against existing inequalities. The Stoics accepted the institution of slavery without approving it, and their philosophy inspired, not a general attack on the practice, but merely a greater willingness on the part of individuals to set their slaves free. It was the same with the Christians, who thought the slave as capable of virtue and salvation as his master, but advised him to accept his earthly lot cheerfully. The early Christians were no reformers; they despised this world too much. Man was only on a pilgrimage through it, and it was foolish to set much store on the comforts of the journey.

The Christian Fathers regarded government, slavery and property as effects of man's fall, partly as punishments for his sinfulness and partly as remedies. If Adam's posterity had been as innocent as he was before he disobeyed God, there would have been no need for the institution of government on this earth; all men would have been free and would have held all things in common. But in a world of sinners, coercion and therefore government are necessary, and what is for one man's use must be carefully distinguished from another's. It was comparatively easy to prove that government and property are useful, and therefore established by God for man's benefit. The case with slavery was different. It was not possible to prove it a remedy against the violence and intemperance of sinful men, nor even to show how it could be a punishment for sin. For since all men are sinners, why should some be slaves and the others not? The Fathers did not even pretend that slaves were worse than their masters, but thought them just as likely to receive grace and to merit salvation. St Augustine, in particular, condemned human slavery as unjust.

The Christian Fathers, in proclaiming equality, merely repeated what the Stoics had said before them; and they drew from the common dogma no novel conclusions of any practical importance. Indeed, unlike the Stoics, they invented a new kind of inequality not known before. They divided mankind into two parts: those who receive God's grace and are destined to reign eternally with him, and those who do not receive it and who, through their own sinfulness, are condemned to perpetual torment. The great exponent of this doctrine

9

was St Augustine, who described the community of the elect, the City of God, to which all men who have received grace, but they only, belong. Theologians have argued for fifteen hundred years about the conditions under which men, according to St Augustine, receive grace, but what they have never denied is that he believed that there could be no true justice in pagan states, and that, as a rule, infidels are eternally damned and only Christians can be accorded grace. Far from adding anything to the Stoic doctrine of equality, the Christian Fathers took something precious away from it – the idea that at all times and in all places virtue and happiness are offered to all men on the same terms.

Christianity was nevertheless destined to affect European political theory profoundly – not because of anything particularly new in its morality, but because it was a kind of religion not known when the major Greek philosophies were elaborated. It was cosmopolitan, dogmatic, and monotheistic; its priests were not state officials like the Roman flamens; and its organization was necessarily quite separate from that of the State, however much its ministers might preach submission to the Emperor. It was not the only religion of this new kind, but it was the one that triumphed. When Constantine adopted Christianity as the official religion of the Empire, he undertook the duty of protecting it and was expected by the Church to help maintain the true doctrine. The Church, of course, did not expect him to decide what the true doctrine was; but since, when it was divided, both parties to the controversy asked for his support, it was the party to which he gave it that prevailed and whose doctrine was received as orthodox.

The Church, before it became official, had not been able to persecute heretics, and had not even wanted to do so. But after it had become official, it gradually (and none too slowly) changed its mind. It mattered immensely that the truth should prevail, and any means that caused it to do so were thereby justified. This change of heart is illustrated in the life of St Augustine, who had been against persecuting the Manichaeans, on the ground that sincere belief alone is valuable and cannot be forced, but who afterwards favoured persecuting the Donatists. He had, in the interval, noticed that persecution can be effective; that, though it may not enlighten the obdurate, it does at least prevent the timid (and they are the great majority) from falling into temptation. We may well agree that his psychological insight had increased, but whether we think that his goodness of heart had done so as well must depend on the moral assumptions we make.

The very existence of a Church claiming to be universal and to preach a dogmatic religion independent of the Temporal Power created a situation not known before. For the Church, however much it laid on all men in God's name the duty of obedience to the Emperor, also claimed their allegiance for itself. It was a society quite separate from the State, having different ends and using different methods. While there was one Empire and all Christians were inside it, and while the official church was still young, it stood very much in need of imperial protection; its clergy were therefore inclined to be obedient and deferential towards the temporal powers. The Empire still had immense prestige, and the Church had no hope of becoming in fact universal except under the wing of the Emperor.

When the Empire disintegrated, the situation was quite altered. The new barbarian kingdoms had none of the prestige of the old Empire, and they were in any case relatively small. The Church could not depend on any one of them as it had depended on the Emperors, and it was aware of itself as a society more extensive than they were and needing to maintain jealously its separate existence. Not that the Church became stronger when the Empire fell. On the contrary, it became weaker for losing its strongest support. But it did at least learn to regard all secular states as short-lived and of restricted jurisdiction, and itself alone as enduring and universal.

St Ambrose, in the fourth century, was the first important Christian writer to define the relations of Church and State more or less clearly. He asserted that the Church exercises a spiritual jurisdiction over all Christians, however exalted, and does so independently of the Temporal Power, which is therefore necessarily limited. It is for the Church alone to declare what the true religion is, and to decide the terms on which men can be admitted to its sacraments. The Emperor has no right to control the Church in its exercise of its spiritual functions, but has a duty to protect it. On the other hand, Ambrose did not claim that priests are not amenable to temporal courts for temporal offences, and he admitted that church property, like any other, was held subject to civil law. His position bears a resemblance to that taken by the Catholic Church today, but was very different from the claims put forward soon afterwards and successfully maintained for over a thousand years.

The collapse of the Empire in the West naturally strengthened the hand of the Pope against an Emperor reigning in Constantinople. Pope Gelasius I, at the end of the fifth century, first defined what became in the Middle Ages the official theory of the Church about its relations to the State. God has instituted for the benefit of mankind two Powers on earth, he maintained, the Spiritual and the Temporal, both subject to certain limits. Each is supreme in its own sphere, kings being subordinate to bishops in spiritual matters, and bishops to kings in temporal matters. Though each Power is independent of the other and has a quite different purpose, the persons entrusted by God with the exercise of them – that is to say, priests and temporal magistrates – cannot avoid relations with one another. Gelasius did not draw a precise line between the two spheres, but he went much further than Ambrose in asserting the claims of the Church. He was eager, not merely to defend the independence of the Church in spiritual matters, but also to withdraw priests from secular jurisdiction even when they committed secular offences. He was apparently the first to claim for the clergy what might be called extra-territorial rights. Just how far he meant to go we do not know; but apparently much further than anyone before him. It was, broadly speaking, his view of the relations between Church and State that prevailed in the Middle Ages.

III. LAW AND THE STATE IN THE LATE MIDDLE AGES

I mean here to do no more than offer a sort of inventory of the political ideas inherited by the Reformation and Counter-Reformation from the late Middle Ages. Those ideas changed as they were used by different thinkers for different purposes. But that, after all, is the nature of ideas. If they are merely weapons, as the Marxists say, in a war of interests which they do not cause, they are certainly strange weapons; for their shape seems to change as they are used, and with their shape, the character of the battle.

I propose to consider the political thought of the Middle Ages under six main headings: the nature and functions of government; the notion of law; tyranny and the right of resistance; the effect of the study of Roman Law on mediaeval conceptions of government; the relations between Church and State or, as it was put then, between the Spiritual and Temporal Powers; and, finally, the intellectual legacy of the Middle Ages.

1. Mediaeval Ideas about the Nature and Functions of Government

For mediaeval political thinkers, few things seemed more certain than that government is conventional, established rather on account of man's iniquity than as a means towards his perfection. Indeed, this is so not only of government, but marriage and property as well, and all the great institutions of society. Man, in the Middle Ages, was not thought of as essentially a political animal. More than that, even society was not thought of as primarily political. Mediaeval writers spoke of the Temporal Power rather than of the State or of civil society; and the Temporal Power was only one of two.

Government, property and all other institutions were perceived as consequences of the Fall. If man had been what God originally made him, if Adam had not sinned and human nature had not been corrupted, these artefacts would never have been invented. That, however, does not mean that they are themselves evil – that man, as he has become since the Fall, would be better without them. On the contrary, they are divinely established as remedies for sin; they exist to protect men from each other's evil passions. Man is by nature what God made him, and God made him innocent; if he were still innocent, he would not need government and property. It is in that sense that government is not natural; it is a restraint put on a creature who has not been true to his nature, who has fallen away from what God intended him to be. When mediaeval writers call government and property conventional, it is of this they are thinking much more than of historical origins. No doubt, remembering how God, through His servant Samuel, placed Saul over the Jews as their king, or even how Romulus founded Rome, mediaeval political writers also thought of government as deliberately set up. It was for them conventional and perhaps even artificial in that sense also; but what they had chiefly in mind was its function. Aquinas no doubt sought to reconcile Aristotle's philosophy with Christian theology, in the light of which government might be conceived not only negatively, as a remedy for sin, but positively, as a means to virtue, since he thought the State framed the earthly dimension of man's moral nature. But even allowing for such attempts as this, mediaeval writers on politics and law did not really think of the State in Aristotelian terms. For Aristotle had supposed that it was man's natural environment in a quite different sense, in that outside it he had no truly human identity. In perfecting human nature, the State alone, according to his philosophy, provided for the salvation of men's souls.

Neither did mediaeval political writers distinguish, as we do now, between private and public law, between men's rights and obligations as ordinary members of the community and their rights and obligations as holders of public office. They often used the same word, *dominium*, to mean both property and authority. They knew, of course, that some men have much more power than others, and that most men have very little; indeed, they recognized a hierarchy of Temporal Power, which was as real to them as the hierarchy of Spiritual Power, the order of priests, or the Church in the narrower sense. But they did not, as we do, distinguish between two kinds of rights and obligations, those which a man has merely as an agent or servant of the community, and the others. They admitted that all rights and obligations are conditional. Having no use either for absolute power or for absolute rights, they had a profound respect for law and believed that a man's rights spring from his duties. They had, very obviously, a deep sense of community; they were not in the least what we should call individualists. Still less were they worshippers of power. While both Roman Law and canon law could acknowledge the establishment of a civil power as a composite representative of its various members, the modern distinction between individuals and the State – between private persons and what is sometimes called the public person – meant nothing, or almost nothing, to them.

Nor, in the Middle Ages, before the fourteenth or fifteenth centuries, was the Temporal Power so organized as to incline men to think of it as directed from one centre. There were, of course, lesser and higher authorities, and there were all kinds of reciprocal obligations between them; there was system and there was hierarchy. But feudal superiors did not control feudal inferiors in the way that modern governments control their servants. Feudal inferiors had, of course, obligations to their superiors, who could often coerce them if they did not carry out those obligations. Inferiors owed certain kinds of service to their superiors, and had revenues and authority on condition that they did the service they owed, but they were not their agents or instruments of their policy and were only to a limited extent responsible to their superiors for what they did with their revenues and authority. Their *dominium*, their property and authority, was almost as much their own (though, of course, smaller in extent) as the property and authority of the Emperor or the King were his. They did not hold it unconditionally; they had duties to both their inferiors and their superiors. But they were neither officials nor delegates. Neither in England nor in France, still less in the Empire, was there anything like the machinery of a modern State, a hierarchy of public officers and courts standing to one another in such relations that the whole system of power can be said to be firmly controlled from one centre. If, in England, it may appear that a largely centralized political power had already been established briefly in the course of the twelfth century by King Henry II, in the thirteenth century such power came to be successfully challenged and undermined before it was subsequently assembled once again. In this sense, which is the essence of what we nowadays mean by the word 'state', there were no enduring states in the Middle Ages before the fourteenth and fifteenth centuries.

Already in those two centuries, which are by tradition included in the Middle Ages, we can see emerging in England, in France and in Castile, the lineaments of the modern state. For the growth of the royal power, the extension of the authority of royal courts, and the more frequent meetings of legislative assemblies supposed to represent the entire national community, are precisely the beginnings of what we call the State. Linguistic habits, however, change slowly, and usually more slowly than men's social environment. Political theorists and lawyers went on speaking of the Temporal Power in the fifteenth century much as they had done in the thirteenth. The more abstract, the more philosophical, their treatises, the less their habits of speech and thought changed. A writer, who, like Sir John Fortescue in fifteenth-century England, sets out to describe an actual system of government, will often, if he is shrewd, give a fairly accurate and convincing account of it; but the pure theorist will contrive, at least while he is theorizing, to ignore the realities. There is nearly always a very considerable gap between abstract political theory and descriptive political writing.

Apart from the great nation-states, there were also emerging, over roughly the same period, though the process began even earlier, states of another kind. They no longer survive today, but they were for several centuries of immense importance in the intellectual and artistic, and even political, life of Europe. I mean, of course, the small republics or city-states, in Italy especially but also elsewhere. These states emerged by a process exactly the opposite of the one that produced the nation-state; they emerged, not where the highest among the mediaeval hierarchy of temporal powers grew strong at the expense of the lower, but where it decayed. The kings of France and England eventually made themselves effective masters of their kingdoms, but the Emperor did not. Hence the virtual independence of the Italian republics. These republics were compact, wealthy and civilized; they were, for their size, much more important than the northern kingdoms. They were also, as might be expected, less bound by feudal traditions; they could apply to their communities, much more readily than to other people, the old Greek and Roman conceptions of the State. Already in the fourteenth century, in Marsilio of Padua's *Defensor pacis*, we find a political theorist speaking of civil society almost as seventeenth-century theorists were to do so, as if it were a well-integrated whole with a structure of government enabling it to act effectively in all matters of common concern. It is all too easy to treat mediaeval writers as more modern than they actually were, to read more into their words than was ever in their minds, but the impression of modernity created by the *Defensor pacis* is strong. Though Marsilio was writing to defend the claims of the Emperor against the Pope, the way he described civil government seems much more in keeping with how it actually worked in the Italian republics of his day than with the feeble structure of the Empire, He spoke of the fractured mediaeval Empire as if it were something like the old Roman Republic, which was perhaps all the more attractive to him because he was an Italian, because he came from a part of Europe where there already existed compact, articulate, enterprising, highly self-conscious political communities such as we imagine states to be.

2. The Mediaeval Conception of Law

The primary social and political conception that prevailed in the Middle Ages was not that of power but law. Let me elucidate my meaning. These two things, power and law, are intimately related, for there can be no government without law. Government is a *regular* exercise of power, so that where there is government there must be laws, and there cannot be stable and effective power without government. These two ideas are at once fundamental and interconnected; we cannot think or speak about politics unless we use them both. It is, however, possible in the light of these ideas to have very different notions of government: we can either, like Hobbes, regard government as primarily the exercise of power, or we can regard it as primarily the enforcement of law. It is, of course, always both; but it is not a matter of indifference that we should be inclined to think of it as primarily the one rather than the other. In the Middle Ages, while it was sometimes recognized by both ecclesiastical and secular authorities that legislators should not enforce their own decrees, men habitually thought of government as the enforcement of law.

This way of conceiving government is not confined to the Middle Ages; it is the oldest and perhaps most obvious way; we find it among the Greeks and Romans, and it is still common today. But today it has to be interpreted differently, because our whole conception of law has changed, or rather has been elaborated and refined. We are much more conscious than men were in the Middle Ages that governments not only enforce but make law. Now, if they make law effectively, it must be in virtue of their power. And so, we are also inclined to think of government as an exercise of power, to put as much emphasis on this aspect of it as on the other. We accept, with qualifications, both the mediaeval conception of government and the conception of Hobbes; but we cannot effect this reconciliation between them except by insisting on certain distinctions that mediaeval writers either knew nothing of or else virtually ignored. Mediaevalists, with a very natural desire to enhance the virtues of the society they study, like to say that in the Middle Ages everyone, or nearly everyone, believed in the supremacy of Law, perhaps forgetting that rule by divine right, as was claimed on behalf of the Capetian and Valois dynasties of France, for instance, could locate the king's authority above the law. For the most part, however, it was the law, and not the ruler, which it was thought must be supreme.

The mediaeval conception of the supremacy of law is not to be confused with constitutional government in the modern sense, and still less with what writers like Dicey have called the rule of law. The rule of law, as Dicey interprets it, can only apply in countries where a distinction is made between men's actions in a private and a public capacity, for it asserts that they ought to be responsible for both kinds of actions to the same courts. But in the Middle Ages, the distinction between private and official actions was seldom made or perceived, and at the same time, there were several separate jurisdictions and spheres of law. There were ecclesiastical courts and secular courts; and among the secular courts, some were royal and some manorial. There were all kinds of immunities and privileges. There never was a time when Dicey's rule of law was less observed.

Nor did the supremacy of law, in the Middle Ages, mean what it means today in countries like the United States. With the exception of the Church itself and perhaps a small number of Italian cities, there were no written constitutions, and no courts with an acknowledged right to set aside statutes made by the highest legislative body. There were hardly even *unwritten* constitutions, as we now understand them, for the conventions that rulers were expected to conform to were far too vague; apart from the settled procedures of canon law, there were no elaborate treatises on constitutional practice, and there was much less agreement then than there is today about the precise limits of different kinds of authority. Though there is no document called the British Constitution, and no fundamental law by reference to which British courts can decide that an Act of Parliament is not good law, there does exist an elaborate, precise, coherent, and generally accepted body of rules, long studied and often described, to which British governments do in fact conform. This body of rules is what we mean by the unwritten constitution of Britain. But it clearly is *not* unwritten in the same sense as the simple, not very coherent, body of custom defining the authority of mediaeval kings, parliaments and courts which prevailed throughout the early Middle Ages. For what mere custom defines, what is not systematically discussed and carefully described, is always defined uncertainly. If it is not exactly wrong, then it is misleading to speak of unwritten constitutions limiting the powers of mediaeval governments; for the word constitution, even with the adjective 'unwritten' before it, suggests something more precise, coherent, and uniformly interpreted than existed in the Middle Ages prior to the fifteenth century (even in England where, however, in the late twelfth century, custom did begin to get transcribed as law).

Before we can appreciate just what the supremacy of law meant in the Middle Ages, we must remember that law was then classified very differently from how we classify it today. Certain distinctions, very familiar to us and so simple as to seem obvious, were not then made, or else were made so confusedly as not to bring out their implications. The distinctions that were made between different kinds of law turned much less on intrinsic differences than on supposed origins or on the manner that men got to know them. All law was thought to be at bottom God's law, either as made directly by Him or as derived from His law by His creatures, just as all authority was thought of as coming ultimately from God, whether the persons who actually exercised it were elected by the people, or were appointed to their offices, or succeeded to them by hereditary right.

Aquinas's account of law, which is an unusually clear and well-presented summary of what is best in mediaeval thought devoted to the subject, can serve to make clear to us just what distinctions were made, or were not made, in the Middle Ages. Aquinas tells us that God the Creator gave a law to all things, animate and inanimate. This law, which is the Reason of God manifest in the world created by Him, Aquinas calls 'eternal'. But those of God's creatures endowed by Him with reason are subject to His law in a manner peculiar to their kind. They are not blind subjects of law, for they partake of God's reason. By the light of the reason given them by God they discover the part of the eternal law relating to creatures like themselves; and this part Aquinas calls the Law of Nature. It is a law which is the same for all men everywhere, for it applies to them in virtue of their very nature as men. But men's circumstances are not always the same, and they therefore require a law suitable to each kind. This law is human, conventional and variable. In order to be true law, in order that men should have a real duty to obey it and a right to enforce it, it must, however, be in keeping with the Law of Nature; it must be the Law of Nature adapted to the circumstances.

Apart from the Law of Nature and the conventional law that derives from it, there is another kind of law to which men are subject in this world. Aquinas calls it 'divine', not because it owes more to the will of God than does the Law of Nature, but because it is made known to men by God directly and is not discovered by the mere use of human reason. This divine law is revealed in the Old and New Testaments; it is rational because all the laws of God express His Reason and therefore cannot contradict the Law of Nature. God has endowed man with reason, but that reason is limited and is not enough to enable him to discover his final end, or God's purpose for him. Yet God is rational and benevolent; He would not create man for a purpose and then leave him without the means of attaining it. Since man's reason is not enough to enlighten him about that purpose, God gives him a law supplementary to the Law of Nature, which, if he follows it, will enable him, in spite of his defective reason, to attain God's purpose for him. Aquinas adds other reasons why man needs a special divine or revealed law, but this is the most important.

The Law of Nature, moreover, as he tells us, is a part of the Eternal Law. The creatures who obey it do so in a manner peculiar to their kind; their obedience is rational. But the law, whether merely eternal or both eternal and natural, is treated as if it were, at bottom, one kind of law. There is no clear distinction made between natural uniformities of behaviour and rules of action voluntarily accepted because they are thought to be just – between what we should call natural and what we should call moral law. There is, of course, some kind of distinction made between them, for Aquinas does not treat natural law as if it were just the same as eternal law applied exclusively to man; he does recognize that it not only applies specifically to man but applies to him in a peculiar way. Yet Aquinas clearly does not understand the full implications of this difference, or he would not speak of natural law as a species of eternal law. He introduces the notion of command into his account of both kinds of law, as if God ruled the non-rational part of the universe and received obedience from it in much the same way as He rules and is obeyed by man. This manner of speaking about law, which to the modern mind seems inadequate and confusing – because it ignores (or at least belittles) what to us appears the most important and obvious distinction – comes naturally to persons whose deepest and most constant belief about the universe is that it was created and is now controlled by God. No doubt many of us, perhaps most of us, still think of the world in this way, but we find the idea of inanimate things obeying God at best a metaphorical use of language; and we think it odd that uniformities in nature should be called rational laws. We may discover them by the use of our reason, but in themselves they are neither rational nor irrational, for they are only ways in which things behave. Nor, finally, do we think even of moral laws as being quite literally commands, divine or human; but that is precisely how Aquinas thought of them.

By 'human' or 'conventional' law, mediaeval jurists and philosophers meant both custom and the statutes, ordinances or decrees made by some person or persons having the customary right to make them. Ordinarily, they thought of human law as being primarily custom, and of consciously enacted law as being either a declaration of what custom is, made necessary by doubts or disputes about it, or as supplementary to custom. This was the earlier conception of how statutes and ordinances stood in relation to custom, and even when, in the thirteenth and fourteenth centuries, rulers in many parts of Europe found it convenient to convoke representative assemblies, this view of the primacy of custom continued to hold. The business of estates and parliaments was perceived not so much as that of making laws as of voting subsidies and presenting petitions. When the prince, after consultation with them, promulgated a new law, it was not thought of as superseding custom. On the contrary, it was precisely because princes were held under an obligation to rule in accordance with custom that it was thought right that they should consult their subjects before making new laws; for laws made after consultation with the different classes and communities of the people were thought more likely than others to conform to custom. The notion of an unlimited legislative power, either in the prince or the people, was repugnant to most mediaeval thinkers, however attractive it came to seem to certain rulers, particularly popes, who sought to establish an absolute power unfettered by customary restraints. No doubt, as estates and parliaments met more frequently and statutes multiplied, legislators felt themselves less and less inhibited by custom, more and more at liberty to interpret it as they liked. The belief that custom must take precedence over statute correspondingly grew weaker, not consciously rejected so much as unconsciously modified. And yet even in England, where, by the fifteenth century, Parliament had already become a more effective institution than any of the continental estates, its supremacy was thought of as less legislative than judicial. Although it had come to be admitted that what Parliament declared to be law was law, this admission meant no more than that Parliament was the highest court, the pre-eminent interpreter, of law. All courts interpret the law, for by describing how law applies to particular cases, they declare what it is. To say that what Parliament declares to be the law is the law does not therefore amount to claiming for Parliament sovereignty in the Hobbesian and modern sense of the word; it is not to say that Parliament has a legally unlimited right to make whatever law it pleases. Neither is it to say the contrary. In the fifteenth century, men did not distinguish, as clearly as we do now, between the legislative and judicial functions, between the making of law and its interpretation. We thus cannot argue that when they called Parliament the highest court in the land, from whose decisions about law there was no appeal, they were denying that it had the right to make law as well as to declare it, or were trying to set precise limits on its law-making powers. Historians who write as if, in the fifteenth century, the sovereignty of Parliament, in the sense we now understand it, was either denied or affirmed are equally wide of the mark. Until the law of nature was recognized as a determinate body of moral principles, and hence as law in a quite different sense from those rules which were enforced by the courts; until, moreover, a clear distinction was made between the legislative and judicial functions of government; and until the relation of custom to statute law was clearly defined, there could be no real conception of sovereignty, and therefore no assertion or denial that kings or parliaments are sovereign in our modern sense.

It should be evident that the supremacy of law, to people who have nothing like the Hobbesian notion of sovereignty, cannot mean quite what it means to people who have it. Aquinas may have perceived law as a promulgated expression of will, but for most mediaeval thinkers before and after him, law is not primarily a human command. It is, above all, custom, deliberately enforced but not deliberately made. When we say that the law is supreme in a particular country, we either mean to deny that there is a sovereign legislature in it, because there is a body of law – a written constitution or a declaration of rights – recognized by the courts as superior to ordinary law; or, if there is a sovereign legislature, we mean that there are fairly rigid and precise conventions which governments in fact obey, though there are no laws or customs that the supreme legislature cannot amend or abolish. Alternatively, if we mean neither of these things, we mean something like what Dicey called the rule of law. When we speak about the supremacy of law, we nearly always have in mind some fairly precisely formulated and well-established body of rules, which governments and their servants are either legally obliged to obey or else in practice dare not disobey. In either case the law that is supreme is what Aquinas would call conventional or human. No doubt, the supremacy of law in the Middle Ages did mean part of what it means to us; no doubt it did contain in embryo the idea of constitutional government, not in the American sense, but in the sense of government carried on in a traditional manner, according to long-established usages (though the usages were not, by our standards, at all well defined). But it also meant something more; it meant respect for the law of nature, for a supposedly universal and unchanging system of law which was neither thought of exactly as we think of moral principles nor clearly distinguished from them.

If we enquire how mediaeval jurists and philosophers came by their opinions of what the law of nature actually prescribed, we find that they got them by comparing the customs of different peoples and seeing what was common to them; or from the Bible (from the examples set by God's chosen people and from the precepts of Christ and the Apostles); or from Roman Law, which was peculiarly venerable to them, as the law of an Empire which had included almost every part of the world they were familiar with and which was already Christian at the time its law was codified. But though they got their notions of the law of nature from what they knew of human law, they none the less distinguished it, in principle, from all customs and laws made by man. Their presumption might be that custom, just because it seemed enduring and was generally accepted, did conform to natural law, and that statutes, properly made in the ways established by custom, would very probably do so as well; but they knew that customs vary and that statutes are easily changed, while the law of nature they took to be always and everywhere the same. The authority of custom and of human law generally seemed to them to derive from this relation to the law of nature, which made even conventions and statutes seem more than merely human, on account of their being, at bottom, fixed by the law of reason, the law of God, adapted to the circumstances of particular communities.

What was implied by this manner of speaking about law, both human and natural? Did mediaeval courts, ecclesiastical or secular, in fact set customs or statutes aside on the ground that they did not conform to a higher law? The truth is that they very seldom did so, though they no doubt habitually interpreted them in the light of their conceptions of the law of nature. But if they did not set them aside, if they nearly always assumed that they in fact conformed to the higher law, what exactly was the point of calling that law superior to them?

Perhaps our question is misconceived. The distinction we frequently make between moral principles and ordinary law does not require that our courts always set aside laws they judge immoral. Indeed, they may never do so. Why, then, should we dismiss mediaeval ways of thinking about law as fundamentally confused for neglecting to draw practical consequences from ideas which have a similar foundation? The law of nature was supposed to be unchanging in character and divine in origin, a part of the whole scheme of things which is God's universe; it was not separate from custom and foreign to it but was present within it as the true source of its authority. All the functions of government – the making of law no less than its interpretation and enforcement – were deemed legitimate only because they were carried on in customary ways. Custom was the will of the community, sometimes articulated in corporate enactments or ecclesiastical orders, but often not consciously expressed, arising instead naturally among men, as they adapted their lives to their circumstances; it was also the will of God, for the creatures among whom it arose were made by God, enlightened by the reason He placed in them, and destined for the ends He decreed. In a religious, a theological, age, this way of conceiving law was profoundly conservative. The law of nature of the rationalists of the eighteenth century, a law surmised to be a body of precisely formulated abstract rules and individual rights divorced from custom, might be a revolutionary conception; but not the law of nature of the Middle Ages. It gave to all law, as an embodiment of God's purpose for man, a sanctity it no longer possesses, and perhaps no longer needs, now that governments are so powerful and enterprising that their main function is to make law, even to the point of refashioning society.

In the Middle Ages, men could seldom hope, as they can now (though often with too much optimism), to change the conditions of their life, even when they pursued systematically large schemes of reform. Their whole system of government was too crude, too loosely knit, too feeble. Yet the very weakness of the system made abuses of power easy, in so far as law was conceived as something sacred, of divine origin, not to be set over and against custom as a standard by which to condemn it, but to be treated as a moral and divine support of it. Custom might vary from place to place, and might even change from time to time, but it was nevertheless part of the divine order; and no exercise of power, no forcing of some men to do the will of others, could be legitimate unless it rested on custom. For all authority belonged only to God, though men might exercise it under Him. With the law of nature and God's revealed law behind it, custom served both to limit change and to justify such change as was generally acceptable. It did not override statutes in the way that the American Constitution overrides acts of Congress, for the person or body that by custom had the right to make statutes was commonly accepted as the supreme interpreter of custom.

The supremacy of law, as it was conceived in the Middle Ages, is different, therefore, from the modern conception of constitutional government, both in its American and in its English form, though rather closer to the English than the American; it is different also from the idea, now generally accepted, that in every society the authority of government is limited, in fact though not in law, by common notions of morality; and it is different, lastly, from the rationalist and individualist, and therefore potentially revolutionary, conception of the law of nature of the philosophers of the Enlightenment. It is connected with all three of them, both historically and logically, for they emerged out of it; but it is not the same as any of them. How they emerged out of it is, of course, a large part of the history of political thought in the modern age.

3. *Tyranny and the Right of Resistance*

While it eventually, if only occasionally, came to be asserted on behalf of the Papacy, the idea that power can be absolute was largely foreign to the Middle Ages. All legitimate authority was supposed to rest on custom and to come ultimately from God; and even the authority to declare and alter custom likewise rested on custom, and was therefore limited. It was also supposed that custom expressed the will of the community, for it was not imposed upon people by force from above, but endured because it was generally accepted by them. Since authority rested on custom, it derived, so people said, from the will of the community as well as from the will of God.

There is nothing specifically democratic about this way of thinking. Custom is not the conscious will of the people; it is not established by the counting of heads. The persons who by custom in the Middle Ages had the right to be consulted by the king when he took important decisions were not, in our modern sense, representatives of the people. It was not until the fourteenth and fifteenth centuries that national assemblies like the English Parliament or the Estates-General in France took any considerable part in government; and by and large they represented classes and corporations rather than the people generally as a mass of individuals. It was widely admitted that what concerned all should be approved by all; but this principle was not

really democratic in our sense. It did not mean that everyone ought
to be consulted about what concerns him, either personally or through
his delegate; it meant only that when important decisions are taken by
the rulers of a community, they ought to consult those people who
by tradition have a right to speak for the various classes, corporations
and lesser communities that together make up the large one. Such
spokesmen were in fact often not elected, and even when they were,
it was usually by a small number of privileged persons. Democracy,
as we understand it, springs from the notion that all men, merely
as individuals, have a right to a say in the government of their
country. It is in principle different from the mediaeval conception
that all legitimate secular authority derives from the community over
which it is exercised as well as from God. The idea that every man
has a moral right to be consulted in matters of common concern was
wholly foreign to the Middle Ages, more so, even, than the idea of
absolute power.

Aquinas held that a ruler's authority might not be from God, that
is to say, might be illegitimate and tyrannical, either because the
ruler had acquired it illegally, or, alternatively, because he exercised
it wrongfully by compelling men to sin or obey in matters to which
his authority did not extend. In the first case, his authority could
be repudiated; if it was not, it became in the long run legitimate,
since abiding acceptance implies consent. In the second case, men
must disobey the ruler if he tries to compel them to sin, and they
need not obey him if he tries to compel their obedience in matters
that lie outside his authority.

Aquinas was not content to preach merely passive resistance. If
there are legal methods that can be used to restrain the tyrant, so
much the better; but if legal methods prove ineffective, then he
allows that other methods must be used. At least in his later works,
Aquinas did not approve of tyrannicide; he did not think it right
that just anyone should presume to pass judgement on his rulers
and to execute his own judgement. Active resistance must always,
he thought, be undertaken by an established authority, by some
council, court or body of magistrates. But a responsible body of
this kind, acting on behalf of the entire community, may depose a
tyrant and if necessary take up arms against him. Their action will
be unusual; it will not be an exercise of customary right. But neither
will it be, strictly speaking, illegal, since the law of nature, which
is above custom, will justify it. Nor will it be *contrary* to custom,
for the tyrant has himself violated custom and has lost his right to
obedience.

Several mediaeval writers went much further than Aquinas; they even justified the killing of tyrants by anyone whose sense of duty is strong enough to induce him to take the risk. I have considered Aquinas's position because it is moderate and typical. Even this most balanced and cautious of mediaeval philosophers approved of active resistance to rulers who persistently exceeded their authority. By mediaeval custom, emperors and kings were answerable for their actions; there were feudal courts to decide between them and those who complained against them, and if they did not freely accept the decisions, steps could be taken to oblige them, either by a withdrawal of allegiance or by force. Although it had sometimes been claimed that what pleases the prince just *is* the law, the idea that the king could be above the law, in the sense that he was legally answerable to no one for his actions, was not common until the later Middle Ages, when knowledge of Roman Law was more widely diffused, and with it the conception that the prince, as the supreme enforcer of law, cannot be legally subject to anyone. But even this did not mean that he was above the law in the sense that he could not be rightfully resisted if he exceeded his authority.

4. The Effect of the Study of Roman Law on Mediaeval Political Ideas

The revived study of Roman Law in the twelfth and thirteenth centuries had two important effects on mediaeval conceptions of government. First, it made men familiar with the idea that the prince, the Emperor or King – the most highly placed in the hierarchy of secular magistrates – was the representative of the people, of the entire community, the 'bearer of all their persons', to employ a Hobbesian phrase. According to the old Roman lawyers, authority had originally belonged to the Roman people, but they had transferred its use in perpetuity to the Emperor; it no longer belonged to them directly but was exercised on their behalf by the Emperor. Not all mediaeval commentators on Roman Law were of one mind about the nature of the Emperor's authority in their own time; a good many of them argued that the people had never transferred it unconditionally. The people still retained some of it, and could take what they had transferred back into their own hands, if the Emperor abused it. But though there was no agreement about the precise extent of the Emperor's authority, the study of Roman Law did get people accustomed to the idea that the prince, the highest of temporal magistrates, stands in a quite special relationship to the entire community whose head he was. The old Roman Emperors had not been the greatest of feudal overlords: they had been true monarchs, with all lesser magistrates acting in their name as their subordinates. Roman Law, as it has come down to us, is not the law of the Roman Republic, but of the Roman Empire. The *Corpus juris* of Justinian was prepared in the sixth century after the Republic was transformed into the Empire, and after all the great Roman jurists, the Roman philosophers of law, had lived under the Empire. Roman Law, as we know it, is the law of the most powerful and enduring of all European monarchies. That was why the mediaeval Church took to it so easily, and why the champions of imperial and royal authority found it so useful an instrument.

The second important effect of the renewed study of Roman Law was that it made men more familiar with the idea of law as expressing the will of a legislator, as a deliberate creation of human will. What pleases the prince, the Roman jurists had said, has the force of law. There was a great deal of local self-government in the Roman Empire, which formed a collection of semi-autonomous municipalities with an imperial bureaucracy superimposed above them. The Roman Empire was certainly not a highly centralized state, but the Emperor's supremacy inside it was universally acknowledged, and he was recognized as the promulgator as well as enforcer of law. Mediaeval commentators on Roman Law were not all of one mind about how Roman conceptions applied to the Europe of their day. Some of them, even as late as the fourteenth century, still asserted the primacy of custom, though by then most of them agreed that statutes supersede custom. What the legislator declares to be the law, they said, is the law; it is either custom authoritatively defined, or it is a deliberate change in the law made by the legislator, the people's supreme representative, who was most often, although not always, the prince. But it was also held that custom could qualify a statute, if the custom arose after the statute was made and the courts in fact applied the statute in conformity with the custom, as is the case in English common law.

The most fervent of mediaeval admirers of Roman Law never went so far as to assert sovereignty in the Hobbesian sense. Some of the things they said, if they are taken out of context, can indeed be made to look very Hobbesian: for instance, the often repeated phrase, that what pleases the prince has the force of law. But all that was meant by this phrase was that the prince is the supreme interpreter and maker of law; it did not mean that he was exempt from obedience to the law of nature, nor even that he could make law without consulting whatever persons or bodies he was by custom required to consult. There were, in the Middle Ages, almost no advocates for absolute monarchy as the seventeenth century understood it; all or nearly all mediaeval writers believed that princes are bound, under the law of nature, to keep whatever contracts they make with their subjects, and not to dispose of their property without their consent. They did, however, look upon the prince, either alone or assisted by some body which by custom had the right to be consulted, as a maker as well as a maintainer of law.

5. Mediaeval Theories about the Relations of Church and State

The difference between a religious and an irreligious age is not that in the first men believe in God while in the second they do not. Despite the widespread survival of paganism and the prevalence of worldly corruption in the Middle Ages, and notwithstanding the small number of atheists in Europe today, we rightly believe that mediaeval Europe was religious in a way that contemporary Europe is not. It was religious, and deeply religious, in the sense that the entire structure of mediaeval society was profoundly affected by man's conception of God and of God's purpose for man. It does not matter that only a few understood this conception, that they alone could explain it, or elaborate upon it, or argue about it. The beliefs that dominate a society may be fully and intensely alive in only a minority of minds, and yet may affect the lives of all its members.

The true, the passionate, Christian of the Middle Ages believed that man's relations with God are incomparably more important than his relations with men, and that other men are his brothers because they, too, stand, or may stand, in the same position with respect to God. Life in this world is a preparation for life in another. God makes full provision for His creatures on earth; He sees to it that they have the means of preparing themselves for the better life that comes afterwards; He has, through Christ, created a church in this world to instruct them in the faith without which there can be no salvation. This church, to carry out its function, must be independent of the Temporal Power. Its authority comes not from men but from Christ.

Where there is no peace, where men, moved by the evil passions to which they have been liable since the Fall, continually harass and make war on one another, instruction in the faith is not possible. Men therefore need another kind of authority in the world, an authority to keep the peace between them. This authority, the Temporal Power, is not concerned with their souls; it does not have any direct moral or spiritual purpose. If Adam had not sinned, if man were still in a state of innocence, there would of course be no need for the Temporal Power. That Power is a consequence of sin and a remedy for it, but a remedy only in the sense that it protects men from each other's evil passions; it does not purge them of those passions nor make them masters of their souls, for it cannot bring to them the grace of God which alone enables them to rise above their baser selves. That is what mediaeval writers mean when they say that secular rulers have authority over men's bodies only but not over their souls.

Yet the Temporal Power also stems from God. It existed before the birth of Christ, and before the Church was founded. It is indirectly necessary for salvation, since the Church cannot carry out its mission unless there are peaceful and orderly relations among men. One of the most prevalent doctrines of the Middle Ages is that both Powers, the Spiritual and the Temporal, derive equally from God; that neither is subordinate to the other, each being supreme in its own sphere; that man needs both; and that each Power requires the other, for the Church must be protected from violence, while religion strengthens men's loyalty to all legitimate authority. The work of the Church is higher than the work of the State, and its dignity is greater; but this does not mean that the Spiritual Power controls the Temporal.

Such was the prevailing philosophy. As we have seen, we find it as early as the fourth century in St Ambrose, we find it more elaborately in Pope Gelasius I at the end of the fifth century, and we still find it in the thirteenth century in Aquinas. It was the earliest position taken up by Christian thinkers, and the most persistent. As a formula, it was neat enough; but as soon as we try to define more particularly what is involved in each authority's being supreme in its own sphere, all kinds of difficulties arise. I shall not go into these difficulties in detail, nor try to explain how mediaeval philosophers and theologians dealt with them. I shall only point out their general nature.

Mediaeval thinkers characteristically assumed that there could be only one Church: one faith and therefore one Church. That Church existed here on earth; it included all Christians, but was in fact ruled over by priests and bishops, with the Pope at their head. It was the Spiritual Power, but it was also a temporal organization. The priests and bishops could not exercise their spiritual functions unless they had an adequate living. At first, they had largely depended on voluntary contributions from the faithful, and even in the Middle Ages there were the mendicant friars. But the priesthood, as a whole, had to have material security if the Church was to have spiritual independence.

There was no question of priests being paid salaries by the State; and if they had been so paid, the Church could hardly, in practice, have been independent of the State. So the Church owned property, and most of that property, in an agricultural and feudal society, was necessarily in land. Now, attached to the holding of land in the Middle Ages were all kinds of obligations that formed part of the structure of the Temporal Power of feudal society. The inevitable questions arose: To what extent could churchmen be expected to carry out these obligations? How much authority had the secular ruler over the property of the Church?

Again, to safeguard its independence, the Church claimed exclusive jurisdiction in spiritual and ecclesiastical matters. How should this claim be interpreted? Did spiritual authority concern only questions of faith? But the Church also administered sacraments, and marriage was, or eventually became, a sacrament and not just a civil union. The Church was equally the protector of oaths, since oaths were taken in the presence of God. But the feudal tie was created by the oath of fealty. The Church was thus concerned with morals as well as with faith. But who can set limits to the sphere of morality? Just what was involved in the Church's claim to spiritual jurisdiction over all Christians? What, moreover, was involved in the Church's authority over its priests? Priests, after all, are human and capable of other offences besides heresy and breaches of Church discipline. What if their offences are of the kind deemed civil when laymen commit them? Are they then to be tried by secular courts? Logically, it would seem that they should be. But the Church had in fact succeeded in making its priests responsible to its own courts for nearly all offences. Indeed, if it had not done so, its independence even in spiritual matters might have been threatened, for it is always possible to bring false charges against persons in one sphere in order to put pressure on them in another. Soon after Christianity had become the official religion of the Roman Empire, the Church looked to the Emperor for help in its fight against heresy; and ever since it had been current doctrine that civil magistrates must support the Church against heretics. But suppose the Church is divided about doctrine and both sides appeal to the Emperor, and he decides in favour of one? Has he acted as a faithful servant of the Church? Or has he meddled in spiritual matters outside his competence?

I have said enough, I hope, to show how difficult it was, even in theory, to set a precise limit between two kinds of authority, each supposed to be supreme in its own sphere and both exercised over the same persons, when there is no third authority to resolve disputes between them. The difficulty was in practice so much the greater because, for several centuries after the fall of the Roman Empire in the West, all authority had been precarious and variable. The new kingdoms emerging out of the ruins of the old empire had used the Church to help them establish their authority, and the Church had used them against the heretics. The Spiritual and Temporal Powers were in practice so closely and intimately bound up with one another that it was not possible to distinguish between them on any rational principle. When it is virtually impossible to set a definite limit between two authorities, and when there is no third power to judge between them, it is inevitable that each should try to extend itself at the expense of the other. These attempts can be made, up to a point, without questioning the doctrine that there are two authorities, each supreme in its own sphere. But after a time, there arise bolder spirits who either reject the doctrine outright or seek to qualify it drastically.

So it happened in the Middle Ages. As the power of the Papacy grew, so, likewise, did the claims of the Spiritual against the Temporal Power, until in the end we find some champions of the Church contending not only that it is for the Spiritual Power to decide what belongs properly to its own sphere, but even that both Powers were granted by Christ to St Peter, the first of the popes. Therefore the Emperor and all other princes hold their authority from the Pope; they may be elected or they may succeed to their thrones by hereditary right, but they are not truly in possession of their authority until they have been consecrated by the Church. The Church does not itself exercise the Temporal Power, but its duty is to see that that power is exercised properly. It had long been claimed for the Pope that the subjects of a ruler excommunicated by him were released from their allegiance, but excommunication had nearly always been held to be a spiritual penalty for a spiritual offence, or at least for an offence against the Church. Eventually, however, it was claimed as well that princes were responsible, not to God alone, or to God and the people, but to the Church, or rather the Pope, for how they exercised the Temporal Power.

This extreme position never came to be popular, and was brusquely rejected by all secular rulers, but it was vigorously asserted on the Pope's behalf in the thirteenth and fourteenth centuries. The arguments for it were characteristically mediaeval; they were partly biblical and historical, partly metaphysical, partly political. Either Christ had given the keys of both kingdoms, the earthly and the heavenly, to St Peter; or Constantine had acknowledged the supremacy of Pope Sylvester; or several emperors and kings had been deposed by Popes; or the soul

31

governs the body, and therefore the Church which directs men's souls must control the Temporal Power that rules their bodies; or society, to maintain order, must have a single head, who must be the Pope, since his authority alone extends over all Christians.

One extreme led to another. The most extravagant claims for the Church were made towards the end of the thirteenth century, and hence, at the beginning of the fourteenth, there arose equally strong counter-claims on behalf of the Emperor. Marsilio of Padua, in the *Defensor pacis*, argued that, as Christ had assumed no coercive power while on earth, the Church could have none either. Spiritual offences cannot, he said, be punished in this world but only by God in the next. Heresy, if it is punished on earth, is so only as a civil offence, because it is forbidden by civil laws. Christ gave no authority to Peter which he did not also grant to the other Apostles, and that authority was only to preach and to administer the sacraments. All priests, in virtue of their priesthood, have the same powers; the ecclesiastical hierarchy, which places some priests above others, is a merely human institution. The Church consists not only of priests but of all Christians, so that whatever authority belongs to it belongs to the whole community of the faithful, and not to the priests alone, still less to the Pope.

Marsilio's views on the supremacy of the General Council over the Pope within the Church will be considered in a later chapter, and I cannot here go into further details. Few even among the strongest opponents of the Papacy dared go so far as he did. But the contrast he drew between spiritual and secular power was to be elaborated, in different contexts, by subsequent thinkers, such as Wyclif, and later by Protestant writers on the relations between Church and State.

6. The Legacy of the Middle Ages

Political controversy did not become truly secular until the end of the seventeenth century, up to which time most of the arguments used by political writers rested on theological assumptions. Indeed, it is not just the assumptions that are theological, for in many cases the whole body of the argument is as much religious as political in character. God is not a remote creator or a Rational Will manifest in the order and development of the world; He is an omnipotent and invisible but also passionate and exacting master, very much present in the lives of all His servants. What He prescribes for man is not to be discovered merely by a process of inference, by taking stock of the world and then arguing back to the will of a supposed creator; it is recorded in Scripture and testified by the churches. When the philosophers of the eighteenth century spoke about God, they were, as often as not, speaking in a large way about the nature of the world; they were recording their belief that the world is an orderly system governed by reason. God, for them, was above all a necessary hypothesis. But in the sixteenth and seventeenth centuries, this was not so, except for a very few people. To the Huguenots and Jesuits on the Continent, to the Anglicans and Puritans in England, that is to say, to the parties to the most important political controversies of the first two centuries of our period, God was a daily actor in men's lives, an historical person whose more striking interventions in human affairs are recorded in the Bible and in other sacred or venerable books, who has spoken through the prophets and holy men, who has set precedents for mankind. He is also, of course, the Creator and Governor of the universe, manifestly reasonable and supremely benevolent; but these conceptions of the Deity were not yet separate in men's minds from the more personal, angry, jealous and enterprising God of the Jews before the dispersion.

The political writers of the sixteenth and seventeenth centuries still use the same kind of arguments as were used in the Middle Ages; they still appeal to the recorded activities of God and of divinely-inspired persons as much as to the general purposes that can be logically attributed to a Rational and Omnipotent Will governing the universe. They still mix up abstract and philosophical suppositions with historical claims. The history of the Jews, as recorded in the Old Testament, is still for them full of valid precedents for what Frenchmen or Englishmen should do in the seventeenth century. God was once very closely concerned with the affairs of His chosen people, and what He prescribed for them must still be good law for their successors, the peoples redeemed by Christ.

The great political argument of the Middle Ages about the proper relations between Church and State continued well into the seventeenth century. Indeed, it continued much longer, and has not yet come to an end, but it is not now, and has not since the seventeenth century been, the most urgent of political controversies. The theories of the social contract and of the divine right of kings, and modern arguments for limited and absolute secular power, actually arose out of this controversy, which belongs as much to the Middle Ages as to the Reformation. Of course, as a result of the Reformation, it changed in character, and it is easy to see that it must have done so. Arguments about the proper relations between Church and State are likely to be very different when there are many churches as compared to when there was only one – when the State is strong and growing stronger as opposed to when it scarcely existed as we know it today.

An old controversy which is pursued into an epoch different from the one that gave birth to it necessarily changes its form, but it does so slowly and without the parties to it being aware that it has changed. Old ideas and arguments continue to be used, though their altered significance is unnoticed. We can see how this has happened in our own day with Marxism, which was quite transformed by the Bolshevik revolution and the triumph of the Stalinist bureaucracy. It has come to be no longer what it was in Marx's time, or even in the years between Marx's death and Lenin's seizure of power in 1917. It is not merely that Marxists now act differently; they also think differently, though they still use the old vocabulary and even the old arguments. And yet how they think and act is profoundly affected by the doctrines laboriously put together by Marx. So it was with the political thought of the sixteenth and seventeenth centuries; the weight of the Middle Ages is heavy upon it, and yet it is not mediaeval. It too is revolutionary, moreover; it is a moral revolution of the first order, for it brought to birth, slowly, painfully, confusedly, our modern idea of freedom. With Hobbes and Locke, with Grotius and Pufendorf, we leave behind us the older methods of controversy, the war of texts and precedents, the arguments by crude analogy; we come to the more systematic treatises, of which only Marsilio had provided a true model in the Middle Ages, purporting to reach general conclusions from self-evident premises by a process of transparently clear reasoning. With the change in method comes a change in manners. Controversy becomes more polite; for men who seek to convince one another by rational argument have nothing to gain from vituperation.

These large assumptions, which were supposedly self-evident, and the logical arguments erected upon them by the political and legal philosophers of the late seventeenth and eighteenth centuries, were by no means all new. Many, perhaps most, of them had been current in Europe for centuries. What was new was chiefly the systematic treatment of them, and their separation from the older discarded ideas, theological and historical, with which they had previously been associated. No doubt, politics and law are not abstract and *a priori* sciences of the kind imagined by philosophers such as Hobbes and Locke, but they did gain immensely from this invasion by rationalist philosophy. The theology until then mixed up with them was largely irrelevant, and the history was almost wholly false. These systematic, secular and philosophical thinkers, by extricating in this way the basic concepts of politics and law from the foreign matter in which they were embedded, helped to clarify them. They made it possible to discriminate carefully between ideas long used but never before properly separated. Much more clearly than their predecessors, even including John of Paris and Marsilio who had put forward similar claims hundreds of years earlier, they drew a distinction between the legislative and the judicial functions of government, and between the legislative and executive; they recognized that the conception of law as a moral or rational principle is altogether different from the conception of it as a command; and they gave a much more precise content to the notions of consent and legitimate authority. Above all, they presented to us, in the shape in which we still use them, two ideas unknown to the Middle Ages and to Greek philosophy: first, the idea of sovereignty, and, second, the idea that the preservation of individual freedom is one of the basic duties of governments.

These two ideas, sovereignty and freedom, emerged out of controversies which were as much religious as political, in the sixteenth and early seventeenth centuries; and those controversies, as I have already said, though in essential respects different from mediaeval disputes, were carried on in terms of mediaeval ideas and arguments. To understand the significance of the controversies and the exact nature of the revolution in political and moral thinking implicit in them or brought about by them, we have to look at the political thought of the Middle Ages. We have to look at it, not systematically or historically or in great detail, but just enough to see what the stock of ideas was that the political writers of the sixteenth and early seventeenth centuries, of post-mediaeval and pre-rationalist Europe, inherited from the Middle Ages. For all these writers, except one, were steeped in the mediaeval Christian tradition; and that one exception, Machiavelli – who, while familiar with it, preferred to draw upon more ancient sources – was not a rationalist and systematic political philosopher in the manner of Hobbes or Locke, but a self-consciously unchristian patriot and republican of a kind scarcely to be found in Europe outside Italy before the nineteenth century. Machiavelli is either a very modern thinker indeed or else a refugee from the Rome of the last century before Christ. He profoundly affects the main course of European political thought but seems hardly to belong to it.

CHAPTER 2
Machiavelli

I. INTRODUCTORY

Machiavelli stands outside the main tradition of European political thought. He thinks and speaks of society and government differently from the great mediaeval writers, and differently, too, from the great writers of the sixteenth and seventeenth centuries, men like Bodin and Hobbes, Hooker and Locke. The mediaeval writers were mostly concerned with problems of definition, and with deriving men's rights and obligations from these definitions. They put such questions as: 'What is the Church?', 'What is the Temporal Power?', 'What purposes do they serve?' Those purposes seemed to them to flow from the nature and present condition of man. They therefore also asked, 'What is the nature of man?' This last question was, in their eyes, equivalent to asking, 'What are God's intentions for man?' The rights and duties, both of magistrates and of subjects, derived, ultimately, from these intentions of God, from the limitations of human reason as created by God, from the condition of man following the sin and fall of Adam, and from God's conditional promise of forgiveness brought to the posterity of Adam by Christ. Mediaeval political theory was rooted in theology, and sought to explain the authority of Church and State and the limits of that authority by reference to the will of God and the nature of man as created by God.

The political theory of the sixteenth and seventeenth centuries was also, for the most part, rooted in theology. That theology was, of course, different from the theology of the Middle Ages: very obviously so in Protestant writers but also, though less so, in Catholic ones, for they too were affected by the Reformation. Yet, though the conclusions reached by these political theorists might differ greatly, they continued to use much the same methods as their predecessors had done in the Middle Ages. They put the same questions: 'What is the essential nature of man?', 'What are God's purposes for him?' And they derived their conclusions about Church and State, about the rights and duties of magistrates and priests, on the one hand, and of their subjects and flocks, on the other, from the answers they gave to these questions. They used the same method: they offered definitions, and from these definitions, they derived conclusions about men's rights and duties. These definitions were answers, not to questions about empirical facts, but to questions about the purposes of God and the essential nature of man. That is what makes them definitions: definitions in the Aristotelian sense. The political philosopher who defines the nature of man does not purport to tell us how man actually behaves but rather what his end or destiny is, what he is created for.

This method was not the only one used by political writers even in the Middle Ages, but it was the traditional method; the only method that many writers used, and the method that nearly all writers used, though they might use other methods as well. Even if we take an unusually worldly, untheological mediaeval writer like Marsilio of Padua, we find the same concern with definitions and the same belief that moral rules can be derived from them. It was a method brought to the highest point of subtlety and elaboration in a theological age, but it by no means appealed only to men who accepted what the theologians taught. And it lasted long after the Middle Ages.

Some who openly rejected the method were less well rid of it than they imagined. Hobbes spoke scornfully of the 'essences' of Aristotle and of definitions which purport to tell us what things are for, what their destiny is, what they tend towards, and do not merely point to those of their observable characteristics which distinguish them from other things. He had no use either for the definitions of Aristotle or for the mediaeval glosses upon them produced by Christian theology. Yet he too made definitions, albeit of a different kind, and drew conclusions from them about the rights and duties of rulers and subjects. His conception of human nature, so different from Aristotle's and different too from that of the theologians, is yet no more than theirs got from experience. Indeed, if we compare his idea of man with Aristotle's or even Aquinas's, it is more inadequate, less true to the facts. Hobbes puts another kind of definition in the place of the kind he rejects, and then proceeds to his conclusions. To some extent, despite his deliberate break with tradition, he uses a traditional method and even traditional ideas; he argues with the mediaeval thinkers and those who follow their example to some extent on their own terms. He tries to prove them wrong.

Machiavelli does nothing of the kind. He cares nothing for traditional arguments, because he does not put traditional questions. He does not, as Hobbes and the Utilitarians do, no less than Aquinas, put these two questions: What is man? and What are his rights and duties?, seeking in the answer to the first question a key to the answer to the second. He offers no definitions, and never seeks to explain why, and to what extent, subjects have a duty of obedience. He is not, in the same sense as Aquinas, Bodin, Hobbes or Locke, a political philosopher. The question which to them seemed the most important, the question of political obligation, does not interest him. He wants to know what makes government strong, what makes freedom possible, how power is most easily obtained and preserved. In trying to answer these questions, his appeal is always to history; his books are full of examples. He seldom makes a generalization or gives a piece of advice without producing evidence in its favour.

Since he is so clearly not a political philosopher in the traditional sense, Machiavelli has sometimes been called a political scientist. He tries to support his conclusions by an appeal to the facts. He is interested in man, not as he ought to be, but as he is. True, he is concerned to do more than explain how governments function; he does not merely describe, he also prescribes; he gives advice about what should be done to create or to restore strong government. But he does not speak to men of their destiny or of ends which they, as rational creatures, are obliged to pursue. He takes it for granted that they want strong government, and confines himself to advising them how they can get it.

I think it misleading to call Machiavelli a political scientist. His indifference, when he speaks of government, to the destiny of man or to God's purposes for the 'most excellent' of His creatures, is not enough to make a political scientist of him. The Utilitarians share this indifference; they take it for granted that man in fact wants happiness, and confine themselves (so, at least, they think) to giving advice about how happiness is to be obtained. So, too, Hobbes takes it for granted that man wants security, and is chiefly concerned to advise him how he can get it. Hobbes and the Utilitarians both start from what they take to be the actual desires of mankind; they, too, are concerned with man as he is (or as they think he is) rather than as he ought to be, and the advice they give him is grounded in their estimate of what man actually is.

There is nothing specifically scientific about this attitude. A writer on politics is not scientific merely because he is interested in facts rather than ideals, and rests his advice on what he takes to be the facts. An account of what men want and what they ought to do in order to get it is not scientific merely because it is not an account of what they ought to want. It is scientific only if it uses suitable methods to establish what the facts are, what men actually do want and what experience has shown to be the most effective way of getting it. In this sense, Hobbes is not scientific, nor are the Utilitarians, nor is Machiavelli.

It is true that Machiavelli appeals to history as Hobbes and the Utilitarians do not. But he does so at random to support whatever conclusions he happens to be interested in. He has no conception of scientific method, of the making and testing of hypotheses. He never makes a systematic study of any one political order, let alone a comparative study of several. His generalizations about men and government, as also his practical advice, are the fruits of experience much more than of systematic study. They are the fruits of his experience as a civil servant in Florence and his reflections upon contemporary Italy. He uses history to support the conclusions reached by reflection on personal experience and observation. Machiavelli is shrewd, realistic, imaginative; he sees further than other men with as wide an experience as his own to reflect on. If this were not so, we should not be interested in him; we should not look upon him as one of the greatest of political writers. But to say all this is not to concede that he is a political scientist.

Of Machiavelli's two most famous books, one, *The Prince*, discusses a limited problem: how to acquire enduring and absolute power with the least effort. The other, the *Discourses*, is a commentary on another book, on the first decad of Livy's *History of Rome*. It is a series of reflections suggested by the reading of Livy, and is roughly divided into three main topics: how states are founded and governments organized; how states are enlarged by conquest and by other means; and how their inevitable decay can be prevented for as long as possible. Though these topics are discussed much more elaborately and realistically than they ever had been in the Middle Ages, they are not discussed systematically.

They are discussed for their own sake, and not in order to draw from them support for some kind of theory about the rights and duties of subjects and rulers. The discussion rests on assumptions not derived from theology and reaches conclusions which are not moral rules. Yet, untheological and morally neutral though the discussion is, it hardly deserves to be called scientific. The questions that Machiavelli puts are, of course, questions about matters of fact; the answers to them are not essential definitions in the Aristotelian sense, and they are not moral principles. They are empirical generalizations; they are based on observation. And yet they are not scientific because Machiavelli has no idea, however vague, that there are appropriate rules, that there is a proper method, for testing such generalizations. He does not do for the study of society what Galileo tries to do for the study of nature; he does not use, let alone define, methods appropriate to testing the sort of conclusions he reaches. It is only persons who follow such rules, who use such methods – or who feel, at least, the need for them and try to discover them - who deserve to be called scientists. Machiavelli felt no such need, and it is therefore misleading to call him, as some writers have done, the first political scientist – or the first since Aristotle. He was intelligent, original, penetrating and hard-headed; he had some of the qualities that go to make the good scientist. But he was not methodical and never aspired to be. Though the questions he put were new, he never seriously addressed himself to the problem of what is the best way of answering them. He wrote essays about politics, and not scientific studies, however tough, however inadequate.

When I say that Machiavelli is not scientific, I do not mean merely that many of his conclusions are questionable or even superficial. A writer who is not a scientist may sometimes be right where a scientist is mistaken. For example, I should say that Montesquieu comes much closer than Machiavelli to being a political scientist, though he too reaches many questionable and superficial conclusions. Montesquieu expresses opinions about a much wider variety of subjects, and is therefore probably much more often wrong than is Machiavelli. Though he, too, is imaginative and original, he is less hard-headed and more credulous than Machiavelli. But he does at least attempt to make a systematic study of different types of government; he takes many examples; he aims at an exhaustive classification; he is concerned about the methods he uses. We may say that his study is not as systematic as he thought it was, that his examples are not well chosen, that his classification is not exhaustive, and that his ideas about his methods are confused; we may say all this, and yet concede that he aims at making a scientific study of society, that he has some notion of what distinguishes a scientific from an unscientific study. But we cannot say this of Machiavelli. He is not, as is Montesquieu, a very imperfect social and political scientist; he is not a political scientist at all but a man of genius with considerable practical experience writing about politics.

If we compare Machiavelli, not only with mediaeval political writers but even with such writers as Hobbes and Locke, nothing is more striking than the keen interest he takes in history. Most of his arguments are supported by copious examples taken from the past and the present. But this interest in history has sometimes been misinterpreted. Some of his admirers claim for him that he was the first writer on politics to use what they call the 'historical method'. They may not claim for him that, because he uses this method, he is a political scientist; they may even avoid the term 'political scientist', perhaps because they think that only the natural sciences are truly scientific. There are many scholars, especially in England, who are reluctant to speak of the 'social sciences', preferring to call them the 'social studies'.

I no longer share this reluctance. Of course, the social studies do not use the same methods as the natural sciences, and they reach less precise and more questionable conclusions. Nevertheless, there are methods appropriate to the social studies, and I should call anyone who used these methods a social scientist. That there is still controversy about the methods does not make it improper to call the student of society a social scientist. Provided the student recognizes that his study is empirical and makes a real effort to use what he thinks are proper methods to test his conclusions, I should say that he deserves to be called a scientist. If Machiavelli had used an historical method to establish political conclusions, if he had had definite ideas about how history should be used to reach or to test such conclusions, I should not hesitate to call him a political scientist. But I find no evidence that he used such a method or had any such ideas. To support political principles with historical examples is not to use the historical method in the study of politics; it is merely to drive points home by selecting vivid illustrations.

True, Machiavelli is steeped in history. Yet, like nearly all his contemporaries, he lacks what, for want of a better word, I shall call 'a sense of history'; he lacks the sense that society changes from age to age, so that to see the past as it really was requires a great effort of the imagination. He sees history as little more than a kind of extended experience enabling the wise man to learn more about human nature than he could if he had to rely merely on his own personal experience, on his own memories. He uses the records of the past as he uses those of his own time; the historians speak to him as his contemporaries do; they tell him of what he could not see and hear for himself. He ponders what they tell him as he ponders his own memories; he is greatly indebted to them. But the past of which they speak seems to him very much like the present which he knows. Men, he thinks, find themselves again and again in similar predicaments. If their actions are recorded, others can learn from their examples and mistakes. Human nature, at bottom, is always and everywhere the same. Put a man in the same situation, and he will act the second time as he did the first, unless he remembers the consequences of the first action and decides to avoid them. History provides us with a much larger store of examples and warnings than we could otherwise have; it is the memory of mankind; it is a treasury on which any man can draw provided he has the wish to do so.

This is the use of history to Machiavelli; it is the abundant and fascinating source of practical wisdom, adding greatly to our understanding of ourselves and our neighbours. But he has almost no conception of moral and cultural change. The ancient Greeks and Romans are, in his eyes, much the same as the Italians of his own day. He does not deny that ancient Rome differs in many ways from Medicean Florence, but then so too do Venice and Milan. That the old Romans, belonging to a society profoundly different from all the states of Renaissance Italy, thought and felt in ways peculiar to themselves and difficult for him to appreciate, never really occurs to him. The old Romans are, in his eyes, merely better men than the modern Italians, braver and wiser and less corrupt. He speaks of Caesar and Alexander, and even of Moses, much as he speaks of any famous Italian of his own day whom he has not met. He might agree that men in antiquity were better than they now are, that there has been a sad falling away from the dignity, the manliness and the courage of the past. But he does not see how different were their values, their philosophies, their conceptions of themselves and of the world.

Of necessity, by our standards Machiavelli knew little history. He knew most about ancient Rome and the Italian republics of his own day. He knew much less about the Greeks. There was little enough history in his time for anyone to know, and much of it was inaccurate. Most of it consisted of annals and not of descriptions of how institutions and custom had changed. Machiavelli could scarcely use it to deepen his understanding of how societies develop and institutions and ideas are transformed; he could use it only to deepen his knowledge of human nature.

Those who call Machiavelli a political scientist, or who say that he was the first to use the historical method in the study of politics, are moved to do so because they feel that he is, in some sense, an innovator. He breaks with tradition; and they are hard put to it to explain just how he breaks with it. They see that he is chiefly concerned to show how power is obtained and preserved, and that he abounds in examples taken from history. He wishes to explain the facts and uses history to help him do so. That, they think, is enough to make a scientist of him; or, if not a scientist, then a political theorist using the historical method.

They are right in saying that Machiavelli is an innovator, but they miss the sense in which he is one when they call him a scientist or a user of the historical method. I do not know what word to choose to mark how Machiavelli differs both from mediaeval political writers and the exponents of divine right and the contract theory. I might be tempted to call him a positivist, if that word were not already associated with the theories of Comte and his disciples. He does not consciously put forward any ultimate moral principles; he takes it for granted that men want security and need strong government, and he tells them how to get what they want and need, appealing always to the facts in support of his arguments. He is not to be placed in any category; he is neither Platonic nor Aristotelian, neither Stoic nor Epicurean; he cares nothing for theology and deals only in human purposes; and yet he does not, like Hobbes and the Utilitarians, rest his political theory on an explicit psychology. He does not first tell us what man is like and then argue that a certain type of government suits him best; he appeals, not to psychology, but to history. He is *sui generis*.

Machiavelli puts new questions; or rather he puts questions neglected for centuries, since Aristotle's time. What makes the State endure and government strong? How can a state already on the way to dissolution be reformed? What kinds of morality and religion strengthen the State? And he puts these questions, as even Aristotle had not done, for their own sake, and not because he needs the answers to help him solve a moral problem, to help him discover the political conditions of the good life. In putting these questions, and in trying to answer them, he makes assumptions which are either new or were never made so boldly and unequivocally before him.

It may be that he never sees clearly how these assumptions are related to one another, nor even what they are. Certainly, he does not make them explicit, nor does he use them to construct a systematic theory of government. Yet he makes them and holds fast to them. Together, they make up an attitude to life, to man and society and government, which is as little Greek as it is mediaeval. It is new in the intellectual history of Europe. In this sense alone does Machiavelli have a philosophy; he has a new way of looking at man and society rather than a new theory about them. It is so sharp and vivid, so clearly his own, so much the fruit of a single, strong, imaginative and independent mind, that it deserves to be called a philosophy. It is a very personal criticism of life, which is the product of long reflection and great intelligence. Machiavelli's writings are not a random collection of second-hand ideas of the kind that any educated man picks up during the course of his life; they have a character peculiar to them, an aesthetic unity, because they are all the products of a highly idiosyncratic and vigorous mind. Machiavelli has a philosophy in the same sense as Montaigne has one, or even as Molière has one. Though there is no systematic theory, there is a consistent attitude, or a coherent set of attitudes. There are characteristic reactions that go easily together.

Machiavelli's philosophy is secular. This distinguishes it as much from Greek as from mediaeval philosophies. The Greeks did not distinguish the divine from the human, the sacred from the profane, as we have learnt to do since the emergence of Christianity. But by Machiavelli's time the distinction had been made, and his peculiarity is that he attends only to the human and the profane. The Greek, not less than the mediaeval, idea of man forms part of a conception of a universe in which are unfolded greater than merely human purposes. But Machiavelli is as entirely secular as Bentham or Bertrand Russell.

Machiavelli's philosophy is entirely secular, and to that extent, if you like, modern. Yet it is not entirely, nor even predominantly, modern; for Machiavelli is in some ways as foreign to us as he is to the Middle Ages and to antiquity. His is the classic, the purest, the most self-assured, the most uncompromising, expression of an attitude to life – to human life, taken in the round, and not just to the political side of it – which is not mediaeval or ancient or modern, but belongs only to the Renaissance, and above all to Renaissance Italy, an Italy still untouched by the Reformation. It does not so much reject Christianity as turn its back upon it, and has no use either for the Greek notion of the good life or for modern faith in progress. Machiavelli is as indifferent to Christian morals as to Christian theology, whereas our morality, even when we are agnostics or atheists, still owes a great deal to the faith with which it was connected. Machiavelli is more completely unchristian than any of the sceptical philosophers of our century.

Even in the narrower field of politics, Machiavelli is as unmodern in some ways as he is modern in others. He is so partly because his moral assumptions are different from ours and partly because the kind of state with which he is most familiar, the small Italian republic, is neither feudal nor national. He is aware that there are states very different from the Italian republics, and he sometimes discusses them, and yet, when he speaks of the State, it is clear that he usually has in mind a polity essentially similar to the Florence or Milan or Venice of his own day. That is why, the better to understand his political theory, we must first take a look at the Italian republics of the fifteenth and early sixteenth centuries.

II. ITALY AND FLORENCE IN MACHIAVELLI'S TIME

Italy, in the early sixteenth century, was, and long had been, the least feudal of the civilized countries of Europe. Her towns were the largest, richest and most independent; her civilization was the most urban and the most secular. The authority of the Emperor had worn so thin as scarcely to deserve the name of authority. The Emperor did not rule any part of Italy; he merely had better excuses than other princes beyond the Alps for meddling in Italian affairs. Less feudal than England or France, Italy was also less united, less close to becoming a single nation and a single state.

The Italian municipality or commune, when it first emerged as a privileged community, had been weak; its inhabitants had felt themselves more dependent on associations inside it, such as the guild and the family, than on the commune itself. But as the commune grew strong and developed into the city-state, these other ties weakened. The Florentine or Milanese learnt to regard himself as primarily a citizen of Florence or Milan and to set great store by such political rights as he had. The largest and most powerful community he belonged to, the city, was small; its rulers were much closer to him than the rulers of their country would be to Englishmen or Frenchmen of that period. The ordinary Florentine was more absorbed in the life of his State, better aware of what his rulers were doing, politically more restless and enterprising than the ordinary subject of the English or French king. He was much closer to thinking and feeling as a citizen. The ties that bound him to the largest community he belonged to were stronger. Even if he loved his country no better, he had more to fear and to hope for from the day-to-day actions of his rulers. He felt himself to be, as an individual, more important, precisely because his city was small and intimate. He was freer of lesser associations and also apt to be more self-centred.

The Italian commune had not developed a representative system; it was no doubt too small to feel the need to do so. As it grew larger and more independent, direct government by free citizens became unmanageable unless the number of the citizens was kept small, because direct popular government must either be on a narrow basis or else must lapse into anarchy. At the same time, to maintain its growing independence, the Italian commune needed to increase its resources and to extend the territory under its control. It had therefore to multiply its subjects while restricting the number of its citizens; in other words, it had to become an oligarchy. Florence in 1494, when Savonarola restored what was called democracy, had 90,000 inhabitants but only some 3200 citizens.

Restricted citizenship and the weakening of the old ties that bound men to guild and family caused great discontent, which one class of citizens could exploit against one another, or an adventurer against the whole body of citizens. Hence the weakness of the narrow regimes that fifteenth-century Italians called democratic, and the ease with which they were replaced by oligarchy or tyranny. Of the three greater Italian republics, Venice had by Machiavelli's time become, for good and all, an oligarchy, and Milan a tyranny. Only in Florence was there still reasonable hope of re-establishing democracy – that is to say, of making good the political rights of the less than twentieth part of the inhabitants of the city who had a hereditary claim to take part in its government and in the control of the territories subject to it.

During the greater part of the fifteenth century, Florence had been a tyranny, but an especially mild one. Her feudal nobility had long since lost most of their power, and the sharpest conflicts among the citizen body had, in the early fourteen hundreds, set the Major against the Minor Guilds, the rich merchants against the small tradesmen, the oligarchic party against the democratic. The Medici, though they belonged to one of the Major Guilds, took up the cause of the Minor ones, and used the conflict so cleverly that they got control of the State. They were not oligarchs but demagogues.

Variety and instability of government, deliberate change, remodelling of the machinery of State, were nowhere to be seen as much as in Italy. Any student of politics who, like Machiavelli, contemplated the recent histories of the Italian republic could discover more kinds of government and more frequent changes in forms of government than in all the other Western countries put together. Florence had transformed her government several times in the hundred years before Machiavelli began to write about politics.

For thirty-five years, from 1429 to 1464, she had known the mild and disguised tyranny of Cosimo de' Medici, who had preserved the forms of the constitution. Then, for twenty-three years, from 1469 to 1492, Lorenzo de' Medici had continued to rule by Cosimo's methods, but more blatantly and arbitrarily. Lorenzo's son, Piero, fled in disgrace from Florence in 1494 when the French invaded Italy. Florentine democracy was restored that same year by the Dominican friar, Savonarola, a fearless and austere demagogue who attacked luxury and corruption. Machiavelli was twenty-five when Savonarola gained control of Florence and set the poor against the rich. He was both fascinated and repelled by Savonarola – fascinated by his ascendancy over the people, repelled by his fanaticism and political crudeness. Savonarola cared only for purifying morals; he did nothing to reform institutions or to consolidate his power. While the people listened to him, he was all-powerful; but as soon as they began to grow tired of him, the party of the rich easily contrived his downfall and death in 1498. But the rich were not strong enough to put an end to the democracy he had restored, which survived until 1512, when the Spaniards took Florence and brought back the Medici.

Two months after Savonarola's death, Machiavelli entered the State service; and it is worth bearing in mind that all his practical experience of politics was as a servant of democracy, or of what passed for democracy in sixteenth-century Italy. He was familiar by hearsay with the tyranny of the Medici, and had directly observed the fanatical omnipotence and sudden ruin of Savonarola.

III. MACHIAVELLI'S CAREER AND HIS WORKS

It would be quite beside my purpose to give an account, however brief, of Machiavelli's life. I am concerned with his ideas and not with his life or his character, except to the extent to which they throw light on his ideas. We do not ordinarily need to know how a man comes by his ideas to be able to understand what they are, but sometimes, in order to get the full significance of his theories, we need to know more than a man tells us about his purposes in constructing them. This is certainly true of Machiavelli, who was a civil servant for many years before he was a writer, and who learnt more from experience and observation than from books. Moreover, he wrote his books, and especially the most famous of them, in enforced retirement and to prepare the way, if possible, for a return to active political life. Machiavelli wrote because he could not act; he took no pleasure in his withdrawal from politics, and was always as eager to affect a situation as to understand and describe it. Even as an historian, he put himself into other men's shoes, considering the alternatives open to them as if he were placed as they were and had to make a decision. No one was readier to praise and to blame than he was; and yet he passed his judgements nearly always as a politician and hardly ever as a moralist. He praised men for knowing what they wanted and knowing how to get it, and he blamed them for not knowing what to do or not daring to do it; he scarcely ever passed judgements on their ultimate purposes.

Until July 1498 Machiavelli was almost unknown, even in his native Florence. In that month, at the age of twenty-nine, he was appointed secretary to the Council of Ten, the second most important executive council in the Republic. The Council of Ten combined the functions of a War and a Home Office, and its secretary was therefore an important servant of the State. There were wars in Italy all the time that Machiavelli held office, and he was sent on many missions to Italian and foreign princes: to the Pope, to the King of France, to the Emperor Maximilian, to Cesare Borgia, and to other persons less well remembered by posterity. Four years after he had started his official career, it was decided that the Signoria, the chief executive council of the Florentine Republic, should have a president, or gonfaloniere, elected for life. The man chosen to fill this post, Piero Soderini, was a friend of Machiavelli, who therefore, though only a civil servant, contrived to have a considerable say in the making of policy. Perhaps he was never as important as he later, in the days of his retirement, persuaded himself that he had been, but he was important. He was close to the centre of affairs, had strong opinions about them, and was able to get a hearing.

When the Medici returned to Florence in 1512, Machiavelli lost his job. He had served the republic for nearly fifteen years and had acquired a taste for the active political life. Though he knew that he could not aspire to govern, he still allowed himself to hope that he might be in the future what he had been in the past, an important official in close touch with the makers of policy. He tried hard to win the favour of the Medici and to get employment from them, but he was compromised by his long service of democracy. That service had not even weakened his preference for democracy. He blamed several persons – and not least Piero Soderini – for the disasters that befell the republic, but he was by no means convinced that the absolute rule of the Medici was the best suited to Florence. He merely accepted that rule because he believed that, in the circumstances, it was impossible to get rid of it; and since the Medici were restored and he wanted active employment and could get it only from them, he did what he could to win their favour. But he was never an admirer of their methods of government. He was never won over to them; his heart was never with them. He continued to believe that, where conditions allow it, democracy or free government is better than monarchy or princely rule, and he was by no means certain that nothing could have been done, before the return of the Medici, to ensure that Florence should be both free and strong enough to defend her free institutions. The Medici were right in not being persuaded of Machiavelli's devotion to their interests; they kept him out in the cold for fourteen years, merely encouraging him to write the history of Florence, and when at last he was partly restored to favour, he had only a year to live. He died in June 1527.

It was after 1512, during the years of his retirement, that Machiavelli wrote his four books on government, on war and on history. The shortest and most famous, *The Prince*, was written in 1513, and Machiavelli hoped it would attract the attention of the Medici and induce them to employ him in affairs of State.

But *The Prince*, though its author hoped it might bring him employment, is not an insincere book; we cannot say of it that it does not contain Machiavelli's true opinions but only what he thought would please the Medici. The arguments of *The Prince* are perfectly consistent with the arguments of the much longer *Discourses*, in which Machiavelli expresses his strong preference for popular government. As has often been noticed, there is scarcely a maxim in *The Prince* whose equivalent is not to be found in the *Discourses*. *The Prince* contains only a part of Machiavelli's political thought, but that part is quite in harmony with the rest. It does not assume that princely rule is better than popular government; it merely confines itself to considering how princely rule is best established and preserved in the sort of conditions that prevailed in Italy at the time it was written. It is a well-made book, a treatise, terse and vigorous, on practical politics.

If Machiavelli had been a courtier by temperament, he would have written, to attract the favour of the Medici, a very different book from *The Prince*. He might have given the same advice but would have given it differently; he would have wrapped it up in soft words, he would have made it more palatable. Princes, not less than other men, like to think of themselves as high-minded; they like to disguise their motives and the true character of their actions, not least from themselves. The advice given in *The Prince* is too direct, too bold, too naked not to appear cynical even to persons who would be quite willing to act upon it if only they had the courage to do so. So lucid, so unadorned, so stark a book, such strong meat without sauces to soothe the delicate stomach, is not a fit offering for princes.

Machiavelli was disappointed; his book did not dispose the Medici to employ him. He was, though perhaps he did not know it, above all a writer and an artist rather than a practical man; he lacked discretion, and was carried away by his theme.

Of the men whom Machiavelli visited on his various missions, none impressed him more than Cesare Borgia, an unscrupulous political adventurer and the son of Pope Alexander VI. Borgia had tried to carve out a principality for himself, and had stopped at nothing in the attempt. He had failed, not for lack of courage or skill, but because the odds against him were too great, and above all because his luck did not hold. When the Pope, his father, died, he was, at a critical moment of his career, taken ill, and was unable to do what he should have done to defend his interests. It has often been said that Machiavelli admired Cesare Borgia and took him for his model when he wrote *The Prince*.

Certainly, Machiavelli admired Borgia greatly, and the portrait of the Prince is taken from Borgia more than from anyone else. Yet Borgia was a tyrant, while Machiavelli was a partisan of popular government. Machiavelli did not believe that men like Borgia make the best rulers, or even nearly the best; he believed only that they are at times a desperate remedy for a desperate disease. And he believed that Italy suffered from that disease. The Italians had, he thought, become so depraved and corrupt that only a resolute, clear-headed, hard and unscrupulous prince could save them by uniting their country under one government. Machiavelli was too much a realist ever to have believed that Borgia could have united Italy; even if Borgia had succeeded in his enterprise, he would have made himself master of only a small part of Italy and would have had many Italian rivals to contend against. His success might have made Italian disunion even more painful to Italy than it already was. But, though Borgia could not have united Italy, anyone who could have done so would have needed to have (in Machiavelli's opinion) the qualities of Borgia; and among those qualities were several which we should call vices.

Machiavelli certainly admired Borgia, but the admiration was not unqualified. When he wrote *The Prince*, Machiavelli's feelings for Borgia were already more mixed than they had once been. Not because Borgia had failed in his enterprise, but because, when luck had turned against him, with the death of his father and his own illness, he had for a time lost his nerve. His illness had prevented his opposing the election of Pope Pius III, and Machiavelli could not blame him for that; but Pius III had died soon after being elected, and Borgia, though at that time he was no longer ill, had allowed his partisans to vote for Cardinal della Rovere, who became Pope Julius II, and whose enmity Borgia should have foreseen. He had miscalculated from pusillanimity, and had not simply made a mistake; he had, in Machiavelli's opinion, shut his eyes to the dangers that faced him because he was too dispirited to take bold action. The portrait of the prince is not exactly the portrait of Borgia as he appeared to Machiavelli at the time that he wrote his most famous book; it is rather a portrait of what he had once believed that Borgia was. It is an idealized portrait, a deliberate embellishment, an image inspired by his reflections on what he had seen of Borgia rather than a sketch of what he really took Borgia to be. It is inspired to some extent by disappointment in Borgia, by the desire to improve on him, as well as by admiration for him.

That Machiavelli was an Italian patriot, who was humiliated by the intrusion of foreigners into his country and who desired the union of Italy, cannot be denied. But it would be a mistake to treat *The Prince* as a book inspired by simple patriotism. Though Machiavelli desired the union of Italy, he could hardly have believed that it was possible in his day. Did he suppose that the Medici were able to achieve it? We know that, in spite of his endeavours to win their favour, he did not admire them. They were too petty and too weak for so great a rôle. There is no evidence that Machiavelli believed that what Florence could not do might be achieved by Venice or Milan. He regarded the Papacy more as an obstacle in the way of Italian union than a promoter of it. Machiavelli was a man of strong passions and vivid imagination; his zeal for Italy is unquestionable. But it is difficult to believe that he thought it possible that Italy as he knew it could be united. *The Prince* is inspired by more than the dreams of an Italian patriot; it is inspired by curiosity. Machiavelli took it for granted that strong government is desirable, and he knew that strong government is not always popular government. He was interested for its own sake in the main question posed in *The Prince*, which is this: What qualities must a man have and what methods must he use to establish a strong and enduring monarchy?

The Art of War treats of politics only in relation to war, and *The Florentine Histories* put forward no political opinions not to be found in *The Prince* and the *Discourses*. The entire political theory of Machiavelli is therefore to be found in just two works; and not only the political theory but also the philosophy of life implicit in it. *The Prince* and the *Discourses* are important not only for what they tell us about how power is to be gained and preserved; they are also important for the philosophy contained in them but never made explicit. I shall be as much concerned to expound and criticize that philosophy as the political theory which goes with it.

Machiavelli's character is of a kind that is easily misunderstood because it is so uncommon, so free from the sentimentalities and illusions in which most men take comfort. His intelligence is keen; he lays bare our baser motives with a matter-of-factness which makes us uneasy. He is imaginative and lucid. His lucidity and cynicism make him seem cold to persons accustomed to look at the world through a comfortable haze. But he is not cold; he is as much capable of passion as of cynicism. He is not a man of very wide sympathies; but what he sees, he sees clearly and in sharp outline. He has few illusions about himself and still fewer about his friends. His terse, direct, exact descriptions are disturbing to those who like the warmth of ordinary make-believe. Neither his detachment nor his passions appeal to the modern taste, especially the northern taste; he is too cold when his intelligence alone is at work, and his passions are no longer ours. What excited his admiration does not excite ours, or excites it much less. He admired singleness of purpose, intelligence, courage and pride above all other qualities. We are more often struck by his cynicism than his admirations; for his style appears to us more the style of the cynic than of the admirer. The northern admirer is apt to enthuse, and enthusiasm is apt to be long-winded. By temperament Machiavelli is perhaps further removed from us than any of the other great political writers since the Middle Ages.

Many have found it difficult to believe that a man who could speak so cynically, and even coarsely, of his love affairs, who could describe so precisely the faults of his friends, who could discuss his own ambitions with so little reserve, could be anything but heartless or selfish. But all this may well have been an effect of pride, of a determination never to be deceived by anyone, not even by himself; and also, in part, of the bitterness of a disappointed man. He was, in fact, sincere and clear-sighted and therefore rather more loyal to his principles than most men are; and also, I suspect (unless loyalty consists merely in a disposition to praise), not less loyal to his friends.

IV. MACHIAVELLI'S POLITICAL THEORY AND HIS PHILOSOPHY OF LIFE

I have denied that Machiavelli was a systematic thinker and that he had an orderly and well-constructed political theory. To extract a comprehensive and neat system of ideas out of his writings would be to force those ideas into a frame which was not his own. At the best we should have, not a structure designed by him, but a structure of our own built out of his materials. I have also said that he had no explicit philosophy of life, no set of opinions about man and his place in the world which he ever troubled to put together into a system. That philosophy, though it has in fact an inner consistency and a definite character, is merely implicit in *The Prince* and the *Discourses*, and is never there expounded.

I shall consider Machiavelli's political theory and his philosophy or attitude to life by discussing in turn those of his assumptions, beliefs and preferences which seem to me most characteristic of him: his conception of the State, his belief that men are to a considerable extent masters of their environment, his interest in the psychology of rulers and the ruled, his concern for morality as a social force, his alleged lack of morality, his opinions about religion, and his preference for popular or free government.

We have seen that Machiavelli neglects the problems which seemed the most important to political thinkers before him, mediaeval and Greek. He never undertakes to analyse the concepts that politics uses; he never puts or answers such questions as 'What is the State?', 'What is law?', 'What are rights?' If we want to discover what he understands by these words, we have to see how he uses them. It is obvious that he speaks of society, government and law differently from the mediaeval writers, and differently also from Plato, Aristotle, the Stoics and the Sceptics. But he is not himself aware of these differences, and therefore never feels the need to explain the terms he uses or to prove them more adequate than others. Though, no doubt, he uses them much as they were currently used in his own day, he gives no sign of being aware that, by doing so, he is marking himself off from the great thinkers of the past.

Though Machiavelli says nothing about the duty of obedience and the limits of authority, though he entirely neglects this perennial theme of political philosophy, he is by no means – as we shall soon see – morally neutral. He has strong preferences. The idea that he has not is an illusion created in the unwary by the tone he often affects to discuss what he likes and dislikes. Some men are better able than others to look at their own preferences dispassionately, to speak of them as if they were not their own but someone else's. Machiavelli has this ability more than most men. He has it, not because he is cold or morally indifferent, but because his sympathies, though they are not wide, are strong. He can put himself in other men's shoes, he can appreciate what it feels like not to feel as he does himself; and with this capacity there goes the ability to see himself, as it were, from the outside. He expresses his own preferences clearly and vigorously, and very often does so without attempting to justify them. He is not without deep moral preferences, although he is not a moralizer.

1. Machiavelli's Conception of the State

In the Middle Ages political writers spoke of the Temporal Power more often than of the State.[1] They conceived of the whole of Christendom as one vast community with two kinds of authority established in it, the Spiritual and the Temporal. By the Temporal Power they understood the whole body of magistrates exercising authority outside the Church. They saw the Temporal Power as a hierarchy of persons standing to one another in many kinds of often rather loose relations, defined by custom and not easily changed. They often spoke as if all the civil magistrates in Christendom formed one hierarchy, with the Emperor at the top, though they also knew, what was indeed obvious, that the Emperor's authority did not in fact extend over the whole of Christendom, there being other Christian princes as supreme in their dominions as he in his. All Christendom formed, in theory, one community, and yet there were acknowledged to be in practice several kingdoms inside it independent of the Emperor. Within the Temporal Power, whether it was conceived of as a single Empire or as many separate kingdoms, nobody had absolute power. Not only was the authority of the Temporal Power, taken as a whole, limited by the authority of the Church, but the authority of every magistrate within it was limited by custom and also – so it was argued – by the Law of Nature, the same for all men everywhere though modified by custom to suit the circumstances of particular peoples.

From the thirteenth century onward, these ideas were considerably altered by the study of Aristotle's *Politics* and of Roman Law, and also by the continual growth of royal power, especially in the western kingdoms. Already in the fourteenth and fifteenth centuries, we have the beginnings of the modern conception of the State. Yet the feudal idea of temporal authority as a kind of private property still persisted; as, too, of course, did the claims of the Church, the Spiritual Power, and the old conception of civil government as primarily a remedy for

[1] The theme of this and the succeeding paragraph also figures in ch. 1 (see pp. 14–15 and 26–27 above).

sin. No political thinker of the Middle Ages, except perhaps Marsilio of Padua, spoke of the State as we do now: as an all-embracing and supreme authority; as a compact, precisely articulated, centralized body, with so strong a hold on its members' loyalties that it almost seems natural to speak of it as having a mind or will of its own. The modern State, even in its federal form, is highly centralized if we compare it with the strongest mediaeval kingdom; every part of it responds much more quickly to impulses received from the centre. The rights and duties of officials and citizens are more definite and elaborate. There is either a single system of courts enforcing a uniform law; or, if there is more than one system, the spheres of their competence are strictly defined.

Machiavelli's conception of the State is already ours. He does not think of it as a hierarchy of magistrates whose authority and relations to one another are defined by custom, but as a single structure, closely-knit and all-controlling, all of whose parts respond to one centre. The State is not, for him, co-ordinate with the Church; it contains within itself (or, at least, ought to contain) all the authority there is within the territory it embraces. Only the family is prior to the State, and nothing is superior to it or not to be questioned by it. This conception of the State squares with the notion of sovereignty, as we find it fully developed by Hobbes; but it squares also with the even more modern notion of federalism, which allows of no Hobbesian sovereign. The pillar of a federal state is its constitution, which divides, deliberately and carefully, a whole mass of power among bodies whose mutual relations are defined by law. There is nothing left out of account, nothing that lies outside the sphere of the State; all authority is exercised either by the State or with its permission. From the point of view of the State, the Church is either a part of itself, a State Church, or a voluntary association whose rights are defined by it.

Of course, we do not find in Machiavelli the explicit notion of sovereignty that we find in Bodin and Hobbes; we find only the conception of the State which eventually gave birth to that notion. For the doctrine of sovereignty is a deliberate rejection of mediaeval ideas about the limited authority of government, ideas which Machiavelli not so much repudiated as ignored. Machiavelli took it for granted that the well-constructed State is all-powerful within its frontiers, enjoying the undisputed loyalty of all its citizens. He did not openly contest the authority of the Church; he merely spoke of the State as if all public authority belonged properly to it alone.

The modern, the Machiavellian, conception of the State is not just an old Greek idea revived. Unlike the Platonic and Aristotelian *polis*, Machiavelli's State is morally neutral. It is an organized mass of power used by those who control it for the pursuit of whatever ends seem good to them. It is not thought of by Machiavelli, as the *polis* was by Plato and Aristotle, as forming the minds of its citizens, as the means to their moral improvement, as the environment enabling them to develop their faculties harmoniously. Machiavelli was not indifferent to morals; he often insisted that the State cannot be strong if its citizens are pusillanimous and dishonest. But he never tried to explain or justify it as the condition of their perfection or improvement. Indeed, he never tried to justify it in any way. He took it for granted that nearly everyone wants to belong to a powerful and respected political community. It may not be all that he wants, or even what he wants most intensely, but it is the one wish he shares with the great majority of his compatriots. The State is the society which, above all others, excites men's loyalties and ambitions. It is also, in a different but related sense, the complex of institutions which gives to that society its cohesion, its individuality and its power. The State has a structure, and the better constructed it is, the greater its stability and its strength. Machiavelli's conception of the State is more Roman than Greek; but above all it is modern.

2. Machiavelli's Faith in Man's Ability to Change his Environment

In the Middle Ages it was taken for granted that institutions rest on custom, that time has made them what they are, and that they are not to be changed. The Temporal and the Spiritual Powers were explained as instituted by God for the preservation and redemption of man. Man's nature and his needs are unchanging, as are also God's purposes for him. The institutions of Church and State are adapted to his nature and destiny, for man is a sinful creature who may yet be saved by the grace of a merciful God. Because man's predicament is always the same, so too is the frame of his world, his institutions. The purpose of all civil institutions, of government, law and property, is to preserve man from the consequences of the evil in him; he needs to be restrained, to be saved from his own and other people's unbridled passions. To restrain him is the function of the Temporal Power. The function of the Spiritual Power, the Church, is to bring God's Word to him, offering him the sacraments and so putting him in the way of salvation. The order of the world, the structure of authority inside it, Spiritual and Temporal, is unchanging.

When mediaeval writers call institutions like government and property *conventional*, they mean that they are consequences of the Fall, of the corruption of man's nature by Adam's sin, and would never have come to exist if man had remained true to his nature as God first made him. Though they admit that government and property rest on custom and serve human needs, they do not allow that men, having made them for their use, may change them as they please. For, though they arose among men to protect them from one another, and are therefore means to security, they are also remedies for sin, divinely instituted. The condition they are meant to remedy is permanent, and so too are they. They are adapted to what is enduring in the fallen nature of man.

It is enough to read only a few pages of Machiavelli to see how differently he looks at law and government. He does not deny the obvious; he knows that habits change slowly. He does not despise custom or deplore its hold on man. He even believes that states and nations decay, and that the process, if it has gone far, cannot be stayed. He is very much aware of the many obstacles in the way of anyone who wants to make great political changes. Yet he greatly admires the man who wants to make them and knows how to set about doing so. The only purposes he takes account of are men's own purposes for themselves; and all institutions are, in his eyes, human contrivances for human ends. What man has established to suit himself, he can also change, provided he knows how.

Hence the intensely practical and yet broad and deep interest that Machiavelli takes in politics. He invites us to be enterprising and cautious. We are not, as citizens and social creatures, caught up in purposes larger and more sacred than our own; we are men living among our own kind, each with only one life to live and make the best of. We cannot attain our purposes unless we study ourselves and our social world, unless we know what is possible and what is not. Arrogance is foolish, but so too is the tame acceptance of our lot.

Men cannot do what they please with their institutions. What they can do is limited by the character of what they work with. But they can take thought and refashion what they have inherited from their ancestors; they are not bound to accept it unchanged. They must take large account of custom, and ought always to build upon it where it offers a secure foundation. Machiavelli was too much a realist to suppose that men can remodel the State as they like to achieve whatever purposes they have in mind. He knew that innovators and reformers are exceptional men, apt to be misunderstood by their contemporaries and frustrated by the inertia and stupidity of the herd.

Yet he believed that they could, if they chose the right moment and the right methods, achieve a great deal.

For all his caution, Machiavelli exaggerated the extent to which men can change their institutions to suit their ambitions and ideals. He took the Roman and Greek historians literally; he believed what they told him about Lycurgus, Solon, Romulus and Numa Pompilius; he had no means of separating the mythical from the true in their stories. The founders of states are, he said, to be counted among the greatest of men, if the states they found endure. He believed that history provides many examples of founders and restorers of states, of men who, almost single-handed, set up new political societies or transformed old ones. He seems also to have believed that, at least in the parts of the world best known to him, in the Mediterranean countries, the power of the elect, of heroic natures, to create and to reform had been greater in the past than it had since become. There men had grown corrupt, and, the more corrupt men are, the more difficult it is to find a remedy for whatever weakens the State.

Machiavelli's ideas about how states are created and reformed may seem to us rather too simple. We may protest that the deliberate creation or reform of a political system is much more likely in an advanced than in a primitive society, and that it is truer today than ever it was in early Greece and Rome that systems of government are human contrivances for human ends. We may also be readier to admit than he was that our ability to make exactly the changes we want is severely limited, that political reforms always have consequences not foreseen by their makers, that achievement always falls far short of intention. The social structure is more complicated than Machiavelli imagined it to be, and the political structure is only a part of it; our understanding of it is imperfect, and when we act upon it, we can never rely on getting from it precisely the reactions we want. Nevertheless, we are still perpetual reformers, trying to adapt our institutions to our purposes; though with different and perhaps larger reservations, we still share the faith which Machiavelli was the first among modern political writers to take for granted.

Augustin Renaudet[1] has noticed that Machiavelli was interested only in political reforms. To explain the disorders to which states are liable he often pointed to rivalries between the rich and the poor. Indeed, it would have been difficult for a Florentine not to do so. But he proposed no social reforms; he did not think it important to keep inequalities of wealth within limits. He had no strong feelings

[1] In his *Machiavel*, 2nd ed. (Paris 1956).

for or against any class, with only one exception – the feudal nobles, whom he abominated. Thus, on the whole, he accepted the social order as it was. He noticed that a prince, to increase or preserve his power, must treat different classes differently; their attitudes to government differ and so too must the attitudes of government to them. He was not unaware that forms of government and types of social order are closely connected; he could see that a wealthy commercial city cannot be governed in the same way as a poor and simple agricultural community. Yet he sought only political remedies for whatever seemed to him defective or evil in the State.

He disliked the feudal nobles, not because they were rich or raised up high above other classes, but because they weakened the State; they were not, as he saw them, a privileged class inside the State so much as a privileged class against the State. They had usurped some of the prerogatives of the State; they had rights of private jurisdiction and private war, and, as long as they had them, there could not be a powerful State. Machiavelli disliked the feudal nobles only because they had made private rights of what belonged, or should have belonged, to the State. He thought it desirable that they should lose these rights, but he did not want to deprive them of anything more.

There is also another way in which the modern reformer differs from Machiavelli. He often believes, as Machiavelli does not, in progress. He believes in more than the remedy of abuses; he believes in indefinite progress. He is not primarily interested in strengthening the State or in putting off, for as long as possible, its inevitable decay. He has some conception, more or less vague, of a desirable social and political order, and, though he admits that men may never reach it, or not for a long time to come, he believes that they can approach indefinitely nearer to it. He may or may not believe that this progress is inevitable, but he believes that it is at least possible; whereas Machiavelli, like several of the philosophers and historians before the Christian era, believed in cyclical change.

No doubt, there are men today who are reformers and, who yet do not believe in indefinite progress. They may reject the very idea of progress, or they may, without rejecting it, think that indefinite progress is unlikely. If they do not reject the very idea of it, they may hold that the forces likely to impede it are stronger than the forces likely to favour it. Yet they may still be reformers. They may hold, quite reasonably, that they ought to do their best to improve the world even though it is unlikely, in the long run, to prove a better place than it is now. They may, by their efforts, ensure that, at least for a time, it is better than it would have been without those efforts.

But they may reject the very idea of indefinite progress. They may hold that, as society changes, so too do men's values. They may argue something like this: 'If one generation act to improve society by certain standards, they help to bring into existence other standards which move their descendants to make changes which by the earlier standards are not improvements. Though, no doubt, there are some standards common to all epochs and all societies, it is seldom by reference to them that an epoch or society which claims to be superior to another can justify its claim. By the standards common to Englishmen in the tenth and twentieth centuries, modern England is no better than the England of a thousand years ago.' And yet even those who argue like this can still be reformers, and not unreasonably; they can have their own standards, and can seek to live by them as well as they can, leaving it to later generations to look after themselves.

These reformers who, for one reason or another, do not believe in indefinite progress, still differ greatly from Machiavelli. Their scepticism rests on a conception of social change quite foreign to him; they think of it as going on endlessly, neither repeating itself nor coming indefinitely closer to some desirable goal. They do not believe, as he did, in cyclical change; they do not believe that there is a natural or *normal* course of growth and decay through which all states move unless some force external to them prevents their doing so. In the last two hundred years, most believers in a *normal* course of social and political change have also been believers in indefinite progress; they have seldom been attracted to the idea that social change is cyclical.

It may be that one reason for this is the great accumulation of historical knowledge; we know too much about too many very different types of society to believe that there is a normal cycle of change which they would all complete if external causes did not destroy them prematurely. We know too much to believe that long ago other societies passed through the phases through which our societies are now passing. But history does not, in the same way, prevent our believing in progress. It may be that the more steeped we are in history, the less inclined we are to believe in progress. I do not say that it is so, but I suggest that it may be. And yet history does not, in this case, clearly refute us, as it does in the other. There is overwhelming evidence against the belief that all social and political change is cyclical, except when the community involved in it comes to an untimely end; there is nothing like the same clear evidence against the belief in indefinite progress.

Since Machiavelli believed that all states, unless external causes disrupt them, pass through the same cycle of change, from youth through maturity to decay, he thought it the mark of a great statesman that he gave his State a solid constitution, prolonging its maturity for as long as possible. He saw this maturity as the period of the State's greatest strength and vigour, when it is least likely to succumb to external blows. Just as a man may be struck down in his prime, so too may a state, if it is exposed to destructive forces of exceptional power; but the greater its vigour, the greater its expectation of life.

Machiavelli took this idea of cyclical change from Polybius. It is easy to see what makes it attractive. Renewal and decay are the law of life, of the vegetable and animal kingdoms, and men have always been apt to argue by analogy from the biological to the political. Though there is nothing about political change, as they experience it, to suggest that it is cyclical, they are ready to apply to it ideas suggested to them by the changes they see in themselves. There are some beliefs which, given the state of our knowledge, come easily to us, though there is no real evidence of their truth, and which we later abandon only with difficulty, after we have accumulated overwhelming evidence against them and have come to understand the significance of that evidence. It is now easy to see that one belief of this kind is belief in cyclical change, and perhaps in the future it will be as easy to see that another is belief in indefinite progress.

Today we have a conception of political and social change foreign to Machiavelli; we see it as unending, unrepetitive and all-embracing, transforming all communities. This conception does not logically require belief in indefinite progress, but is compatible with it.

3. The Psychology of Rulers and the Ruled

Machiavelli does not enquire, as Hobbes and so many other political thinkers were to do, into the psychology of natural man, into human nature as it might have been outside organized society. There is, with him, no argument from the psychological to the social and the political. He is not concerned to show, as Hobbes is, that man, since he has by nature such and such characteristics, can get security only under a certain type of government, nor yet to prove, as Locke tries to do, that man, by reason of his nature, has rights which can be made good only if he is governed with his own consent. Nor does he hold, with Aristotle, that man has a nature which is fully realized only in the State, where he becomes actually what he is potentially. We never find Machiavelli speaking as if man were somehow more true to his essential nature in society and the State than outside it. Though he sometimes hazards opinions about universal human nature, they are with him merely remarks made by the way. No important political conclusions are derived from them. He takes it for granted that men, without the discipline of government, would know nothing of justice and honesty, but he does not labour the point or use it to justify government.

Machiavelli is interested, not in natural man, but in social man – man as citizen, soldier, prince and public official. He is interested, above all, in political psychology, in the passions and opinions which inspire political behaviour. He is interested both in individual and in mass psychology. In this respect, he is a precursor, not of Hobbes, Locke and Rousseau, but of Montesquieu, Burke and Tocqueville.

There is nothing specifically modern about this interest in political psychology. When I say that Machiavelli was, in this respect, a precursor of Montesquieu and Burke, and not of Hobbes and Locke, I am merely pointing to something about him that distinguishes him from the political theorists of the Middle Ages and of the sixteenth and seventeenth centuries. Both Plato and Aristotle were interested in political psychology, as well as in essential human nature. They saw that the passions and prejudices that inspire political behaviour differ in different types of State. So, too, did several of the Greek and Roman historians.

Given the questions which Machiavelli was concerned to answer, it is easy to see why he should have been so much interested in political psychology. He wanted to know how states are established, how they grow strong, and what causes them to decay. To ask 'How ought this State to be governed?' was, in his eyes, equivalent to asking 'What sort of government should it have to make it enduring and strong?' At the same time, he knew that conditions are not everywhere and at all times the same; he knew that what makes some states strong weakens others. He saw connections between political institutions and political psychology. He took it for granted that men are, at bottom, very much alike in all societies, or at least that, though they differ considerably as individuals, much the same types are to be found everywhere. Your Caesar differs from your Pompey, and yet you must expect to find men of their types in any society. Machiavelli did not trouble to consider how far what is common to all mankind is due to all societies being in many respects alike and how far it consists of inborn characteristics; he merely took it for granted that much the same types of men are to be found in all societies. He took this for granted, and yet at the same time, and not inconsistently, believed that the passions and motives inspiring political behaviour differ considerably from State to State. Where there is popular government the type of man that gets power is apt to be different from the type that gets it in a closed oligarchy or monarchy. The attitude of the citizen to public affairs and to his government is different in a democracy from in a dictatorship, though men in both communities can be sorted out into much the same psychological types. We can imagine some men – as, for example, Savonarola or Hitler – getting power only where certain quite exceptional conditions hold, and we can imagine others – Caesar, perhaps, or Washington – getting it under much more varied circumstances. Different circumstances bring out different sides of a man's character; and so we can say that the qualities needed to make a Roman dictator and a President of the United States are different, even though we believe that Caesar had them all.

I am tempted to say that Machiavelli was the most political of all the great political theorists, that he confined his interest almost entirely to man's political behaviour. As we shall see, he was not indifferent to morals or to religion. Quite the contrary. But he was more concerned to discover what makes the good citizen than what makes the good man, and cared more for the political effects of religion than for what it is in itself. As I hope to show later, his concern for religion was closer to being exclusively political than his concern for morality, and yet his concern for both was primarily political.

We cannot blame a man for confining his interest to one part of human and of social life, but we can blame him if he speaks as if it were the whole of it or the most important part. Machiavelli is one-sided, not because his interest in man and society is limited, but because he seems not to understand how limited it is. He is more than one-sided; he is also untouched by much that is human. Man, as he depicts him, is a creature concerned above all to impose his will on other men or to impress them; he is primarily a political animal, though in a sense different from Aristotle's. He is not political as being capable of realizing his potentialities only in a political community; he is political as being a lover of power and reputation, as being self-assertive, as being a creature who strives to achieve his ends by controlling others, and whose dearest wish is to raise himself above them. No doubt, these qualities are much more to the fore among leaders than among the people generally. But, then, Machiavelli, to the extent that he is interested in the individual for his own sake, is interested in the man who achieves or aspires to political greatness. Though he does not say, as Nietzsche was to do, that ordinary men exist only to give scope for the activities of heroes, his interest is confined mostly to heroes and would-be heroes, and his heroes are not poets or artists or philosophers but only men of action. He does not exactly despise the humble; he merely ignores them, except in the mass, when they begin to count politically. He does not ask what the State does for them, beyond giving them security; he is not interested in the sort of men they are or the lives they lead. And yet he is interested in the men he thinks of as great or as aspiring to greatness; he is interested in them because of what they are in themselves and not only because of the political consequences of what they do. He admires Borgia for being the sort of man he is as well as for trying to establish a powerful State.

4. Machiavelli's Concern with Morality as a Social Force

It is to *The Prince* that Machiavelli owes his reputation, and especially his evil reputation. At the worst, *The Prince* has been called a wicked book; at the best, a book not concerned with morality. And yet, as Pasquale Villari and others have shown, there is no unscrupulous maxim or repulsive advice in *The Prince* whose equivalent is not to be found in the *Discourses*, a milder, fuller and less offensive book. It is easy to accuse Machiavelli of immorality or of cynicism. No doubt, he sometimes was immoral, in the sense that he advocated courses which must be condemned by anyone who accepts certain very common beliefs about how people should behave. No doubt, too, he was often indifferent about matters which most people think morally important. It is not only useless, it is even impertinent, to try to defend him against some of the charges levelled at him. He had rather a good opinion of himself, and also an acute sense of the ridiculous. If he had lived to hear his accusers, he would have been indifferent to most of them, and amused by some. Frederick the Great, who both took his advice and denounced him for giving it, would probably have been a favourite with him. He would probably have found most ridiculous of all the people who have taken it upon themselves to defend him. It was no part of his ambition to be thought a good man by respectable persons.

I certainly do not wish to defend Machiavelli against the charges of immorality or cynicism. They are charges that can be brought, on occasion, against many important politicians and political writers; and their being brought more often against Machiavelli than against others seems to me not to matter very much. It is, I think, more important to notice that few writers about government and society have had as much as Machiavelli to say about society's need of good morals; he had some new and also true ideas about the social functions of morality.

In the second chapter of the first book of the *Discourses*, Machiavelli, discussing the origins of states, says that the sentiments of justice and honesty arose among men after they had chosen to live under chiefs for their common protection. Though this argument is not repeated in his other works, it is nowhere denied; and it would, I think, be fair to say that he believed that there is no morality prior to society. He believed that men, if subject to no discipline, would seek to satisfy their appetites by every means open to them, restrained only by fear. Before law and government have bridled them, men are creatures of passion and reason; but they are neither moral nor immoral. It is the discipline of law that makes them honest and just. Take this discipline away, and they soon lapse into selfishness, dishonesty and injustice.

It often happens, when men are observed to share one belief, that they are taken to share another, because the observer mistakenly supposes that the two beliefs are logically connected. It has been noticed that Machiavelli and Hobbes both look upon justice as an effect of law; and therefore, since Hobbes (so it is said) believed that men are always self-regarding and that positive law is the *only* measure of the just and unjust, it has sometimes been taken for granted that Machiavelli also believed this. The assumption is gratuitous; the first belief does not entail the second, and there is no evidence that Machiavelli held them both.

Hobbes went to great trouble to make his meaning clear, to prove that, from first to last, man, savage or civilized, amoral or moral, is entirely self-regarding. Man is just and honest in civil society because it is there made worth his while to be so; but his purpose is always the same, the pursuit of his own good, which is peace for the sake of felicity; and felicity is continuous success in satisfying desire. From first to last, man lives for himself alone. We can know that Hobbes thought this because he went out of his way to drive the point home.

Machiavelli tells us only that men are by nature immoderate, and that, without the discipline of law, they are neither just nor honest. He never undertakes to show, nor anywhere takes it for granted, that honesty and justice are refined forms of egoism. To hold that morality is an effect of law and social discipline is not to be committed to hold that man, by necessity of his nature, is always selfish, or that there is no difference between merely obeying the law and having a sense of justice. For example, Rousseau believed that man in the state of nature is a mere creature of appetite, and that only life in society, by putting him under the discipline of law and opinion, makes him capable of justice; and yet Rousseau was emphatically not a psychological egoist. Nor did he equate justice with legality.

But I must take care not to suggest that Machiavelli stands closer to Rousseau than to Hobbes. In Rousseau's writings there are, as there are not in Machiavelli's, several arguments meant to show how the discipline of social life makes man moral and just. Where Hobbes and Rousseau are explicit, coming to opposite conclusions, Machiavelli is silent. The state of nature, which means so much to them, means nothing to him. Machiavelli is no more to be classed with Rousseau than with Hobbes. All that can be fairly said of him is that he believes that honesty and justice, and their opposites, are qualities acquired by men in society, and that he always speaks of these qualities, as we all do when we have no theoretical axe to grind, in ways which do not imply that they are refined forms of egoism or that justice is merely obedience to positive law.

Yet the critics who say that morality, to Machiavelli, is something different from what it is to most people, are not entirely wrong. There is some truth in what they say, but they exaggerate. They do so because they misunderstand the distinction he makes between what he calls *virtù* and ordinary goodness. Since Machiavelli thinks *virtù* indispensable to the citizen and the State, and sometimes says that goodness is harmful to them, it is easy to conclude that he makes a sharp distinction between private and public morality, between what makes good men and what makes good citizens. This, I am sure, is a mistake; there is a distinction, but less sharp and more subtle than is often supposed.

By *virtù* Machiavelli means vitality, or energy and courage without regard to their objects, energy and courage both for good and evil; and by goodness he means what most people of his time meant by it, namely, the qualities generally admired in European society. Most of these qualities – honesty, justice, devotion to duty, loyalty and patriotism – are, he thinks, necessary to the good citizen. So that the *virtù* proper to the citizen is not energy and courage for good and evil indifferently, but for good alone – that is to say, displayed in honest and just causes for the public good.

That Machiavelli thinks a high level of private morality necessary to the State is shown by what he says about the Swiss and the Romans. Of the peoples of his own time, he admires the Swiss most; he argues that they are free and formidable because they have a high sense of duty to their neighbours as well as to their country. The Romans, he says, lost their liberty because they neglected their duties as citizens; but it was the same causes that made bad citizens of them and that corrupted their morals. Nobody is more interested than Machiavelli in the moral causes of political strength and weakness. This is what we should expect, for no one with his interest in psychology could neglect the moral factor or suppose that private and public virtues are not closely related.

But Machiavelli is not a Christian moralist. He is, as he has often been called, a pagan. He dislikes some of the qualities most admired by the whole-hearted Christian. He dislikes excessive humility; he dislikes asceticism, and patience under injustice; he likes a man to have a proper sense of his own dignity, to resent an insult even more than an injury; he has a high notion of what man owes to himself as well as to his neighbour. Meekness is an invitation to others to be unjust, and therefore a bad quality in a citizen. He approves of ambition, of the passion for worldly fame, because he takes it for a mark of vitality; and the State needs strong men. All citizens should be honest, just and patriotic; but the ablest of them are most likely to make full use of their talents under the spur of ambition. Ambition is dangerous; but it is also necessary, if the State is to be well served. The problem is not to destroy it but to direct it into proper channels. In the independent and self-governing State, the State whose citizens are free, ambition and public spirit sustain one another. Machiavelli believes that the desire for fame increases men's fortitude and courage. Hence a certain distaste for Christianity, the religion that teaches humility and unworldliness.

It is the *worldliness* of Machiavelli, much more than his belief that the end justifies the means, which makes the morality he commends so unmediaeval and unchristian. He admires the ancient Romans more than any other people. What he admires most about them is their fortitude in adversity, their strong sense of public duty, their readiness to make great sacrifices for the republic; and all this, not for the sake of eternal happiness, but from motives of honour and patriotism. The Roman felt that he owed it to himself and to others to live with courage and dignity, and when he sought fame, he sought it in serving his country. Machiavelli does not admire the man more occupied with the condition of his own soul than with his neighbours and his country.

The qualities admired by Machiavelli are, for the most part, the qualities in men which make for strong political communities. But it would be a mistake to suppose that he admires these qualities only for their political effects. That is not the impression that his writings, taken as a whole, create on the unprejudiced reader. He admires the Romans for being the sort of men they were, and not only because Rome was powerful. Because he is at pains to show how their virtues made Rome formidable, it does not follow that he cares for the virtues only on account of their political effects; any more than it follows that Christian moralists who tell us that the reward of virtue is Heaven approve of what they call virtue only on account of its reward. Machiavelli admires the greatness of Rome and the virtues of the Romans; he believes that the virtues produced the greatness, and perhaps also that the greatness encouraged the virtues. Since he speaks of both with admiration, it is to read more into his words than he puts there to suppose that he cares for the virtues only for the sake of the greatness they produce.

The truth is that the order of Machiavelli's moral preferences is different from ours, and even more different from that of the mediaeval Christian. How he differs from the mediaeval Christian I have already tried to explain; and now, in order to make his position, as I see it, clearer, I shall try to show how he differs from us. He admired courage, intelligence and resourcefulness much more than we do, and kindness and modesty much less. He liked men who are true to the passions they really feel, who dare to live the lives that seem good to them, who are not slaves of opinion. He despised the man who is honest and mild, not from principle, but from timidity. He did not say, with Shakespeare, that conscience makes cowards of us, but he did believe that we often think we are acting conscientiously when in fact we are merely afraid. He was apt to speak contemptuously of persons who refrain from crime only because they fear the consequences of it; and this has too often been mistaken for approval of crime. He admired courage, intelligence and tenacity of purpose wherever he found them, even in the criminal, and he expressed his admiration boldly, as people no longer care to do.

In saying all this, I am not seeking to make him out better than he was. My only concern is to make his position clear. He was, I dare say, too ready to mistake the promptings of conscience for cowardice. Whether a man is courageous or cowardly, he will more readily do something dangerous which he believes to be good than something dangerous which he believes to be evil. The horror that a man feels at the thought of committing what he believes to be a great crime, even when he is strongly tempted to commit it, ought not to be confused with fear of the consequences. Though this horror has something of fear in it, it is fear of a special kind. It is fear of the act more than of its consequences. If we compare him with Plato or with any of the great tragedians, ancient or modern, we cannot say that Machiavelli had a deep insight into the mind of the criminal. But that, after all, is not a harsh judgement to pass on a mere political theorist.

Machiavelli, who set no great store by veracity, seems to have admired people who have no illusions about themselves, who can themselves face the truth even though, from policy, they hide it from others. And he had no pity for those who fail because they are poor in spirit, whether their ambition is noble or criminal; he had no pity for them, not because he worshipped success, no matter how obtained – for he was never as vulgar as that – but because he admired singleness of purpose, and the courage, subtlety and resourcefulness which so often bring victory when to the timid defeat seems inevitable. He could speak of failure with sympathy and respect, provided it was not an effect of cowardice or stupidity. He could also condemn success (as he did Caesar's) when a man gets power for himself by destroying freedom and corrupting the State. He was not interested in an eternal or universal morality; he approved the most strongly the moral qualities that make political societies free and strong, and individuals enterprising, bold and public-spirited.

5. Machiavelli's Attitude to Religion

Nothing separates Machiavelli more sharply from his mediaeval predecessors than his attitude to religion. He was concerned with it only as an influence on political and social behaviour, as a system of beliefs and ceremonies strengthening some motives and weakening others. He put founders of religions even higher on the roll of honour than founders of states. All founders of religion are, in his eyes, worthy of honour, provided the religions they found lend support to the kind of morality he admires or finds useful. His attitude to religion, unlike his attitude to certain moral qualities, is entirely utilitarian. We have seen that he valued honesty, justice, courage and patriotism for their own sake as well as because they make the State strong, but religion he valued only for what it brings, for the morality it promotes. The man who cares more for his relations with God than with men, the man who is truly pious in the Christian sense, was distasteful and perhaps incomprehensible to him.

He approved of the religion of the Romans because, in his opinion, it encouraged virtues useful to the republic and created ties to draw citizens closer together, producing supplementary loyalties to strengthen their patriotism. He even claimed for the Romans that they had been more religious than other peoples, and therefore less easily corrupted and more devoted to the State. Roman piety bridled the passions and directed them to ends useful to the republic; it kept morals pure and strengthened social ties, reminding men of their duties to their families, their neighbours and the community. Though Machiavelli cared little for Christian piety, he cared a great deal for the old Roman kind – for the kind which is not reverence for a Being infinitely greater than oneself, but a decent respect for the forms of worship and sacred myths of one's own people. This kind of piety is more a matter of practice than of faith.

Since Machiavelli's time, we have learnt to distinguish between dogmatic and undogmatic religions – between religions preaching doctrines which their adherents are required to accept and religions which impose no doctrines and require little more of their adherents than their taking part in certain ceremonies. No doubt, for many of its adherents even a dogmatic religion consists mostly of ceremony and ritual; they pay lip service to the doctrines without understanding them and without admitting, even to themselves, that they do not understand them. They are comforted and encouraged, not by doctrines which mean nothing to them, but by forms of worship. And yet, where religion is dogmatic, though there are many who take part in it in the same spirit as they would do if it were undogmatic, there are others who take the doctrines seriously. In their case, religion does not serve merely to strengthen loyalties and affections useful to the community; it may, and often does, bring them into conflict with the community, or it absorbs spiritual energies which otherwise might be devoted to it. Machiavelli did not distinguish, as we do now, between dogmatic and undogmatic religions, but he did have a sense of the difference between them, as his different attitudes to Christian and Roman piety show. And he preferred undogmatic to dogmatic religions.

Yet his conception of religion, even of undogmatic religion, is inadequate. He speaks with great respect of founders of religion; they are more to be admired even than founders of states. But it is the dogmatic religions, rather than the undogmatic, that have founders: Buddha, Christ and Mohammed. The origins of the older, pre-dogmatic religions are unknown to us. They may in fact serve to strengthen communal loyalties but they were not deliberately created for this purpose. The dogmatic religions arose when men had become more sophisticated; they arose along with philosophy; they were attempts of man, no longer satisfied with the simple pieties and amorphous beliefs of primitive societies, to provide himself with a coherent and comprehensive picture of the world and of his place in it. Dogmatic religion is a response to a need which arises in man when he has become self-conscious and self-critical, and critical also of the society in which he lives; it is essentially 'unworldly'.

Even men for whom religion is much more a matter of practice than of doctrine, if they are truly pious, do not share Machiavelli's attitude to religion. Religion is, to them, something valued for its own sake and not for its political effects. It is a communion with others which is deeply moving, even when it has little or nothing to do with explicit beliefs. They see in religious ceremonies the solemn expression of feelings which they deeply respect. No doubt, they also see religion as something which brings men closer to one another, deepening the emotional ties between them, adding colour and dignity to their lives, and filling them with a sense of awe for what is permanent in the human condition. Yet they value this communion for its own sake without asking themselves whether it strengthens the State. Men need ceremony; they need to come together to give ritual expression to emotions shared in common. They need to hold up to outward reverence certain common aspects of life; they need to honour the ties that bind them to one another; they need to clothe life in ceremony.

It may be that Machiavelli understood these needs; he certainly understood how greatly men are governed by the imagination. And yet, though he understood the need for undogmatic religion, he does not appear to have shared the piety even of the undogmatic. He believed that Roman piety was useful to the republic, but he does not seem to have admired piety, even of the Roman kind, for its own sake, as he admired courage, intelligence, tenacity and public spirit. He was by temperament almost entirely irreligious. Certainly, he was quite without sympathy for the man who feels intensely the need for a faith to live by and a personal relation with God. He knew, of course, that there are such men, but he did not understand their need.

When Machiavelli died in June 1527, less than ten full years had elapsed since Luther had nailed his theses to the church door at Wittenberg. Both *The Prince* and the *Discourses* were written before Europe had heard of Luther. We do not know how Machiavelli would have reacted to the Reformation if he had lived long enough to take account of it. Yet it is not pointless to make a guess. Machiavelli was nothing if not definite in his opinions, and his attitude to religion is clear enough to make it worthwhile considering how he might have interpreted Luther's attack on the Church and the Papacy.

Though Machiavelli was repelled by Savonarola's fanaticism, he approved of his condemnation of corrupt and worldly priests. Religion, if it is to do what it ought to do, if it is to strengthen social ties and encourage virtues useful to the State, must be held in respect, and it will not be respected unless priests live exemplary lives. Machiavelli would almost certainly have sympathized with Luther's denunciation of papal and ecclesiastical abuses. Nor did he care, for its own sake, for papal supremacy inside the Church. He was concerned only with the social and political effects of religion, and not with the organization of the Church, and there is nothing in his writings to indicate how he believed that the Church should be organized so as best to ensure that religion had the desired effects.

Machiavelli would probably have condemned Luther for challenging old beliefs. He would not have done so because he was attached to those beliefs, but because he disliked disputes which might weaken the State. Religion should draw men together and not divide them. If Machiavelli had found that men could in practice differ in their religious beliefs and yet share a common devotion to the State, he would presumably not have minded how much they differed. The old Romans had not all shared the same beliefs; they had taken part in the same religious observances in spite of considerable differences in their personal beliefs. Machiavelli presumably cared nothing for uniformity of belief, merely as such. He would not have blamed Luther for not sharing established beliefs. But he probably would have blamed him for the sort of attack he made on those beliefs, for helping to create an atmosphere in which it was difficult for men to have different religious beliefs without coming to blows. Luther was not content to abandon the old faith; he felt the need to denounce it. He raised passions which weakened what were, in the eyes of Machiavelli, the primary loyalties, to the family and (above all) to the State. He may not have intended to do this, but that is what in fact he did. It was not enough for Luther that he should abide by his own opinions; he wanted to proclaim them to the world and to pour contempt on the opinions he rejected, thus confusing men and bringing them into conflict with one another and with their rulers. To denounce abuses which debase religion is praiseworthy; to hold privately to beliefs different from the established ones is allowable; but to set people quarrelling furiously over obscure points of doctrine unintelligible to most of them is both absurd and dangerous. This, I suspect, would have been Machiavelli's reaction to Luther.

Though Machiavelli was not intolerant, neither was he a believer in liberty of conscience, for he merely took little interest in what people believed. He neither asserted nor denied liberty of conscience, since the issue was never brought home to him. It would no doubt have seemed absurd to him to try to force beliefs on others on the ground that they are necessary to salvation. He says nothing to suggest that he would have condoned persecuting beliefs on any other ground than their being harmful to society. Yet he does not assert man's right to hold and publish whatever beliefs he chooses, short of committing slander or libel or inciting to violence. He says nothing about freedom of thought and speech and publication, and there is no evidence that he cared for it either for its own sake or for its consequences. We can say that in practice he was not intolerant; but we cannot say that, as a matter of principle, he was either for or against toleration. He lived before the era of religious wars and dissensions, and so we must not speak of him as if he had taken a stand on an issue which was gradually raised to the point of clarity only during that era.

Machiavelli disliked the Papacy entirely for political and Italian reasons. He was too much a realist to suppose that Christianity could be replaced by the undogmatic national cults of antiquity, by anything like the religion of the virile and public-spirited old Romans whom he admired so much. Though he said that Christianity made virtues of some qualities harmful to the State, he admitted that it encouraged others indispensable to it. Men need some religion, and in Europe they could scarcely have any other than Christianity. Machiavelli did not object to the claim of the Roman Catholic Church to be the one true Church, the Universal Church. Whatever he may have thought privately of the claim, he was not concerned to deny it publicly. He did not contest the Pope's spiritual authority over all Western Christendom, though he strongly disliked papal or priestly interference in temporal affairs and always spoke of the State as if its authority within its own territory were unlimited. Yet he never troubled to put forward any theory about the proper relations between Church and State. There was no need for him to do so; the issue was not most vital in Italy in his time.

The popes of his day were not perhaps to be taken seriously as spiritual rulers trying to extend the authority of the Universal Church at the expense of princes and republics. They were formidable in Italy much less as rulers of the Church than as rulers of the papal states. Machiavelli disliked the Papacy because he saw in it the chief obstacle to the union of Italy. The popes were too weak to unite the country, and yet were unwilling to let anyone else unite it. He resented their political influence, which was so much greater than the size and resources of the papal states gave them a right to. If he resented their spiritual authority, it was not because they were using it to limit the Temporal Power (for they had never been less inclined to use it for that purpose); it was because they were using it to push the interest of the papal states at the expense of other states in Italy. They held a trump card denied to the other players competing for political supremacy in Italy; and this Machiavelli objected to, not because he wanted fair play, but because he thought that the Pope's ambitions, as a temporal ruler, were bad for Italy.

Machiavelli, though himself probably without religious beliefs, was clearly not an enemy of religion – not even of dogmatic religion. Christianity, by his standards, was by no means the best of religions; but that does not mean that he wanted to weaken its hold on men, for he had no hope of anything better taking its place. He was personally without religion but not therefore against religion. He saw in religion chiefly a means of discipline, and what to many people is the heart of religion meant nothing to him. There have been avowed atheists who have understood better than he did what Christianity and the other great dogmatic religions mean to the faithful.

6. *Machiavelli's Preference for Popular or Free Government*

Machiavelli's severest critics, who have accused him of immorality, cynicism and even superficiality, have not denied his strong preference for popular or, as it was often called, free government. He admired the Roman Republic, not the Roman Empire. As democracy was understood in his own day, he was a democrat. He did not want every adult male in Florence to take a part in government, but he did want the artisans and small traders to do so as much as the great merchants and nobles. Popular government or political freedom meant, in his day and country, government responsible to the whole body of citizens and not to all adults within the State. Within the citizen body were included most native Florentines carrying on an independent business, and the excluded, apart from women and children, were mostly foreigners, servants and other dependants. Thus the citizens, though only a minority of the people, included most of the native-born men with (to use an expression once popular in England) 'a stake of their own' in the country, and who could therefore be expected to be patriotic and independent, and to take a keen interest in public affairs.

Freedom, as it was understood in Machiavelli's time, did not include liberty of conscience. Champions of freedom in his day were not much concerned to protect the rights of dissident minorities or of individuals who rejected commonly received principles. There is a wide difference between the freedom desired by Machiavelli and the liberty expounded by John Stuart Mill. Yet Machiavelli had a high regard for personal dignity and independence. We have seen that he greatly admired the Swiss because they were free and uncorrupt. He ascribed their freedom to their self-respect and independence of spirit combined with a strong sense of duty to their neighbours and their country.

Many people who have not shared our concern for liberty of conscience – who have not even conceived of such a liberty – have put a high value on independence of spirit. The Athenians, in the fifth and fourth centuries before Christ, the Romans under the republic, the English long before they had learnt to be liberal and tolerant, were remarkable for their love of independence. They respected a man who stands for his principles, who does not bow to the multitude, who has the courage of his convictions. It is important to distinguish this respect from concern for liberty of conscience. The Romans had no tenderness for purveyors of what they took to be perverse or immoral opinions; they did not admire the man who rejects principles respected in his community time out of mind; they abhorred the iconoclast. They did not respect the man who, for conscience' sake, challenges the most cherished beliefs and principles of his community; they respected only the man who stands by those principles when most other men, swayed by passion, have lost sight of them. They admired integrity; they admired moral courage; they admired the man able to stand alone against the multitude. They could do all this without caring in the least for, or even having any idea of, what we call liberty of conscience. This is the independence of a free people, as Machiavelli understood it. It is to be found wherever there is a strong tradition of popular government or of popular participation in government; it is even to be found among many primitive peoples, whereas concern for liberty of conscience is something altogether more sophisticated and more rare.

We have seen that the man who could write *The Prince* could also count Julius Caesar among the worst of tyrants. Now Caesar, as much as any man that ever lived, possessed *virtù* in the Machiavellian sense; he had energy and courage enough to serve the greatest ambition. He was intelligent and resourceful; he could easily deceive others but had few illusions about himself; he desired fame and strove to make the world suit his purposes. He, if anyone, should be a hero to an admirer of power and of unscrupulous courage used to establish a strong and enduring empire. Yet we find Machiavelli, who could praise a petty adventurer like Cesare Borgia, condemning an incomparably greater and more important man. Machiavelli's reason for condemning Caesar is that he destroyed Roman liberty when he might have saved it. A man aspiring to fame should, he said, wish to be born in a corrupted State, not utterly to spoil and subvert it, as Caesar did, but to remodel and restore it. Caesar's crime was that he took advantage of corruption to get power at a time when it was still possible to restore liberty; and liberty cannot be restored except by destroying corruption. If Caesar had lived in Renaissance Italy and had used the same methods to get power, Machiavelli would not have condemned him, as he did not condemn Borgia.

It is astonishing what large claims Machiavelli makes for free government. We are told in the second chapter of Book Two of the *Discourses* that 'experience shows that no state ever extended its dominion or increased its revenues, any longer than it continued free'. This claim is bold to the point of extravagance; history does not bear it out. Machiavelli's argument in support of it is worth noticing, for it is more typical of the late eighteenth century than of the early sixteenth. What makes a state powerful, enterprising and prosperous is, he says, the citizens' steady preference for the public good; but this preference is nowhere as likely as in a republic, because the public good is the advantage of the majority, whose will, in a republic, must always prevail. This perhaps too simple argument reads almost as if it came straight from Rousseau.

Machiavelli makes other and more modest claims for the people. Unrestrained by law, they are capable of enormities; but not more than princes are. They are good judges of men; better usually than princes, who often prefer servility to independence of judgement. Easily misled when they hear only one side of a question, the people are good judges of the merits of alternative policies put to them by rival orators. They are impetuous and need guidance; they must have good leaders whom they trust. They are less often moved by avarice than princes, and less given to jealousy and suspicion. Popular government, in the eyes of Machiavelli, is clearly something nobler, more generous, more enterprising than monarchy or oligarchy. It is the form of government best suited to a vigorous and healthy people.

Though Machiavelli says nothing about the rights of the individual or of minorities, he does say that freedom thrives on controversy. Now, controversy will not thrive except where there is real independence of judgement. Roman liberty, he said, was preserved for centuries by the unceasing conflict between patricians and plebeians. That conflict turned on the Agrarian Law, on the question of how property in land should be distributed; and the disputes it led to in the end destroyed liberty. This, says Machiavelli, has led many people to conclude that faction destroys liberty; but the conclusion is facile, and only partly true. Faction can destroy liberty, and in the end did destroy it in Rome; but Roman liberty would never have survived so long if the plebs had not successfully challenged patrician supremacy. Anyone can understand that faction easily grows bitter, and that if it grows too bitter freedom is destroyed. What is equally true, but less obvious, is that, where there are no disputes to divide men and make them rivals for power, there cannot be freedom.

Machiavelli, when he used this argument, was not thinking of the competition for power between rival parties, the competition which is supposed to preserve freedom in modern democracies; he was thinking rather of a division of offices between different classes in the community, with each class jealous of its rights and critical of the others. Yet, at bottom, his conception is not very different from ours. Freedom is preserved by a competition for power kept within bounds by respect for law, and also by a common loyalty to the State. This competition, so long as the law is respected, does not weaken the State but makes it stronger, because it requires vigilance, energy and courage in the competitors.

Though Machiavelli preferred popular government to any other kind, he thought it difficult to establish, and almost impossible to revive, once corruption had destroyed it. It is the best and strongest of governments, but not therefore the most common or the best suited to most states. When a people have become corrupt, the mere revival among them of the institutions they had when they were free will not restore their freedom; because a corrupt people will misuse the instruments of freedom. The institutions needed to reform a corrupt State – and reform, for Machiavelli, means the restoration of freedom – are different from those that maintain freedom in an uncorrupt State.

Freedom can, he said, be restored either gradually or by violence: gradually, when some wise and farseeing person guides the State slowly back to freedom, persuading the people of the need for change; and by violence, when the change is made all at once and the opponents of democracy are ruthlessly cut down. Machiavelli thought it unlikely, though not impossible, that either method would succeed. The rulers of a corrupt State profit too much from the power they hold to allow a reformer to take it away from them peacefully and by degrees. The kind of men most apt to use violence, moreover, are not likely to use it to restore freedom. Freedom is their pretext rather than their aim.

Machiavelli therefore did not condemn monarchy. When a people are corrupt, they must, for their own good, be subject to a single powerful ruler. Incapable of freedom, they must still have order, and must therefore get it in the only way open to them. Machiavelli preferred an absolute to a feudal monarchy, thinking it better that the people should have one master than many. As a citizen of a great mercantile city, which had long been the cultural as well as the financial centre of Europe, he heartily disliked the feudal nobility. He approved of the efforts of the kings of France to increase their power at the expense of the nobles. Yet, even here, he was moderate; for he also approved of the supreme courts of law in France, the *parlements*, whose activities very considerably limited the royal power. For the Estates-General, the French equivalent of the English Parliament, he had no sympathy. As the French *parlements* were hereditary corporations of lawyers and the Estates-General were the nearest thing in France to a body representing the whole nation, this preference may seem odd in an avowed admirer of popular government. It is not, however, as odd as it seems, for the *parlements*, while they restrained the monarchy, sympathized with its endeavours to make France law-abiding, united and strong, whereas the Estates-General were dominated by the nobles and the priests, who cared more for the privileges of their class or order than for the good of the State.

7. *Machiavelli's Reputation for Immorality*

I have tried to explain just how much and for what reasons Machiavelli cared for morality, why he thought religion necessary and also why he preferred popular government to every other kind. How then did he acquire his world-wide reputation as an immoral writer? How is it that the word 'Machiavellian' is nearly always used in a pejorative sense? Is it really possible that for centuries people have so misunderstood Machiavelli as to take him for the opposite of what he was – as to take him for a cynical apologist of tyranny?

No doubt, Machiavelli has been misunderstood; and partly by his own fault. It is not his fault, of course, that most people who have read him have read only *The Prince*, which gives a much stronger impression of cynicism than the *Discourses*.[1] It is also not his fault that his preferences are not ours, that he is hard where we are soft, cold where we are sentimental, awed and fascinated by what we grudgingly admire. He did not have our respect for the over-tender

---

[1] There is no advice, however unscrupulous, given in *The Prince* that is not repeated in the *Discourses*. But in the *Discourses* there is much more besides, to reconcile Machiavelli with the modern reader.

conscience, nor our patience with the well-meaning fool. He felt a strong sympathy for the man of principle, capable of heroic self-sacrifice, but not for the man tormented by scruples. It is often said that the West is no longer truly Christian. This may well be true as regards our beliefs (or lack of them) about God and the universal order. But our morals are still largely Christian, much more so than our beliefs; and it is there that we differ most from Machiavelli. He was not much repelled by Christian theology, for he gave little thought to it; he was repelled by Christian morals, which seemed to him to rob men of the pride and self-assertiveness needed for a full life. It takes some imagination and even an effort of will on our part to persuade ourselves that Machiavelli was perhaps not less concerned than we are that men should behave well, but merely had different ideas about what constitutes good behaviour. Though we can, by taking thought, come to realize this, it is still not easy, when we come upon some of his opinions in all their nakedness, to avoid being shocked by them. Machiavelli is so explicit, so bold, so eager to drive home conclusions repulsive to us that the impression of cynicism remains even after reason has sought to dispel it. Of course, by our standards he sometimes was immoral; but he had his own standards which mattered as much to him as ours do to us.

Yet there is another, a more specific and damaging, charge of immorality brought against him: that he excused in the powerful, in those who rule, actions which, when others do them, are plainly wrong, even by his own standards. This charge is not that he was mild where we are severe, or treated as innocent what we condemn; it is that he argued that what is wrong for most people might be right for some. This charge has been generalized (and weakened) into the accusation that he held that the end justifies the means.

There is nothing really vicious about the doctrine that the end justifies the means. It all depends on the end. The Utilitarians, for instance, taught that an action is right if it promotes the greatest happiness of all whose happiness is in question; and this, of course, is to say that a particular end (the greatest happiness) justifies any means to it. Many people have thought the Utilitarians wrong-headed, and some have found them dull; but scarcely anyone has accused them of immorality. We may hold that some actions are wrong no matter how good their consequences, and yet not be shocked by someone who holds the contrary opinion. Nor is it vicious to argue that some people, because of their special position in society, may do things which it would be wrong for anyone, not in that position, to do.

Our trouble with Machiavelli is that the end he puts forward as justifying all means to it seems to us lamentably inadequate. To say with Bentham, 'Do anything that promotes happiness', sounds well enough; we may not agree but we are not shocked. But to say, with Machiavelli, 'Do anything that establishes the State's power more firmly or increases its extent', sounds downright wicked. It would have sounded wicked in the Middle Ages, and at almost any other period of European history; and it still sounds wicked today.

But, in justice to Machiavelli, we ought to remember that, in his opinion, the *only* end that justifies any means to it is the establishment or preservation or enlargement of effective power, of the State, which is, he thinks, the first condition of order, and also, under favourable (though admittedly rare) circumstances, of freedom as well. Machiavelli admired the man who gets power, by whatever means, to make a weak and corrupt State strong; but he condemned the man who gets it by weakening the State, by corrupting it, or by taking advantage of its corruption when it is still possible to restore freedom.

Where, as in sixteenth-century Italy, there was almost no freedom to destroy and almost no hope of restoring it, Machiavelli was willing to support a tyrant in all his wickedness, provided that the wickedness was really needed to bring order and unity to the country. Hence the portrait of the single-minded, bold, subtle, unscrupulous prince, who will stop at nothing to get what he wants, and who is justified (in the eyes of Machiavelli) because what he wants is to bring all Italy under his rule and to drive the barbarian invaders out. The prince may be ambitious and evil, more concerned to get power for himself than to do good to Italy; and yet he ought to be supported and his crimes condoned, because, if he gets what he wants, Italy will have domestic peace and orderly government.

It is true that Machiavelli cared for national greatness for its own sake, as well as for its good effects. He wanted Italy united, not only that Italians might be saved from anarchy, and from the miseries and humiliations that anarchy brings, but also that Italy might be great. This ideal of national greatness, which meant so little in the Middle Ages, has been important among nations of European stock since the sixteenth century; and Machiavelli was its first great exponent. His maxims were, with rare exceptions, accepted almost without question by sixteenth-century governments. Deceit, treachery and cruelty were common in high places, not only in Italy, but also in the northern countries; though the Italians were perhaps bolder in their crimes and less hypocritical about them. There was nothing Machiavelli wanted his prince to do that had not already been done many times over. He did not corrupt the rulers of Europe but merely found excuses for their corruption. And we must not forget that he condemned their stupidity, which caused them to commit many unprofitable and therefore unnecessary crimes. It is the clever tyrant who can most often afford to be mild, because, when he is severe, he is so to good purpose. He makes each crime go further, and so can afford to commit fewer crimes.

Machiavelli was not much condemned until the seventeenth century. By that time the hold of many governments over their subjects had been greatly strengthened; the modern State was more solidly organized and relations between states more regular, and therefore more honest. Richelieu, who wanted national greatness for France just as much as Machiavelli wanted it for Italy, found that he could achieve it without resorting to many of the crimes committed by Italian tyrants in the early sixteenth century. The *Political Testament*, attributed to him, condemns what Machiavelli excused. Princes, it says, ought to keep faith with one another, even when it is not their interest to do so. France was by this time so united and powerful a kingdom that her rulers could more easily distinguish between immediate and permanent interests; they could see that it was worthwhile, in the long run, making considerable sacrifices to preserve France's good name. The predicament of an Italian ruler of the early sixteenth century, fighting for survival against unscrupulous enemies, was altogether different. Honesty was a rather better policy in Richelieu's Europe than in Machiavelli's Italy. By Richelieu's time, Europe was almost ready to accept a new version of the law of nations from the hands of Grotius – to admire it in theory and to try to make the facts look as if they were in keeping with it. Machiavelli's advice was still sometimes taken, but his reasons for giving it were roundly condemned. He had become the whipping-boy of philosophic statesmen.

8. Machiavelli's Great Omission

I have not, I hope, neglected any important aspect of Machiavelli's political theory. That theory is not a systematic whole, but a set of assumptions and opinions about man, society and government which reveal what is, taking it all in all, an extraordinarily fresh, sharp, intelligent, secular, many-sided and realistic philosophy of life. Machiavelli had precursors, no doubt, as all great thinkers and writers have; the further we carry our researches, the clearer it becomes that no man is as original as at first sight he may appear. Nevertheless, it is with Machiavelli that modern social and political theory really begins. Indeed, he is often more modern in outlook, more untheological, less *a priori* and more down-to-earth than many of the great men who come after him.

But there is one omission which cannot help but strike anyone who has studied his writings at all closely. Though Machiavelli knew that the future lay with the larger States and therefore wanted Italy to become one of them, he gave almost no thought to the problem of how a great State should be governed. His scattered comments on the government of France, the only great State he knew at all well, shrewd though they are, amount to little. Still less did he consider what institutions might be necessary to establish or preserve or restore freedom in a large State. The kind of popular government he had in mind and approved of had never existed except in small republics. He was not interested in representative government, which alone makes popular government possible in large States. Though he loved freedom, the only free institutions he took serious account of could not work except on a small scale. And yet he also loved Italy, and wanted her to be great. We never find him, like Rousseau, arguing that popular government is possible only in small States; nor did he prefer small to large States. Yet, though he knew that small States could not survive in the face of the large ones, he was not made anxious for freedom by this knowledge. He never succeeded in reconciling his two strongest passions: for political freedom and for the independence of Italy. Indeed, he never even felt the need to reconcile them.

CHAPTER 3

The Reformation and Liberty of Conscience

Europeans, on both sides of the Atlantic, are apt to speak of freedom as if it were something peculiarly European, or at least of European origin, though the peoples of Asia and Africa are now also coming to understand and desire it. They speak as if the concept of freedom, born in Greece, perfected in Christianity, and realized in practice through institutions developed by the English, the French, the Americans and other Western peoples, were Europe's gift to the world. They speak also as if the attainment of freedom were the supreme achievement of mankind; from which it seems to follow that the liberal peoples of European stock are, if not inherently superior to others, at least more advanced than they are.

The sophisticated Chinese or Indian, learned in the traditions of his own country, will perhaps be struck by the arrogance of this claim. He will perhaps be moved to protest that freedom has been valued by non-European peoples long before they began to be influenced by Europe. Freedom is as much Asian, as much African, as it is European; it is human. Men have set store by it in all kinds of communities; it is, and long has been, a value acknowledged everywhere, though not everywhere in quite the same terms. Europeans are merely being provincial when they claim that freedom is now thought desirable in Asia and Africa only because the Europeans have taught other peoples to know and desire it. The world now speaks of freedom much as the Europeans first learned to speak of it; the modern vocabulary of freedom is largely European. But freedom, though it now wears European dress, is not therefore peculiarly, or even originally, European.

This protest against European arrogance and provincialism is not misplaced. The Europeans, in this matter of freedom, have made altogether too large and too simple a claim for themselves. The love of freedom is rooted in sentiments and habits to be found everywhere in the world; it is, in essence and origin, no more European than Asian or African. Those who say that man is by nature free because he is rational are, I think, right, though they sometimes read more into this dictum than is acceptable. It may not follow that man ought to be free because he is rational; but it cannot be denied that, unless he were rational, he would not put a value on freedom. He is provident and critical and self-critical; he organizes his life; he becomes attached to a way of life or strives to achieve an ideal, and makes a claim against other men that they should allow him to live as seems good to him or to strive for what he finds desirable. He does this in Asia and Africa as well as in Europe and America.

All this is true. The peoples of European stock have made too large and too simple a claim. And yet there is a claim which they could make, and which perhaps they intend to make, even though they seldom find the right words for it. Freedom is not a simple idea. Or perhaps it would be better to say that the word is used to cover several ideas, which are closely connected and easily confused, but which need to be distinguished from one another. I think it can be claimed for the Europeans that they have done more than other peoples to define and elaborate these different, though closely connected, ideas of freedom, and also that they have produced most of the institutions which make it possible to realize them in large and complex communities. It can, moreover, be claimed for one of these ideas, much more confidently than for the others, that it is originally European; I mean the idea of liberty of conscience, which is scarcely to be found even among the Greeks. It is an idea which slowly emerges in the West in the course of the sixteenth and seventeenth centuries; and yet today, in the eyes of the liberal, it is that liberty which is the most precious of all.

This revised claim made for the Europeans is more modest than the other. But it is not quite as modest as it may at first appear. The definition and elaboration of moral concepts is not a mere exercise in lexicography and logic; it is not even a merely intellectual operation. In the process of examining our values critically, we enlarge and refine upon them; and we do this also in the process of acquiring the institutions which help us to realize them. We cannot, for example, say that what the English-speaking peoples understood by freedom in the sixteenth century is precisely what they now understand by it, since they now use different words to define it and different institutions to preserve it. By applying their minds to it, by disputing about it, and by aiming deliberately at its preservation and enlargement when reforming their institutions, they have, for better or worse, greatly changed their conceptions of it.

Though my present purpose is to explain how the idea of liberty of conscience emerged in Western Europe in the sixteenth and seventeenth centuries, I am not interested, for its own sake, in the question of origins. It is merely that I believe that one of the best – and sometimes even *the* best – method of getting a firm grip on a moral idea is by seeing how it arose and by contrasting it with the other ideas closely related to it. There were champions of freedom and martyrs for it long before anyone stood up for liberty of conscience, and these were also advocates of toleration. How then does liberty of conscience differ from other forms of freedom? And how does it differ from mere toleration?

In all societies there are limits to what men will put up with from one another and from those set in authority over them; in all societies it is admitted that men ought not to be prevented from doing what the law, in the broadest sense, does not forbid, and ought not to be compelled to do what the law does not require. As Hobbes insisted, law and freedom are correlative terms. We can agree with him here without also agreeing that law, as he defines it, is properly defined as command. Wherever there are accepted rules of conduct, there is some idea of freedom; or, in other words, wherever men recognize obligations, they also ordinarily claim that they ought not to be compelled where they are not obliged. It is not merely, as Hobbes said, that they are in fact free to do what the law does not forbid; it is also that they are held to have the right to do it, in the sense that any attempt to prevent them is condemned. Freedom, in this sense, is not the mere absence of obligation or compulsion within a given sphere; it involves the notion that interference is wrong. Freedom is therefore the right to do what is not forbidden and to refrain from doing what is not required. In this obvious and important sense, there is freedom wherever there are obligations, or accepted rules of conduct; and there are such obligations or rules in all societies.

Again, in all societies the authority of rulers is held to be limited. Either it is not recognized that they have authority to make laws, or it is held that, if they have it, the authority is limited, legally or morally. In primitive societies rulers are bound by custom; their functions are judicial and executive rather than legislative. If they disregard custom, they are held to have acted oppressively. Where the ruler's legislative authority is admitted, it is nearly always held to be limited by a higher law. The doctrine that the ruler has a legally unlimited right to make law is scarcely older than the seventeenth century, and is in any case confined mostly to philosophers and lawyers. And even they, with rare exceptions, admit that the right, though legally without limit, is not unlimited morally. Everywhere, among non-Europeans as much as among European peoples, it has been widely held that rulers do not make but merely enforce the law, or that their right to make laws is limited by a higher and unchanging law, or (where law and morality are distinguished) that it is their moral duty not to make laws which are immoral. These doctrines, since they set limits to the authority of rulers, are assertions of freedom.

In all societies man has a sense of his own dignity. He feels himself entitled to certain courtesies. He resents insults; he resents interference. He resents them, not only because they frustrate his desires, but because they humiliate him. As a social creature, he is both dependent and independent; he cannot live without others, and must serve them and be served by them. But his dependence is regular; it is subject to rules which both bind and protect him. Outside the sphere of his dependence, he is independent and is jealous of that independence; he is watchful to preserve it, more for the sake of his dignity than because he expects material advantages. This is as true of primitive as of civilized man, and as true of civilized man in the East as in the West; it is true of him in all kinds of communities and under all forms of government. If we bear that in mind, we can give some meaning to the assertion often made that man is 'by nature' a lover of freedom. True, he is 'by nature' other things as well which often prevent his being free.

By freedom is also meant a man's right to take part, directly or indirectly, in running the affairs of his community. This is political freedom. There is nothing specifically European about it. Among primitive peoples all over the world, there has quite often existed a form of tribal democracy. Or perhaps it would be nearer the truth to say that in simple societies, government, such as it is, is apt to be mixed; it often has elements of monarchy, oligarchy and democracy about it. Nor is the popular element in government confined, except in Europe or where European influence is strong, to primitive societies. Indians claim that in their country, before the coming of the British, there were powerful village communities in which oligarchy was often very much tempered by democracy. There is nothing surprising about this. In non-industrial societies, the village is often almost self-supporting and is also, to a considerable extent, self-governing. The local rulers, who are not mere agents of the central government but enjoy a considerable autonomy, may, of course, be oligarchs, but they need not be. Authority may be widely diffused in the community, and the men who have it may be quickly responsive to popular opinion. The central government of a great empire may be despotic and yet allow a considerable measure of popular control at the village level. Ottoman rule was not merely despotic; it was also arbitrary and oppressive, and yet the Christian village communities subject to the Turk were largely self-governing and to some extent democratic. The Turk was chiefly interested in gathering taxes, in money and in kind; and, provided he got what he asked for, he cared little enough for what the Christians did with themselves. Even in the West, in the mediaeval manor, the serfs had some powers of self-government; there were some matters which they decided for themselves or in consultation with their lord or his officers, and the same was true in Russia before the great emancipation of 1861. There is nothing peculiarly western about popular government in this rudimentary sense.

The most that can be claimed for the West – and it is a large claim – is that it has evolved institutions and ideas making possible popular government and the protection of individual rights in very large and complex communities. The western peoples, by their subtle and careful analyses of moral, legal and political ideas, by their systematic and lucid codifications of law, and above all by developing courts of law having strict procedures and high professional standards, independent of the other branches of government, have made possible the precise definition of rights and their scrupulous and impartial protection. Custom alone, or custom combined with a rudimentary judicial process, may protect the individual and the family adequately in simple and slow-changing societies; but where society is complex and changes quickly; where men depend for the necessities of life, not on a small village community, most of whose members are known to them, but on a vast and intricate economy, freedom, in the sense of the secure enjoyment of rights, must be precarious, unless judicial processes are elaborate, refined, scrupulous and free from interference by the executive. There must be what western jurists have called the rule of law. In this sense, the rule of law is also necessary if democracy is to be possible on a large scale, if intimidation and corruption are to be prevented, if the ordinary citizen is to have a truly independent vote.

I have spoken of two kinds of freedom: the secure enjoyment of established rights (or freedom from arbitrary interference), and the right to take part in running the affairs of the community (or political freedom), which are not specifically European, even though it is nations of European stock which have evolved the ideas and institutions making possible their realization in vast and complex communities. I have also spoken of a third kind of freedom, liberty of conscience, that is peculiarly European in a sense in which the other two are not. By calling it European, I do not mean to imply that only Europeans desire it and set a value upon it, or that only Europeans are capable of realizing it. I mean only that, for a variety of reasons which have (so far as I know) nothing to do with any racial or inherited characteristics peculiar to peoples of European stock, it first emerged among them. It is the least common, the most recent and the least easily understood and established form of freedom. And yet, where it is established, it is apt to be considered the most precious of all freedoms – precious above all for its own sake, though precious also for the sake of the other two kinds. For in the modern world, where the power of governments over the bodies and minds of their subjects is so enormously greater than ever before, neither political freedom nor the enjoyment of established rights can be really secure where there is no liberty of conscience.

Liberty of conscience is the right to hold and profess what principles we choose, and to live in accordance with them. Like any other right, it is not unconditional; it is limited, as all rights are, by other rights and duties, and also by the need to ensure that some people do not so use it as to deprive others of it. The liberal admits that I can rightly be forbidden to live according to my principles, when by doing so I injure other people, and that I am not entitled to obtrude my principles upon them when they would rather not listen to me. I can also sometimes be rightly forbidden to give public expression to my principles, if by doing so I provoke violence, even though I have no intention of provoking it. Whatever the right we exercise, we have a duty to consider the consequences to others of what we do. But they too have a duty to act so as to enable us to exercise our right. Where a decision has to be taken in common, for example, and our principles are relevant to that decision, they ought to listen to us when we expound those principles, and ought not to turn deaf ears to us on the ground that they find our principles shocking. The right to profess what principles we choose implies the right to criticize the principles we reject, and both these rights are limited in similar ways.

Liberty of conscience was not admitted in the Middle Ages, and even the Athenians, for all their passion for freedom, scarcely knew it. The Greeks were a highly critical and intellectual people; they discussed many problems quite freely, and were capable at times of remarkable tolerance. So, too, though in a lesser degree, were the Romans, especially after they had absorbed Greek influences. Indeed, the Romans, though less inventive, less imaginative, less critical and intellectual than the Greeks, were not less open-minded. Scepticism and tolerance were at times as widespread among the educated classes in the ancient world as ever they have been in the West. Yet the ancients did not value liberty of conscience as we have learnt to do. Why was this so?

I cannot give a confident answer to the question, but I am struck by the fact that, if we consider how liberty of conscience came to be valued in the West, we notice that it was first asserted and cherished in an age of strong beliefs. It was first asserted among peoples who adhered, as the Greeks and Romans did not, to dogmatic religions, among peoples who had been taught for centuries that nothing was more important than to have the right beliefs, and who had recently become divided in their beliefs beyond hope of ever again reaching agreement. To Europeans in the West it seemed to matter enormously, not merely how men behaved, but what they believed. It mattered that they should hold sincerely the right beliefs and not merely that they should speak respectfully of traditional beliefs. This was, no doubt, the source of fanaticism and persecution, but it was also, I suggest, the source of a new conception of freedom. Liberty of conscience was born, not of indifference, nor of scepticism, nor of mere open-mindedness, but of faith. 'Faith is supremely important, and therefore all men must have the one true faith.' 'Faith is supremely important, and therefore every man must be allowed to live by the faith which seems true to him.' These are two quite different arguments, and yet it is not difficult to see how the first gradually gave way to the second in a part of the world which had long been accustomed to think of itself as a single community of the faithful and now found itself divided into several. This new conception of freedom emerged out of controversies which raged in a divided Christendom about the limits of toleration. These controversies, in their turn, were closely connected with disputes about the proper relations between Church and State in the only part of the world where such disputes were possible. The idea that men could belong to two communities, separate from one another and each supreme in its own sphere, was peculiar to the West; it was not accepted in the eastern part of Christendom, where the Spiritual was subordinate to the Temporal Power, and it was inconceivable outside Christendom. I want now to consider these disputes about the relations between Church and State and about the limits of toleration, and to show how a new conception of freedom slowly emerged out of them. I must go back for a moment to mediaeval times, but only for a moment.

I. TRADITIONAL CONCEPTIONS AND THE REFORMATION

1. *The Middle Ages*

In the Middle Ages the rights of the Christian against authority were often and vigorously asserted, but those rights did not amount to what we should call liberty of conscience. The Christian was held not to be bound to obey commands contrary to the Word of God; he was said to be bound in conscience to obey God rather than man. Yet this claim on his behalf did not go so far as to say that he was responsible to God alone for his interpretation of that Word; it did not make him the final judge. In practice, the claim was made against the Temporal Power, and was a weapon used by champions of the Church against that Power. It was never made against the Church. No doubt, both Popes and lesser priests were often criticized. There were also disputes about where final authority in spiritual matters lay inside the Church. But it was not disputed that it did lie in the Church. God's Word is above all human laws, but the only authoritative interpreter of the Word is the Church.

The great political controversies of the Middle Ages had turned on the relations between the Spiritual and Temporal Power, as the champions of each claimed more for it in theory than they tried to get in practice. In the eleventh and twelfth centuries, the Church gained authority at the expense of temporal rulers; but from the beginning of the fourteenth century it lost ground rapidly. With not many exceptions, controversialists on either side, though claiming more for their own side than the other would accept, had admitted that both powers were, each in its own sphere, supreme, each needing the other and yet neither subordinate. Inside the Church, the authority of the Pope came to be increasingly challenged. The mediaeval Church had grown strong under the wing of the Papacy, and had done great service, cultural and moral, to the peoples of Western Europe. But in the fourteenth century, owing first to the removal of the Popes to Avignon from 1309 to 1377 and then to the Great Schism of 1378 to 1417, the prestige of the Papacy had declined rapidly. The religious zeal of earlier centuries had subsided; monks and friars had grown worldly and immoral; while the Church had come to be rich and the clergy unpopular. It was the age of Boccaccio and Chaucer. The Church had become corrupt and the Popes seemed unable or unwilling to reform it. The most pressing question was much less that of asserting the Pope's claims against temporal rulers, or of defending the latter against him, than of saving the Church from eventual collapse. Men therefore reverted to a belief of the early Christians, a belief that had never quite died out, that the authority of the Church belongs properly to the whole community of the faithful, laymen as well as priests. This revived fundamentalism slowly developed into a challenge to papal rule.

During the early Middle Ages, together with the power of the Church had grown the authority of the Papacy. The government of the Church had become more and more a monarchy. Then, in the fourteenth century, that monarchy had moved to Avignon into partial subjection to French kings; and later still, when it had returned to Rome, there had arisen rival claimants to it. The Papacy was discredited and therefore weakened. It had gone against the grain both with the English and the Italians to acknowledge a succession of seven French popes; and in any case all the secular princes, most of them busily extending their authority inside their own dominions, resented the Pope's having so much power. The less the Universal Church was governed from a centre outside their control, the better it would suit them. It was only natural, therefore, that the drive to regenerate the Church should take the form of an attack on papal supremacy inside it.

No mediaeval monarch, not even the Pope at the height of his power, was absolute. Just as it was taken for granted that temporal rulers were subject to a customary law resting on popular consent, so it was thought that the Spiritual Power resided in the whole Church and not in the Pope alone. The idea of authority belonging primarily to the whole community and only secondarily to the actual rulers, the agents of the community, was widely popular in the Middle Ages. But it was not an idea clearly embodied in mediaeval institutions, either secular or ecclesiastical. There was no settled procedure to ensure that rulers were in fact subject to communal authority. There were constant disputes about the nature of papal supremacy in the Church and of royal supremacy in the State, but no institutions that effectively determined the precise limits of authority.

Even the most powerful king was not, in the modern sense, sovereign. He was subject to law, which was primarily custom; and when the need to make statutes supplementary to custom appeared urgent, he was expected to consult, not the people generally, but the more important classes and corporations among them. Though the king summoned his estates to advise him what to do, he was not thereby made subject to laws imposed on him by those estates. The estates were nothing without him, and could not even meet unless he summoned them; and he took at least as great a part as they did in making statutes. The king was not sovereign, either alone or with his estates or Parliament; for all secular authority was limited by custom. But custom notoriously sets uncertain limits on authority; it has to be interpreted, and can be interpreted variously. As I have already observed in my first chapter, even in the strongest of mediaeval states, even, that is, in fifteenth-century England, the King-in-Parliament, though the admitted sovereign, was so as the interpreter of custom and not as one who could dispense with it. The King-in-Parliament was the highest court in the land, but was not yet, in our modern sense, a sovereign legislature. It was, no doubt, well on the way to becoming one; but that was not how it appeared to fifteenth-century Englishmen. Custom, embodied in the common law, was still thought supreme; and yet it was also admitted that what Parliament declared to be law could not be questioned by any inferior court. There was no Hobbes in England to point out the logical absurdity of holding these two positions at the same time. And in no other European country was there a body whose supremacy was as generally recognized as Parliament's in fifteenth-century England. Lack of definition, self-contradictoriness, perpetual fluctuation: these were the characteristics of nearly every form of mediaeval authority.

The distribution of authority within the mediaeval Church was even more confused and precarious. The old idea, that the Church is the community of all the faithful, lay and clerical, with whom authority ultimately rests, was by no means dead. In practice, however, authority had in the course of centuries passed to the clergy; and within the clerical hierarchy to bishops and abbots, and eventually to the Pope. The mediaeval Church had not produced inside itself the institutions needed to make effective the authority of all the faithful. It just could not be democratic; and so it became an oligarchy inclining more and more towards monarchy. By the fifteenth century it was a kind of constitutional and elective monarchy; but the precise nature of its constitution was far from certain. The internal structure of the Church was vast, intricate and obscure; its clergy had acquired immense wealth, most of it monastic and episcopal, and had meanwhile become worldly and sometimes corrupt.

When, in the eleventh century, the Church had been reformed and purified, the reformers had worked from (or at least through) Rome, so that the process of regeneration had enormously strengthened the Papacy. But in the fourteenth and fifteenth centuries the diminished authority of the Church and of religion was partly an effect of the decline of the Papacy. The Church appeared rotten at its head; and it was therefore natural that those who sought to reform it should seek to restore it to health, not so much through Rome, as in spite of it. They believed that the Church, the entire Christian community, must reform itself; it must meet together through its spokesmen in the General Council – an institution which, though it had long fallen into disuse, had never been repudiated – and they must consider how best to put an end to corruption and to schism. Marsilio of Papua and William of Occam were the two ablest exponents of this doctrine.

Marsilio, to be sure, was not even friendly to ecclesiastical pretensions. In setting the General Council above the Papacy, he was less anxious to strengthen the Church by reforming it than to weaken the Pope for the benefit of lay rulers. The ecclesiastical hierarchy, he contended, is an entirely human institution, popes and bishops having greater authority than other priests only because it had been found convenient that they should have it. He admitted the sacred character of all priests, but denied that any priest had, by divine right, greater authority than any other. Though, by virtue of their consecration, priests alone can perform religious rites and administer sacraments, the government of the Church no more belongs to them than to ordinary Christians. Only the whole Church, lay and clerical, assembled in General Council, has authority to pronounce finally on matters of faith and discipline; and the General Council, to be authentic, must be an elected body representing all Christendom.

Marsilio's voice could not carry much weight with good churchmen, for he was notoriously anti-clerical. He believed that the clergy, except as agents of the Temporal Power, have no right to exact penalties for spiritual offences; and that heresy, if it is punishable in this world, is so only as a civil offence. All the rights of the clergy are civil rights, granted to them by the Prince or the Republic. Nevertheless, though Marsilio's anti-clericalism was repulsive to good churchmen, his suggestion that ultimate authority in the Church rests with the entire Christian community was too much in keeping with mediaeval ideas about government not to be attractive to much better Christians than he was.

William of Occam, an English contemporary of Marsilio's, an exemplary Christian and loyal churchman, and also one of the greatest of the mediaeval philosophers, declared for the same expedient: a broadly representative General Council consisting of laymen and clergy, to be the supreme authority in the Church. William hoped that the General Council would reform the Church; he did not think that the Council would be infallible, nor did he claim for it sovereign authority in the Hobbesian sense. Its business was to

93

declare and interpret law rather than to make it; for the fundamental law of the Christian community is the Word of God, which men cannot change. William conceived of the supremacy of a General Council in much the same way as the English lawyers of his time conceived of the supremacy of Parliament, which was supreme, not because its will was law, but because no one was competent to challenge its interpretation of the law. Nor, of course, was William a democrat; he did not want the General Council to represent the Christian peoples in strict proportion to their numbers. He wanted it to represent Christendom as it actually was, as an hierarchical and diverse society. He was not even hostile to the Papacy; he merely wanted papal power limited by a General Council in something like the way that the King of England was limited by Parliament. Nor was he consciously putting forward an English solution to a problem that concerned all Christian peoples. In the fourteenth century, there was nothing specifically English about the notion of limited monarchy, nor yet of the supremacy, as an interpreter of law, of the monarch in consultation with the spokesmen of the more important classes and corporations of his realm. The mediaeval conception of a society asserting itself through its representatives was not democratic; the people as a whole were not thought of as choosing their spokesmen, but rather as spoken for by their natural leaders, by the barons and knights, and in the towns by the more important burgesses. The right to sit in Parliaments, Diets and Estates-General, or to vote for those who sat there, was in actual practice narrowly confined; and yet it was taken for granted that these bodies spoke for the whole people: not, of course, as sovereign legislatures but as supreme interpreters of law. It was in just this way that William of Occam conceived of the General Council of the Church.

General Councils were in fact made use of in an attempt to reform the Church and to provide it with a constitution which would prevent future abuses or make it easier to correct them. The two General Councils that actually met in the fifteenth century, first at Constance from 1414 to 1416 and then at Basel from 1431 to 1449, were far indeed from being the bodies representative of all Christendom, lay and clerical, that Marsilio and Occam had wanted; and, in any case, the Councils did not succeed in reforming the Church or abridging the Pope's authority. It had been fairly easy to bring the Schism to an end, because nearly all Christians were genuinely shocked by it; and it was still taken for granted that there could be only one Church, and therefore only one Pope. But there was no general agreement about the best means of limiting papal authority or of ensuring good discipline in the Church. It was proclaimed in principle, both at Constance and at Basel, that the General Council representing the Catholic Church derives its authority directly from Christ, and that therefore everyone, not excluding the Pope, is bound by its decisions in matters of faith and discipline. Unfortunately, though both Councils were sufficiently of one mind to declare for the same principle, they could not decide how to put it into practice. They found it impossible to agree about how Church government should be reformed; they admitted that authority belongs ultimately to the whole Church, but they did not know how to make this authority real, by setting up institutions to ensure that the Church as a whole could act as they were agreed it should act. One thing, however, they did do; they made it clear, by their condemnation of John Hus, that they would not tolerate democracy in the Church. For John Hus was a popular leader in Bohemia, a demagogue who had appealed to the people against the hierarchy. To the dignitaries assembled at Constance and Basel, the ultimate authority of the Church, of the Christian community, did not mean the present will of the Christian peoples; it meant what is agreed upon by those who, in virtue of their position in the Church and in society generally, have a right to speak for the Church. It meant something subtle and ambiguous, something that the Councils of Constance and Basel could not translate into an acceptable and workable constitution for the Church.

But I am not concerned with those Councils, with what they attempted and why they failed. I want to point out only that the opponents of the Papacy were not asserting the rights of the individual Christian against the Church; they were asserting the right of the Church, a community of laymen and priests, against the Papacy. They were not even claiming for every Christian the right to take part in running the Christian community. The delegates they had in mind, who were to meet together in General Council to speak authoritatively for the whole Church, were not to be chosen by the Christian population generally, but were merely the eminent and the powerful, both churchmen and laymen, from all parts of Christendom, the 'natural' leaders of society, the persons who by custom had the right to speak on behalf of their local communities. William of Occam's idea of Church government was in fact more aristocratic than democratic. If it had come to anything, it might have made the Church easier to reform and more tolerant. There would probably have been considerable diversity of opinion in a General Council consisting of laymen and priests from every part of Western Europe, and the system could not have endured unless they had learnt to make compromises and to tolerate one another. But, as we shall see, there can be toleration and willingness to compromise within fairly broad limits without there being true liberty of conscience. The failure of the Church's attempt to reform itself led eventually to another schism, greater and more permanent than the one brought to an end at Constance. This greater schism was caused, not by rival claimants to the Papacy, but by a determination to achieve Church reform even in defiance of the Pope and the hierarchy. The makers of this new schism were moved partly by a desire for a purer religion, and partly by other more worldly passions.

The reformers, Luther and Calvin most prominent among them, were scarcely at all innovators in the realm of ideas. I am referring, of course, not to their theologies, about which I am not competent to judge, but to their theories about the relations of Church and State. Luther made no claims for the Temporal Power that Marsilio had not made before him; while Calvin's position was almost entirely orthodox. What Calvin wanted for his reformed Church in its relations with the State was more or less what the unreformed Church had always wanted for itself; he merely, being weaker than the Pope, was more cautious, and therefore apparently more willing to make concessions to princes. In practice, as we shall see, he was no less determined than even the most powerful of mediaeval popes to make the State an instrument of the Church; while his ideas about Church government were certainly no closer to being democratic than those of, say, William of Occam.

The reformers, in my opinion, contributed nothing new to political and social theory. Whatever virtues they possessed as political thinkers, originality was not among them. Nevertheless, though they lacked new ideas, the Reformation they made faced political thinkers with a problem unknown to the Middle Ages. Neither Luther nor Calvin had wanted to replace the Universal Church with many separate churches; the ideal of universality remained strong long after the Reformation. But by the end of the sixteenth century, men were already growing used to the existence of several churches. The old problem of what should be the relationship between Church and State was thereby profoundly altered. The Temporal Power might prefer one church to the others, and yet find it impossible to destroy those of which it did not approve. The question of how the State should treat several churches is in practice quite different from the question of how it should treat only one; and so, too, is the question of how one church among several should behave towards the State different from the question how only one church should do so. The old Universal Church, older than all the states among which it lived, could effectively make demands upon them scarcely possible for many smaller churches only recently created. The Reformation, as we shall see, brought to birth political and moral problems hardly known to the Middle Ages; but it did so without the reformers having desired that it should.

It is true that the Reformation in the end caused men to put a greater value than ever before upon individual freedom and tolerance; but it did so only by placing them in such altered circumstances that they could no longer live peaceably together unless they discarded some of their oldest prejudices. It is not true, though many have said it, that respect for freedom and tolerance were originally Protestant virtues. They were no more Protestant than Catholic, but were in the end accepted by Protestant and Catholic alike after repeated failures by each to force the other to accept his own beliefs.

2. Luther

Luther, who asserted the priesthood of all believers, who said that every Christian can interpret God's Word for himself, and that faith alone is enough for salvation; Luther, who said these things, must surely have believed in liberty of conscience! That is the claim sometimes made for him. Now, it is true that these doctrines can be understood in a sense which implies liberty of conscience. It was therefore an important step towards the attainment of that liberty when Luther published those doctrines with a force and eloquence unique among reformers. Luther was one of the greatest, one of the most fervent and colourful, pamphleteers and propagandists that ever lived, and the seed that he scattered so widely has had an immense and, on the whole, a liberating influence. But that does not mean that Luther himself understood liberty of conscience as we do now; not even when he first defied the Papacy and before the excesses of the Anabaptists and the Peasants' Revolt made him a fierce and even brutal champion of authority.

Luther certainly defied authority for conscience' sake. At the beginning of his quarrel with Rome, in October 1518, when there was still hope of healing the breach, he wrote to Cardinal Cajetan, 'I know that neither the command nor the advice nor the influence of anyone ought to make me do anything against conscience or can do so. For the arguments of Aquinas and others are not convincing to me, although I have read them . . . and have thoroughly understood them . . . . The only thing left is to overcome me with better reasons'. In the tract on *The Freedom of a Christian*, published in November 1520, Luther said, 'One thing only is necessary for a Christian life . . . and freedom . . . the gospel of Christ . . . . Perhaps you ask: What is this Word of God and how is it to be used, for there are many words of God? . . . Faith is the sole salutary and efficacious use of God's Word, for the Word is not to be grasped . . . but by faith alone'. And in a sermon at Wittenberg, in March 1522, he remarked, 'I shall not with force constrain anyone, for faith must come freely without compulsion. Follow my example. I opposed indulgences and all the papists, but not with force: I only wrote, preached, used God's Word, and nothing else. That Word, while I slept and drank beer with Melanchthon and Amsdorf, has broken the Papacy more than any king or emperor ever broke it'.

These things Luther said within five years of his first defiance of Rome, and before Anabaptists and rebellious peasants had brought home to him the dangers of excessive freedom. They belong to the first and most liberal phase of his public career. Later, he greatly modified his opinions, but not, I think, as greatly as may appear at first sight. For we are apt to read more into his early pronouncements than he put into them, to interpret them in too liberal a sense. If anyone now were to say what I have quoted Luther as saying, we should infer that he believed in liberty of conscience, and our inference would probably be correct. But if we make the same inference in Luther's case, we should probably be wrong. For many things that are now taken for granted were not so taken in his time, and he made assumptions we no longer make. That Luther was more liberal before 1525 than he was afterwards is certainly true; but that he began by believing in liberty of conscience and afterwards gave up that belief is almost certainly false. Or, to put it another way, he understood by liberty of conscience something different from what we understand by it.

All Christians are, he says, priests; and this implies that every Christian can understand the gospel. But, then, who is a Christian? Not, clearly not, *any* man who can read the gospel and claims to understand it; for an atheist can do that. The Christian must have faith. He must accept what the gospel teaches, if he is really to understand it. That much Luther certainly believed. To assert the priesthood of all believers does not therefore imply that anyone who rejects the gospel has the right to do so. Liberty of conscience is only for believers. And what exactly is the extent of this liberty? Have believers the right to read anything they like into the gospel? Or must their interpretations of it be reasonable? And if that stipulation is made, who is to decide what interpretations are reasonable?

Again, faith is presumably sincere. What is to prevent a man who has no faith from pretending that he has it, and from reading into the gospel whatever he chooses to find in it? And who can put himself forward as an infallible judge of the sincerity of others? The closer we look at this formula about the priesthood of all believers, the more obscure and less liberal it looks. Used as Luther used it in defiance of the Pope, it has great emotional force. Luther believed in the gospel, and on that belief rested all his hope of salvation. We can argue, in the light of what history we know, that his act of defiance served the cause of liberty. But we have no warrant for saying that, at any time of his life, he asserted what we now understand by liberty of conscience.

Luther believed, at least before 1525, that we ought not to use force to constrain belief, 'for faith must come freely without compulsion'. Indeed, by 1520, he had explicitly rejected all the claims of authority made on behalf of the Papacy and had taken up a position as extreme as Marsilio's. No coercive power, he said, belongs to the clergy, who are as entirely subject as any other class of people to the secular magistrates. He distinguished between the invisible and the visible Church, between the mystical community of the faithful, all of whose members are priests and kings, and the actual Church, the community of priests and laymen, organized for the propagation of faith and the due worship of God. The invisible Church is beyond the reach of political theory, for no earthly government can touch it; and to Luther it was the true Church.

It is, however, quite possible, quite consistent, to hold this belief and yet deny that anyone has the right to profess what faith he pleases. Everyone ought to believe the truth sincerely, and therefore it is wrong to use force to compel belief; but it does not follow that it is wrong to forbid the profession or teaching of false doctrines. In a letter to Joseph Metsch, in August 1529, Luther wrote, 'No one is to be compelled to profess the faith, but no one must be allowed to injure it. Let our opponents give their objections and hear our answers. If they are thus converted, well and good; if not, let them hold their tongues and believe what they please. . . . Even unbelievers should be forced to obey the Ten Commandments, attend church and outwardly conform'. These sentiments and others like them Luther mostly uttered after the Anabaptist and peasant troubles, but they are not inconsistent with the doctrines he preached during the first years after the breach with Rome. While Luther was a rebel, his arguments were devised to justify his rebellion; later, when he had to consider how order should be preserved in Germany, he used other arguments. Though the early arguments do not imply the later ones, they are quite compatible with them. It is possible to hold them simultaneously without contradiction.

If we look at what Luther taught about the organization of the Church and its relations to the Temporal Power, we can see how far he was from understanding what liberty of conscience implies in practice, what institutions must exist to make it good. The Church, not long before Luther's time, in the fifteenth century at the General Councils, had made a half-hearted and abortive attempt to reorganize and cleanse itself. Luther, like Wyclif before him, despaired of the Church's ability to reform itself, and thus looked to the princes, the Temporal Power, to reform it. He therefore argued that the clergy are as entirely subject as the rest of the people to the secular magistrates. They have no coercive power, for Christ gave none to them, and their function is merely to instruct in the faith. To carry out this function, they need property, which they receive from the prince. It is the right of the prince to appoint to all benefices within his dominions, and to see to the moral discipline of the clergy. Yet the Church is not a mere fellowship of believers, an association of persons who instruct and sustain one another in the faith. It is a mystical body, divinely instituted, through which God, by means of the sacraments, gives His grace to the faithful. There is no faith outside the Church, and no salvation without faith. But neither is there, inside the Church, any order of persons, any priesthood in the Catholic sense, to whom God gives special powers which He does not give to all true believers. The clergy are merely instructors in the faith, and their selection, training and discipline are matters for the prince to decide. The Church, as a community of the faithful and an organ of grace, is a divine institution, but as an organization of pastors, of instructors in the faith, it is merely human, and no one, in virtue of his place in that organization, can be any the less subject to his prince.

Though Luther taught that it is for the prince to establish and maintain the visible Church – to organize the ministry, to appoint pastors, to provide for them and to ensure good discipline among them – he also denied that the prince has authority in matters of conscience and faith. Not for him to decide how the Scriptures, which contain God's Word, shall be interpreted. To us it seems odd that Luther should not have seen that whoever appoints to the ministry and provides for it will in fact decide what it shall teach. How can the Church depend on the secular power in matters of discipline and organization, and yet retain its spiritual independence? Luther seems also to have believed that the Church, the community of the faithful, is universal, so that there never can be more than one true Church. Yet he knew that there were many independent princes, and he wanted each prince to organize the ministry in his own dominions. How could a Church be only one body if there were inside it many separate ministries controlled by as many independent princes? And why should Luther assume that princes would care more than bishops and popes for the purity and good discipline of the Church?

His opinion about the relations of Church and State hardly deserve to be called a political theory; they leave too much out of account and make too many simple assumptions. Yet Luther must not be set down for a crude German worshipper of power. He leant on the princes, not because he was afflicted with a German's supposedly inordinate love of power, but because he felt he had nothing else to lean on. He had reacted violently against the old Church order, which was independent and yet (in his opinion) worldly, corrupt and incapable of reforming itself. He cared above all else for man's immortal soul and its relation to God. Politics and worldly institutions concerned him much less. And yet, by his defiance of the Pope, he had made a great stir in the world; he had therefore made powerful enemies and needed powerful friends to protect him. He found them among the German princes.

Luther had an even stronger motive for clinging hard to the princes. His example was catching, and there were soon people willing to carry his principles much further than he had done. Why, these people asked, if God's Word is contained entire in the Scriptures, which every faithful Christian can interpret for himself, why have an organized Church at all? Why have any discipline in matters of faith? The Church is the community of the faithful, but only God can know who the truly faithful are. The true Church is therefore invisible except to God, and there is no need for a visible Church organized by men. Others went less far, admitting that the faithful ought to form voluntary associations to sustain one another in the faith, but also denying the need for a Church as Luther understood it. Some denied the two sacraments, Baptism and the Eucharist, which Luther still retained; some condemned property, marriage and other institutions; some denied the legitimacy of any kind of authority of man over man, spiritual or temporal. These people, who formed not one sect but many, were called Anabaptists, because many of them believed in adult baptism. Most of them were harmless, though some were aggressive and violent. But even the most pacific of them tended, in the name of principles proclaimed by Luther, to treat established authority as a nuisance to be borne with patiently. At Mühlhausen they went so far as to attempt to establish their rule by force; and having to defend themselves against attack, they developed an economy that Lenin would have called war communism. At Münster, they wanted to exterminate the ungodly. The Anabaptists were mostly much more peaceful and much less dangerous than their enemies made them out; but the belligerence of a few of them and the anarchist leanings of many others frightened all Germany. Their theories were denounced as subversive, and Luther, who was no doubt aware that their extravagances were partly an effect of his own successful defiance of the Established Church, was anxious to dissociate himself from them and to see them put down.

Luther saw the danger of allowing anyone, no matter how ignorant or fanatical, to preach what doctrines he pleased. Yet, lacking a true conception of liberty of conscience, he did not know how to reconcile the claims of faith with the need for order. He proclaimed both the priesthood of all believers and the need for strong discipline in Church as well as State. His defiance of Rome had excited the Anabaptists, who used his principles and authority to reach conclusions abominable to him. Socially and politically, he was, as most of them were not, deeply conservative. Not, as some hostile critics have said, because he worshipped power, or served as the blind instrument of princely anti-clericalism and greed for Church lands, but because he believed that, without the social peace which rests securely on custom, men are distracted from God. Luther, though his detractors have often said otherwise, had no great respect for temporal rulers. No one has spoken more contemptuously of princes than he sometimes did. He was a deeply religious man and a mystic, with an acute sense of men's spiritual needs, but not much understanding of political and ecclesiastical institutions. The old faith in the visible Church as a self-governing community capable of reforming itself, the faith of William of Occam and of the Conciliarists of the fifteenth century, he altogether gave up. The Church had not reformed itself, and must therefore be reformed by the Temporal Power. For Luther, though he thought the invisible Church the true one, also believed that men need an actual Church, an organized community in this world, to convey God's Word to them. The leaders of that community must be kept to their duties, and can be kept so only by the secular power. It does not much matter, he thought, what kind of order there is in the world; what matters is that what order there is shall be secure, so that men can take the world for granted and turn their thoughts to God. A man as deeply religious as Luther (and no one denies the strength and sincerity of his faith) is not inclined to worship power, even when his anger is most fiercely turned against disturbers of the peace.

As Luther saw it, it was the Anabaptists who were worldly, and not he; for they were concerned, as he was not, about how worldly power and wealth were distributed. He believed that unless there is security and peace on earth, men's minds are distracted from God. He wanted worldly discipline for the sake of spiritual freedom, and could not see how this freedom could be made more secure by changing the social and political order, which was of no importance for its own sake. What did seem to him to matter was that order should be stable, so that Christians might have time enough to think of less worldly things. He lacked a political sense; he had no idea how to get what he wanted, how State and Church should be organized to make possible the quality of life most precious to him. He longed for freedom but did not know how to make freedom at home in the world. The Anabaptists frightened him, and he clung the more closely to the order familiar to him.

Luther preached total submission to established authority, excepting only that commands contrary to God's Word must not be obeyed. The Christian must never actively resist his prince or combine with others against him. He must disobey only when obedience involves sin, and never for the purpose of weakening the authority of the prince. The Christian has only one right against established Power: the right meekly to suffer unjust punishment, bearing witness to the truth as Christ did on the Cross.

3. Calvin

Calvin was even less inclined to liberty than Luther. In his political and social theories, he was not a deep or subtle thinker, a questioner of accepted principles, a framer of new concepts and hypotheses. He was almost entirely derivative. This is true, apparently, even of his theology, which mostly comes from Luther, though it emphasizes some aspects of Luther's teaching much more than Luther did, and neglects others. Ernst Troeltsch, in his remarkable book on *The Social Teaching of the Christian Churches*, says that Calvin was a more lucid, consistent and systematic theologian than Luther, but also speaks of his 'doctrinaire logic which is peculiar to men of a second generation, due to their sense of possessing a secure inheritance'.[1]

---

[1] Troeltsch, *The Social Teaching of the Christian Churches*, first published in 1911 (London 1931), vol. 2, p. 581.

Calvin's theology does not concern us, but his political theory has all the qualities that Troeltsch ascribes to his theology: it is lucid, consistent, systematic and entirely second-hand. It comes, however, not from Luther, who really had no political theory, but from mediaeval and early Christian sources. To be more precise, his conception of the relation between Church and State is essentially mediaeval, while his theory about the internal government of the Church is early Christian rather than mediaeval. In any case, his political theory, whatever its sources, is illiberal; it scarcely leaves room for liberty of conscience. There is not in Calvin, as there is in Luther, a yearning for liberty which finds no adequate political expression. Although much more a politician than Luther, he was not a monk but a student of law, less a mystic than a moralist. God, for him, is a master to be obeyed; God's law must therefore be made certain, and proper measures taken to ensure that it is obeyed.

According to Calvin, the Bible, which takes precedence over custom and all man-made laws, prescribes how the Church, the community of the faithful, is to be governed. He believed that the Bible is fundamental for all societies, though the New supersedes the Old Testament where the two differ. It is not for the Temporal Power to govern the faithful, he claimed. The Church alone has authority to declare true doctrine, and also to control the moral life of the community. Temporal rulers do not derive their authority from the Church; they too get if from God, either through the people or directly. Church and State are therefore separate, and neither is subordinate to the other. Now this, as we have seen, is the typical doctrine of the Middle Ages, though extremer champions of papal or imperial claims had denied it.

Temporal rulers – and this too is good mediaeval doctrine – are obliged to support the Church, to favour the true doctrine and worship against all others, and to extirpate heresy, if necessary by force. But this doctrine, in Calvin's time, had different practical implications. In the Middle Ages there had been only one Church, and temporal rulers, though they might have doubts how far to go in supporting the Church, did at least know what Church to support. After the Reformation, matters stood differently; it was no longer as obvious as it had been which Church was worthy of support. It might be obvious to Calvin or to the Pope, but in the minds of temporal rulers there was more room for doubt.

In the Middle Ages, the Conciliarists had wished to reform the Church from the centre outwards, by trying to provide it with a central authority, other than the Papacy, strong enough to impose its will over all Christendom. Calvin sought to reform it piece by piece, as it were, from the circumference inwards, by first reorganizing it in every locality where there were true Christians strong enough to reform it. The ideal of a Universal Church he never abandoned; he thought of himself as reforming the old Church rather than as creating a new one. It is because the old Church survived his efforts to reform it, and in the end reformed itself on principles quite different from those he advocated, that he appears to us as the creator of a new Christian Church and not as the restorer of the old one. He himself, however, never doubted that he was bringing the Church back to its true principles. He was appealing from the clerical hierarchy to the entire community of the faithful, to the Church against the priests who perverted it.

Calvin's conception of how the Church should be organized, though contrary to ecclesiastical institutions as they had in fact developed since the early days of Christianity, was quite in keeping with ideas that had never ceased to be popular. It was merely a question of how those ideas could be applied in practice. The Church, for Calvin as well as for William of Occam and the later Conciliarists, was a self-governing community of pastors and laymen. True, Calvin, unlike William and even unlike Marsilio, denied the sacred character of the priesthood; he did not believe in the uninterrupted transmission of spiritual powers through a succession of bishops from St Peter downwards. But scepticism of this kind was nothing new; it had been known in the Middle Ages. And, in any case, belief in the sacred character of the priesthood had not prevented quite a few mediaeval doctors, who took pride in their orthodoxy, from asserting that ultimate authority in the Church belongs to the whole body of Christians, lay and clerical.

Calvin declared that the Church is independent of the State, and also admitted that the State is independent of the Church. There is, he said, only one true Church, which it is the duty of the State to support. But how, in a Europe where there were already several churches claiming to be the one true Church, could it be ensured that the State shall support *the* true Church? It could hardly be done unless the true Church makes the State subordinate to it. This, at least, was the conclusion to which Calvin was driven in practice, though he never admitted it in theory.

In Geneva he set about making the Church supreme. Without, for a moment, denying the independence of the State, he so contrived matters that the Church should be certain of the State's support. And certain it could not be unless the State was in fact subordinate to it. In Calvin's Geneva, though supreme civil authority belonged to the City

Council, and supreme ecclesiastical authority to the Consistory, in fact both bodies were dominated by the Congregation of Pastors. As the elders outnumbered the pastors, and as they were all appointed by laymen, it might indeed appear that the City controlled the Church. But this was not so in reality. The pastors, unlike the laymen, were a unified body; their Congregation met weekly; they catechized whom they liked and interfered as they liked in private matters; and they also controlled the schools. Though pastors were officially appointed by the City Council, they had first to be examined by the Congregation. Just as in some parts of the world today, ultimate authority belongs, not to the highest organs of the State, but to the leaders of a political party, so, in Calvin's Geneva, the City seemed to be supreme while the Church was so in fact. No doubt, when Calvin first went to Geneva in 1536, the City ruled the Church; the Bishop and the Duke had recently been driven out, and all their powers taken over by the Council. But this situation did not long survive Calvin's coming. It was he who organized the Church and established it in such a way as to make it virtually supreme. Anyone excommunicated by the pastors lost his civic rights.

All this may seem odd, when we consider that, according to Calvin, authority in the Church belongs to the entire community, laymen as well as pastors; but in no other way could he have achieved his object. Just as the Conciliarist doctrine that the Church belongs to the whole body of Christians had not meant democracy to the mediaeval doctors who asserted it, so, as the organization of the Genevan Church abundantly proves, it had no such meaning for Calvin. In no part of Catholic Europe, outside the papal states, was the hold of the Church over the State as great as in Geneva. It took Calvin many years to establish this supremacy; but he knew from the beginning exactly what he wanted, and he worked for it consistently. The Roman Church scarcely needed such a hold, for its claims on the State had long been admitted. It could rely on old loyalties and old habits.

Calvin preached the doctrine of obedience to established civil authority almost as fervently as Luther. It could not endanger his position in Geneva; for where the Church in fact dominates the State, there is no need for it to contest the State's authority. The more the State is an instrument of the Church, the better the Church can afford to preach complete submission to the State; and by preaching it Calvin could help his disciples outside Geneva. He well understood that his victory in Geneva had been made easy by circumstances not likely to be often repeated, and he did not expect the true religion to triumph quickly everywhere. He knew that, outside Geneva, the position of his adherents was precarious, and that it was essential for them to be patient – especially in his native France, where the most the Calvinists could hope for, for a long time to come, was toleration. To earn this toleration, they had to avoid appearing dangerous to the king, and had also to strengthen their influence at court, which they could best do by admitting as unreservedly as possible their duty of obedience. There is, therefore, a surface resemblance between Luther's and Calvin's teaching about the obligations of subjects to their rulers. They both tell men to obey God rather than man, and also never actively to resist established authority, because, in the words of St Paul to the Romans, 'the powers that be are ordained of God'. To resist the prince is to resist God.

This resemblance, masking a difference between two almost opposite conceptions of how Church and State should be organized, did not last long. For a quarter of a century, Calvin hoped to win over enough influential converts to his cause in France to permit the Huguenots to establish themselves so thoroughly that no one would dare to harm them. Throughout that period, nothing seemed more useful to the Huguenots in their endeavours to win over French public opinion than a loudly proclaimed respect for the Crown, and this is what Calvin believed until the 1560s. But as soon as he saw that the Huguenots could not win the support they needed at the French court to enable them to get secure privileges for themselves, and so work peacefully to bring the whole country over to their way of thinking, he added a rider to the doctrine of non-resistance which quite changed its character. Under the influence of pressure from his co-religionists in France, he argued, in a letter to the Huguenot leader, Coligny, that though, in general, subjects must never actively resist their rulers, yet, if Princes of the Blood, supported by the *parlements*, gave the lead, it was allowable, on the authority of these magistrates, to take up arms in defence of legal rights, even against the legitimate sovereign. At first sight, this rider to the doctrine of non-resistance seems mild enough, for the rights to be defended with arms must be generally recognized and also admitted by the highest judicial authorities. It was a doctrine admirably suited to the special needs of the Huguenots. Though they were only a minority in France and could not hope to control the Estates-General, many of them were noblemen or wealthy merchants, who held the chief magistracies and controlled the highest courts of their own provinces, principally in the South and West. Calvin's doctrine of active resistance by lesser magistrates to the sovereign or supreme magistrate justified their using their local privileges in defence of their faith, when they came to despair of obtaining enduring protection from the Crown. Since they had few adherents among the lower classes, even in the provinces where they were strongest, no doctrine asserting a merely popular right of resistance could suit them. They needed a right of resistance they could use wherever they were socially predominant, but which could not be used to stir up against them the lower classes who were strongly Catholic in almost every part of France. The highest French judicial authorities and magistrates were not all concentrated in Paris; there were still much greater provincial autonomies in France than in England, existing not for the benefit of all classes, but of the upper classes alone. The Huguenots meant to use them, if necessary, to defend their religion against the centralizing royal power. Yet Calvin's doctrine, slightly altered to meet their needs, was at bottom only the old mediaeval theory of resistance, as we find it in Aquinas, which asserts, not a right of individual or even popular resistance, but a right of official or privileged resistance. According to this theory, only those who already have authority have the right to resist authority. The mere citizen or subject has no such right.

Calvin and the Huguenots had to be careful; they had to prove just enough to suit their rather special needs, and no more. But Calvin had, in Scotland, a disciple who could afford to be less cautious in advocating open resistance to established authority; who was not content to argue that, under certain circumstances, lesser magistrates can use force to defend established rights against higher magistrates; who boldly affirmed that, no matter what the established rights might be, the people can always set them aside on the authority of the Bible, if these rights are used against the true religion. This is the argument of John Knox's 'First Blast of the Trumpet Against the Monstrous Regiment of Women'. It was the duty of the English people, he implied, to depose Mary Tudor, who was persecuting the true faith. Though her title to the throne might be good by English Law, that law stood for nothing against the authority of Holy Scripture, which has prescribed woman's subservience to man. Of course Knox's real objection to Mary Tudor, who was under what he called 'the malediction and curse pronounced against Woman', was that she regarded persons like himself as heretics. The argument is curious, for Holy Scripture does not forbid the succession of women to the throne; it merely in a general way places woman under the government of man. The 'First Blast' is an attack on a very restricted class of persons, on women who happen to be queens regnant and who persecute the faith of John Knox. In his later writings, in the 'Appellation' against the sentence passed on him by the Scottish bishops, and again in his 'Letter to the Commonalty of Scotland', Knox broadened his argument, taking it to its logical conclusion. Everywhere the faithful have the duty to depose impious rulers and to establish the true faith, he claimed. It was scarcely possible to make a wider breach in the old doctrine of non-resistance. Knox went further, much further, than Calvin had done; he was a more violent and reckless controversialist. It was not, however, mere recklessness that sustained him, for the Calvinists were stronger in Scotland than in France, and could afford to be bolder. Knox's doctrine of resistance is entirely in keeping with Calvin's conception of the proper relations between Church and State. He was merely drawing a conclusion more sweeping than Calvin – who was more concerned with France than with Scotland – could afford to draw himself.

The right of resistance is confined by Knox to the faithful, to those who believe in the true doctrine. Sincere believers in false doctrines have no right of resistance against true believers seeking to establish uniformity of worship. Knox was no respecter of persons. No matter how humble a true believer, he has the right to resist. The privilege of fighting for the faith is not confined to the well-born and powerful. Knox was, if you like, a democrat. But he cared nothing for liberty as such; he cared only for the liberty of people who agreed with him. He believed in liberty of conscience about as much as most Communists do today.

The early Calvinists, in Geneva, in France, in Scotland and in England too, were quite unambiguous. We cannot say of them, as some people (though, in my opinion, mistakenly) have said of Luther, that they put forward a claim to liberty of conscience, which they then belied by making other claims incompatible with it, without noticing the incompatibility: or that they began by believing in it and afterwards gave up the belief. They never believed in it, and were never any closer to doing so than the Pope.

4. The Jesuits

It is instructive to compare the Calvinist position with that of the Jesuits, as we find it especially in the writings of Molina[1] and Suárez[2]. Although the Jesuits were the Pope's most devoted servants in the struggle to reunite Christendom under the authority of Rome, their

[1] *De justitia et jure* (1597).
[2] *Tractatus de legibus ac Deo legislatore* (1612).

conception of the proper relations between Church and State is at bottom the old mediaeval conception as we find it, not in the extreme papalist writers, but in Aquinas. It is merely adapted to the new situation created by the reformers. The Jesuits stand out among the political controversialists of the sixteenth century by their lucidity, their respect for logic and their better manners.

They distinguished sharply between the authority of the Pope and the authority of temporal rulers. The Pope's authority comes directly from Christ; it does not come from the Church, the community of the faithful. But the authority of temporal rulers is vested in them by the community they govern; though it also comes from God, as all legitimate authority must do, it comes from God through the people. Princes and other temporal rulers are the delegates of their peoples, and their authority is therefore limited. What the people have created for their convenience and happiness they may resist or remove when it does not serve the purposes it was meant to serve. Both Molina and Suárez asserted the people's right to depose their rulers for misgovernment.

The Jesuits admitted that temporal authority is by its origin independent of the Church, and that the Pope has no right to interfere with purely temporal matters. But it is his duty to see to it that men are not governed in such a way that their salvation is imperilled. Though the Temporal Power is independent of the Church, it has no right to obstruct the end and purpose of man's life, which is spiritual as well as temporal. The Pope, *ad finem spiritualem*, may depose a prince, or at least may excommunicate him, thereby releasing his subjects from obedience to him.

The Jesuit doctrine in this matter is at bottom the same as the Calvinist, except that, where Jesuits speak of the Pope, Calvinists speak of the Church, meaning in practice the morally respectable and the godly, led by their pastors. Arguing from first principles, the Jesuits, who did not have to suit their doctrine to the conditions of any particular country, always insisted on the popular origins of temporal power, and never confined the right of resistance to inferior magistrates. The Church, for them, was essentially a monarchy, but the State could have whatever form its people had chosen to give it; whereas the Calvinist ideal, in both Church and State, was aristocratic, the rule of the godly. There were other differences between them, but their conceptions of the relations of Church and State were broadly similar. Neither allowed room for anything like true liberty of conscience. To them the liberty of the faithful meant only the rights of the Church against the State.

5. The Sects

The Catholics, the Lutherans, the Anglicans, the Calvinists, all had this in common: they believed that there could be only one true Church. Whatever their views about the internal government of the Church and its relations to the State, they all agreed that the Church is not a voluntary association of believers, a merely human institution which men may or may not join as they please. It is through the Church that God's Word is brought to man, and through it also that man receives from God the gift of grace without which he cannot be saved. Though Luther and Calvin proclaimed the priesthood of all believers, and said that the Bible alone contains the whole Word of God, the entire truth necessary to salvation, they did not believe that men could receive the Word and be saved outside the Church, or that there could be several churches, each interpreting the Word differently from the others, and yet all equally acceptable to God. Luther and Calvin, no less than the Catholics and Anglicans, believed in uniformity of faith and worship.

We have so long been used to there being several Christian churches that it is difficult for us to enter into the minds of persons who took it for granted that there could be only one. Indeed, in this matter, the Catholic argument, that a single Church can have only one head, is perhaps the most easily intelligible to us, even when we are Protestants, because it is more in keeping with modern ways of thinking about what constitutes a community. How can there be only one Church for all Christians unless they all recognize one authority as supreme over them? How could Luther, who left it to each prince to organize and provide for the ministry within his own dominions, believe in only one Church? How could the Anglicans do so, and yet recognize the King of England, whose kingdom included only a small part of all the Christians in the world, as supreme governor of their Church? Calvin, at least, appears rather more logical to us. Though he held that it is for the faithful in every locality to establish their own Church, which, if it is truly based on God's Word, will have full spiritual authority, he also wanted to have a kind of federation of Protestant churches united against Rome.

Christians in the sixteenth century did not think of the Church as a society which owes its unity to being under a single government. Nor did they think of it as merely a group of persons having the same religious beliefs. They thought of it as a divinely instituted community, a brotherhood in Christ, possessing – in the Bible, in the sacraments, in certain forms of worship – the means of faith and of union with God. I am not a theologian, and I must take care not to

111

get out of my depth, but I believe that to be united in the faith with other people is not just to share their convictions or to be under the same Church government. It is to stand to God in the same relation as they do, a relation that no man can stand in unless he receives God's grace, which he can do only through the means to grace provided by God, which are the Word and the sacraments. Catholics, Lutherans and Calvinists might disagree about what Holy Scripture meant and about who had the right to interpret it, and also about the number, character and effects of the sacraments; but they all agreed that there were specific means to grace provided by God, without which no man could be saved. These means were provided through the Church, the only true Church, so that nothing should matter more to any man than that he should belong to that Church.

Let us try to see how this conception of the Church, even when combined with the doctrine of the priesthood of all believers, stands in the way of liberty of conscience. Like the Catholics, the Lutherans and Calvinists thought it the duty of the one true Church to bring the Word and the sacraments to all men, and so put them in the way of receiving God's grace. Yet, while the Catholics believed that the head of the Church had divine authority to interpret the Word to all men, Luther and Calvin held that Holy Scripture is such that any man of good will, sound intelligence and sufficient knowledge cannot help but understand its plain meaning. But this Protestant idea, that the correct interpretation of the Word somehow comes of itself, through the mere power of the Word, had in practice to be modified – for the very simple reason that there cannot in practice be uniformity of belief unless it is imposed from above. There is no salvation without the truth, and there is only one truth, revealed in Holy Scripture. How then is it to be contrived that all men of good will, sound intelligence and sufficient knowledge shall interpret Holy Scripture in the same way? If they interpret it differently, how can it be known who possesses the truth? How can there be only one truth acceptable to God and only one true Church, and yet all believers be priests?

Luther and Calvin denied that Holy Scripture, in fundamental matters, can be honestly and reasonably interpreted in more than one way, and also implied that every man of good will, sound intelligence and sufficient knowledge will interpret it aright. Now, this denial and that assertion, taken together, must lead to great difficulties, logical and practical. The logical difficulties are perhaps insuperable, but the practical difficulties can be got over after a fashion. There is, *ex hypothesi*, no need for a single authorized interpreter of Holy Scripture, since anyone possessing certain qualities can be relied upon to interpret it correctly. All that is needed is some authority to decide whether or not a man possesses these qualities. In Calvin's Geneva, this authority was the Consistory. Since it contained only men of good will, sound intelligence and sufficient knowledge, it felt justified in concluding that anyone who understood Holy Scripture in a way not acceptable to itself did not possess these qualities, and was either malicious or incompetent. It was as simple as that. Though not in so many words, yet implicitly, a claim was made which I believe I do not distort if I put it thus: 'Any morally and intellectually competent person can understand the Scriptures as well as we can; but since we are competent, anyone who understands them differently from us proves himself incompetent, either morally or intellectually.' There could be no question of setting up other criteria for testing good will, intelligence and knowledge, that is to say, for testing moral and intellectual competence; for then it might happen that people who passed the same tests differed fundamentally about Holy Scripture. The only safe criterion, if there is to be only one true Church and one true doctrine, is the criterion used by the Genevan Consistory. Any competent person can know the truth, but the only mark of his competence is that he agrees with us who also know it. Those who, like the Consistory, are strong enough to coerce others need only assume their own competence to feel justified in concluding that anyone who does not agree with them does not know the truth, and is therefore incompetent and deserves to be silenced. How much more modest is this claim than the one made on the Pope's behalf! And yet, in practice, it comes to much the same thing. No one, no man or group of men, assumes supreme authority from God to interpret God's Word; nobody assumes anything more than that he is morally and intellectually competent.

No doubt, it is not self-contradictory to hold that there is only one true Church teaching the doctrine necessary to salvation and yet to allow full liberty of conscience. It is not illogical to hold that no one will be saved unless he accepts certain beliefs and belongs to a certain community, and at the same time to admit everyone's right to believe what he pleases and to join any community. But this position, though there is nothing inconsistent about it, is not attractive to people who believe that there is only one true Church. They are driven back upon it only when experience has taught them that there is no hope of bringing everyone into their church and that the cost in suffering of trying to force them in is altogether excessive. It is the position they gradually fall back on the longer they have to put up with several churches, each claiming to be the one true Church.

Not everyone adhered to this idea that there can be only one true Church because, by virtue of its very nature, the Church is universal. Even in the Middle Ages there had been people who denied the need for a Universal Church, who rejected the sacraments as means to salvation, and who had no more use for an organized ministry than for priests in the Catholic sense. These people, the Catharists and Waldensians in the north of Italy and the south of France, had been persecuted without pity and their heresies almost rooted out. During the Reformation the Anabaptists adopted very similar beliefs, and this time there was no longer a single Church over the whole of Western Europe strong enough to put them down. Among the Anabaptists there were some who denied the need for any kind of organized church, but most of them were content to say that a church is only a voluntary association of believers, so that there can be any number of churches, each as truly a Church as any other. Anabaptist ideas passed from Germany to Holland, and thence to England, and eventually to the English colonies across the Atlantic, either directly from Holland or through the mother country. By the middle of the seventeenth century the sectarian conception of a church as a voluntary association had taken firm hold among politically important minorities both in England and America. People for whom their church is merely a voluntary association of believers, and who therefore do not look to the State to provide for only one true Church, need evolve no elaborate theory about relations between Church and State. All they need ask of the State is that it should let them alone, provided they do nothing to disturb the peace. All they need ask for is toleration.

Not just Catholics, but Lutherans, Anglicans and Calvinists asked for more than this. Yet, in a Europe permanently divided among several churches, they could not continue asking for more indefinitely, and everywhere. Somewhere or other, each of these churches was weaker than the others, and therefore found it expedient to abate its claim. As might be expected, it was the weakest among them that made the first concessions. The Calvinists were both more widely and more thinly spread over Europe than the Lutherans and the Anglicans. They were therefore the least well placed, except in one or two countries, to induce the State to do what they wanted. They were less numerous and powerful than the Catholics, and less congenial to princes than the Lutherans and Anglicans. In several countries, they had to reconcile themselves to being, for a long time to come, a small minority, and were therefore disposed to give up the claim that the State should support the one true Church against all others. They adopted what came to be called the 'free church' principle. The

Church must rely on itself alone to maintain faith and good discipline among its members, and can require no more of the State than to be tolerated. The first English Calvinists to adopt this principle were the Congregationalists. There were not many of them, and the most they could hope for was to be let alone. But the Calvinists were driven back on the 'free church' principle by their weakness; whereas the sects, rejecting the traditional conception of a Universal Church, were from the first more inclined to toleration.

Old ideas die hard. Even the Congregationalists, though they wanted no support from the State, still expected it to suppress what they called idolatry and blasphemy, which meant in practice any forms of worship very unlike their own. They were prepared to admit that other people could differ from them, provided they did not differ too much. The weakness of this early Calvinist belief in toleration is plainly shown by what happened to the Congregationalists when they got to America. When they found themselves a majority in some of the New England colonies, they became as eager as Calvin had been to use the civil power to make their church supreme.

Though the 'free church' principle, once firmly established, leads inevitably to toleration, it took the Calvinists a long time to accept its implications. Belief in toleration among the religious comes more easily to groups which either, like the Anabaptists in Germany and Holland and their Baptist and other successors in England and America, from the first conceive of the Church as merely a voluntary association of believers, or which, like the Socinians, though they think a Universal Church desirable, do not require uniformity of belief. Toleration and liberty of conscience are not, as I shall try to show, by any means the same; but they are intimately related. I want now to consider them more closely: how they differ, how they are connected and how they spread.

II. THE GROWTH OF TOLERATION AND LIBERTY OF CONSCIENCE

So far, I have been considering traditional ideas about the nature of the Church, its relations to the State, and the rights of the Christian conscience. I have tried to show how equivocal the great reformers were, how what they gave with one hand they took away with the other, and how far they really were from a true conception of full liberty of conscience. Protestant apologists, not of the sixteenth but of the nineteenth and twentieth centuries, have spoken enthusiastically of the connection between the growth of freedom and the spread of their religion. Yet there is nothing particularly liberal about the doctrine that all the truths of religion are contained in the Bible and are plain enough to be understood by any honest man with a sufficient education. Protestants as well as Catholics thought it important that what they considered truth should be taught and believed; and there is nothing to choose, as far as freedom of conscience is concerned, between the infallibility of the Church or the Pope and that of the Bible. A man may accept ecclesiastical or papal infallibility and yet believe in freedom of conscience; for he may also hold that other people are free to reject what he himself has freely accepted. No doubt the Protestants of the sixteenth century claimed freedom of conscience against the Pope; they claimed the right not to be forced to conform to a religion they believed to be false. But then Catholics claimed the like liberty of conscience against Calvin or Knox or Queen Elizabeth. It is not by claiming freedom for themselves that men prove its true champions, but rather by respecting the claim when others make it. And this Protestants were no more willing to do than Catholics. People could admit that belief in true doctrine has no value unless it is sincere and yet deny that men must be free to choose what they shall believe. It was possible to value sincerity without respecting freedom. So was it also possible to condemn persecution as a cause of insincerity without respecting freedom. Yet it transpired that the very equivocation of the great reformers advanced the cause of freedom. No doubt, they did not concede in practice what they seemed to offer in theory; but they did seem to offer it. They spoke of the individual Christian's competence in matters of faith as the mediaeval Church had not done, and they successfully defied authority, spiritual as well as temporal. They helped indirectly to prepare Europe for intellectual freedom, far though they themselves were from understanding and desiring it. I now want to consider how the full conception of this freedom gradually emerged, and what arguments were used in its favour.

By the end of the seventeenth century it had fully emerged. Of course, the fight against intolerance continued long afterwards, and still continues today. The right to profess and practise the religion of one's choice was still far from universal in Europe in Locke's time. It was indeed still the exception and not the rule. But by Locke's time, the case for liberty of conscience had been clearly put; though not all its implications had been drawn, the assumptions the case rested on had been clearly stated. It had, moreover, ceased to be primarily a theological argument. The right asserted was not that of mere freedom of worship and religious belief; it was the right to hold and profess any opinions. Religion was in those days held so important that to allow people to hold what religious beliefs they wanted was virtually to concede full intellectual freedom. If men were free to accept or reject beliefs long held necessary to salvation, why should they be bound in lesser things? So the doctrine was put about that a man is not responsible to other men for the opinions he holds, and may profess them freely, provided that by so doing he does not promote disorder. This is essentially the doctrine of Locke's first *Letter Concerning Toleration*, published in 1689. Not long afterwards we come to the age of Voltaire, when the champions of religious and intellectual freedom could afford to take the offensive, and believers in persecution first began to look more foolish than dangerous. By that time freedom of thought and expression, understood as we now understand it, was already widely, though not yet often legally, acknowledged in the West as among the most precious of the rights of man. It was also widely disputed, but much less confidently than before.

1. Arguments for Mere Toleration

Long before Locke there were many advocates of toleration. But we must not confuse what they understood by toleration with positive belief in liberty of conscience. It is possible, for all sorts of reasons, to condemn persecution without conceding that men have a right to hold (and express) what opinions they choose and to order their lives accordingly, provided they do no harm to others. To forbear from persecution, and even to advocate such forbearance, is not to assert a right to freedom of thought and expression.

People can believe in persecution or toleration for two quite different kinds of reason: political and religious. They can hold that uniformity of belief is necessary to the security of society or the State, or at least that the suppression of some kinds of belief is necessary to that end; or they can hold that the attempt to establish uniformity of belief will be so costly or painful as not to be worthwhile. These are political reasons for advocating persecution and toleration. With only them in mind, we can quite consistently advocate persecuting some beliefs and tolerating others, or persecuting some beliefs at one time and tolerating them at another. The party of mainly moderate Catholics in France known as the *Politiques*, though most of them thought uniformity of belief desirable, were against persecuting the Huguenots because they believed that the Huguenots could not easily be suppressed by force; and so they argued that to tolerate them was better than to

continue the civil war. No doubt many of the *Politiques* would not
have wished to persecute the Huguenots even if it had been possible
to do so without ruining France; but the argument they thought it
advisable to use against persecution was that, if persisted in, it would
ruin France. Queen Elizabeth, in England, persecuted the Catholics
and the Puritans, not because she was offended by their religious
beliefs or because she cared overmuch for the welfare of their souls,
but because she thought them dangerous to the State. The Catholics,
she feared, might put their allegiance to the Pope above their allegiance
to herself, and the Puritans, she thought, wanted to set up in England
forms of worship, Church government and moral discipline which
most of her subjects disliked and which seemed to her dangerous to
the peace of society. Elizabeth was just as tolerant in her way as the
French *Politiques* were in theirs, or, rather, her motives for intolerance
were as political as theirs for tolerance. She was as anxious as they
were, for the sake of domestic peace, to persecute as little as possible.
If she was mildly intolerant, that was because she feared the much
greater intolerance of two classes of her subjects.

Political motives for toleration and for persecution were frequent in
the sixteenth century, and some historians, J. W. Allen among them,
have been inclined to think that they were the most frequent of all.
Perhaps they were, among the persons whose motives mattered most
politically – among the actual rulers of states, who alone could decide
whether to persecute or not. Among their subjects other motives were
probably stronger; and the feelings of their subjects must have had
a large influence on the decisions of the rulers. Some kings, who
might have been glad to be tolerant, could not afford to be so for
fear of losing the loyalty to their subjects or of offending some
powerful group. The greatest crime of the sixteenth century, the St
Bartholomew massacre, was forced on a reluctant king by persons
and groups he was too weak to defy.

Political arguments for the persecution or toleration of beliefs, even
though they are the most frequent in high places, are always, in a
sense, derivative and secondary. For, unless it is supposed that men's
beliefs affect their political behaviour, there are no political grounds
for deciding to persecute or tolerate these beliefs. Faith must affect,
or be thought to affect, politics before politics takes notice of faith.
The religious motives for persecution or toleration are not derivative
in the same way; they spring from concern with the nature and quality
of men's beliefs and of human life generally, with what is believed and
how it is believed, and with the consequences to the individual himself
of faith or the lack of it, and not from concern with the political effects

of belief. It was, as I shall try to show, from religious arguments for toleration that the conception of full liberty of conscience gradually emerged. These arguments were first put by the smaller sects that did not accept the idea of only one true Church or only one set of beliefs acceptable to God.

If God has a purpose for man, a purpose which must be attained to enable man to get eternal happiness and to escape eternal misery; and if it cannot be attained unless man stands in a certain relation to God, which he cannot do unless he has the true faith, it must matter enormously that he should have that faith. He may not want to have it; he may not understand its value, or he may not believe that it has the value attributed to it by those who have it. But if the faith has that value he should have it; and it is therefore the duty of those who already have it and know its value to do their utmost to see that he gets it. They may not succeed, but they should at least try.

Everyone who values faith believes that it should be sincere. Indeed, unless it is sincere, it is not faith; for to pretend to believe is clearly not the same thing as to believe. From this premise those who, from religious motives, believe in toleration derive their strongest arguments. They do not admit that it does not matter what a man believes; they do not deny that it is the duty of those who have faith to bring it to those who do not have it. But certain methods, they say, are ruled out by the very nature of the end to be achieved. You cannot force belief, and it is therefore absurd to try. Not only absurd but harmful. For to pretend to believe when you do not is an even worse condition than not to believe. When force is used, it is impossible to tell the sincere from the false believer, the faithful from the hypocrite. Even among the persecutors there may be hypocrites, who persecute not for the faith but to serve their own ends. If error is made dangerous, faith itself shines the less brightly, for it cannot be distinguished from hypocrisy.

This argument for toleration was quite familiar to the sixteenth century, though it was perhaps less frequently used than the political arguments. To some people it seems so obvious and so strong that they cannot understand how it has come to be so often rejected. Yet there have been persons who, having used it themselves, have afterwards abandoned it, who have seen the force of it and have found that force insufficient. St Augustine began by condemning persecution on the ground that it makes hypocrites rather than believers, and ended by admitting its necessity; and so too, over a thousand years later, did Martin Luther. They came to believe that the persecution of heretics discourages the propagation of false doctrines, that it silences error and

119

thus prevents the seduction of the irresolute. The heretic has always been persecuted, less for his own sake than for the sake of others. It was not to force the truth upon him that he was tortured and burned, nor even to add a little agony in this world to the everlasting torments he would endure in the next; it was rather to purge society in a striking and solemn manner of a seducer and corrupter of souls.

Liberal critics of persecution have sometimes argued that persecutors would not resort to terror if they really believed that reason was on their side. Why persecute if you can convince? This argument is not sound. Men are not merely rational creatures; they are sensual, lazy and passionate as well. It is a doubtful assumption that the best arguments must in the end convince. The zealous persecutor of the sixteenth century was certain that reason was on his side, but he knew that men are not always amenable to reason – not so much from lack of intelligence as from pride or because the flesh is weak. It is notoriously a hard thing to be a good Christian; it requires self-discipline, self-sacrifice and humility. It is hard for the lazy and the restless, and still harder for the proud. The ordinary, sensual, lazy man is easily tempted away from a religion requiring so much of him, and the restless man quickly falls a victim to new and strange doctrines, to anything that encourages him to throw off the accustomed burdens. The proud man loves to defy authority, to take the measure of his own courage, to prove himself better and wiser than other people.

The obdurate heretic – so thinks the persecutor – is the most dangerous heretic of all; he is the peculiar victim of pride. His virtues may be greater than other men's, but he has also, much more than they have, the sin of pride, the sin which can turn even a man's virtue to evil purpose. The zealous persecutor, when he destroys the obdurate heretic, is not using force to make up for the weakness of his arguments; his arguments, he thinks, are rejected, not because they are weak, but because men who have fallen prey to evil passions will not listen to reason when reason points to conclusions they dislike. It is therefore right to silence the proud, even by death, if the lazy, the weak and the restless, who are the great majority, may thereby escape corruption. To the conscientious persecutor, the argument that, where thought is free, the truth must in the end prevail, seems paltry and sentimental, an argument attractive only to men lacking courage to exert themselves in defence of the truth.

2. The Socinians and Castellion

Belief in true liberty of conscience, in man's right to hold and profess what opinions he pleases, limited by the need to protect the same right in others, scarcely existed in the sixteenth century. It is a belief which emerged, slowly and painfully, out of disputes about toleration, and did not find clear and adequate expression until the seventeenth century. At the same time, belief in toleration, inspired by political motives, was quite common in the sixteenth century. Fairly common, too, was belief in toleration inspired by concern for the purity and sincerity of religious belief. We find it in Erasmus, in some of the early tracts and letters of Luther, in Bodin, in Montaigne and in Hooker. I mention these names only to show how wide was the diversity of beliefs held by men who, for one reason or another, advocated a fairly broad toleration. They cared not only for domestic peace but also (and sometimes much more) for the quality of men's beliefs; they wanted to put as little strain as possible on tender consciences. 'God', said Luther, 'desires to be alone in our consciences, and desires that his Word alone should prevail'. We are not to suppose this opinion less typical of the age than the opinions of the persecutors. Luther could say this, and then take up other positions putting him in the camp of the intolerant.

The friends of toleration, especially when they defended it from religious rather than political motives, were seldom leaders of strong parties; they were not, for the most part, demagogues but quiet and scholarly men. It may be – and we certainly have no good reason for supposing the contrary – that their sentiments found an echo in many hearts; but these champions of toleration were more isolated from one another and less vociferous than the persecutors, and they lacked organized support. To consider only the men I have already mentioned (and there were many more), Erasmus was concerned to prevent religious disputes rather than to stand up for toleration as a principle; Luther was equivocal and confused; Bodin never dared publish the book which was his ablest defence of religious liberty; Montaigne disliked controversy too much ever to wish to engage in it, and had little faith in the power of argument; Hooker was scholarly and abstruse. There were many believers in toleration, and yet there was widespread persecution. To win toleration it was necessary to fight for it, to engage in active and sometimes dangerous controversy; and these great men, among the greatest writers and thinkers of their age, were mostly not fighters. Luther, of course, was a great fighter, brave and stubborn, but he was also moody and muddle-headed and more often intolerant than tolerant. The others were either not fighters by temperament or else gave the best of their energies to other causes.

The cause of toleration in the sixteenth century, and the first half of the seventeenth, was sustained less by these great men than by some of the sects and by liberal groups inside one or two of the larger churches; by the Socinians and Unitarians, by the Anabaptists and Baptists, by the Arminians in Holland, and by the Latitudinarians in the Church of England. They argued the case for toleration before the triumph of rationalism in the West; before Spinoza, Locke and Bayle; before the argument was refined and brought back to first principles; before it was cleared of biblical and historical encumbrances and received the simple, untheological and universal form which made it popular in the eighteenth and nineteenth centuries – that is to say, before it ceased to be merely an argument for religious toleration and became an argument for full liberty of conscience. These early champions of toleration were moved, not by political motives, but by a deep concern for the quality of religious belief.

The Socinians or Antitrinitarians were originally a small group of Italian reformers who took refuge in Switzerland. Less dogmatic, more scholarly and more gentle than most of the northern reformers, they had already, before they left Italy, made converts among the German Anabaptists. But they did not exert their greatest influence until after they had moved to Switzerland. Most prominent among them were Laelius Socinus, from whom the group got the name Socinians, George Blandrata and Bernard Ochino. Calvin was quick to notice the moderation of these men, whom he called 'academic sceptics'. His attacks obliged Blandrata and Ochino to flee to Poland, and Socinus contrived to stay in Switzerland only by keeping very quiet. From Poland, Blandrata moved to Transylvania, where he was joined in 1578 by Laelius Socinus's nephew, Faustus, who had inherited his uncle's unpublished writings. Laelius was the gentle and retiring thinker, and Faustus the active disciple. In the sixteenth century, Poland, till the Jesuits got control of it, was among the most tolerant countries in Europe, and Transylvania was even more so. It was in these two countries that the Italian Socinians, together with their disciples, came to be known as Unitarians.

The Unitarians and the Anabaptists were strongly attracted to one another by a common belief in toleration. But there were also profound differences of opinion and temperament between them. The Anabaptists disliked most kinds of external discipline; they inclined to anarchy in both social and religious matters. In Germany, some of them had attacked property and had used force to overthrow the established order. Most of them were not revolutionaries, but they were, or affected to be, indifferent to worldly affairs; they wanted to withdraw themselves from the ordinary run of men, either into spiritual isolation or into fellowship with the few who shared their own beliefs. The world was an oppression or a snare to them; and when they were not rebels (as most of them were not) they were inclined to be escapists. They were mystics or quietists or believers in the simple life. They disliked hierarchy, complexity and ceremony, as much in society as in religion. They cared little or nothing for letters or tradition and were almost untouched by the humanism of the Renaissance. Let the faithful, they said, form communities or churches if they feel the need to do so; but let them ask nothing of governments except to be left alone.

The Socinians were not at all inclined to anarchy; they accepted the need for hierarchy and organized discipline. They had a sense of history and respect for tradition; they believed that primitive simplicity was no longer possible, that men must accept society and make the best of it. They were, especially the Italians among them, humanists. In the religious sphere, they made a sharp distinction between Church affairs and matters of faith. It is not for temporal rulers, or for anyone else, to decide what men shall believe. From this, however, it does not follow that temporal rulers must have nothing to do with the government of the Church. On the contrary, it is their duty to establish a Church, make adequate provision for it, and see to it that it carries out its duties. But the Church should be as broad, as encompassing, as hospitable to all forms of Christian belief as possible; it should teach doctrines acceptable to all or to nearly all Christians, for though Christians now passionately disagree about some things, they agree about many others. What they agree about sufficiently embraces what is really essential to the Christian faith. There should be one Church opening its doors wide to all believers, but no one who refuses to enter should be persecuted. The Socinians did not want many small sects or churches, narrow and perhaps ephemeral, each separate from the others and lacking sympathy for them; they wanted to preserve the old mediaeval sense of a universal brotherhood in Christ. They cared for toleration as much as the Anabaptists did, but they cared for other things as well; about their conception of the Church there is a generosity and a breadth which is in sharp contrast to the rather narrow sectarianism of the Anabaptists. Their device was not 'Let each of us go his own way', but rather 'Let us agree to differ and yet still remain united in Christ'.

The Socinians believed that the essentials of Christianity are contained entire in the New Testament, and that only those parts of the Testament accessible to reason can be matters of faith. There may be, in the New Testament, matters beyond human understanding, but nothing in it can be contrary to human reason or to the common sense of mankind. Every man must therefore be allowed to judge Holy Scripture for himself. So far the Socinians were of one mind with Luther and Calvin. But they drew from these premises conclusions that neither Luther nor Calvin would accept. Where every man judges for himself, they said, there must be diversity of opinion; and this diversity, since it is inevitable, must be accepted with a good grace. The first Socinian *Confession of Faith*, published in 1574, roundly condemns the persecution of dissidents. The famous *Catechism of Raków*, published in Poland in 1605, comes nearer to proclaiming full liberty of religious belief than any earlier manifesto issued by an organized body of Christians: 'Let each man be free to judge of religion: this is required by the New Testament and by the example of the primitive Church. Who art thou, miserable man, who would smother and extinguish in others the fire of the divine spirit which God has kindled in them?'

Long before the *Catechism of Raków*, there had appeared an important book arguing for toleration on purely religious grounds, Castellion's *De haereticis, an sint persequendi*, published in 1554 under a pseudonym. The book was so markedly Socinian in character that it was widely attributed to Laelius Socinus himself, though the author was actually a Frenchman who had once been attached to Calvin but had afterwards turned against him. An open attack on Calvin, it was inspired by the burning as a heretic in Geneva of the Spaniard Servetus, whose death shocked all Europe, but especially the milder Protestants, who had taken it for granted that only Catholics would resort to so extreme a measure. The dispute between Castellion and Calvin is worth studying because it reveals just how far one of the noblest champions of toleration in the sixteenth century still was from arguing on broad principles for full liberty of conscience.

Castellion never once said that man has a right to profess what beliefs he pleases; he never asserted full liberty of conscience. He spoke *against* persecution rather than *for* liberty and merely condemned the persecution of beliefs about matters that God has not made plain to man. Christians, he said, are all agreed about some things, while about others they have disputed for centuries. But what has always been disputed cannot be known for certain, and what cannot be known for certain is not necessary for salvation. Since God is good and just, He must have made it possible for men to know for certain whatever is necessary for salvation. Therefore, the only beliefs necessary for salvation are those that Christians have always agreed about. We must accept frequent disputes as evidence that the beliefs they relate to are not necessary for salvation. For otherwise, since the people we dispute with may be right, we risk persecuting them for the truth; and even if they are wrong, we should still be persecuting them for holding to what they honestly believe to be true. God cannot wish us to force others to assent to what they believe is false, even when it happens to be true.

Though we sympathize with Castellion's motives, we must admit that his argument is weak. For he did not say, any more than Calvin did, that every man has the right to believe what he chooses and to assert his belief. On the contrary, he believed, with Calvin, that a man, to be saved, must be a good Christian – that is to say, not just a good man, but a man having certain beliefs. He merely disagreed with Calvin about what beliefs are necessary to salvation, excluding from that category some of the most important of Christian doctrines. Now, the beliefs around which Christians divided in Castellion's time seemed to them just as plain and important as the beliefs they held in common. Calvin did not for a moment deny that the beliefs necessary for salvation had been made plain to men by God; he merely denied that what is often disputed cannot be plainly true. And surely, on this point, he was right. It is notorious that men are often led by their passions and prejudices to reject the plain truth. To the modern liberal, Castellion's argument may appear more reasonable than Calvin's, but, if anything, it is less so. The liberal looks more favourably upon Castellion's case because he prefers the practical conclusions drawn from it. He, like Castellion, thinks it dreadful that Servetus should have been put to death for what he honestly believed. That, however, has nothing to do with the quality of the two arguments. Neither Calvin nor Castellion believed that every man has a right to his own religious opinions, whatever they may be. They both believed that certain truths, to be found in Holy Scripture, are necessary to salvation; and they also agreed that God must have made His meaning clear about what is necessary to salvation. They differed only about what those truths were. For Castellion, what men have long disputed cannot be plain truth necessary to salvation; whereas to Calvin it seemed obvious that it could be. Calvin's argument here is just as well grounded as Castellion's. Holy Scripture, being the Word of God, must, he assumed, have a plain meaning; for we cannot suppose, either that it is beyond God's ability to make His meaning clear, or that He could wish to confuse His creatures. Since we cannot deny either God's lucidity or the fact that men have quarrelled about the meaning of Holy Scripture, we cannot conclude that what they have quarrelled about is not necessary to salvation. Calvin believed that the meaning of Holy Scripture is plain to every reasonable and literate man, unless his reason is obstructed by his passions.

Towards the end of the century, Bodin, in a manuscript not meant for publication and in fact not published until long after he was dead,[1] went further even than Castellion and the Unitarians; he was for tolerating all religions, Moslem and Jewish as well as Christian, on the ground that all sincere belief and worship are acceptable to God. He used rather better arguments to reach conclusions even more liberal than Castellion's, and there may well have been thousands who thought like him without troubling to set down in writing what they could not safely publish.

Yet even this argument, which condemns persecution, not for its harmful social effects, but because it attacks sincere belief, does not amount to a fully conscious respect for freedom as such. I do not mean merely that the people who used it set limits to toleration – that Bodin would have no truck with atheism, and that Castellion never made it clear what should be done to people who reject Christianity altogether. I mean rather that to condemn persecution as wrong is still not to assert men's right to full liberty of conscience. It is still not to assert that men may hold, publish and propagate what opinions they choose, provided they do not threaten the peace or destroy one another's reputations. There is a difference between saying that it is wrong to make people suffer for their opinions and saying that it is their right to hold and teach what opinions they choose.

Castellion would almost certainly have denied that it does not matter what a man believes, provided his belief is sincere; or that all men should be allowed to propagate their religious opinions freely so that everyone can choose for himself what he shall believe; or, indeed, that heretics should not only remain unpersecuted but should be given all the privileges and opportunities of the orthodox. Even Montaigne, who had a genius for saying the boldest things in the most unprovocative and charming way, apparently never went so far. What he may have thought we cannot know, but he never put anything like such ideas into his *Essays*. There was still a considerable difference between the most tolerant published opinions of the sixteenth century and the sentiment attributed to Voltaire: 'I do not agree with what you say, but I shall defend to the death your right to say it.'[2] Voltaire was

---

[1] The *Heptaplomeres*, first published in 1841.
[2] These are not in fact the words of Voltaire, but rather those of a modern interpreter of his philosophy. Voltaire did believe in freedom of speech; though how far he would have gone in defending another man's right to it, I do not know.

not, perhaps, the stuff that martyrs are made of; but the assumption behind the words put into his mouth is clear. Voltaire may have seen himself, for a moment, as a possible martyr for freedom; but in the sixteenth century there were martyrs only for faith.

It is not my purpose to describe the spread of toleration; I am concerned not so much with the propagation of ideas as with the ideas themselves. The Counter-Reformation drove the champions of religious liberty out of Hungary and Poland, and the sects fared badly in Germany. In the seventeenth century, it was in Holland, in England and in some of the English colonies across the Atlantic, that this kind of liberty made the greatest progress. Most of its advocates were Protestants, because in Protestant countries, where religious minorities were more varied and vociferous, there were more people with little hope of imposing their beliefs on the majority. Bitter experience taught them that they had more to gain than to lose by allowing to others a liberty which they claimed for themselves. The Catholic Church, the largest and most international of Christian Churches, was the least interested in toleration because the most hopeful of supremacy. Catholics, where they were in a minority, might demand toleration, not only for themselves, but for Christians of all kinds, and might even come to believe in it sincerely; but most Catholics lived in countries where they were the majority. Moreover, the Catholic Church had for centuries been the only Church in the West, and it was peculiarly difficult for Catholics to reconcile themselves to the loss of this monopoly. It was only to be expected that the organized bodies of Christians pressing the most strongly for a wide toleration, and eventually for complete religious liberty, should be Protestant and not Catholic.

It is, however, important to notice that the attitude of the different churches to toleration and liberty of conscience depended almost entirely on their relative sizes and hopes of predominance. Calvinists were not by temperament more tolerant than Lutherans and Anglicans; they were merely more thinly distributed over a wide area and were everywhere in a minority except in a few small states and distant colonies. Toleration and persecution are social doctrines and practices, and have no clear logical connection with purely theological beliefs. If we know only how Catholic theology differs from the Lutheran or Calvinist varieties, we should have no good reason for supposing that Catholics would be less inclined to be tolerant than Lutherans or Calvinists. Even the doctrine that there is no salvation outside the Church does not logically imply that it is right to persecute unbelievers. If we are to understand why some varieties of Christians

127

were more inclined than others to be tolerant, or came more easily to believe in liberty of conscience, we must look, not at their religious beliefs, but at the position of their church or sect in relation to the State and to other churches. And, in the case of the Catholics, we must look at the traditions of their Church in its dealings with the Temporal Power and with heretics – traditions built up over the centuries, and owing more to history than to theology.

As a matter of fact, many good Catholics were tolerant, even in the sixteenth and seventeenth centuries; and some of them proved it when occasion offered. While the colony of Maryland was predominantly Catholic, every form of Christianity was tolerated there. Anglicans and Puritans oppressed in other colonies flocked to Maryland, until the flood of immigrants made the colony more Protestant than Catholic and toleration came to an end.

3. Liberty of Conscience and the Philosophers

In the sixteenth century, political arguments for toleration were the most frequent, and next after them religious arguments; but, as time passed, a third type of argument, broader in scope, came to the fore, a type which, for want of a better word, I shall call *philosophical*. It rests, not on considerations of expediency, nor on concern for the sincerity of religious beliefs, but on an ultimate principle: that every man has a right to hold and profess what opinions he chooses, provided the opinions are not seditious. Princes and parliaments got used to having subjects with different religions, and learnt by experience that they could rely on their loyalty provided they did not ill-treat them; and private persons got used to having neighbours who, though they did not share their most cherished beliefs, were yet found to be trustworthy and benevolent. As princes and peoples got used to toleration, from putting up with it because they could not safely do otherwise, or from inertia or indifference, or because they feared the spread of hypocrisy, they passed gradually to approval of it for its own sake. They passed gradually from the practice of toleration to a positive belief in liberty of conscience. Let a man hold and profess any opinion, as long as he does not stir up disorder or promote treason, they contended. This moral conviction, that everyone has a right to think and live as he pleases, is tolerance in a deeper sense. The conviction is, in its origins, no more Protestant than Catholic, and is in fact compatible with all forms of purely religious belief. It is, in itself, an opinion not directly about God, His purposes and our relations with Him, but rather about what worldly authority ought to disregard in matters of religion. There were already, by the end of the seventeenth century, many educated persons who accepted such a principle.

They were not content, in supporting this principle, merely to quote Holy Scripture or to argue that persecution is ineffective or weakens the State or promotes hypocrisy. They continued to use the old arguments for toleration, and sometimes even improved on them, as Locke did in his *Letter Concerning Toleration*, but they also put liberty of conscience forward as a natural right. They asserted it, either as a part of the law of nature or as a valid inference from it. True, they did not all understand natural law and natural right in the same way. Spinoza, for instance, did not understand them as Locke did. Yet they both produced, for allowing men to profess any opinion which is not seditious or subversive, arguments derived from what they took to be fundamental law, which men can discover by the use of their reason. It is arguments of this type which, to distinguish them from the others, I call philosophical, not because philosophers who believe in liberty of conscience have always employed such arguments (for many would not employ them today), nor because the philosophers who used them in the seventeenth century used only them, but because the arguments rest on assumptions essential to their philosophical systems. Though Spinoza's argument for liberty of conscience, if we compare it with Locke's, is more abstract and owes less to the Socinians and other sixteenth-century religious champions of toleration, his principle that liberty of conscience is a natural right is affirmed just as clearly by Locke, and in a form more generally acceptable, because Locke, unlike Spinoza, does not give a peculiar sense to the term *natural right*.

The principle of liberty of conscience was clearly and boldly asserted by Spinoza and Locke, and by other writers too, in the second half of the seventeenth century; but this does not mean that all the conclusions later drawn from the principle were already drawn in their time. It usually takes a considerable period for the main implications of an important doctrine to be drawn. Even the philosophers who advocated freedom of thought in the seventeenth century were chiefly interested in religious freedom, though they did not qualify their principle in such a way as to confine it to religious opinions. They spoke of man's right to profess any opinion which is not seditious, and not merely of his right to profess any religious opinion. But they did not trouble to make a distinction between the seditious and what offends against commonly received ideas about morality, and they therefore did not assert a right to profess beliefs which offend against such ideas but are not seditious. We should certainly be going further than we have any right to go if we were to say, for example, of Locke, that, because he argued that men should be allowed to profess any opinion which is not seditious, he would have admitted that they ought not to be prevented from professing beliefs which are morally offensive. He may even have thought that such beliefs are always seditious in the sense that they advocate or condone practices which subvert public order. Or it may be that, if it had been brought home to him that beliefs might be morally offensive without being seditious, he would have been moved to say that man has a natural right to profess only opinions which are neither seditious nor immoral. We should certainly be wide of the truth if we supposed that the *Letter Concerning Toleration* is as liberal as J. S. Mill's *On Liberty*. Yet Locke is already closer in spirit to Mill than to Castellion and Bodin and the other sixteenth-century champions of toleration. He asserts man's fundamental right to profess what opinions he chooses. He clearly asserts such a right, though he may set limits to it that Mill would not set, and that we should not set. And we all agree, including Mill (who would not have tolerated slander and libel), that this right, like every other, must be limited.

The ablest exponents, in the seventeenth century, of what I have called the philosophical case for toleration or the case for liberty of conscience, were undoubtedly Spinoza and Locke. Spinoza's argument is to be found chiefly in the twentieth chapter of the *Tractatus Theologico-politicus*, published in 1670, fifteen years before Locke wrote his first *Letter Concerning Toleration*. But, apart from these two arguments, there is a third which also deserves attention because it raises issues not raised by Locke and because it had a profound influence in France, the country where, in the next century, the attack of the philosophers against religious intolerance set a model for all Europe. Pierre Bayle's *Philosophical Commentary on these Words of Jesus Christ, Compel Them to Come In* was published in 1686 in Amsterdam, one year after Locke, while he was hiding in Holland to avoid extradition to England, had written his *Letter*, which he did not venture to publish until 1689, after the revolution which brought Dutch William to the English throne.

Spinoza, as an advocate of liberty of conscience, is less attractive then Locke, not because he believes less strongly in what he advocates, but because the assumptions on which he rests his arguments are less familiar. Locke's conceptions of natural law and natural right are traditional, while Spinoza's are not. For Spinoza natural law is not prescriptive; it does not consist of maxims of prudence or of moral rules or of divine commands. It consists of scientific laws, which are, for Spinoza, necessary uniformities of behaviour. The laws of nature, as they apply to man, do not differ from the laws of nature as they apply to the rest of the universe; they are ways in which man necessarily behaves. Man is both passionate and rational; but, whereas he shares the passionate side of his nature with other animals, he alone among them is rational. When therefore he acts rationally, he acts in accordance with the nature peculiar to him, and when he does this, he is free. It is a law of nature that man does what he believes to be in his own best interest. Reason is merely the power to form adequate ideas and to grasp necessary connections; to act rationally therefore involves having an adequate idea of one's interest and of the means to achieve it. If a man has this adequate idea, he necessarily acts in what is truly his own best interest; but even if he does not have it, he necessarily acts in what he believes to be his own best interest.

For Spinoza, natural law and natural right are not correlative but identical terms. Man has a natural right to do whatever he does necessarily, by the law of his nature, and all his actions are necessary. Since man is rational, or, in other words, since he reasons by necessity of his nature, he has a natural right to do so. And so we find Spinoza saying,

> It is impossible for thought to be completely subject to another's control, because no one can give up to another his natural right to reason freely and form his own judgement about everything, nor can he be compelled to do so. This is why . . . a sovereign is thought to wrong its subjects and to usurp their right, if it seeks to tell them what they should embrace as true and reject as false, and to prescribe the beliefs which should inspire their minds with devotion to God; for in such matters an individual cannot alienate his right even if he wishes.[1]

The 'natural' and 'inalienable' right to reason freely and form judgements about everything, as Spinoza conceives it, is by no means a natural and inalienable right in the ordinary sense. It is merely a power of which man cannot in fact divest himself, even should he wish to do so; it is not a right that other people are obliged to respect. That is why Spinoza has to admit that a ruler 'has the right to treat as enemies all who are not in complete agreement with him on every point'.[2] He has the right to do it provided he has the power, and he may have the power to treat them as enemies even though he lacks the power to compel them to agree with him. Spinoza, moreover, greatly underestimates both the extent to which beliefs can be controlled and also man's capacity to abandon the power to reason freely. The man

---

[1] *Tractatus Theologico-politicus*, ch. xx, in *Spinoza: The Political Works*, ed. and trans. A. G. Wernham (Oxford 1958), p. 227.
[2] Ibid., p. 229.

who habitually submits to another's judgements may freely decide on this submission, but if he does decide on it and acts accordingly, there is an important sense, not discussed by Spinoza, in which he gives up the right to 'reason freely and form his own judgement'. And submission need not be voluntary; a man may pass, without ever having decided to do so, very much under the influence of other men. A complete submission may perhaps be impossible, except in extreme pathological cases, where a man is so inert and suggestible that he is incapable of any but 'reflex actions' unless someone else has put ideas into his head. But there are many degrees of submission short of these extreme and rare cases.

So far, given the peculiar sense in which he uses the terms *natural law* and *natural right*, Spinoza's assertion of man's natural right to reason freely and form his own judgements may not, from the point of view of the ordinary believer in liberty of conscience, amount to much. For Spinoza, power and right are identical, whereas the believer in liberty of conscience is not asserting a power but a right, and therefore understands by right something different from what Spinoza understood by it. But the matter is not as simple as that. Spinoza did not arbitrarily choose to use the word *right* in a sense peculiar to himself; he did not believe that he was telling other people how he proposed to use a word, but rather that he was explaining to them the true nature of what they, as well as he, called by that word. And though he did not conclude, as the ordinary believer in liberty of conscience would do, that since man has a natural right to reason freely and to form his own judgements, the sovereign has no right to punish his subjects for professing opinions different from his own, he did conclude that he is acting against sound reason when he does so. Though we may say of Spinoza, even more confidently than of Hobbes, that his philosophy leaves no room for moral obligation as it is ordinarily understood, that philosophy does not prevent his showing that the attempt to establish uniformity of belief is unreasonable. The sovereign would not make the attempt if he had an adequate idea of his own interest and of the means to achieve it. Spinoza's philosophy being what it is, when he calls an action reasonable or unreasonable, he is getting as close as he can to what is ordinarily meant by calling it right or wrong.

Moreover, though a philosopher constructs a theory which fails to take proper account of an important element in common experience, his theory is not therefore free of that element. While rights and duties, as commonly understood, have no place, logically, in his theory, they still have a place in his thinking; he continues to use arguments which are conclusive only if there are rights and duties in some ordinary sense, which is different from the sense he has defined, though he may not know it. Spinoza argues that the sovereign acts unreasonably if he attempts to establish uniformity of belief, and that he acts reasonably if he allows his subjects openly to express all opinions which are not seditious. If we substitute 'wrongly' for 'unreasonably' and 'rightly' for 'reasonably', we have here the creed of the believers in liberty of conscience.

Unlike Hobbes, Spinoza did not believe that the purpose of the State is merely to give security to its members, to liberate them from the constant fear of death; its purpose is to enable men to 'live in harmony' and 'to enjoy peace', which 'is not mere absence of war, but a virtue based on strength of mind'. He says that 'a commonwealth whose peace depends on the apathy of its subjects, who are led like sheep because they learn nothing but servility, may more properly be called a desert than a commonwealth'.[1] No State is solidly established unless it serves its members' interests; but men, by necessity of their nature, seek more than merely to keep alive; they seek also to reason freely and to form their own judgements. For, as we have seen, to say that they have the natural right to do this is, for Spinoza, the same as to say that they have the power (which here includes both the will and the ability) to do it. Or, as we might put it, using the idiom of Rousseau, man is by nature free, and the political order which promotes that freedom is the more solid for doing so. Spinoza does not believe in a God who offers men salvation on condition that they hold certain beliefs sincerely; he does not advocate toleration primarily because he fears that intolerance will encourage hypocrisy, nor yet because he fears that the attempt to achieve uniformity of belief will incite more conflicts than it appeases. He advocates it because he puts a high value on freedom of thought.

Locke was much more directly influenced than Spinoza by the arguments of the Socinians and other pious champions of toleration. He was no pantheist but a practising Christian who believed in a personal God. In one place in the *Letter Concerning Toleration* he even admits that there are beliefs necessary to salvation. 'Every man', he says, 'has an immortal soul, capable of eternal happiness or misery; whose happiness depends on his believing and doing those things in this life which are necessary to the obtaining of God's favour, and are prescribed by God to that end'.[2] But he believes, as Castellion had

---

[1] *Tractatus politicus*, ch. v, in *Spinoza: The Political Works*, p. 311.

[2] Locke, *Second Treatise of Government* and *A Letter Concerning Toleration*, edited by J. W. Gough, 3rd ed. (Oxford 1966), p. 153.

done, that only a sincere faith is acceptable to God, and that such faith cannot be compelled. 'Whatsoever may be doubtful in religion, yet this at least is certain, that no religion which I believe not to be true can be either true or profitable to me. In vain, therefore, do princes compel their subjects to come into their church communion, under pretence of saving their souls.'[1] The doctrines imposed on men as being true and necessary to salvation differ from country to country; and so, since there is only one body of truth which really is necessary to that end, it follows that many are persecuted for refusing to profess erroneous doctrines.

Such arguments as these – and they make up a considerable part of the *Letter* – though perhaps put more simply and persuasively, go no further than the Socinians had already gone. They are arguments congenial to the lover of liberty, but, as we have seen, they take no account of some of the strongest arguments put on the other side. Those who persecute the purveyors of what they think are false and damnable beliefs do so less to bring true and sincere faith to their victims than to prevent their corrupting the still uncorrupt. They hold that, since there is a truth necessary to salvation, God must have made it plain to His creatures, for it is unthinkable that a benevolent God should make salvation conditional on true belief and yet leave it open to reasonable doubt as to what that belief is. It is absurd to suppose that the beliefs necessary to salvation are those about which all men are agreed, because, since there are atheists in the world, we must conclude either that there are no such beliefs or that, if there are, they do not relate to God.

But Locke has other arguments than these old ones inherited from the Socinians. His conception of the State enables him to deny that it has authority to concern itself with men's souls. 'The commonwealth', he writes, 'seems to me to be a society of men constituted only for the procuring, preserving, and advancing their own civil interests'.[2] And by men's civil interests Locke means those things for the preservation of which they have put themselves under government, such as life, liberty, health and external possessions. We have here another version of the same doctrine that we find in the *Second Treatise of Civil Government:* the authority of government is limited by the nature of the end which it is established to serve, and it is established by men to preserve life, liberty and property. Government may use force to preserve these things but may not use it for any other purpose.

[1] Ibid., p. 143.
[2] Ibid., p. 128.

Any man who believes that something is true and important has a right to try to persuade other men of its truth. But this is no more the right of rulers than of their subjects: 'Every man has commission to admonish, exhort, convince another of error, and, by reasoning, to draw him into truth; but to give laws, receive obedience, and compel with the sword belongs to none but the magistrate. And upon this ground I affirm that the magistrate's power extends not to the establishing of any articles of faith, or forms of worship, by the force of his laws.'[1]

Locke has the same conception of a church as the Anabaptists in Germany and the Independents in England. It is a free and voluntary society whose members have joined it of their own accord to worship God in the manner which they think acceptable to Him. It follows from this that no church has any authority directly from God to teach the true faith. Yet every association, no matter what its purpose, needs some discipline, some rules, if it is to endure and to have any hope of doing what it is established to do. To maintain its discipline it may admonish and exhort its members, and if any of them persist in disobeying its rules, it may expel them. Expulsion or (as churches like to put it) excommunication is the ultimate sanction; it is the severest penalty that any church can impose. No church is entitled to deprive its members of any of their civil rights or to call upon the civil magistrate to do so. Expulsion from a church deprives a man of no more than the rights he acquired by joining it, and he acquired them on condition of respecting its rules. 'Nobody, therefore, in fine, neither single persons nor churches, nay, nor even commonwealths, have any just title to invade the civil rights and worldly goods of each other upon pretence of religion.'[2] Locke says here on *pretence of religion* because the intolerance he is attacking happens to be religious; but it clearly follows, from what he says about states and churches and the limits of their authority, that no one is entitled to injure anyone merely on account of his beliefs.

Just as the magistrate has no right to suppress beliefs which he considers heretical, so he has no right to suppress practices which he considers idolatrous. Anything which is lawful in the ordinary course of life is lawful as a form of worship: 'Meliboeus, whose calf it is, may lawfully kill his calf at home, and burn any part of it he thinks fit. . . . And for the same reason he may kill his calf also in a religious meeting.'[3] But infanticide is unlawful in ordinary life,

[1] Ibid., p. 130.
[2] Ibid., p. 137.
[3] Ibid., pp. 147–8.

and is therefore intolerable as a religious practice. If idolatry is in fact offensive to God, it is undoubtedly a sin; but it does not follow that the magistrate ought to punish it. It is sinful to tell lies, but a lie is not punishable merely as such; it is punishable only when the liar, by his lie, injures other men or the commonwealth. The argument of the *Letter Concerning Toleration*, like that of the *Second Treatise*, is that no man is to be punished unless he has offended other men, unless he has injured them in their rights. Now, logically, it follows from this that no man ought to be punished for any action which is merely immoral and not injurious. Yet Locke did not actually draw this conclusion, as Mill was to do in *On Liberty*. We can only say that it follows from what he said; we cannot say that he said it; and experience teaches us that men do not always accept what follows logically from their own principles. Locke's peculiar concern in the *Letter* is to argue that men may profess what opinions they choose, especially in matters of religion, provided the opinions are not seditious, and that they may, in any association which they form, and especially at religious meetings, do anything which it would not be unlawful for them to do outside it.

The word *seditious* is scarcely used in the *Letter Concerning Toleration*; I use it because it seems to me as well suited as any other to convey Locke's meaning. I might have used the world *subversive*, which conveys Locke's meaning just as well; but I have avoided it because it has been so much used in recent controversies. Locke is laying down a very general principle: all opinions are to be tolerated unless they are dangerous to society or, as he puts it, unless they are 'contrary to human society, or to those moral rules which are necessary to the preservation of civil society'.[1] Locke's periphrasis conveys no more precise impression than the single word *seditious*. What opinions are 'contrary to human society'? What moral rules are 'necessary to the preservation of civil society'? Is a man to be punished for professing any opinion which would be dangerous to society if more than a few men acted on it? Is he to be punished, for example, for condemning the use of violence under all circumstances, even though he is so little listened to that the government can recruit all the soldiers and policemen needed to defend the country from invasion and to maintain order? Or, is an opinion only to be punished if there are enough persons likely to act on it to constitute a public danger? Are opinions to be tolerated which excite deep and widespread indignation but which would not be dangerous if they did not excite it? These are

[1] Ibid., p. 156.

all issues which Locke does not raise. I do not criticize him for not raising them; there was no need for him to do so in a discourse whose object was to condemn religious persecution. It was enough that he should have asserted, as clearly and boldly as he did, so important a general principle. Mill, in *On Liberty*, does not improve upon it; he merely works out some of its implications, raising issues that Locke, for his purpose, had no need to raise.

Locke believed that it was rare indeed for a church to profess opinions 'contrary to human society' or to denounce moral rules 'necessary to the preservation of civil society'. He believed that scarcely any of the opinions for which men were punished in his day were dangerous to society. It would, he thought, be folly for any church or sect to put forward, as religious doctrines, opinions which manifestly undermine the foundations of society. But, nevertheless, on rare occasions, what they dare not say plainly and nakedly, men will say covertly. No church, for instance, teaches openly that men are not obliged to keep their promises, but some do teach that faith is not to be kept with heretics. Or again, though no church teaches that a king may be dethroned by those who differ from him in religion, some do teach that an excommunicated king forfeits his crown and kingdom. These, Locke tells us, are doctrines dangerous to society and are not to be tolerated. No church has a right to be tolerated whose members admit an allegiance to a foreign prince, for to tolerate it is to allow a foreign jurisdiction to be set up in one's own country. Lastly, atheism is intolerable because atheists, being without fear of a God in whom they do not believe, cannot be trusted to keep their promises.

It would appear, then, that Locke would not have tolerated atheists or the Catholic Church. True, Locke does not actually say in the *Letter* that the Catholic Church ought not to be tolerated, but he clearly has that Church in mind when he speaks of a church teaching that faith is not to be kept with heretics and that an excommunicated prince forfeits his crown, and whose members admit an allegiance to a foreign ruler. Locke, a Protestant, was not unprejudiced in his attitude to the Catholic Church, nor was he careful to distinguish between the authoritative doctrines which every Catholic was required to accept and doctrines taught by the Jesuits and by others, which a man might reject and still remain a good Catholic. The great majority of English Catholics probably did not accept the doctrines to which Locke objected. The Catholic is, of course, obliged to put what he considers to be the law of God before the law promulgated by man, but then so, too, is any other Christian. He admits the authority of his Church to pronounce on moral issues as well as on questions of theology, but then so, too, in practice, do most other Christians. The Lutheran or the Calvinist is just as likely as the Catholic to look to his Church for moral support when he refuses to obey a law made by men on the ground that it is contrary to God's law. That the Catholic believes, as the Calvinist and Lutheran do not, that his Church, when it pronounces on certain matters, is infallible, does not really make it more likely that he will refuse to obey the law of his country on religious grounds.

Locke's intolerance of atheism is inspired by the same doubtful beliefs as Rousseau's advocacy, in the penultimate chapter of the *Social Contract*, of a civil religion. A man cannot be a good citizen, thinks Rousseau, unless he believes in God, and so any man who lacks this belief is to be banished from the State, not because he is an unbeliever, but because he is unfit for society. The assertion that a man who does not believe in God is unfit for society purports to be a statement of fact, and may be refuted by producing the true facts.

The limits which Locke places on toleration are narrower than most people now think proper. His imputations against Catholics and atheists may strike us as false to the point of absurdity. But at least they are charges that can be easily rebutted. They detract nothing from Locke's principle that a man's beliefs are his own concern, and that government must allow him to give free expression to them, unless they are seditious, unless they advocate or provoke conduct dangerous to society. The modern liberal disagrees with Locke, not about his principle, but about the facts: he denies that atheists do not keep their promises or that Catholics cannot be relied upon to be loyal.

Pierre Bayle's *Philosophical Commentary on these Words of Jesus Christ, Compel Them to Come In* is much longer than Locke's *Letter Concerning Toleration*; it is more polemical, more personal, more highly coloured, and goes much more into details of the controversies of the period. Yet it is not less philosophical than the *Letter*, because it too rests its arguments on clearly enunciated first principles of universal application; it too treats liberty of conscience as a right that men have everywhere merely by virtue of being rational creatures. But inevitably, since the book is diffuse and polemical, and goes minutely into controversies that have long ceased to be interesting, the general argument stands out less sharply than it does with Locke and Spinoza.

I would not say that Bayle believed more strongly in toleration than either Locke or Spinoza, but he was less interested than they were in the problem of how public order is to be maintained, and was therefore less concerned to set limits to toleration than to argue against the limits proposed by other people. He was also, perhaps, by temperament bolder than Locke and less apt to see dangers where there were none. He argued that, if you want to put an end to error, you defeat your own purpose by resorting to force, which may silence your opponent but will not convince him. To fight error with blows is no less absurd than to try to take bastions with speeches or syllogisms. Christ, moreover, never used force to compel belief, and those who speak in His name should follow His example. Coercion has been used to turn Catholics into Protestants, and Protestants into Catholics, to turn Christians into Moslems and Moslems into Christians. It is incredible that God should have authorized the use, in the service of truth, of a means used to such diverse effect.

Unlike Locke, Bayle would not exclude atheists from toleration. The man who errs has as good a right to his opinions as the man who possesses the truth. Bayle was no unbeliever; nor did he reject Christianity. But he attacked those he called the 'half-tolerant', who would allow a considerable diversity of beliefs but would not tolerate anyone who denied what they took to be the fundamentals of Christianity. If any belief is open to criticism, then all beliefs are so. There is nothing which it is wrong for men to call in question, not even the truth about God.

Bayle even says, as Locke does not, that diversity of faith may be pleasing to God, just as a choir of many voices may be more pleasing than the singing of one voice alone. And to say this is to come close to suggesting that there are no minimal beliefs necessary to salvation – that, though there are true beliefs about God, a man may find favour with God without holding them. If men hold incompatible beliefs about God, then some of these beliefs must be false. If men who hold false beliefs about God are acceptable to Him, why should not unbelievers be so too? Locke, for all his advocacy of toleration, seems to have accepted the notion that there are beliefs necessary to salvation. He speaks in the *Letter* of 'there being but one truth, one way to heaven',[1] and says that 'if any man err from the right way, it is his own misfortune'.[2] It is true that, in one place,[3] he admits that, if there were several ways to Heaven, there would be no excuse left for religious persecution, but the general impression conveyed by the *Letter* is that he accepted the orthodox notion of a truth necessary to

[1] *Letter Concerning Toleration*, p. 130.
[2] Ibid., p. 135.
[3] Ibid., pp. 140–41.

salvation. Bayle, who was no less a believer than Locke, came much nearer to rejecting it.[1] Now, to reject this notion, as even Locke for one moment admitted, is to reject the assumption on which the whole case for persecution, in order to save men's souls, rests.

Bayle excluded only the Catholics from toleration. They are not to be tolerated because they are themselves intolerant. This exception, made at a time when the Huguenots in France were being cruelly persecuted, is not surprising. Bayle's concern with large questions of principle combined with a keen interest in the controversies of his own day (a combination which made him 'philosophical' without being remote or arid), together with his freshness and pungency, his combativeness and generosity, his vivacity and irony, attracted Voltaire and the Encyclopaedists, who borrowed heavily from him during their prolonged assault on the Church. They put some of his arguments with greater economy and elegance than he could master, but they added little that was substantial to them.

Bayle's belief that the intolerant ought not to be tolerated still has its adherents today among people who call themselves liberals; it seems to them eminently just. But they are, I think, mistaken. If we believe in liberty of conscience, if we assert every man's right to hold and profess what opinions he chooses, then we ought, logically, to tolerate the intolerant, provided their intolerance is not dangerous. A man's right to profess whatever faith he chooses does not depend on the content of his faith, not even when part of that faith is that other faiths ought to be suppressed. His right is limited only by the need to protect the rights of others. If, in a particular situation, the profession of that faith is dangerous to others, and if the danger can be averted only by preventing those who hold it from professing it, then it is right to prevent them. We have no right to punish or obstruct the intolerant merely because they are intolerant; we have the right to do so only when their activities are in fact dangerous to freedom or otherwise injurious, and it is incumbent upon us to make sure that there is no other likely way of averting the danger or injury. The liberal is committed to the view that the enemies of freedom have as much right to it as its friends, that right being in all cases limited by the need to protect freedom and to prevent injury. No doubt, the enemies of freedom are usually – though by no means always – more dangerous to it than its friends; but that does not affect the point at issue.

---

[1] How far Bayle's beliefs were Christian, and Locke's orthodox, are matters of dispute which do not concern us here.

By the end of the seventeenth century the new faith in intellectual freedom, in liberty of conscience, had found adequate and bold expression, though many of the implications of that faith still stood in need of elaboration – as indeed they still do today. The origins of that faith were not Dutch but European generally, but it was in Holland, then the freest country in Europe, that a Jew, an Englishman and a Frenchman gave to it the form it still, essentially, wears today.

CHAPTER 4
Bodin

I. HIS PHILOSOPHY IN GENERAL

My purpose is not biographical or historical; I do not want to explain how Bodin came by his opinions or to show the place of his theory in the political, social or intellectual history of his time. I am concerned with expounding and criticizing a political and social theory which is certainly interesting in itself, but which is also something more. It is also important because it introduces into political and social thought, or provides good examples of, ideas which we still use to describe society and government or whose criticism increases our ability to think clearly about them. But sometimes a political theorist is so much wrapped up in the affairs of his country that it is scarcely possible to consider his theory without also considering, however briefly, the political circumstances in which it was produced. This is especially true of Machiavelli and Bodin.

The two great political theorists of the sixteenth century have several things in common which distinguish them from many of their successors. They were both for a considerable time servants of the State, and their political thought was deeply affected by their practical experience. Bodin had been in the royal service for several years before his greatest book was published in 1576. He was elected that same year a deputy by the Third Estate of Vermandois to the Estates-General meeting at Blois, and later he was in the service of the Duke of Alençon, whom he twice accompanied to England. Bodin did not, like Machiavelli, write his books after he had left the public service; he wrote them while he was still active in public affairs. When he wrote about politics, however generally, he had the situation and the needs of his own country very much in mind. Much more so, for example, than Hobbes. True, Hobbes would not have written as he did had he not been an Englishman reflecting on government at a time when his country was on the brink of, or plunged into, civil war; and yet we can take in and appreciate the message of *Leviathan* without considering its historical setting. But some of the distinctions made by Bodin seem pointless, and some of his conclusions absurd, unless we see him as the champion of the royal power in France during the wars of religion.

Bodin is like Machiavelli also in this, that he is a political theorist immersed in history. Indeed, he read more widely than did Machiavelli, and was a more learned man. In 1548, when he was eighteen or nineteen (the exact date of his birth is unknown), he left his native Anjou for Toulouse, where he remained, first as a student and then as a teacher of law, some twelve years. He even succeeded in getting a Chair in Roman Law shortly before he gave up academic life and moved to Paris to practise at the Bar. At Toulouse, being an opinionated and pugnacious (and perhaps even a jealous) man, he had come to look upon himself as a rival of Cujas, the greatest Roman lawyer of his day, the man who first expounded Roman Law as the law of a unique society very unlike the countries of Western Europe in the sixteenth century. Though Bodin never acknowledged a debt to Cujas, he did treat law much as Cujas treated it; he explained it historically and socially, always bearing in mind the type of society where it flourished. He possessed, though in smaller measure, one of the great qualities of Cujas, a sense of history.

He possessed this quality probably in greater measure even than Machiavelli. No doubt, Machiavelli was an artist and a great writer, as Bodin conspicuously was not. This, indeed, is one reason, and perhaps the most important, why Machiavelli is still remembered, and Bodin is not, except by academic students of political theory. Machiavelli had much more imagination than Bodin. When he speaks of Caesar or of any other historical person, be brings before us a live man; at least, he comes much closer than Bodin to doing so. His understanding of human nature, though limited, is much more sure, and his ability to recreate character much greater. But a man may have this kind of imagination and yet lack historical imagination, a sense of history. He may present us with an image of a Caesar or a Pompey which is psychologically convincing, and yet may see him more or less as he would see one of his own contemporaries, without understanding how greatly Caesar's environment differed, socially and morally, from his own. And conversely, a man without much insight into individual character, a man like Bodin, may have historical imagination. He may have a lively sense that societies differ greatly in both structure and ethos from one another, and that the past must not be recreated in the image of the present. Clearly, if he has this kind of imagination, it is likely to affect his political and social theory; he will not suppose that what is best for his own country is also best for others.

Today, of course, we are very much aware that societies differ greatly, and we need not be more than ordinarily imaginative to have this awareness. We have been copiously warned against attributing our own ideas and values to men in countries and ages remote from ours. We live at a time when man's image of himself and his environment has been deeply influenced both by the study of history and by the comparative study of widely different societies. But in Bodin's time it was not so.

Bodin was less narrowly *political* than Machiavelli. He had larger intellectual ambitions. He aimed, as it still seemed possible to do in the sixteenth century, at universal knowledge. He was a student of theology as well as of law, history and government; he took an interest in mathematics, astronomy, physics and medicine. He could read Hebrew, Greek and Latin, and among modern languages, Italian, Spanish and German. He wanted to explain the universe and man's place in it; he aimed, as Machiavelli never did, at systematic and comprehensive knowledge.

Evidently, with such wide ambitions as these, he failed of his purpose. He never constructed a systematic theory out of such knowledge as he did acquire; he merely aimed at system without achieving it. Yet he had some ideas worth noticing both about how the sciences differ from one another, and about the use of history to the political and legal theorist. In the *Methodus ad facilem historiarum cognitionem*, published in 1566, he claimed that it was possible, by comparing the laws and institutions of different countries, to reach a set of principles which could serve as a universal standard of criticism. It was possible to discover what standards and purposes were common to men everywhere, and then to estimate what institutions and what laws would come nearest to realizing them under varying conditions. For Bodin never supposed that any one political or social system could be the best for all peoples at all places and at all times. But, though he recognized that peoples differ in their environments and even in their inborn qualities and dispositions, he thought it possible, by the comparative method, to discover principles accepted by them all. He thought it possible to make the discovery, but it can hardly be said that he went far towards making it.

Nevertheless, he did use history for a different purpose from Machiavelli's; he did not use it merely as a store of examples from which he could select those needed to illustrate his maxims; he used it to show how much one political community can differ both in structure and ethos from another, or how a system of government gradually emerges.

Bodin, as might be expected of a sixteenth-century philosopher and jurist, went further than to say that there are important principles accepted by all mankind, principles discoverable by the method he advocated. He took it for granted that these principles are not merely universal but are also rational in a sense in which principles peculiar to only a few peoples and ages are not, because reason can show them to be adapted to man's essential nature. They are the laws of nature, manifestations in man of the divine wisdom. Bodin, despite his advocacy of the comparative method, was in many ways more traditional than Machiavelli. He was not content to find out what all men actually want or actually think good; he wanted to know what is good absolutely, and believed that his comparative method could help him to discover it.

He attempted what Machiavelli attempted, but also had other aims more like those of the mediaeval philosophers. He too wanted to know how to strengthen the State and how to prevent its decay; he too was aware that a political or social remedy must be adapted to a system which already exists and which cannot be greatly changed. But he was also interested in questions of legitimacy, which he did not distinguish from questions of fact. In his day political theorists had not yet come to make this distinction. Not even Machiavelli made it. He merely happened to be interested only in questions of the one type and not the other. But Bodin was interested in both, and his meaning is sometimes difficult to seize because he did not make distinctions which we are in the habit of making and think important.

Bodin is more comprehensive, more traditional and more systematic, at least in intention, than Machiavelli, and at the same time less direct, less lucid and less persuasive. By the standards of his day, he was a man of vast erudition, and by any standards he was a man of immense intellectual energy. Though it was more than he could do to put his ideas into good order, he was continually excited by them. He never gives the impression, as learned men quite often do, of being weighed down by a burden of knowledge too heavy for them; he is seldom flat or dull or weary. But he is tortuous, obscure, repetitious and disorderly. He lacks elegance; he is scholastic and pedantic. He often gets lost in the labyrinths he has created, little though he may know it. In these respects and others, he reminds me very much of Marx; there is the same irrepressible energy, the same power of rapid assimilation, the same claim to competence in many different spheres, the same impatience of criticism, the same boldness of conjecture, the same recklessness, the same preoccupation with questions of method. Both Bodin and Marx claim to know how society should be studied, and yet neither explains his method clearly nor uses it consistently. It is almost as if they cannot bear not to be able to give an immediate answer to any question which occurs to them; as if they cannot put up with ignorance, however temporary; as if their minds, like the nature of the mediaeval philosophers, abhor a vacuum. Where they do not know and cannot easily discover by using the methods they advocate and misdescribe, they promptly make a guess and support it by whatever reasons seem at the moment to serve their purpose.

Bodin was aware – much more so than most learned men of his time – that different methods are appropriate to different fields of study, that some are deductive while others are based on experience. Politics he put very definitely in the second category. Yet he could not in practice bring himself to accept the limitations which he placed on this empirical study. Sometimes he used the method he advocated, but at other times he reverted to other methods which he had himself condemned as inappropriate. He remained in some ways very much a mediaeval philosopher, with a passion for definitions, multiple distinctions, *a priori* principles and teleological arguments. He often cared more for symmetry than for logic or for facts. If there were three of one thing, there must be three of another to suit the arrangement which he had decided upon for reasons often left obscure.

He could use the oddest and most irrelevant arguments. To prove that men are the superior and governing sex, he thought it enough to observe that Nature had given them beards to make them more honourable. Though he divided the sciences into the deductive and the empirical, he never lost his respect for what he called the 'occult sciences' and the wise men of the East who practised them. Though he told his readers that they must put up with ignorance where they could not get properly attested knowledge, his passion for omniscience prevented his taking his own advice. Though he warned them that they must not take an opinion on trust merely because it was to be found in the works of Aristotle or in some other book venerated for centuries, he made one of the interlocutors in his dialogue on religion argue that we can accept Christ's being born of a virgin on the ground that in the Old Testament there is talk of the spontaneous generation of birds and fishes, that Plato speaks of earth-bound men, and Virgil of mares that become full by turning their nostrils to the wind. Bodin was a mixture of scepticism and credulity, as so many learned men were in the sixteenth century. But what is remarkable about him is not his being credulous; it is rather the breadth of his scepticism. And yet he is not as free as Machiavelli or Montaigne or Rabelais of the superstitions of his age. We cannot imagine any of them writing, in perfect good faith and eager to save his fellow mortals from a pressing danger, a book like the *Demonomania of Sorcerers*, where Bodin describes how those who have sold themselves to the Devil and who seduce others for him may be known by their behaviour, and how legal action may most conveniently be taken against them. This learned treatise, which Bodin published towards the end of his life, was immediately translated into Latin and, thus raised in dignity, was used by the courts as a legal text-book for several generations.

Bodin was not as narrowly political and practical as Machiavelli, and not as consistently sceptical as Montaigne and Rabelais. But he had his moments of rare insight, and he was eminently constructive. He was a philosopher, in two different senses of that word, as Machiavelli was not. His political theory is only part of a larger theory about the universe and man's place in it; it is a political theory attached to a cosmology, as most political theories had been in the Middle Ages. That is to say, though the mediaeval producer of a political theory may not himself have produced his own version of a theory of the universe, he usually took for granted some traditional version and related his political theory to it. Again, Bodin asked what knowledge is and what are the proper methods of acquiring it. He was, in his own very tentative and inadequate way, a philosopher in the manner of Descartes as much as in that of the mediaeval theologians. No doubt, he is unimportant as a philosopher; it is perhaps no loss to philosophy, in either of these senses, that his contribution to it is not studied. But it is important that he was a philosopher, that he reflected, however inadequately, on how politics should be studied. For, had he not reflected on this matter, he might never have attempted to produce the sort of political theory which he did produce. He tried to do what he believed had not been attempted before him; he tried to compare political systems, not merely in order to classify them, but to discover which are best suited to what conditions.

Roger Chauviré, whose excellent book about Bodin[1] was published as long ago as 1914, lamented that Bodin was forgotten. 'Evidently',

---

[1] *Jean Bodin, auteur de la République* (Paris 1914).

he said, 'it is Montesquieu who has killed him, by saying the same things better than he did, and other things besides'. This verdict was premature. Bodin is no longer forgotten, at least not by historians and political theorists, and many competent judges would agree with J. W. Allen that he is, with Machiavelli, one of the two great political thinkers of the sixteenth century.

Bodin is famous as a champion of royal power. Yet his greatest work, *Six Books on the Republic*, was attacked for not being royalist enough as well as for being excessively royalist. In 1576, the year in which he published his remarkable argument for the absolute sovereignty of the French monarch, Bodin, as a deputy in the Third Estate, persuaded that body to refuse a subsidy for which the King was asking. No doubt, it was mere chance that Bodin's own defiance of the royal will should have coincided with the appearance of his most vigorous defence of monarchy. But it is worth considering why Bodin persuaded the Third Estate to refuse the King's request. The three Estates had voted in favour of a motion calling for religious uniformity, and Henry III was asking for a subsidy to enable him to establish that uniformity by force of arms. Bodin could not persuade the Third Estate to reject a motion which he thought dangerous to peace, but he was able to persuade it not to vote the money which would enable the King to enforce what the motion called for. He defied the King for the sake of religious toleration and peace. He believed, moreover, that Henry III, by attacking the Huguenots, would weaken his authority. He would not only drive the Huguenots into open rebellion; he would also put himself in the power of the extremer Catholics. The King could best strengthen his authority by refusing to lead one part of the nation in arms against the other. He could save France by raising the monarchy above the religious factions.

In England in the seventeenth century the king was a party to civil war; he defended his prerogatives against the encroachments of the two Houses of Parliament. In France, in the sixteenth century, the king was not, in the same obvious sense, a party to the religious wars. The Huguenots were not, to begin with, any more concerned than anyone else to challenge the royal authority; they came to challenge it only because the kings of France took up the cause of the extremer Catholics. And the Huguenots, as soon as their leader, Henry of Navarre, became the legitimate heir to the throne, quickly forgot all their arguments for limiting the royal power; they were suddenly transformed into ardent royalists. Neither Charles IX nor Henry III had been a fanatical Catholic; they had taken up the Catholic cause partly because it was the more popular and partly because they had feared the Catholic League. The real initiative against the Huguenots had not come from them.

Bodin, soon after his arrival in Paris from Toulouse in 1561, had made friends with men who were later to form a group opposed to both the main parties to the civil wars. These men – the brothers Pithou and Étienne Pasquier prominent among them – came to be known as the *Politiques*; they were champions of religious toleration and of royal power. They believed that religious uniformity could not be achieved in France by force of arms, and that there could not be enduring domestic peace unless the Huguenots were tolerated. Only the king, if he made bold use of the authority traditionally vested in his office, could be strong enough to impose toleration and to maintain peace. The Estates-General could not do it; they lacked the authority of the monarch, and in any case, having come to be dominated by the Catholic party, were unwilling to come to terms with the Protestants. So the champions of religious toleration tended also to be champions of royal power.

II. HIS VIEWS ON TOLERATION

Some of the *Politiques* were lukewarm in matters of religion, but Bodin was not. He remained throughout his life a deeply religious man. He was born a Catholic and died an ardent champion of religion, though probably without being strongly attracted to any form of Christianity. At one time he may have been a professing Calvinist, for he seems to have gone to Geneva in 1552, staying there for several months – an unlikely journey for a young Frenchman in those days unless it were made from religious motives. There also survives from him a letter which reveals strong leanings towards Protestantism. But Calvinism, if ever he adhered fully to it, can have been only the religion of his early manhood. In his last years, he was very probably a deist, rejecting all forms of Christianity. Yet his deism, if deist he was, was not the mild sentiment of some of the eighteenth-century philosophers. The god of his old age, if no longer the Christian God, was never a remote deity uninterested in human affairs, the god of Voltaire. He was much more than an hypothesis which Bodin could not bring himself to reject or a still undiscarded remnant of childhood piety. God, for Bodin, was always a real person, omnipotent and omnipresent, a God worshipped, feared and loved, a God close to man, the most excellent of His creatures made in His own image.

Of the complaints made against his *Six Books on the Republic*, perhaps the most bitter was that it advocated religious toleration. Yet the views expressed in that work are mild indeed compared with those which Bodin reached in his old age. By 1593 – some three years before he died – he had completed a dialogue about religion called *Heptaplomeres*, which he dared not publish and which first saw the light of day long after his death.

Heptaplomeres is an imaginary conversation about religion between seven people: A Catholic, two kinds of Protestants, a Moslem, a Jew, an adherent of natural religion, and a broad-minded friend of all religions which are not fanatical. We may take it that the last two come closest to sharing Bodin's own beliefs, for he puts most of the best arguments into their mouths. They dispose of myths and dogmas in the name of reason, and yet, like Bodin himself, are sometimes unreasonable. The most consistent of the seven is the broad-minded Senamus, who distrusts revelation, rejects most dogmas as absurd or meaningless, and will have nothing to do with miracles; he is Bodin at his most sceptical. Senamus believes in a single, eternal and benevolent God, in the freedom of the will and in a life after death, which does not last forever but only long enough to ensure that virtue is rewarded and that those who have suffered unjustly in this world are compensated in the next. These, according to Senamus, are the only beliefs attested by reason; and no others are needed to support morality.

The three Christians in the dialogue get the worst of it, and are the most often reduced to silence. Bodin's attitude to them reveals his distaste for the theological disputes of his age. But the Christians are not roughly handled; and above all – and this is what really matters – they are *not* converted. The seven champions of seven creeds, when they separate, are left with the beliefs they brought to their meeting; their arguments have given them, not new religious convictions, but a greater tolerance and good will. The moral of *Heptaplomeres* is clear: all religions are acceptable to God if they are sincere, and if they admit the truths attested by reason and necessary to good morals.

Bodin, towards the end of his life, was very probably a deist friendly to Christianity but sceptical of all specifically Christian dogmas. Chauviré suggests that Senamus, the most sceptical and light-hearted of the seven interlocutors, expresses only one side of Bodin's attitude to religion. Toralba, the adherent of natural religion, who thinks it possible to defend the divinity of Christ on purely rational grounds, is almost as formidable in argument as Senamus; and it is clear that Bodin has great respect for his views. Solomon the Jew is also gently handled, and none of the interlocutors challenge the authority of the Old Testament, of which Solomon is admitted to be the most competent interpreter. Bodin, in his attitude to religion as in other aspects of his thought, reveals an equivocation much less uncommon among intellectuals in the sixteenth century than it is now: a bold scepticism alternating with submission to the authority of sacred texts. He had a special affection and respect for the Old Testament, partly perhaps because he was proud of his knowledge of Hebrew, a rare accomplishment in his age. Bodin, if ever he ceased to be a Christian, which he probably did, must have given up the ancestral faith reluctantly.

All things considered, Bodin's attitude to religion is not unlike that expressed some two hundred years later by Rousseau's Savoyard vicar. Like the vicar, Bodin values religion for two reasons: because it is a support to good morals, and because without it man does not feel at home in the world. Bodin takes it for granted, as Locke and Rousseau (and many others) were to do, that man can scarcely have adequate motives for behaving well unless he believes in an after-life and an omniscient Being aware of his innermost thoughts. He also takes it for granted that man needs the sense of living in a world shaped by much larger than human purposes if he is not to be cynical and hopeless, if he is not to feel lost in a mindless universe, if life is not to lose its savour. Like the Savoyard vicar, Bodin has a horror of atheism and materialism, which seem to him both demoralizing and depressing. Man is hopeful, brave, benevolent and capable of self-sacrifice because he sees himself living in a world governed by a Being infinitely greater than himself, a Being to whom he is nevertheless important. This horror of atheism is far removed from Machiavelli's approval of religion on purely utilitarian grounds; it is a sentiment perhaps unknown to Machiavelli. It is like the fear of death but also unlike it; it is the fear of insignificance. It is not a man's fear that he may cease to exist; it is the fear that, though he exists, there is no point to his existence. It is a feeling, strong in some men and perhaps unknown to others, that, unless there is a God, it is unbearable to be a man.

III. HIS POLITICAL THEORY

Bodin's *Republic*, like almost everything he wrote, is badly arranged and repetitious. It would be absurd to follow his order in discussing his political theory. It is perhaps best to begin by discussing some of the concepts he uses, above all the concept of sovereignty, passing on to consider his views about the various forms of government, their advantages and defects, and ending with a brief look at his defence of the French monarchy.

1. Power, Right and Sovereignty

Bodin does not begin his treatise on politics, as Hobbes and Locke were to do, with an account of rights. He does not speak of a state of nature and says very little about the first origins of government. He thinks it probable that most states were created by force, though some grew out of the family or were set up by agreement. He does not use the notion of covenant or contract to explain what are the functions of government or what makes it legitimate. He takes it for granted that a government, no matter how it arose, is legitimate provided it maintains order and acts for the good of its subjects.

The doctrine of the social contract is, no doubt, artificial and misleading. If we suppose that the allegiance of a subject arises from a contract or a promise, from an act having the juridical or moral character connoted by one or other of these terms, we get involved in all sorts of difficulties, verbal and real. But, as a matter of history, the doctrine did bring to the fore the question of political obligation, and did incline the thinkers who used it to distinguish rather more sharply between questions of fact and questions of right. Admittedly, the contract theorists often failed to distinguish between these two types of question, but at least they came closer to doing so than mediaeval political thinkers had done. Moreover, the inadequacies of their theories in the end brought home the need to make this distinction clearly. It is not an accident that Hume and the Utilitarians, who between them killed and buried the contract theory, were among the first to explain this need.

Bodin, writing before the social contract had become a fashionable device of explanation, seldom (if ever) troubles to distinguish between what makes government effective and what makes it legitimate. He does not argue, as Hobbes has been accused of doing, that might makes right; he does not try to show that government is legitimate to the extent that it is effective. To argue as Hobbes does, or as he has been accused of doing, a philosopher would need to be aware of the distinction he is denying or treating as unimportant. If his critics are right, Hobbes is either saying that others have made a distinction where there is no difference or that they have drawn improper conclusions from that distinction. But Bodin, because he does not distinguish might from right, must not be supposed to have held that might makes right. Certainly the mere failure to make this distinction does not imply that he held that opinion.

There is no evidence that Bodin believed that anyone strong enough to get obedience is for that reason alone entitled to it. But he does seem to have believed that enduring power is probably being exercised for the benefit of the persons subject to it. Power used capriciously is unlikely to endure because men will not long submit to it. Thus Bodin presumed, as Burke did, that, if a ruler has enduring power, he has a good title to it because he uses it for the common good. He either makes use of it wisely or he follows custom, which has become what it is because it has been found useful. Bodin venerated whatever in society is long established and regular in operation; he believed that it conforms with men's more permanent needs as determined by their nature, and therefore also with the will of God, who created that nature. 'True wisdom', says Chauviré, interpreting Bodin, 'is to study facts objectively and in their wholeness; to determine their order, which, owing to God's goodness, conforms with the general good, and to follow that order in one's theories and actions'.[1] Things can be as they ought not to be; for God has given to men the power to choose, and they may make evil or mistaken choices. But they suffer the consequences of evil and error, and wish to be rid of them. Therefore whatever is long acceptable to them is very probably for their good. Lasting authority and wisdom are closely allied, not because those who have authority are necessarily wise, but because their authority is exercised in traditional ways, adapted to human nature and to the peculiar circumstances of those subject to them.

This kind of argument was apt to be more convincing in the past than it is now. All governments in the sixteenth century, if we compare them with ours, were weak. Law-breakers escaped justice more easily than they do now, and it was almost impossible to enforce a widely unpopular law. Central governments depended, if they were to have effective authority, on the loyalty of local bodies and potentates whom they would have been hard put to coerce. If, then, their authority was effective and enduring, the presumption was that it was exercised in ways which seemed just, if not to the illiterate and the poor, then at least to the better-to-do and the locally prominent, who

[1] Ibid., p. 290. The translation is mine.

were taken to be spokesmen for the people generally. The authority of kings, to be effective and enduring, had to be exercised in ways approved of by this part of the people, who were assumed to be virtually the whole people, though numerically only a small part of them. And it was further taken for granted that the authority of this part over the rest of the people, if it was enduring, was so because it too was exercised for the common good.

Writers on politics in Bodin's time and for nearly two hundred years afterwards were much less concerned with the attitude of the poor and the illiterate to the classes above them, of whom they spoke as if they were the whole people, than with the attitude of these classes to the central government. If the 'people', in this narrow sense, did not contest the authority of the government, then, since the government's power to *oppress* them (that is to say, to govern them in ways which seemed to them contrary to the common good) was slight, the presumption was that the government was not oppressive. The people, thus conceived, were not incapable of judgement or of taking action against their rulers. Their acquiescence was not the acquiescence of the ignorant, and their obedience was not the obedience of the impotent. Therefore their acquiescence and obedience could be taken to be virtual consent, which was free, though tacit, to the authority of their rulers. And, of course, it never occurred to Bodin to ask whether the acquiescence and obedience of the poor and the illiterate were of the same kind, whether the unquestioned authority of the socially superior classes over their inferiors was also good evidence that the authority was exercised for the common good.

Though the assumption implicit in much that Bodin says is that enduring power is legitimate because its endurance is evidence that it is exercised for the common good, he sometimes uses arguments inconsistent with this assumption. For example, he does not hold that the authority of conquerors over the conquered becomes legitimate only by being used for their good; he accepts the commonly held opinion that, since victors in war have the right to kill the vanquished, they can rightfully become their rulers by offering them their lives in return for obedience. Even when victors are aggressors, even when they make war from no other motive except desire to extend their dominion, their victory gives them a right to rule over the vanquished, and even to deprive them of their property and their personal freedom. This was allowed by the *jus gentium*, as academic lawyers interpreted it in the sixteenth century, and that is enough for Bodin, the one-time professor of law. There was property and there was freedom, he admits, before there were governments. He dislikes slavery[1] and sets great store by the right of property, but that does not move him to question the teaching of the jurists that conquerors, though they are also aggressors, can rightly deprive the conquered of their freedom and their estates. He does not pretend that it is for the common good that they should do so; on the contrary, he admits that it is not. He therefore admits, at least by implication, that force can be legitimate even when it is not exercised for the common good. Thus there is not in Bodin's political theory one consistent doctrine of legitimacy.

Bodin treated the family, not the individual, as the basic unit of social life. He defined it as 'a right government over several subjects under obedience to a head of the family, and over what belongs to them'; and he said of it that it is 'the true source and origin of every republic, and the principal member thereof'. He found it weakened by the immorality and insubordination resulting from civil war, and wanted to strengthen it by increasing paternal authority, even to the point of giving a father the right of life and death over his children.

Property, being an institution older than the State, ought to be respected by the State. The family, the primary community on whose solidity and health all other communities depend, rests upon it. Who destroys property weakens the family, and therefore the State also, which is made up of families.

Bodin defined the State as 'the right government of several families, and of what is common to them, by a sovereign power'. The word 'right', in this definition, implies that the power is exercised for the common good or in accordance with the laws of nature. Sovereignty is defined as 'the absolute and perpetual power in a republic'. It is 'perpetual' because, whoever has it, though he acts through agents, does not lose it; it is perpetual in the sense of *inalienable*. It is absolute because whoever has it 'holds it, after God, only by the sword'; it is absolute in the sense of *unconditional*. The sovereign makes the law, which is his mere command, and himself is not subject to the law which he makes. Law is defined as the 'command of the sovereign touching all his subjects generally on general matters'.

The sovereign acts necessarily through agents; but, no matter how extensive the powers he delegates, no matter what rules he lays down or permits to arise concerning the passing of these powers

---

[1] When he objects to slavery he does so more from the master's point of view than the slave's. The slave, he says, hates his master and is therefore his enemy. He is the most dangerous enemy of all, the enemy in the household; and yet he is little use to his master unless the master keeps him close to him. The slave is less profitable to his master than a free servant working for a wage.

from one person to another, they are always exercised on his behalf. The authority is always entirely his, even though others exercise it in his place, and he cannot be held to have lost any part of it merely because he has allowed them to exercise it for a long time. In other words, those who exercise authority under the sovereign have no prescriptive right to that authority which they can appeal to against the sovereign if he decides to deprive them of it. The right of the subject to his external possessions does not derive from the sovereign, nor does his authority within his own family. But all temporal authority which is not paternal belongs properly to the sovereign and is exercised by him directly or through agents. Whoever holds the authority of the sovereign and claims if for his own offends against that sovereign.

The doctrine that the sovereign's authority is inalienable was directed against the feudal lords, both temporal or spiritual, who claimed rights of jurisdiction in temporal matters otherwise than as agents of the sovereign. The temporal lords claimed that these rights were hereditary, that they were inherited from their ancestors along with their estates. The bishops and abbots claimed that they were rights attached to their benefices. Bodin protested strongly against this assimilation of rights of jurisdiction with rights of property. He insisted that they are quite different in kind, since the first kind are exercised for the protection of the second. Kings may in the past have found it convenient to grant rights of jurisdiction to holders of certain properties, and may have allowed these rights to pass to their heirs or successors; but this could never convert authority into property, because the two are by nature different. No public office can be a part of any man's private estate, and whoever has rights of jurisdiction holds a public office. To hold any public office, except the highest, is to be an agent of whoever holds the highest office, of whoever is the sovereign.

Bodin did not want to deprive the lords temporal and spiritual of their jurisdictions; he knew that in practice it would be impossible to do so. He could not, as a Frenchman who had been in the king's service, echo Machiavelli's almost unqualified condemnation of feudal nobility; he knew that the king, to make his power effective, needed the support of the nobles. They were part of the established order, and there was no civil service capable of taking over their functions. The most that Bodin could hope for was that the nobles would acknowledge that they held such authority as was theirs in trust from the king.

Bodin is given the credit of being the first to put forward clearly the conception of sovereignty as the legally unlimited power of making law. That power, he said, is perpetual (i.e. inalienable) and absolute; and he also suggested that it is indivisible, for he denied that there could be a mixed state, that is, one in which the supreme law-making power belongs to more than one person or assembly. He distinguished custom from law, saying that law is the sovereign's command and always takes precedence over custom. Now, the modern idea of sovereignty is precisely that it is supreme legislative power, 'absolute', 'inalienable' and 'indivisible'. When sovereignty is vested in an assembly, it is not thought of as divided between its members, but as belonging to the whole body. Yet the conception of sovereignty, as we find it in Bodin, is still, for all its modernity, in some respects very unlike what it has since become. Bodin had nothing like Hobbes's gift for disentangling his ideas; whatever is new in him is stuck fast in the old, and takes much of its colour from its surroundings.

Though Bodin called sovereignty absolute, he also said that it is limited in three ways: by divine and natural law; by the law of succession (the law in virtue of which sovereignty is acquired by whoever rightly possesses it); and by the right to private property. Hobbes also spoke of laws of nature existing before there was sovereign power, and called them the commands of God; but he did not think of them as limiting the sovereign's authority. He went out of his way to argue that they must be taken to be whatever the sovereign says they are. Indeed, he even went so far as to suggest that they are not laws, properly so called, until there is a sovereign to enforce them. Bodin, however, thought of them as somehow limiting the sovereign's authority, even though no one could justly use them as an excuse for actively resisting him.

It might be objected that this is making a distinction where there is no difference. Bodin said that the sovereign is responsible to God alone for how he uses his authority, and denied that subjects may resist him on the ground that he has broken the law of nature. To make this objection is, I think, rather to miss the point. We are discussing a political idea and not the practical consequences drawn from it. Bodin never suggested that the laws of nature, though binding on the sovereign, are not properly laws unless there is a sovereign to enforce them, nor yet that they are whatever the sovereign says they are. He did not distinguish, as Bentham was to do, moral principles from positive laws. He always spoke of laws of nature as they were traditionally spoken of, as divine commands superior to the sovereign's commands and not always in keeping with them. He saw no contradiction between speaking in this way and calling the sovereign's authority absolute, and made no distinction between legal and moral obligation.

Bodin did not believe that subjects are bound to assume that every command of the sovereign is in keeping with the laws of nature; he forbade only active resistance to the sovereign, and allowed the subject to disobey only if he were convinced in conscience that what the sovereign commanded was contrary to God's law. He also said that the sovereign has no right to take his subjects' property without their consent, or to change the law of succession. The rule that establishes his right to govern is a rule he cannot change.

Hobbes, of course, knew as well as Bodin did that no human power is in fact absolute. But his purpose was to show how what must, of its very nature, be limited in fact, can be without limits in law. His purpose was different from Bodin's, and his conception of sovereignty clearer and closer to the modern one. Yet Bodin's originality was considerable; he was the first who clearly ascribed to sovereignty the attributes of inalienability and indivisibility, and who first classified states according to where supreme legislative authority lay within them. By monarchy he meant, not the government of one man whose authority is primarily executive and judicial (though he may also take part in making law), but the government of one man who by tradition alone has the right to make law. Aristocracy and democracy he redefined on the same principle.

2. Forms of Government

Like other political philosophers, Bodin unconsciously passed off some of his own preferences as statements of fact. There are, he said, only three basic types of state or republic: monarchy, aristocracy and democracy. Because sovereignty is indivisible, there cannot be a fourth type. Sovereignty must belong either to one person, or to a minority, or to a majority of the people. Even when it belongs to more than one person, it belongs entire to the whole group that has it, and is not shared among them. To say this is to imply that, where there is no sovereign, there is no State; for Bodin makes sovereignty part of his definition of the State.

Yet, in spite of his definition and would-be exhaustive classification of states into three main types, Bodin knew that in fact the power he called sovereign is sometimes shared by several persons and bodies; he knew that there are mixed types of states, and therefore states without sovereignty as he defined it. When he said that there are no mixed types, he really meant that there ought not to be any. He believed that states where the supreme legislative power is divided cannot perform their proper function, which is to afford security. Denmark, he said, has never enjoyed secure peace since the king was forced to share sovereign power with the nobles. Bodin made full use of the old prerogative of the political philosopher; he could annihilate something by definition, and then calmly go on to discuss what was wrong with it where it existed.

This tactic, though logically indefensible, is rhetorically effective. To speak of what ought not to be as if it could not be, though in fact it is, is somehow to make the condemnation more absolute. By putting the concept of sovereignty into the definition of the State, Bodin adds weight to his argument that the State cannot be stable nor its members secure unless supreme legislative authority belongs entire to one person or one body of persons. He also suggests, what he appears to have believed was true, that there is everywhere a tendency for this authority to be concentrated in the hands of one person or assembly. This, presumably, for two reasons: because every person and body among whom the powers which constitute sovereignty are divided will strive unceasingly to increase his or its share until one of them succeeds in engrossing the whole; and because it is the common interest that this should happen and the people will come to see that it is so and to acquiesce in it. Men need the State to give them security, and this it can best do when there is a sovereign inside it. There is therefore a strong bias towards sovereignty, and the bias is good. The State tends to become what it ought to be. This is not exactly what Bodin says, but it is, I think, suggested by his making sovereignty, as he defined it, an essential characteristic of the State.

Bodin distinguishes three kinds of monarchy: the royal and legitimate, the seigneurial or lordly, and the tyrannical. In the first the prince respects the laws of nature and does not interfere with his subjects' property; in the second he has rights over the persons and properties of his subjects and yet rules them for their good as well as his own; and in the third he disregards the laws of nature and treats his subjects as if their persons and estates belonged to him. These distinctions, which are primarily moral, illustrate a confusion, or at least an inconsistency, in Bodin's mind as to what makes human authority legitimate.

How, we may ask, does the seigneurial monarchy differ from the tyrannical? Bodin is ambiguous. Does the seigneurial monarch ruling his subjects for their own good exercise his rights over their persons and properties? Or does he, though the rights are his legally, refrain from exercising them? Does the tyrant's tyranny consist in his exercising rights which he does not have, or in his not ruling his subjects for their own good? In what does ruling subjects for their own good consist, if not in giving them security of person and property? Certainly, in the sixteenth century, to provide this security was thought to be the essential function of the Temporal Power. That being so, it would seem that the seigneurial monarch, when he rules his subjects for their own good, gives them security of person and property; it would seem that he rules in the same manner as the royal and legitimate monarch. Getting his power by conquest, he has a right not to rule his subjects for their own good, not to give them security of person and property; but he chooses not to exercise his right. If he did exercise it, he would be a bad ruler, though not a tyrant. For the tyrant is not merely the ruler who fails to give his subjects security of person and property; he is the ruler who fails to give it to them when he has no right to withhold it. He is the ruler who treats his subjects as if he had over them the right of a victor over the vanquished, when in fact he has no such right. It might seem that, logically, Bodin should have allowed for four, and not just three, types of monarchy; he should have distinguished the seigneurial monarch who chooses not to exercise the right which conquest gives him from the one who does exercise it.

Why then did Bodin not do this? Presumably because he was loath to admit that the ruler, no matter how he comes by his power, has the right to disregard the good of his subjects and to rule them entirely for his own good. But, since he accepted what the jurists had taught about the *jus gentium*, he could not bring himself to deny that the conqueror acquires a right over the persons and properties of the conquered. So he spoke as if the conqueror, while exercising this right, while ruling his subjects as the father of a family rules his slaves, might yet be ruling them for their own good, even when he disposed of their persons and properties as if they were his own. He spoke as if government might be good, might be in the interest of the governed, even though it did not give them security of person and property. But, if the function of government is to provide this security, if the good of the governed consists in their having it, how can a ruler govern for his subjects' good if he treats their persons and property as if they were his own? This is a question which Bodin could not answer. He did not reject the assumption commonly made in his day, and indeed for long afterwards, that the proper business of government is to give this security to the governed, that the public good consists in their having it; he did not suppose that political authority serves the same purpose as paternal authority. Nor did he hold that some men are by nature slaves and that therefore it is for their good to be treated as such. He could not reconcile his belief – that what makes power legitimate is that it is exercised for the good of those subject to it – with what he had learnt from the jurists about the *jus gentium*. So he persuaded himself that it was possible to rule men for their good while depriving them of their personal freedom and property, and never troubled to ask what that good could then be. He found it possible to assert both that the seigneurial monarch, treating his subjects as slaves, could act for their good, and that the tyrant, by so treating them, must harm them. Unprovoked aggression against foreigners, if successful, creates a right to treat them as slaves, while unprovoked aggression against one's own subjects or compatriots does not. Clearly, the moralist and the lawyer in Bodin never came to terms.

Bodin, loving symmetry, having distinguished three forms of monarchy, goes on to distinguish three forms of aristocracy and three of democracy; but he speaks of them so perfunctorily that there is little to be gained by considering them in detail. What he says about the three main types of government is more interesting than what he says about the three forms within each type.

Each type of government has its distinctive devices, customs and merits, which the statesman must understand if he is to preserve it and them. He must learn to distinguish the customs and devices which strengthen a form of government from those which weaken it. Bodin, despite his preference for monarchy, could see the virtues of other kinds of government. Popular government, he said, is prolific in great men, and its civil laws are closest to natural justice. The advantage of aristocracy is that it rests on natural inequality, which is permanent among men. It gives authority to those most worthy of it, to the able, to the rich, to the well born. Bodin seems to have believed that nobility and riches are usually effects of character and talent, that men who rise to high places mostly deserve to do so. Even when the heirs to wealth and honours are the most ordinary of men, their privileges are not unjust; for their ancestors excelled in some way or other, and it is right and expedient that able men should be rewarded in their posterity. Bodin could see virtues in both popular government and aristocracy. He prided himself on his open mind. There is not a trace in the *Republic* of the doctrine of the divine right of kings.

Yet Bodin's standard of good government was monarchy and, above all, French monarchy. The King of France seemed to him the best of all royal and legitimate monarchs. Not necessarily the actual king, the man who happened to be on the throne, but the king as he might be if he made full and wise use of the authority that tradition gave him. Popular government, even at its best, is unstable. It stimulates all ambitions, and therefore all talents, but it also gives opportunities to the selfish, unscrupulous or foolish. It is not true that the people are good judges of men; the qualities they most admire are not the qualities that make good rulers. To give control to the people is to hope for wisdom from what is by nature superficial and impetuous. Though aristocracy avoids some of the evils of democracy, it encourages others as much or more. It is by nature factious. When the nobles quarrel, one party seeks the support of the common people against the other, to the great damage of the State. Aristocracy, almost as much as democracy, lacks secrecy and despatch in the conduct of public affairs. It creates a wider gulf than either monarchy or democracy between the privileged and unprivileged, and so makes it dangerous to arm the people, thus weakening the State militarily.

Monarchy has its disadvantages: sudden changes of policy when one prince succeeds another, disputed succession, regencies, the corrupting influences of undisputed power. But it is, take it all in all, the best of possible governments. When the monarch is hereditary, reverence for him grows from generation to generation; he knows that his authority is lasting and will pass after him to his natural heirs, and is therefore strongly inclined to work for posterity. Getting power without seeking it, he values it less for itself than for what he can do with it. To live in his people's memory, he must use power well; he must care for all classes of his subjects, and stands only to lose by allowing one class to oppress another. He can protect small groups against the people, and in the public interest can prefer their advice to the clamour of louder and more powerful factions. Though Bodin admitted that unlimited power corrupts, he thought it so necessary to public security that the risk was worth taking. His own belief in God was strong, and he probably took it for granted that kings, unless they were foolish or wicked, would feel their responsibility to God. The fear of God, he thought, is a reasonable fear, and therefore a considerable motive with every properly educated man. The modern argument, that responsibility to God alone is virtual irresponsibility, would probably have seemed impious to him, as it would have to most people in the sixteenth century.

Bodin distinguished between three kinds of justice: the commutative or arithmetic, the geometric and the harmonious. The first, which is proper to popular governments, treats all men alike, whatever their personal qualities and social standing. It treats every offence or claim or contract on its intrinsic merits, as a situation which might affect any man; it treats the individual, whoever he may be, as an abstract possessor of rights and duties. 'Geometric' justice, which is aristocratic, takes account of the social standing of the offender or plaintiff, treating him differently according to his circumstances, his wealth and the class he belongs to. The best justice is neither 'arithmetic' nor 'geometric' but harmonious, taking into account the nature of the act or claim, the wealth and standing of the agent or claimant, and the needs of society. This 'harmonious' justice, which accepts inequality but keeps it in bounds, is proper to monarchy.

These distinctions are not quite as clear as Bodin takes them to be. He treats harmonious justice as a kind of happy combination of the other two, and implies that each of the others is one-sided. Geometric justice takes account of the wealth and social standing of the offender or claimant, and so too does harmonious justice. How then do the two differ? Clearly, geometric justice, just as much as the others, must take account of the nature of any offence or claim on which it has to pronounce; it cannot refuse to consider whether the offence is murder or larceny or whether the claim is for money or for the restitution of conjugal rights. Every kind of justice, whether it is proper to democracy, aristocracy or monarchy, necessarily takes into account the nature of the offences and claims submitted to it; so that the second and third kinds must differ from the first by taking something else into account as well, and this something, Bodin tells us, is the wealth and social standing of offenders and claimants. But, in that case, harmonious justice, proper to monarchy, is not a combination of the other two; it is merely a milder form of geometric or aristocratic justice, taking account of the same things but not attaching the same weight to them.

The justice proper to democracy, moreover, is not really *arithmetic* in the sense defined by Bodin; it does not impose the same penalties for the same offences regardless of the wealth of the offenders. It imposes heavier fines on the rich than on the poor. It aims at maintaining a certain type of social order, and imposes penalties which are adequate deterrents for that purpose. A fine sufficient to deter a poor man will not deter a rich one, while other forms of punishment may bear more heavily on the rich man than on the poor. Only where there is complete equality of wealth and social standing can arithmetic justice achieve its purpose. But Bodin tells us that complete equality is impossible, even though democracy is not. It follows, therefore, that strictly arithmetic justice is not suited to any possible society, not even to a democracy.

Nevertheless, it is worth taking a closer look at the social philosophy which seems to lie behind Bodin's conception of 'harmonious' justice.

He believed that there never had been and never could be a society where there was complete equality of wealth and social standing. If an attempt were made to create this equality artificially, it could not last but would immediately begin to disappear, if only because men's talents differ and some men have more children than others. To maintain equality it would be necessary, at frequent intervals, to put an end to the inequalities which had appeared in the meantime. Every so many years those who had outdistanced their fellows would have to be put back on a level with them. There would have to be periodic cancellations of debts and annulments of contracts, or otherwise creditors would grow rich and important and rise superior to debtors. But that would destroy good faith and therefore undermine the security which government exists to provide. The attempt to maintain equality, if it is seriously and persistently made, must in the long run destroy society.

This argument, unless I am mistaken, implies that, whatever the legal system, whatever the structure of rights and obligations, some people will always contrive to do better than others, becoming much richer and more powerful than their neighbours; so that, if equality is to be maintained, it will always be necessary to change the laws and to tamper with rights and obligations to the detriment of the rich and the exalted and to the advantage of the poor and the lowly. The argument takes it for granted that no stable system of law can be devised which will keep inequalities within fairly narrow limits. This assumption, at a time when no one had thought of death duties or of a graduated income tax, seemed plausible. That taxation could be used to offset the tendency for inequality to grow always greater simply did not occur to Bodin, whose respect for property rights was as great as Locke's. Taxes could be rightly levied, so he thought, only to meet the expenses of government. With such ideas fixed in his head it is not surprising that he could imagine no other way of maintaining equality than by the cancellation of debts and the annulment of contracts.

Bodin was not content to argue that equality is impossible; he also thought it undesirable. He put forward what he believed to be strong arguments in favour of inequality and inherited privileges. It is not enough, he said, to ensure that men are rewarded according to their talents, if they are not allowed to pass on their rewards to their children. For men ordinarily work for their children as well as for themselves; they hope to live on in their posterity. Deprive them of this hope, and you weaken society by weakening a motive that causes men to make the best of their talents. The ablest of them devote their energies to getting glory, power and wealth – to getting whatever raises them above their neighbours and proves their superiority. They also look forward beyond their own lives; they wish to be honoured in their children, to perpetuate themselves and their greatness. A man's concern for his posterity, as Bodin saw it, is clearly not a pure form of altruism; it has a large element of self-love in it. But he believed that self-love, when it works in this way, works for the good of the community.

Bodin admitted that inequality can be excessive and distinctions of class too rigid. Not only do the poor need to be protected from the rich and the powerful, but men of humble birth ought not to be excluded from the highest honours. Society ought to provide men both with security and with opportunities of bettering themselves. Democracy, insisting on an impossible equality, must, in the endeavour to attain it, weaken the bonds that hold society together and the motives that enrich and strengthen it; while aristocracy divides society too much and too rigidly. Monarchy alone both maintains and moderates inequality; it keeps the social hierarchy firmly in place, and yet also enables men of talent to climb to high places. It makes for social harmony, which equality does not; for equals are jealous of equals, while, where privileges are inherited or acquired by merit, ordinary people respect their superiors. Conventional inequalities are irksome chiefly to persons of inferior birth and superior talents, but monarchy provides an outlet for their ambitions.

Though Bodin believed that what he called royal and legitimate monarchy is the best of all governments, he did not think it suited to all peoples. Governments must, he thought, vary with the peoples subject to them. A whole chapter of the *Republic* is taken up with a discussion of the effects of climate and physical environment on peoples. Northerners are tougher, more active physically and also more chaste than other people; southerners are physically weaker, more thoughtful and more sensual. The people in between, living in the middle regions, are less tough but quicker-witted than the northerners, and also tougher and more active than the southerners; they excel in the political arts, and it is among them that we must expect to find the best governments. The southerners excel in the abstract and occult sciences, in mathematics, theology, astronomy; they have founded all the great religions, but politically they are weak.

Mountain peoples, even when they live in southern regions, incline to northern characteristics; whereas plainsmen, wherever they live, are apt to be like southerners. The further west we move, at whatever altitude, the more northern in type the people we find; the further east, the more southern. Bodin did not adhere rigidly to these generalities; he admitted that men of exceptional talent, no matter where they are born, advance beyond a national character largely determined by climate and geography. He also admitted that society can change even when climate does not; for he noticed that Roman society had changed from age to age. Bodin's reflections on the social effects of climate and geography were generally neglected for nearly two centuries, until Montesquieu took them up again to form one of the major themes of his largest work.

In *The Spirit of the Laws*, there is not only a theory about the social effects of climate; there are also arguments favourable to monarchy very like those to be found in Bodin's *Republic*. Bodin's affinities with Montesquieu are obvious, as are also his affinities with Hobbes. There is, however, another great political thinker with whom he has as much in common as with either of them. By Burke's time, Bodin was almost forgotten, and it is improbable that Burke ever studied him. But there are remarkable similarities between them. Both are impressed by the variety of social and political institutions, which they are more inclined to justify than condemn. Both approve of inequality, and go out of their way to explain how it holds society together; both are respecters of tradition and admit the need for reform; both believe that society is weakened unless the claims of birth and talent are alike respected; both see in religion the best preservative of the social order, and yet value it more for its own sake than for its social effects; and for both freedom is an acquired rather than a natural right. Bodin is certainly to be counted among the greater conservative political philosophers.

3. Limitations on Power: The French Monarchy

Bodin believed in a sovereign monarchy, and yet also wanted royal power limited in all sorts of ways. This might be thought a weakness in him when he is compared with Hobbes. He was certainly less consistent than the English philosopher; but he had, what Hobbes had not, a considerable experience of government. He was more realistic, though less lucid, and he appears more inconsistent than in fact he was. He thought it dangerous to allow that anyone had a legal right to set a limit to royal authority, but he knew that the king could not rule efficiently without devices to retard his actions. Bodin wanted royal edicts subjected to close scrutiny; he wanted them responsibly criticized and their defects brought respectfully to the king's notice. He feared not delay but deadlock. No one must have power to challenge the king's authority; no one must thwart

him when his mind is quite made up. The appeal must always be
from the king to the king better advised. The king's will must prevail
in the end; but the king, when making up his mind, should take
account of the opinions of those who, by tradition, have the right to
advise him. The king's will must be established in traditional ways
and with the help of competent persons. His power depends on the
loyalty, the independent judgement and the trust of his advisers and
officials, and also on his people's love. His power is legally absolute
but not arbitrary; it should be exercised after proper deliberation.

Bodin did not reach this position immediately. In the *Methodus*,
published in 1566, ten years before the *Republic*, he was still arguing
that the king is bound by the laws, not of his own good will, but of
right, and that he cannot oblige the *parlements* to register his edicts.
It was the religious wars that changed his mind, causing him to say
unequivocally that the monarch, as their author, is superior to the
civil laws, and that the *parlements*, despite their right of remonstrance,
cannot refuse to register royal edicts if the king, having considered
their objections, still insists on their doing so. The authority of the
parlements and of the estates, general and provincial, comes from the
king, just as do the jurisdictions granted to dukes, marquises and
barons. What the king has given, he may take away. Indeed, he
never really gave it, for his authority, being supreme, is inalienable;
he cannot give away any part of it, he can only appoint agents to use
it in his name. All who have rights of jurisdiction, all who declare the
law and apply it within his dominions, are his officers, and an office
is never the property of the man who holds it.

But though Bodin had by 1576 come to hold this position, he
by no means wanted to reduce either the *parlements* or the estates
to impotence. He thought of the estates less as legislatures than as
assemblies where popular needs and grievances could be discussed and
brought to the king's notice. A meeting of the Estates-General was a
meeting of the sovereign with the representatives of his people. Such
meetings were, in Bodin's eyes, not only useful but indispensable;
the sovereign must keep contact with his subjects, and must not deal
with them only through officials. Meetings of the estates enhance the
king's majesty and strengthen the people's devotion to him. They
are a form of political intercourse making for good government.
They are also necessary if the people are to vote subsidies to the
king, who, being obliged to respect his subjects' property, cannot lay
new taxes on them without their consent. Bodin was perfectly well
aware that the need to get his subjects' consent to new taxes limited
the sovereign's power. He had himself, in the very year when the

Republic was published, induced the Third Estate to refuse a subsidy, hoping thereby to thwart the royal will. But the need for consent to taxation detracted nothing, in Bodin's eyes, from the sovereignty of the French king. This need provided the king with strong motives for not making widely unpopular laws and for not pursuing policies strongly condemned by his subjects. Bodin saw no harm in this. The king was still sovereign; there were no legal limits to his right to make law. No one had the right to resist him on the ground that he had abused his authority. It is one thing to provide the king with strong motives for not using his authority in ways which seem dangerous or wicked to his subjects, and quite another to admit their right to resist him on the ground that he has broken a law superior to his will.

Bodin preferred the *parlements* to the estates. Being himself a lawyer, he saw in these hereditary corporations consisting of lawyers a useful and responsible check on the royal will. He cites with approval many cases of kings giving way to them. They could not claim to be representative of the people; they were royal courts exercising justice in the sovereign's name. They could hardly aspire to be more than guardians of the law and keepers of the king's conscience. Bodin, who had no faith in popular wisdom, had considerable respect for the sagacity and moderation of professional bodies. He exalts the rôle of the lawyer in preventing abuses of authority, just as Montesquieu was to do after him.

He would have liked the king to establish a new kind of army, recruited and paid by the Crown; he would have liked the army to be more professional and less feudal. He distrusted the nobles, and his preference for the *parlements* over the estates may have been due as much to fear of feudal pretensions as to contempt for popular wisdom. He sympathized with the lawyers in their efforts to curtail feudal privileges for the benefit of the monarchy. He argued that the nobles, unless they served their king in time of war without payment, should lose their tax immunities. But he was too conservative, too respectful of tradition, to be whole-heartedly opposed to what was still the most powerful class in France.

Bodin wanted the royal power legally absolute but in practice limited in traditional ways. He appealed to history, and therefore, since (though he might not know it himself) he wanted a stronger monarchy than France had in fact ever had, he interpreted the past to suit his argument. Nevertheless, he wanted to preserve much that had long existed. He wanted to preserve corporate bodies of many kinds, because they, more easily than individuals, can defend themselves against arbitrary power, not by violence, but by making their influence felt. Such bodies must never act conspiratorially, and must never challenge the sovereign's laws. But their very existence, their moderation, their prestige, their number, encourage the sovereign to consider carefully what laws he shall make for the common good, and also provide him with powerful motives for respecting his own laws. Bodin wanted many obstacles to the royal will, but none that was insurmountable. There ought always to be some final authority, some person or persons whose decisions cannot be legally challenged, whom persistently to disobey would be a punishable offence. In France that authority could, he thought, belong only to the king, who could not in practice exercise it just as he pleased, for no authority – not even sovereign power – is absolute in fact as well as in law. What is required for good government is, on the one hand, that no one should be in a position to place his veto on whoever has the highest authority in the State, and, on the other, that the obstacles to that authority (and in practice there will always be some, good or bad) should serve to direct it to the common good.[1]

Bodin had been too long in the royal service to have much admiration for kings. He was a patriot before he was a royalist. The civil wars seemed to him to prove that the nobles, when not under discipline, were too selfish and turbulent to carry out public duties conscientiously; France needed their spirit and their talents but could use them best in the royal service. For the common people, Bodin felt much sympathy but little respect. He found them too ignorant and unreflective to help themselves effectively, and their passions and prejudices made it easy for unscrupulous persons to excite and mislead them. Their anger might endanger order but was likely to be of little advantage to themselves. To Bodin the common people seemed (if I

---

[1] Bodin did not look upon the Church as a useful brake on the royal will. Writing in a country which was overwhelmingly Catholic, he could not deny the autonomy of the Church within its own sphere. He wanted ecclesiastical jurisdiction limited to maintaining discipline within the Church, and argued that clerks should answer to the ordinary courts for all temporal offences. The Church should be prevented from growing too rich, and should be obliged to provide a decent living for everyone in holy orders, no matter how humble his office. Religious unity is desirable, provided it can be maintained without violence and without strong measures against dissenters. The prince is right to forbid attacks on the Established Church, but ought to use only gentle methods to persuade his subjects to adhere to it. Strong action is justified only against atheism, which deprives men of the most powerful motive for acting justly. Bodin, believing strongly in God and in society's need of religion, would not have the prince indifferent to it, nor equally favourable to all forms of it. It is the duty of the prince to promote religion by suitable means, and to preserve religious unity if he can do so without recourse to violent or severe measures. Religious unity is desirable, not because God requires it, but because it makes for social peace.

may so put it) a blind and foolish, but not evil, monster, to be firmly led, decently treated and kept quiet by all suitable means. Distrusting the French nobles and believing that the lower classes were politically helpless, he had no alternative but to be a champion of monarchy. He saw his country in danger and thought that the king alone could save it.

Though Bodin did not admire kings, he idealized the French monarchy. He saw it as an elaborate structure, with the king at its centre, surrounded by the great institutions of State, so disposed about the monarch that he could hardly in practice abuse his authority. Surrounded by conscientious, intelligent and loyal servants, he would have powerful motives for governing well. There was, while Bodin lived, less danger of the king's abusing his power than of its being challenged by unscrupulous factions for selfish ends. Bodin's ideal was the king well served, the monarch supported by an apparatus of power whose regular and smooth working would tend of itself to elaborate and purify his will, making him reasonable and public-spirited.

★ ★ ★

Chauviré ascribes two great qualities to Bodin: originality and good sense. He then goes on to explain how it is that, in spite of these qualities, Bodin is seldom read. His greatest book is ill-constructed, digressive, repetitious, bizarre and verbose; his style is dull and facile, typical of the civil servant and the politician, his similes are mostly borrowed and ordinary, though sometimes fresh and striking; he is frank and naïve, he has considerable vigour (*verve*) and some imagination, but lacks order and polish and lucidity. Chauviré, whose excellent book is clearly a labour of love, speaks of Bodin as of a man destined to be eclipsed by men more brilliant and more gifted than himself. He makes, in the course of his book, every point he can in favour of Bodin, and then in the end passes a verdict on him which, though essentially just, is so cautious as to be almost severe. Perhaps he is afraid of making too large a claim on behalf of a fellow Angevin; perhaps he is afraid of being led astray by local patriotism.

Chauviré might have been less cautious. As an apologist for royal supremacy, Bodin is less eloquent, less lucid, less splendid than Bossuet, but he is also more original and more ingenious. He is a less subtle reasoner than Hobbes but reveals a greater understanding of how government operates. He is less brilliant than Montesquieu but shrewder and less carried away by his own ideas. If we look only at the content of his arguments and not at how they are presented, he produced what was perhaps the ablest case ever made for monarchy, as Europe knew it in the sixteenth, seventeenth and eighteenth centuries. Not the most impressive or persuasive case, especially at the first reading, but the case which makes the most realistic assumptions and stands up best to criticism.

He was not a practical innovator; he proposed no great changes. His originality consists, above all, in a new way of looking at what men were already familiar with: the great monarchies of the West. To explain these monarchies he put forward new ideas, which he did not perhaps define as clearly as they were to be defined after him, but which he used consistently enough to make his contemporaries see what was familiar with fresh eyes. And the State which absorbed his attention and his loyalty was more complicated and more difficult to understand than the small republics of Machiavelli's Italy. He was less narrow, more elaborate and more moderate, more imaginative and more adequate in his views, than anyone else moved to write about politics by the spectacle of a France in the throes of civil war.

CHAPTER 5
Hobbes

I. INTRODUCTORY

Like the *Vindiciae*, like Bodin's *Republic*, like several formulations of
the theory of the divine right of kings, Hobbes's political philosophy
is a product of civil strife and war. But, unlike these others, it does
not take sides. On personal grounds, as a tutor in noble houses,
Hobbes might prefer the Royalists to their opponents; he might
even, on political grounds, prefer the sovereignty of one man to
the sovereignty of a whole parliament of men. The Puritans were
not congenial to him. His sympathies inclined him to one side rather
than the other, but he did not allow them to affect his arguments.
His fundamental position was different from that of either party to
the Civil War.

The Royalists and Parliamentarians quarrelled about the proper
limits of the legislative and executive powers; they quarrelled about
what tradition allowed, and also, though to a lesser extent, about what
was naturally just. Their knowledge of history was slight; they had the
most one-sided and inadequate ideas about their country's past. They
talked a great deal about fundamental law, and accused one another
of subverting it; but they had only vague and confused ideas about
it. Both sides wanted what we should call constitutional monarchy.
Unfortunately, neither side could give a clear account of how that
monarchy should be organized. Both sides were so busy making and
resisting particular demands, so immersed in the conflict, that neither
could see the system of government as a whole or understand how
it had been affected by the early reforms of the Long Parliament
– reforms accepted by most of the Royalists as well as by their
opponents. The old monarchy – the system created by the Tudors

and inherited from them by James and Charles – ceased to exist in 1641, killed by the Long Parliament. But neither of the factions into which that Parliament split understood what had happened. They both believed they were fighting to maintain something traditional, something that had worked well for centuries and was now threatened by the other side.

Hobbes found nothing to attract him in the arguments of either side. They were arguing about how power should be divided, about what tradition allowed and what was required by natural justice. He cared nothing for tradition and had his own peculiar account of natural law. He put two questions that did not interest the belligerents: What is the essential function of government?, and What kind of government can best perform it? His answer to the first question was: Government exists to give as much security as possible to individuals; and to the second: It cannot do so effectively unless supreme authority is all in the same hands. The belligerents were agreed that power must be divided; they quarrelled about the division of it, and yet were not clear in their own minds just how they wanted it divided. But Hobbes knew his own mind perfectly: Power ought not to be divided. If he was right, the war was not worth fighting, and the quarrel that led to it was absurd.

Hobbes, as you can see, was a very superior person, very much *au-dessus de la mêlée*. Here were people drifting into an unnecessary war only because they could not think clearly, because they put irrelevant questions and busied themselves about unimportant matters. He would put the right questions and give the true answers; he would enlighten his generation. Hobbes had great faith in the persuasive power of reason, and also in his own powers as a reasoner. Like many of his contemporaries, he believed that the quarrel that led to war was merely an argument about principles, an intellectual dispute; and he thought himself wiser than the quarrellers for seeing that their dispute rested on misconceptions. The clash of interests that lay behind the dispute was invisible to him.

Hobbes took little notice of politics until the approach of civil war turned his mind to it. He was a philosopher before he became a political theorist, and he applied philosophical methods acquired independently of the study of politics to the solution of political problems. On a prolonged visit to Paris, he had made the acquaintance of Mersenne, Descartes' friend, and of Gassendi, a materialist philosopher. Hobbes professed not to admire the Cartesian philosophy; he rejected Descartes' sharp distinction between matter and mind, and was attracted by the materialism of Gassendi. But his method was like Descartes'; he too began with definitions and with simple and distinct ideas, and erected a whole philosophy on them. It is not always the men we admire most who most influence us.

It was after his return from Paris in 1637, when he was already in his fiftieth year, that Hobbes decided to apply his newly discovered philosophic method to politics. He was stimulated to do so by the already bitter controversies going on around him. His first political treatise, *The Elements of Law*, was completed just before the Long Parliament met in November 1640. Hobbes, who seems to have prided himself on his timidity as other men do on their courage, decided that Parliament would not like his treatise; and so he fled to France. He was the first *émigré*, and he did not return to England for eleven years.

Hobbes's first political treatise was a plea for absolute monarchy. It sought to prove more than the king had ever claimed. But Hobbes was not really more Royalist than the king. His argument for absolute monarchy could easily be, and very soon was, transformed into a general argument for absolute government. Hobbes never really abandoned the position he took up in 1640. In his two greatest works on politics, in *De cive* and in *Leviathan*, he merely elaborated doctrines already put forward before the Civil War began. The first edition of *De cive* appeared in 1642; the considerably enlarged and altered edition in 1647. The first English translation of *De cive*, made by Hobbes himself, was published in 1651, the same year as *Leviathan*. This translation, entitled *Philosophical Rudiments Concerning Government and Society*, forms the second volume of the William Molesworth edition of Hobbes's *English Works*.

II. HOBBES'S ACCOUNT OF HUMAN NATURE

Hobbes's account of human nature is simple. Whatever a man desires he calls good, and whatever he is averse to he calls evil; so that good and evil are not qualities inherent in things but are only signs revealing how the persons who use the signs feel about the things they apply them to. Will is not different from desire but is 'the last appetite in deliberating'. When a man has more than one desire and yet can satisfy only one, he contemplates the objects of his desires and compares them with one another, until at last one desire conquers the others and he acts. Continual success in getting what a man desires is felicity; and his power is his ability to get whatever he may desire. Man, unlike the other animals, is rational; he is aware of himself as a creature liable to many desires and can discover the best means of satisfying them. He has therefore not only his natural appetites to satisfy, but also acquires an appetite for power and for whatever power depends on: riches, honour and command. This appetite, unlike the natural appetites which are quickly satisfied when they recur, is insatiable. A man can never have too much power; he therefore becomes a competitor with all other men for it, and so their enemy. 'Competition of riches, honour, command, or other power, inclineth to contention, enmity and war: because the way of one competitor, to the attaining of his desire, is to kill, subdue, supplant, or repel the other.'[1]

The object of every man's will, says Hobbes, 'is some good to himself'.[2] Imagination can make him interested in another's good, but only because he feels pleasure or pain at the thought of himself situated as that other is. Pity is the grief we feel for the calamity of another arising from the imagination of the like calamity befalling ourselves. Hobbes therefore implies that man is by nature self-regarding and can never be otherwise.

Now, this doctrine, this psychological egoism, which so many of Hobbes's critics have fastened on, is not really necessary to his political theory. Even if Hobbes had described pity and benevolence differently and had not reduced them to manifestations of self-pity and self-love, his political conclusions might have been the same. For pity and benevolence, even if we suppose them genuinely altruistic, are not emotions strong enough to explain the existence of political society. Even Hume, who was so far from being a psychological egoist that he went out of his way to refute that way of thinking, thought that men's purely self-regarding feelings go almost the whole way in explaining their political behaviour. It is in a stable society that benevolent feelings have the largest scope, and they are therefore much more effects than causes of the stability it was Hobbes's purpose to explain. The less orderly and secure men's lives, and the less they are bound by rules, the more ruthless, narrow and selfish they are. On this point, most modern psychologists would, I think, agree with Hobbes. The human child, in his earliest relations with others, is almost entirely selfish; he has to be taught to think of others. In other words, he has to be disciplined. We may quarrel with Hobbes for supposing that men ever were in a state of nature, or for misunderstanding how social discipline affects them and creates new motives in them; but he

[1] *Leviathan*, ch. 11.
[2] Ibid., ch. 14.

was surely much nearer being right than wrong when he assumed that men who had never been under any kind of social discipline would be wholly selfish.

Hobbes denied that society is natural. It is important to get clear just what he meant by the denial, for it has often been misinterpreted. In a note to chapter 1 of his own English version of *De cive*, he makes this statement, commenting on his much criticized assertion that man is not born fit for society:

> Wherefore I deny not that men (even nature compelling) desire to come together. But civil societies are not mere meetings, but bonds, to the making whereof faith and compacts are necessary; the virtue whereof to children and fools, and the profit whereof to those who have not yet tasted the miseries which accompany its defects, is altogether unknown; whence it happens that those, because they know not what society is, cannot enter into it; these, because ignorant of the benefits it brings, care not for it. Manifest therefore it is, that all men, because they are born in infancy, are born unapt for society. . . . wherefore man is made fit for society not by nature, but by education.

In other words, it is education that makes us 'apt for society', which means, not desirous of company, but fit for society; and men in the state of nature are, *ex hypothesi*, without education. It may be that they never were in a state of nature, and therefore never without a social environment moulding their characters – which is education in the largest sense. But if, in order to discover what men gain from society, we imagine them in a state of nature, we must divest them of the qualities they acquire by being subject to social discipline. We need not suppose that nothing in their nature draws them into society, but we must suppose them unfit for society.

Much breath and ink have been wasted denouncing the cynicism of Hobbes. No doubt, men are not as self-regarding as he thought them, and his accounts of several of their passions will not bear examination. His definitions are often too simple. But he was not, by the standards of his time, either cynical or severe. Nobody in the seventeenth century believed that man, untouched by society, is good. Most theologians agreed that man is born evil, with the taint of Adam upon him, and that only by God's grace is he able to attain merit. The peculiarity of Hobbes is not that he asserted man's natural selfishness – for moralists had been busy asserting and denouncing it for centuries – but that he denied his essential wickedness. There is not a word in Hobbes about original sin. On the contrary, he says that 'the desires, and other passions of man, are in themselves no sin. No more are the actions, that proceed from those passions, till they know a law that forbids them'.[1] His contemporaries were not much disturbed by Hobbes's cynicism or his low opinion of human nature. In the writings of religious men they could find much harsher and more terrible judgements. Nearly all the Puritans thought much worse than Hobbes did of human nature; but he, unlike them, did not set himself up above the common run of mankind as one of the elect.

What his contemporaries really disliked about Hobbes was his peculiar attitude to God, which many took for atheism, and his being satisfied with human nature as he found it. This and this, he said, is the stuff of human nature, which in itself is neither good nor bad. Without the discipline of law, men cannot help but behave in ways that make them miserable; but, put them under that discipline, and there is nothing about them that need prevent their happiness. At bottom, they remain always the same, passionate and rational, with reason serving their passions; their real nature does not change, and there is nothing inherently evil about that nature. Create the proper environment, and their nature will do them no harm.

Hobbes did not leave God out of his picture of the world, but he did give the impression that he had first painted the picture without God, and had then put God in afterwards, to save the appearances. His contemporaries were not altogether deceived. Hobbes was saying that men could, by their own devices, get for themselves all the happiness they wanted. In a still theological age, the sin of this worldly and complacent philosopher was not cynicism but pride.

Reason and passion, he thought, together point the way out of man's natural state: 'And thus much for the ill condition, which man by mere nature is actually placed in; though with a possibility to come out of it, consisting partly in the passions, partly in his reason.'[2] Reason gains no victory over the passions. It is merely that, as a result of the terrible experiences of the state of nature, the passions that incline men to peace grow in the end stronger than the passions that incline them to war. This condition is not enduring, and men cannot get peace except by the use of their reason. The office of reason is to serve the passions by discovering the best means of satisfying them. Thus it is that reason suggests 'convenient articles of peace'. It can only suggest but not impose them. Man always remains a passionate creature. His actions are determined primarily by his desires and emotions and only secondarily by reason. While the passions that incline men to war are the stronger there is no hope of peace, for

[1] *Leviathan*, ch. 13.
[2] Ibid.

reason always serves the stronger passions; but the state of continual war is so terrible that the passions that incline men to peace must in the end grow strong enough to cause them to seek peace. It is then only that reason, always in the service of the passions, teaches them the way to get peace. The precepts it teaches are what men otherwise call the laws of nature.

Hobbes's account of the relations between reason and the passions is open to criticism on two grounds: it does not sufficiently allow that reason can affect the quality of men's passions, and it supposes that men are more purposeful and consistent than they in fact are. In other words, it makes too little of reason in one way, and too much of it in another.

It is misleading to say that reason merely serves the passions, that it does not prescribe ends but only discovers the means to them. Hobbes sometimes speaks as if man would still have the same passions even if he were not rational – as if all that reason does for him is to enable him to satisfy his passions more easily. But a rational creature has passions he would not have if he lacked reason; he has, through his reason, conceptions of himself, his environment and his relations with other creatures like himself, which he could not have unless he were rational. All his emotions, all his desires, are deeply affected by these conceptions. The whole quality of his life is altered by them. Hobbes admits that men come to desire some things because they are rational; they desire power, for instance, because it is a means to felicity, and they could not know this unless they were rational. He even admits that power, which is desired at first for what it brings, comes in the end to be desired for its own sake, and often more strongly than any other thing. But he does not see how these admissions undermine his account of how reason stands to the passions. Man can know himself and his surroundings, and can also have illusions about the world and himself, as no animal without reason could do. To speak of him, as Hobbes does, as if he were just a creature of passions like the other animals, and differed from them only in being able to use reason to satisfy his passions, is lamentably inadequate. This shallow psychology was later taken over by some of the Utilitarians, and helps to explain much that is flat and poor about their philosophies.

Man is more deeply affected by reason than Hobbes supposed, and yet also less reasonable in the pursuit of his ends. Hobbes speaks of man as if he were clear in his mind what he wanted, and were therefore easily persuadable by reason. Look, Hobbes says to him, this is what you want, and these are the ways to get it. Take careful stock of your position, and it will then be obvious to you what you should do.

Hobbes would have us believe that all men's troubles come from their not knowing how best to get what they want; it seldom occurred to him that they might come from their not knowing what they want, from confusions of thought and feeling too deep to be unravelled and which yet only creatures endowed with reason are liable to. And so Hobbes, who disparaged reason, also made too much of it; and in this also some of the Utilitarians followed him.

III. THE LAWS OF NATURE

Hobbes's conception of the laws of nature is difficult and requires careful elucidation. He calls these laws dictates of reason and also divine commands. If they were only the first, they would clearly not be moral laws, at least not in any usual sense of moral. If they were the second, they might be moral laws. Whether we conclude that they are or are not depends, of course, on how we interpret Hobbes's meaning.

The laws of nature, as they were ordinarily conceived in Hobbes's time, were supposed to be binding on men even in the absence of all authority of man over man, even in the state of nature. They were both descriptive and prescriptive; they were thought of partly as psychological and partly as moral laws, though the difference between the two kinds of law was seldom made clear. For example, self-preservation was usually treated as a natural law, and yet also as a mode of behaviour and not as a rule of conduct. It was observed that man does, as a matter of fact, seek to preserve himself, and his doing so was called a law of nature. It was also commonly supposed to be his duty not to interfere with other men in what they did to preserve themselves, and this duty too was called a law of nature. The laws of nature, as they were traditionally understood, in part described ends which it was taken for granted that men did pursue, even outside society, merely because they were the sort of creatures they were (or, as it was often put, 'by necessity of their nature'); and in part laid down the rules that they ought to follow, as creatures pursuing these ends, in their dealings with one another. You and all other men, in virtue of your humanity, have certain needs and aspirations. Since you are rational, you can know that other people have these needs as well as you do, and can discover the rules all men ought to follow in order not to prevent one another from achieving the purposes common to their kind.

Men are God's creatures. He made them what they are. By endowing them with reason, He enabled them to pursue their ends differently from other animals. Traditionally, both the needs attributed to men in virtue of their humanity, and the rules which it was supposed reason required them to follow in their dealings with one another, were treated as effects of God's will. The laws of nature were therefore also laws of God, and were supposed to hold good in the state of nature as much as in political society. It was thought that men, because there are rules which they ought to conform to even in the absence of all human government, have natural rights against one another: rights which governments can make secure but do not create. Everyone has a right to require of others that they should keep to the rules in their dealings with him; he would have this right even in the state of nature, and he has it in political society.

It was usually supposed that the ground of natural obligation, of the duty to follow the rules which all must follow if men are to achieve their natural purposes, is the will of God. Our duty in the first place is to God, and to other men only because God has commanded us to love one another. Thus, we do our duty when we do what God requires of us. Now, in itself, this doctrine does not imply that obligation arises either from fear or from self-interest. True, Christian writers delighted to speak of God's power and to repeat that the fear of God is the beginning of wisdom. But they did not put forward God's omnipotence as the only or chief ground of obligation. We ought to obey God, not because we are completely in His power, but because He made us and desires our good. He also threatens to punish our disobedience, and so provides us with a strong motive for obeying Him; but the duty of obedience is not therefore grounded only in His power. The doctrine that the ultimate ground of all obligation is the will of an omnipotent God is not to be reduced to a special case of the principle that 'might is right'.

Though it was usually held that the law of nature is obligatory because it is the will of God, it was also insisted that the will of God is not arbitrary. If it were arbitrary, it could not be discovered by reason. God wills the good of His creatures; and the rules making for this good are the laws of nature. Reason discovers the content of these rules, and God's command that men shall obey them makes them obligatory.

Already, two generations before *Leviathan* was published, a Christian philosopher had denied that the ground of the obligation to obey the laws of nature lay in God's will. Suárez had argued that it follows, merely from man's being the sort of creature he is, that he ought to behave in some ways and not in others. The difference between right and wrong is not an effect of anyone's will, not even God's, though God necessarily commands what is right and forbids what is wrong. A few years after Suárez, we find the same argument in Grotius. 'The law of nature', he says, 'is a dictate of right reason, which points out that an act, according as it is or is not in conformity with rational nature, has in it a quality of moral baseness or moral necessity; and that, in consequence, such an act is either forbidden or enjoined by the author of nature, God'.[1] The law of nature is thus not obligatory because it is the will of God; it is grounded in reason, and God commands us to obey it because it is right that we should do so.[2]

If we compare Hobbes's with the traditional account of the law of nature, and also with the views of Suárez and Grotius, certain differences are immediately apparent. Hobbes does not put together psychological laws or uniformities of behaviour and rules of conduct. His laws of nature are all prescriptive; they tell us what men should do and not how they in fact behave. Again, though the laws of nature, for Hobbes as for Suárez and Grotius and everyone else, are discovered by reason, the discovery is differently conceived. Reason, in Hobbes's account of the matter, does not tell us that, because men are rational and are capable of deliberate choice, it follows that they ought to observe certain rules in their behaviour towards one another; reason does not infer the laws of nature from the nature of man or from God's purposes for men. Nor yet does reason directly apprehend without inference that man ought to keep these laws. According to Hobbes, man, by reflecting on his experience, discovers that, if he is to have peace, he ought to observe certain rules in his dealings with other men whenever he has sufficient grounds for believing that they will do so too. Hobbes's laws of nature are precepts of reason; they are rules of conduct. The question is, are they moral rules?

Hobbes says that a law of nature 'is a precept or general rule,

---

[1] *De jure belli ac pacis* (first published in 1625), I.i.10.
[2] The laws of nature, as precepts discovered by reason, were treated either as inferences from man's essential nature or as self-evident truths. It was sometimes said that, because man is rational and provident and aware that there are other creatures like himself, he ought to keep certain rules in his behaviour towards these creatures. Or else it was put forward as a self-evident truth, directly apprehended by reason, that a rational creature ought to keep these rules. That is to say, the rules were not inferred from statements about man's nature but were treated as ultimate principles not requiring further justification, being themselves self-evident. That moral principles cannot be true or false was, of course, an idea foreign to the natural law philosophers of the seventeenth century.

found out by reason, by which a man is forbidden to do that, which is destructive of his life, or taketh away the means of preserving the same; and to omit that, by which he thinketh it may be best preserved'.[1] The laws of nature have thus been termed 'maxims of prudence'. As a mere precept or general rule found out by reason, as a maxim of prudence, a law of nature is not a moral rule. For a precept of reason or maxim of prudence, merely as such, is only a rule which it is our interest to follow, and is therefore not obligatory in the sense that a moral rule is so.

Nor is it obligatory in the peculiar sense in which Hobbes understands moral obligation; for he speaks as if, where there was no law properly so called, there could be no moral obligation. And he says that law, *properly*, is 'the word of him, that by right hath command over others'.[2] As mere precepts of reason, the laws of nature are 'but conclusions, or theorems concerning what conduceth to the conservation and defence'[3] of those who reach the conclusions. Or, to speak more accurately, they are conclusions about what, given certain conditions, would conduce to their conservation. If then it is said that they ought, if they can, to create those conditions, nothing more is meant than that it is reasonable that they should. The *ought* does not here refer to what anyone, even Hobbes, would call a moral obligation. For Hobbes does not assert the morality of the laws of nature until after he has explained that it is only as commands of God that they can be *properly* laws, even where there is as yet no human sovereign to enforce them.

Speaking of law 'properly' so called, Hobbes says that it is not counsel but command, and is *obligatory* (in some stronger sense than a mere precept of reason is so) only because it is a command. And what makes it a command is not its being couched in the imperative but the commander's power to compel obedience.

Though Hobbes defines law as the word of him that by right has command over others, he uses arguments which imply, not only that there is no right of command without effective power, but also that where there is such power there is always a right of command. For example, he holds that the subjects of a conqueror, as much as those of a ruler established by express consent, are obliged to obey him.

Hobbes also says that all allegiance, at least of man to man, rests on consent, on a covenant express or tacit. Even the conqueror has

---

[1] *Leviathan*, ch. 14.
[2] Ibid., ch. 15.
[3] Ibid.

the consent of his subjects, who must be presumed to have promised obedience to him in return for his not having killed them, which he, having the power to do it, could rightfully have done. Now, if this is consent, it surely follows that a man consents whenever he obeys because he thinks that he has more to lose than to gain by not doing so. If, then, consent, thus conceived, creates a duty of obedience, anyone who can contrive that others have more to lose than to gain by obeying him (and according to Hobbes they will obey him if they see that it is so, for such is their nature) acquires a right of command over them. In other words, where there is effective power to command, there is consent to that power, and therefore a duty of obedience and a right of command.

But if this is consent, it would seem to follow that God's authority, no less than man's, rests on consent; for surely God's position in relation to those who believe in Him is the same, in all relevant respects, as the conqueror's in relation to the conquered. True, God's power is not created by men's submitting to His will because they see they have more to gain than to lose by submission, but then neither is the conqueror's created by the submission of the conquered. In both cases, submission is an effect of power and not a cause of it. Therefore, if submission is an act of consent which bestows authority in the one case, it must surely be so in the other.

Hobbes says or implies in several places that authority springs from the consent of those subject to it, and he does so in contexts which do not always suggest that he has only human authority in mind. Indeed, in one or two places, it would seem that he is speaking of divine as well as of human authority.[1] But why, we may ask, does

[1] Howard Warrender, in the first part of the tenth chapter of his book, *The Political Philosophy of Hobbes* (Oxford 1957), though he does not deny that Hobbes sometimes speaks as if all obligation rested on covenant, says that this is not his true position. Hobbes, he says, does not really hold that even obligations under natural law rest on consent. Yet there are arguments in Hobbes which clearly imply the contrary, as for example the argument that atheism is no sin (see *De cive*, in the English translation, Hobbes's *English Works* vol. 2, pp. 197–9). According to Hobbes, sin, as distinguished from mere crime, is an offence against God's law, though, of course, since God commands those who believe in Him to obey the civil law, any believer who offends against that law is guilty of both sin and crime. But how, asks Hobbes, can a man sin who denies that there is a God, or that He governs the world? For such a man can say that he never submitted his will to God's, not conceiving Him so much as to exist. Though atheists are in God's power, He cannot command them or receive obedience from them; for there can be command and obedience only where the commander makes his will known to those he requires to obey him, which he cannot do if they do not believe He exists. Atheists are *enemies* but not *subjects* of God, for they have not submitted to Him, acknowledging His existence and

he speak of consent at all in this connection? Why is he not content to say, without more ado, that effective power creates an obligation to obey and therefore a right of command? Partly, perhaps, because he wants to turn the tables on writers who, arguing that authority rests on consent, conclude that it is wrong to compel obedience where there has been no consent. Hobbes's reply to them is that, wherever power is effective, it is to men's advantage to submit to it, and that when they submit from this motive (and they cannot submit from any other) the submission is consent. And partly perhaps (and it is then that he has specifically human authority clearly in mind) because it occurs to him that no man can compel obedience of a multitude of subjects unless there are some men willing to comply with his wishes without being compelled. Human power depends on human willingness to obey, as divine power does not. But Hobbes, if he had distinguished more clearly between power and authority, could have admitted this readily without needing to argue that authority (even the human kind) always springs from the consent of those subject to it.

It is perhaps not important to decide whether Hobbes believed that all authority, or only the human kind, is established by consent. For what he says about consent does not explain what he means by obligation, in the stronger sense in which a precept of reason is not a rule which men are obliged to obey, nor yet what he means by *law*, the concept to which he relates *obligation* in this stronger sense.

His power. Now, in Hobbes's view (peculiar though it may be), to submit to power is to consent to it and to oblige yourself to obey its possessor. Indeed, strictly speaking, submission also creates the *power to command* as distinct from the *power to use*. No one, no matter how great his power, can have command over me unless I choose to obey him on account of his power. He may use me as a tool but may not command me unless I submit to his power. Not even if He is God and omnipotent; though, being God and omnipotent, He can, if He chooses, cause me to submit to His power.

It is true that Hobbes distinguishes between God's peculiar authority over the Jews, which was established by express covenant, and His general authority over all men who believe in Him. For this general authority to exist, it is enough that there should be a God who commands men on pain of punishment if they disobey Him, and that men should believe He does so. Authority, as Hobbes conceives of it, requires no more than that those subject to it submit to a power which they believe is great enough to ensure that they stand to lose more than they gain by disobedience to it; and this submission is a tacit covenant as distinct from an express one. But if men are so situated that there is no one already powerful enough to make it worth their while to submit to him, and if they think it their interest that there should be, a tacit covenant is no longer enough. They must then choose someone to submit to and must ensure that he has the power to compel obedience; they must set up a ruler by express covenant, who will be a sovereign by institution.

But it is important to notice that Hobbes, when he describes the laws of nature as laws, properly so called, and treats them as *obligatory* in a stronger sense, always thinks of them as commands. Sometimes he speaks as if they were not properly laws until there is a human ruler to enforce obedience to them, and at other times says that they are laws 'properly' so called merely as commands of God. And it is also to be noticed that Hobbes, though he sometimes says of the laws of nature that, as commands of God, they are moral laws, and calls the obligation to obey them a moral obligation, does not speak of that obligation as if it were different in kind from what the obligation to obey merely civil laws would be in a world in which there was no God. For all that he *sometimes*[1] seems to be arguing that men by consent or covenant can oblige themselves to obey a human ruler only because they are already obliged by God's law to perform their covenants, he never distinguishes between moral and legal obligation. By which I mean both that he fails to explain how they differ and that nothing like an adequate distinction between them is implicit in what he says.

For Hobbes, as for Bentham after him, a man is not obliged to conform to a rule, in the stronger sense of obligation, unless breach of it makes him liable to punishment either by God or by man. But to call a rule *moral* (as Hobbes does) when the breach of it makes us liable to divine punishment, or (as Bentham does) when it exposes us to the ill-will or disapproval of others, is not to distinguish between properly moral obligation and other kinds. It is characteristic of a moral rule that the breaker of it, if he recognizes that it is a moral rule and that he has broken it, *condemns himself* for doing so. No doubt, others may blame him for breaking the rule, but he will not look upon it as a moral rule merely on that account. This *self-condemnation* is quite different from the fear, regret, irritation or embarrassment he may feel when he breaks a rule of some other kind. And if he merely uses a rule to guide his own conduct or to influence the behaviour of others, that is no sign that he takes it for a moral rule; for he may so use what he thinks of as no more than a maxim of prudence. Where there is a moral rule there is an internal censor. And though this aspect of moral rules, being difficult to explain, was not much enlarged upon by moral philosophers before the time of Rousseau and Kant, it was already implicit in the notion of conscience. From Rousseau's time to

---

[1] I say *sometimes* deliberately because Hobbes, when he speaks of the covenant establishing a human sovereign, often treats the laws of nature as mere precepts of reason, forgetting that they are also commands of God.

Freud's, many theories have been produced to explain this internal censorship and its social and psychological causes and functions, but no theory which quite neglects it takes account of what is properly moral obligation.

How, accoᵣ   ᴐbes, are men obliged to obey God's laws? 'To those the   ᴐe power is irresistible, the dominion of all men adhereth naturally by their excellence of power; and consequently it is from that power, that the kingdom over men . . . belongeth naturally to God Almighty; not as Creator, and gracious; but as omnipotent.'[1] According to Hobbes, men are so made that they always act from hope of advantage (or fear of hurt) to themselves. If then there is an omnipotent God who commands and forbids them on pain of punishment if they disobey, they cannot help but obey Him while they actually have in mind how they stand in relation to Him. For they then know that their every thought and action is open to Him and that He can do what he pleases with them. Whenever God is truly present to their minds, they, being the sort of creatures they are, necessarily obey Him. This, I take it, is what Hobbes understands by man's obligation to God, for it is what follows logically from what he says. But, as I hope to show in a moment, in order that men should be so placed in relation to someone that, while they have in mind what that relation is, they necessarily obey him, there is no need for him to be omnipotent. The obligation to obey God, as Hobbes conceives of it, does not differ in kind, but only in extent, from the obligation which some men could have to others even in a godless world.

Long before Hobbes's time, it had been said that men are obliged to obey God because He is omnipotent. This way of speaking was traditional; but it was only a part of the tradition. It had also, and often, been said that men are obliged to obey God because He made and loves them, and desires their good. Thus, to borrow the words of Hobbes, 'the kingdom over men' belongs 'naturally' to God, not merely (or even primarily) as 'omnipotent', but 'as Creator and gracious'. Now *obligation* in this sense (though the writers who speak of it do not define it) is clearly not obligation in the sense understood by Hobbes. If I am obliged to obey God because He made me and loves me (and not only me but other men, whose brother I am as sharing in this love), my obligation clearly does not consist in my necessarily choosing to obey Him whenever His omnipotence is truly present to my mind because I happen to be the sort of creature who always acts from hope of benefit or fear of hurt to himself. Hobbes's peculiar

[1] *Leviathan*, ch. 31.

sense of obligation is not moral obligation as we ordinarily understand it, whereas the traditional conception of man's duty to God may be so, at least in part. I do not mean that we can find in writers before Hobbes an account that we should find satisfactory of what moral obligation is, but only that they habitually speak of man's obligation to obey God in ways that suggest that it is, or may be, a genuine moral obligation.

It has been questioned whether Hobbes seriously considered the laws of nature to be divine commands. He has often been accused of atheism. Whether he was an atheist or not, I do not know. Though God is given a conspicuous part in his political philosophy, that part is equivocal. The laws of nature are properly laws, says Hobbes, only because they are the commands of God; for it is their being so that makes them obligatory. One of the laws of nature is that men should keep their covenants; and temporal authority is established by covenant. It would therefore seem that Hobbes wants to derive the obligation to obey the holder of temporal authority, the sovereign, from a prior obligation to obey God. Yet he also says that in the state of nature the laws of nature oblige only *in foro interno* and not *in foro externo*; or, as he puts it, 'they bind to a desire they should take place: but . . . to the putting them in act, not always'.[1] This seems to mean that in the state of nature we are always obliged to desire that the laws of nature, which are God's laws, should be obeyed, but are not always obliged to obey them. It is odd to speak of our being obliged to desire that something should be done, when nobody may be obliged to do it. And Hobbes is putting it far too mildly when he says that the laws of nature, in the state of nature, oblige *in foro externo* 'not always'. If he had said 'scarcely ever', or even 'not at all', he would have come closer to saying what he meant. For he also says that, in the state of nature, men have a right to all things, even to one another's bodies, which is surely to imply that they have no obligation, at least *in foro externo*.

Howard Warrender, in a notable work entitled *The Political Philosophy of Hobbes*, suggests that by obligation *in foro interno* Hobbes meant something more than just the duty to desire or to intend keeping God's law – that he meant the duty to be always prepared to keep it when it can be kept safely, and to be always seeking for ways to create the conditions which make it safe to keep it. This is a generous interpretation of Hobbes's actual words; but let us not quarrel with generosity. We are always obliged to obey the laws

---

[1] *Leviathan*, ch. 15.

of nature if it is safe to do so; we are obliged *in foro externo* on this condition; but unfortunately the condition almost never holds in the state of nature, for it is almost never safe for us actually to do what the laws enjoin. What, however, we always can do, even in the state of nature, is hold ourselves in readiness to obey the laws when obedience is safe and also seek the means of making it safe. There is, as Warrender points out, a real difference between just desiring that something should happen, and being always prepared to do whatever is needed to make it happen as soon as occasion serves.

According to Warrender, we must, if we are to do justice to Hobbes, distinguish between what makes an action a duty and the conditions which provide a sufficient motive for doing it. Thus, we can say both that it is our duty to obey the laws of nature when we can safely do so only because God has commanded obedience on that condition, and that it is the sovereign who makes it safe for us to obey them. That is, we can say that God lays our natural duties upon us while the sovereign provides us with a sufficient motive for doing them. Therefore, even though it is the sovereign who maintains the social order in which alone nearly all our duties hold, we would have no duty to the sovereign unless we had a prior duty to God. It is my duty to do X under conditions Y only because God commands it, but it is the sovereign who creates these conditions. This is what Warrender understands Hobbes to mean.

To show that Warrender is reading more into Hobbes than is there would be a laborious task requiring close scrutiny of several difficult passages in *Leviathan* and *De cive*. It would also be wasted labour. Perhaps Hobbes did believe that there could be no genuine obligation to the sovereign unless there were a prior obligation to God. But, if he did, he ought not to have done so, for it is a belief that does not square with his own account of obligation. If obligation is what Hobbes says it is, there is no need whatever to derive our duty to man from our duty to God.

According to Hobbes, we are obliged to obey another person when we are so related to him that, if we see that relation clearly, we cannot help but choose to do what he commands. But we can be so related to man and not only to God. True, God alone is omnipotent and omniscient, so that we can say only of Him that we are always obliged to obey *all* His commands. For it must always be true that, if we see clearly how we are related to God, we cannot choose but obey Him. No sovereign is omniscient or omnipotent; no sovereign's punishments are inescapable. It cannot therefore be true of any sovereign that we are always so related to him that, if we see the relation clearly, we can never choose to disobey. But that does not mean that we cannot often be so related to him that, if we see the relation clearly, we must choose to obey. Whenever I stand to gain more than I lose by obeying the sovereign, I am, in Hobbes's sense of obligation, obliged to obey; for if I saw clearly how I stood, I would necessarily choose to obey. Man is so made, Hobbes tells us, that he always acts from hope of benefit or fear of hurt to himself. No more is required to create obligation, in Hobbes's sense, than that someone should be powerful enough to ensure that someone else has more to gain than to lose by obeying his commands. Thus, if we accept Hobbes's account of obligation, we simply cannot say that the duty to obey man must always derive ultimately from the duty to obey God. We can say, of course, that we have a perfect duty of obedience only to God, in the sense that we ought to do whatever He commands; for, being omniscient, He will never command what we cannot do, and being omnipotent can always punish us for disobedience. We can say that the obligation to obey man is limited in ways in which the obligation to obey God is not. But that does not make it a different kind of obligation, or require that it should derive from a prior obligation to obey God.

Suppose we leave God out of Hobbes's political philosophy, and treat the laws of nature as no more than maxims of prudence. Can we then explain how men could come to make a covenant setting up a sovereign and to have an adequate motive for keeping it? It has often been denied that we can explain it, both by defenders of Hobbes who have wanted to put the most favourable interpretation on his theory, and by detractors. The defenders have therefore been inclined to make as much as they could of his doctrine that the laws of nature are commands of God, while the detractors have sometimes treated it as a piece of hypocrisy to mask the true nature of his philosophy. But the truth is that it is not at all difficult to explain how, even in a godless world, complete egoists come to make and keep an agreement to set up a ruler over them. It may be that Hobbes never saw clearly how this could be done; and yet all the elements that go to make up this explanation are to be found in *Leviathan* and *De cive*, though they are there so mixed up with other things that it is not easy to see how they fit together into a consistent whole.

I want now to try to fit that explanation together, and to show that every part of it is to be found in what Hobbes actually wrote. But before I do this, I must utter a word of warning. Though the explanation is all to be found in Hobbes, it is not to be taken for Hobbes's political philosophy, or to be treated as the essential part of it. It is merely extracted from that philosophy, and was probably never seen by Hobbes himself as a single and consistent argument. It would be a solecism to treat it as the core of his theory and what is mixed up with it as padding. It is, however, important historically, because it is the elements in his theory that go to make it up that have attracted the most attention. For it is not as a natural law philosopher in the traditional sense that Hobbes is remembered; it is rather as the writer who tried to explain men's political behaviour entirely in terms of self-interest.

IV. THE MAKING AND KEEPING OF THE COVENANT

Even if we suppose that the laws of nature are not commands of God, and that therefore no one in the state of nature is obliged, even in Hobbes's sense of obligation, to keep them, we can still say that men ought to keep them when it is safe to do so. The 'ought' here refers neither to moral obligation as ordinarily understood nor to obligation in Hobbes's sense; it is not their duty to keep these laws, it is only their interest.

The first two among Hobbes's nineteen (or, rather, twenty) laws of nature are rules that men ought to keep, in this sense of ought, even in the state of nature. The first law is the precept or rule, 'That every man, ought to endeavour peace, as far as he has hope of obtaining it; and when he cannot obtain it, that he may seek, and use, all helps, and advantages of war'.[1] This is a precept which men can follow even in the absence of government; and as it is their obvious interest to follow it, they ought to do so. Now, in the state of nature, as Hobbes describes it, men cannot get peace. The rule that they ought to seek peace is therefore equivalent to the rule that they ought to try to put an end to the state of nature. They have tasted in full the miseries of that state, and have conceived of something incomparably better, which is peace. Being rational and inventive creatures who can learn from experience, men are able both to imagine a condition different from the one in which they find themselves and to devise means of bringing it about. The first rule does not tell them to desire peace (for their miseries in the state of nature are sufficient to make them do that) but to endeavour it: to look out for ways of getting it, and

[1] *Leviathan*, ch. 14.

to be prepared to do whatever has to be done to obtain it.

Though the rule, as a maxim of prudence, is only a piece of advice, there is really as much force to it as if men were obliged, *in foro interno*, to keep it. Their condition in the state of nature is desperate, and their desire to put an end to that state is urgent and strong. By leaving God out of the picture, and doing away with all obligation, even in Hobbes's sense, in the state of nature, we have not really weakened men's motives for getting themselves out of that state. For the state of nature, as Hobbes depicts it, is to all practical intents and purposes a godless state – because men, when they are in it, stand so little in awe of God that they cannot even trust one another to keep God's laws. It is not the urge to obey God but to keep themselves alive which impels them to endeavour peace. Hobbes makes this abundantly clear, for all that he speaks so often of God and of obligation *in foro interno*.

The second law of nature is also a rule which men, in their own interest, ought to keep, even in the state of nature. It is the rule, 'That a man be willing, when others are so too, as far-forth, as for peace, and defence of himself he shall think it necessary, to lay down this right to all things (which he has in the state of nature); and be contented with so much liberty against other men, as he would allow other men against himself'.[1] Anyone who, in the state of nature, in fact renounced his right to anything unless others did so too would be a simpleton, a fool, and would pay dearly for his folly by placing himself at the mercy of others. But if he refused to lay down his right when others were willing to lay down theirs, they would combine against him and destroy him as an obstacle in the way of their getting peace. The second law of nature is a corollary of the first: it tells us what is actually involved in the endeavour to seek peace. As a word of advice, as a maxim of prudence, it is every bit as strong as the first law. Though it is true that in the state of nature men are profoundly distrustful of one another, and for that reason reluctant to make concessions, it is also true that their condition is intolerable and that they are desperately anxious to get out of it. Every man knows that the fears and miseries which are his lot are also the lot of others, and that the others must be as eager as he is to put an end to them. Admittedly, Hobbes's picture of the state of nature is pure fantasy. Yet if we are to see the force of his argument, we must look at the whole of that picture. If men were deeply mistrustful of one another without also being deeply afraid, they would have no strong motive for endeavouring peace and laying down their rights conditionally.

[1] Ibid.

Or if each man were afraid without knowing that the others were so too, no one could reckon on other people's desiring peace as strongly as he himself desires it. But that is not the condition of men in 'mere nature'; for though they are afraid and mistrustful, they also long for peace, and know that others do so too.

Hobbes says of the laws of nature, that 'they have been contracted into one easy sum, intelligible even to the meanest capacity; and that is, *Do not that to another, which thou wouldest not have done to thyself*'.[1] All that a man need do to feel the force of the laws of nature is to put himself in other men's shoes, considering their predicament as if it were his own. The first two laws are preliminary to the rest: they require men in the state of nature to endeavour to create the conditions which make it reasonable for them to keep the other laws. They are equivalent to the precept, *Try to make it safe for everyone to follow the rule, Do not that to another, which thou wouldest not have done to thyself.*

It is with the third law of nature, *That men perform their covenants made*, that our difficulties begin. Can men keep to it in the state of nature? Hobbes tells us that covenants without a power strong enough to enforce them are void, and that in the state of nature there is no such power. And yet a covenant is needed to create that power; for in the state of nature men are equal, and can therefore set up a power strong enough to coerce them only by agreement. It would appear, then, at first sight, that the covenant is both necessary and impossible.

Is this a genuine dilemma? Or can the covenant establishing civil society of itself create the power needed to enforce it? That, certainly, is what Hobbes would have us believe. He distinguishes between two kinds of covenant: those in which the contracting parties do not simultaneously perform what they promise, and those in which they do. Covenants of the first kind require mutual trust, which Hobbes thinks is nearly always unreasonable in the state of nature, there being no power to enforce covenants. For, says Hobbes, 'he that performeth first, has no assurance the other will perform after; because the bonds of words are too weak to bridle men's ambition, avarice, anger, and other passions, without the fear of some coercive power; which in the condition of mere nature . . . cannot possibly be supposed'.[2]

Covenants of the second kind do not require mutual trust, because the parties to them all keep their promises at the same time. It looks therefore as if the covenant setting up the sovereign, if it is really to set him up, must be a covenant of this second kind. Hobbes clearly

[1] Ibid., ch. 15.
[2] Ibid., ch. 14.

thought that it was, for he spoke of all men renouncing their natural rights at the same time. This renunciation somehow creates the power which makes it impossible for those who renounce their rights to take them back again. Having said that 'Covenants, without the sword, are but words, and of no strength to secure [that is, compel] a man at all',[1] Hobbes, a little further on, continues thus: 'The only way to erect such a common power. . .is [for all men] to confer all their power and strength upon one man, or upon one assembly of men, that may reduce all their wills, by plurality of voices, unto one will.'[2] The covenant can set up the sovereign needed to enforce it because the making of it actually consists in a simultaneous renunciation of their rights by all parties to it in favour of some man or assembly that is not a party to it; and this renunciation of rights is a conferring of power.

That is how Hobbes presents the matter; and there can be no doubt that he found his argument convincing. But will it really do? Let us begin by asking: What is involved in all men's conferring power on some one man, in their renouncing rights in his favour? Power and right, after all, are not physical objects which can be handed over at one stroke, on a single occasion, by some persons to others. They are not weapons whose surrender gives overwhelming strength to whoever takes them. A grant of power is a promise made by one man in favour of another, whereby he undertakes so to behave *in the future* that the other will be able to do what he could not do before. If ten men promise one another to obey an eleventh man, that man has no greater power over them than they have over each other, unless they in fact keep their promises. It is not their making the promises but their keeping them that gives him power. If his power alone can make them keep their promises, and yet he has no power unless they keep them, their condition does not change; they remain in the state of nature and have no sovereign over them. Hobbes has confused himself and his readers by taking it for granted that a simultaneous renunciation of natural rights in favour of a particular person or assembly is equivalent to a grant of power to him or them, even when the persons who renounce the rights have no good reason to trust one another until there is a common power over them. The renunciation of these rights is not the *present* performance of the covenant required to make Hobbes's argument valid; it is merely a promise of *future* behaviour which, unless most of the people who

---

[1] Ibid., ch. 17.
[2] Ibid.

make the promise keep it, can create no power capable of coercing the few who may choose to break it. Hobbes tried to show that there can be no confidence where there is no power to force the unwilling to keep their promises. What he failed to see is that there can be no power where there is no confidence.

Are we therefore left with an insoluble dilemma? Only if we pose the problem as Hobbes posed it; only if we insist on saying that in the state of mere nature 'covenants without the sword are but words'. But we do not need to say this even if we accept Hobbes's doctrine of the irremediable egoism of man and his account of the state of nature. No doubt, covenants without the sword have no strength to *compel* a man; and no doubt, too, covenants, of themselves, while no one is strong enough to enforce them, can create no obligation, in Hobbes's sense of the word. If there were an obligation to keep a covenant in the state of nature, it could be only an obligation to God; and in any case, in Hobbes's opinion, if the covenant involved future performance, the obligation could only be *in foro interno* and not to 'putting it in act'. But we have agreed to take no account of God, and therefore must not speak of obligation, even in Hobbes's peculiar sense (and there is no question of any other) in the state of nature. It is a state without obligation, and also without power, since Hobbes tells us that all men are equal in it. And yet, though no one has obligations or power, men can still have an adequate motive for keeping their covenants. I am speaking, of course, of men as Hobbes described them in the state of nature: of creatures entirely self-regarding, without benevolence, honour or pity, and whose passions are apt to get the better of their reason.

Men like that could not, of course, trust one another to keep a covenant when it was to their immediate advantage to break it; they could not trust one another to keep it merely because they had more to gain than to lose in the long run by keeping it. For Hobbes, though he supposes that reason in men is strong enough to enable them to discover what is in their enduring interest, also supposes that they are liable to strong passions which shut their eyes to that interest. They will often be tempted to break the covenant, and the mere belief that it is, in the long run, to their advantage to keep it will not often move them to resist the temptation. Some men, no doubt, are cooler and wiser than others, but, unfortunately, it is not to their advantage to keep the covenant unless they are assured that the others will also keep it. If the unwise and improvident do not keep the covenant, they defeat the purpose for which the covenant was made, so that it is no longer the interest, even of the wise and provident, to keep it. That is why Hobbes insists so much that unless the foolish are frightened into keeping the covenant when they have a mind to break it, the wise would be foolish to keep it.

Hobbes was right to insist on this, but he was wrong to speak of the covenant as involving an immediate keeping of their promises by the parties to it. He was wrong to speak as if obedience and trust were effects of the sovereign's power and not also causes of it. He forgot, at least in this part of his argument, an important fact. Even though no man may trust another to keep the covenant when the other stands to gain by breaking it, he can rely on his sympathy and assistance against any third man who breaks it. For, given the situation as Hobbes describes it, it is the interest of every man that every other man should keep the covenant. It is therefore his interest that the sovereign should have the power to punish any law-breaker except himself. Though he may not trust anyone to keep the covenant who is sorely tempted to break it, he can rely on everyone else being against the breaker of it. The covenant makes the sovereign powerful, not at all because it involves an immediate keeping of promises, but because it creates a situation in which it becomes everyone's interest that some definite person (the sovereign) should get the better of anyone else he seeks to coerce. I want the sovereign to be able to coerce everyone except me, and everyone else has a desire similar to mine. This is enough to ensure that the covenant makes the sovereign sufficiently powerful to be able to punish anyone who breaks the covenant. The sovereign is powerful because he can ordinarily rely on the support of all his subjects except the law-breaker against the law-breaker; his power is not, in the first instance, a cause of trust but an effect of it.

Thus, though it may be true to say that covenants without the sword are of no strength to *compel* a man, it is false that without the sword they are *but words*, if by this is meant that they do not change the situation. There can be no sword, no power, unless they do change the situation. The mere designation of the sovereign creates an interest which did not exist before, an interest which is not an effect of the sovereign's power but a condition of it; it makes it every man's interest that every other man should be obedient to some definite person. Hobbes mistakenly supposes that his two assertions, *covenants without the sword are of no strength to secure* and *covenants without the sword are but words*, are equivalent. But they are not so in the least, though they may seem to be so to the hasty reader. The covenant creates an alliance, which is none the less effective because the parties to it are entirely self-regarding and cannot trust one another to keep their word when they are strongly tempted to break it; it makes every man an ally of the sovereign against the law-breaker except when it is himself that breaks the law.

The makers of the covenant, when they promise to obey the sovereign, undertake not only to keep his laws but also to help him enforce them, if he requires their help; for both undertakings are clearly involved in the promise of complete obedience. Though the passions of an entirely selfish creature may often move him to break the laws, unless he is held in check by fear of punishment, they will hardly ever move him to obstruct the sovereign when he seeks to punish someone else. If the sovereign, as he must, appoints officers to give effect to his commands, he can rely on their loyalty, partly because he rewards their services and partly because it is everyone's interest that everyone else should obey the sovereign and his officers. No more than this is needed to make the sovereign's power effective. No 'one need trust anyone to be wise enough always to prefer social peace, his greatest good, to some immediate advantage, and there need not be (as indeed there cannot be) any simultaneous transferring of right or granting of power, any present performance of the covenant by all the parties to it.

There are passages in Hobbes that show that he knew this – that he knew that men's passions, though often tempting them to break the laws themselves, seldom prevent their siding with the law against other people. He did not, however, see the full implications of this fact, and therefore did not use it as he might have done to support his own theory. By saying that 'covenants, without the sword, are but words'; by insisting so much that confidence is an effect of power and forgetting that it is also a cause of it; by suggesting that completely selfish and imperfectly reasonable men cannot be relied upon to keep their promises except where there is a force strong enough to compel them; by treating the covenant as a simultaneous surrender of rights which of itself establishes an authority able to force people to keep their promises, Hobbes misled both himself and his readers. He quite unnecessarily posed the problem in a way that made it insoluble, and then undertook to solve it by treating the covenant as if it were an act involving a *present* performance of their promises by all the parties to it; whereas what it in fact involves is merely their all simultaneously making the same promise about future behaviour. I surrender, you surrender, he surrenders, we all surrender our rights at exactly the same moment and to the same person or assembly; nobody trusts anyone, and there is no simple-minded reliance on people's not breaking promises they cannot be compelled to keep. 'This', we are told, 'is the generation of that great LEVIATHAN, or rather, to speak more reverently, of that *mortal god*, to which we owe under the *immortal God*, our peace and defence.'[1]

This is magnificent, but it is not good sense.

V. HOBBES'S CONCEPTION OF NATURAL RIGHT AND THE USE HE MAKES OF IT

About Hobbes's conception of law there is no ambiguity; it may be inadequate, but at least it is clear. Law, properly so called, is 'the word of him, that by right hath command over others'. And it follows from Hobbes's account of obligation that anyone who can get himself obeyed has the right of command; for if any man can so place others in relation to him that, when they understand that relation, they cannot choose but do what he tells them, they are obliged to obedience and he has a right of command. But, as we shall see, this sense of right, which is enough to make clear Hobbes's definition of law, is not the sense he uses when he speaks of natural right. It is true that Hobbes speaks with two voices of the laws of nature, sometimes calling them dictates of reason and sometimes divine commands; and that he does not make it clear just how far men are obliged to obey them in the state of nature. This alternation and that obscurity do not, however, affect his definition of law, which is clear enough.

With natural right it is quite different. Hobbes's definition of it is not clear, and in any case offers no clue to either of the senses in which he most frequently uses the term. I shall try to show that Hobbes cannot afford to be clear about natural right – that he has, when he describes the state of nature, to use the term natural right in a sense different from the sense he has to use to explain what makes the sovereign's authority legitimate and absolute. I am not suggesting that Hobbes meant to be obscure; he was merely, as we all so often are, driven to obscurity by the unconscious need to cover up the defects of his argument.

Let us notice the extent of his confusion. 'The right of nature . . . is the liberty each man hath, to use his own power, as he will himself, for the preservation of his own nature. . . . By liberty, is understood . . . the absence of external impediments.'[2] In the state of nature, a man

[1] *Leviathan*, ch. 17.
[2] Ibid., ch. 14.

has a right to everything, even to another's body. Yet this right can be laid aside; it can be renounced or transferred. When a man transfers or renounces a right, he is obliged or bound not to hinder whoever gets the right from the benefit of it. The transference or renunciation of a right is a voluntary act, and the object of every such act is some good to the person who does it. Therefore there are some rights which no man can renounce or transfer, even though he goes through the motions of doing it. A man cannot, for example, lay down his right of resisting anyone who tries to kill or wound or imprison him; for he can have nothing to gain by laying it down. If he promises not to resist, the promise is void.

All this is wonderfully confused. We are told that in the state of nature man has a right to all things, which means, perhaps, that he has a right to anything which he deems necessary to his security, and that he is sole judge of his need. This is the interpretation most favourable to Hobbes, though it is not the only one possible or even the one most in keeping with what Hobbes most often says.[1] But, however that may be, we can see that the word *right* cannot, in this sense, mean *power*, because the right to all things is not a power over all things. In the perilous state of nature, where man is said to have a right to all things, he very clearly is not able to get whatever he wants, or even whatever he deems necessary to his security. And yet, if natural right is called a liberty, and liberty is defined as absence of external impediments, it follows that natural right is a power. The natural right to all things is then the power to get all things – which is absurd, since no man can have this power, and least of all in the state of nature.

Those who say, without qualification, that Hobbes equates natural right and power are mistaken, but so too are those who insist that he distinguishes between them. He sometimes does the one and sometimes the other. No doubt, he does not say, in so many words, that natural right is merely a power, because he wants to set very wide limits to natural right, and indeed usually speaks of it as if it

[1] Ordinarily – and I shall discuss this point again later – Hobbes, when he speaks of the natural right to all things, does not trouble to say 'all things necessary to security'. Moreover, he does say that man, when he acts, *always* seeks his own good and not other people's. Therefore man has a natural right to whatever he thinks beneficial to himself, no matter how much it harms others, provided that what harms them does not also harm him. But my purpose here is to examine how Hobbes uses social and political concepts, and so I do not consider the difficulties he gets into by assuming that man always acts from hope of benefit or fear of hurt to himself.

were unlimited, which power clearly is not; and yet, when he calls natural right a liberty he does suggest that it is a mere power, for that is what follows from his definition of liberty. Though he is aware that power is always limited, and never more so than in the state of nature, Hobbes, at least in his unguarded moments, suggests that, in that state, natural right is unlimited; and even when he speaks more cautiously, he still suggests that it is limited only by the obligation not to harm other people unreasonably – that is to say, not to harm them when by so doing we add nothing to our own security. Hobbes seeks to derive the sovereign's authority from natural right, and also wants to make that authority virtually absolute. He wants to show that the sovereign's authority is both absolute and legitimate because it derives from a transference or renunciation of natural rights which are virtually unlimited.

As a matter of fact, there is a sense of the word 'right' which does allow us to say that all men have a right to all things, though we nearly always use it for a much more limited purpose. Sometimes, when we say that a man has a right to something, we do so without implying that other people have duties to him. When we do this, all that we mean is that there is no law or rule which prescribes what he shall do. Now, it is precisely because we normally think of man as a creature who has obligations that we sometimes feel the need to say that, in a particular situation, there is nothing which he is obliged to do; and sometimes we say this by remarking that he has the right to do whatever he pleases. When we speak in this way, we are putting what is essentially a negative statement in a positive form. What we mean is that he has *no* obligation, and what we say is that he has an unlimited right. In this sense, Robinson Crusoe, while he was alone on his island, had a right to everything. This is not an unusual, and is even a quite proper, use of the word 'right'. But it is worth noticing that when we speak in this way, we are nearly always speaking about moral persons in unusual situations – about persons who, though they normally do have obligations to other people, have none for the time being, situated as they are. We are not inclined to say that the wild beasts in the jungle have a right to everything merely because they have no duties.

Still, we could extend this negative use of the word 'right' to serve a wider purpose than it usually serves. We could imagine a condition of mankind where there were no rules of conduct, positive or moral, and therefore no duties; and we could then say that all men, being in that condition, had a right to everything. It may be that this is what Hobbes was saying, at least part of the time, when he was speaking of natural right. In the fourteenth chapter of *Leviathan* he warns us that we must not confuse *jus* and *lex, right* and *law*; because 'law and right, differ as much as obligation and liberty; which in one and the same matter are inconsistent'. It may well be that, in this passage, Hobbes meant by liberty not absence of external impediments, but absence of law and obligation.

Thus we have in *Leviathan* at least two senses of natural right; the first equates it with power and the second with absence of obligation. The first, as we have seen, clearly will not serve Hobbes's purpose; for a man's power is never more limited than in the state of nature, whereas Hobbes wants to say, at least some of the time, that natural right is unlimited. The second makes better sense on the face of it; for it is not absurd to speak of a complete absence of obligation as an unlimited right, and we can, without formal contradiction, attribute that right to everybody.

But this second sense, though it does not make it nonsense to speak of everyone's having a right to everything, will not do for Hobbes's purpose any better than the first. For Hobbes's purpose is to explain how the covenant, which he calls a mutual *transferring* of right, makes it the duty of subjects to obey the sovereign. Nor does this second sense square with his account of the laws of nature as commands of God.

If the laws of nature really are commands of God, we must have obligations even in Hobbes's state of nature. These obligations may be small but are none the less obligations for that. They are mostly obligations *in foro interno*; they require us, as we have seen, to endeavour peace and to be prepared, as soon as we can safely do so, to treat others as we would have them treat us. We may, in the state of nature, do anything that we think necessary to our self-preservation, and we alone can be judges of what is necessary. But we may do nothing to hurt anyone unless we do it to preserve ourselves; for we are obliged to endeavour peace, and this we cannot do unless, as far as we safely can, we so behave towards others as to cause them to trust us. If, for instance, in the state of nature, we make a promise which we can keep at slight risk to ourselves, we ought to keep it; for by so doing we teach other people to trust us in greater things. If the laws of nature are commands of God, it follows that we have duties even in the state of nature, and therefore do not have a right to everything.

It has been suggested[1] that Hobbes, when he speaks of everyone's

---

[1] By Warrender and others.

right to everything, does not mean to deny that men have obligations in the state of nature, but means only that, in that state, every man is always judge in his own case. God lays down the laws of nature but does not otherwise intervene in human affairs. He leaves it to everyone to decide for himself how these laws apply to particular cases. Until there is a sovereign, there is no one to judge between men. The natural right to all things is not therefore a complete absence of obligation; it is only absence of all responsibility of man to man. In the state of nature, man is responsible to God alone for what he does under divine law. Yet God gives man only the bare law; He neither interprets nor administers it in this world, so that each man must rely only on his own judgement until there is a human judge between him and other men. Therefore a man's right, in the state of nature, is whatever he honestly thinks it is; and this, we are sometimes told, is all that Hobbes means when he says that, in the absence of a common human superior, every man has a natural right to everything.

This argument is ingenious, but it is, I think, straining to do more than justice to Hobbes. It takes for granted that Hobbes ordinarily means, not what he most often says, but what he ought to say (and only sometimes implies) to make his account of natural right square with his account of natural law as divine command. The fact is that, nearly always, when Hobbes speaks of natural right, he does so as if he had forgotten all about the laws of nature being commands of God. We can, if we like, be charitable and put this down to mere carelessness, and so accept a not altogether convincing argument in Hobbes's defence. But, even then, we are left with a conception of natural right which cannot be reconciled with some of the things he says about the covenant establishing the sovereign's authority.

Hobbes speaks in two voices about this covenant. Sometimes, and more often, he speaks as if the makers of it *transferred* their rights to the sovereign, and sometimes, and less often, as if they merely renounced them. He feels the need to speak of it in the second way whenever he takes literally what he says about all men having a natural right to all things. If everyone has all the rights he can have, no one can possibly add to those rights. Thus we find Hobbes saying, 'For he that renounceth, or passeth away his right, giveth not to any other man a right which he had not before; because there is nothing to which every man had not right by nature: but only standeth out of his way, that he may enjoy his own original right, without hindrance from him'.[1] Thus the makers of a covenant, by agreeing not to exercise

---

[1] *Leviathan*, ch. 14.

their own natural rights as they have done hitherto, make it possible for the sovereign to exercise his right much more effectively. They cannot add to the sovereign's right; they can do no more than add to his power.

Now, this account of the covenant simply does not make sense if man's natural right to all things is taken to mean his responsibility to God alone for how he interprets and keeps the laws of nature. Natural right, thus understood, does not include the right to interpret the laws of nature on behalf of other people. If the man chosen to be sovereign did no more than retain his natural right, he would have no authority over others, and therefore would not be sovereign. To be sovereign he must have the right to interpret the laws of nature on behalf of other people; he must acquire a right he did not have before. He acquires it by means of the covenant only because his subjects have agreed that he shall have it. Each of them has agreed with the others that the person chosen to be sovereign shall interpret the laws of nature on his behalf.

Moreover, no man's direct responsibility to God for keeping God's law can cease with the setting up of the sovereign. If I owe it to God to keep His law, I may reasonably conclude that I shall be more likely to keep it, if I can agree with other men on a common superior to interpret and enforce that law on behalf of us all; but I am still obliged to obey that superior only if what he enforces is God's law or a law in keeping with it, and I can never divest myself of my prior responsibility to God. If, for example, I undertake to obey the sovereign whatever he commands, and reserve the right to resist him only when he threatens my life or liberty, I may be failing in my duty to God. I can do my duty to God to keep His law by unquestioning obedience to the sovereign only if this obedience is the best means of keeping God's law. But whether or not it is the best means is a question, not of right, but of fact. If I have one duty, and then, the better to perform it, I undertake another duty, I cannot put the second duty so entirely in the place of the first as to take it for granted that in doing the second I am also always doing the first; I can do the first in doing the second only if I have reasonable grounds for believing that the second is *in fact* a means to the first.

It might be argued that, on the assumptions made by Hobbes, I do have reasonable grounds for believing that by always obeying the sovereign I am also obeying God. For God, according to Hobbes, in requiring me to obey His laws, requires no more of me than that I should act wisely for my own preservation; and this I do if I never resist the sovereign except when he tries to destroy or imprison me.

But that is by no means obvious. By not resisting the sovereign now, when he is ill-treating other people but not me, I may make it more likely that he will destroy or imprison me in the future. To obey God's law I must estimate the danger to myself of the sovereign's action even when he does not now threaten me.

I conclude, therefore, that if we hold that, by man's natural right to everything, Hobbes means man's being responsible to God alone for interpreting and keeping God's law, we must also hold that Hobbes is logically bound to say that the covenant does give to the sovereign rights which he does not already have, and also that the subject can never divest himself of the duty to prefer God's law to the sovereign's, even when the sovereign is not trying to destroy or imprison him. But both these things Hobbes denied, the first sometimes and the second always.

However, I do not believe that this is the correct interpretation of what Hobbes meant by man's natural right to all things. I think it much more likely that he did not know exactly what he meant. It may sound presumptuous to say this about a philosopher who has often been praised for lucidity; but lucid though Hobbes may often have been, he was not so when he spoke of natural right. Even if we suppose that he meant by it merely the complete absence of all obligation, we are still left without a sense of natural right which can be reconciled with his account of the covenant and its effects. Let us see why this is so.

It is obvious that right, if it is mere absence of obligation, cannot be transferred, and Hobbes admits in several places that no right is transferred when the covenant is made. So far, so good. He does, however, say that when the covenant is made, rights are 'laid down' or renounced. What is involved in this renunciation? Hobbes speaks of the covenant as putting the parties to it under obligation. Therefore, to renounce a natural right is to lay oneself under an obligation. But this, too, is an odd way of speaking, for in a situation where there are no obligations of any kind, it is difficult to see how anyone could lay himself under an obligation merely by agreeing to something. As Hobbes himself puts it, 'covenants, without the sword, are but words, and of no strength to secure a man at all'; and, as we have seen already, it is not until the makers of the covenant keep it that there is a force strong enough to compel them to keep it. Unless there is a prior duty to obey God – which there cannot be if the natural right to all things means the complete absence of all obligation – no one in the state of nature can lay a duty on himself merely by being a party to a covenant. All he can do, if he and the others actually do what they say they intend to do, is help create a power which can coerce the recalcitrant; but it is only after the power has come into being that he can be said to have a duty to keep the covenant. All that happens when the covenant is made is that everyone agrees so to behave in the future that the person chosen for sovereign shall be able to compel obedience, and no obligation arises unless the parties to the covenant first keep it without being obliged to do so.[1] This is how we must speak of the covenant and its effects if we assume that the natural right to all things means the complete absence of obligation.

That is not how Hobbes speaks of it. Though he says that there are no rights actually transferred by the covenant, the effects of the covenant, as he describes them, imply the opposite. The covenant, Hobbes tells us, makes the sovereign the 'bearer' of his subjects' persons and their 'representative', and makes them the 'authors' of everything he does. Now, if natural right is only the complete absence of obligation, the covenant cannot have this effect. All that it can do, if the parties to it keep their word, is to make one man or body of men incomparably more powerful than anyone else. The sovereign can be his subjects' 'representative' and they the 'authors' of all his sovereign acts only if he has acquired from them a right, which he did not have already, to act on their behalf. This is implied by the ordinary sense of these words, and also, as the contexts prove, by the sense in which Hobbes uses them.

It is my belief that Hobbes gives at least three senses to 'natural right'. When he calls it a liberty and says that liberty is the absence of external impediments, he implies that a natural right is a power. But this first sense, though worth noticing, is not important; it merely follows from Hobbes's definitions, and is not a sense in which he actually uses the word when he describes the covenant or its effects. Nor is it a sense in which the word is ordinarily used; it is merely an aberration, something implied by certain words actually used by Hobbes but perhaps never seriously meant by him. Hobbes, I think, uses the word in the second sense, which is the complete absence of obligation, *only* when he describes the covenant, though not always even then. He uses it (but without realizing quite what the use commits him to) whenever he insists that there is no transferring

---

[1] If they keep the covenant, they create the power able to compel them on those occasions when they are tempted to break it; they create the situation where there are commands which, if they see their interest clearly, they necessarily choose to obey and are therefore (in Hobbes's sense) *obliged* to obey. But, if the situation arose without their creating it, they would also be obliged.

of rights when the covenant is made; for it is only if right is absence of obligation that it makes sense to say that, because everyone has a right to everything, no right can be acquired by covenant. As soon, however, as Hobbes moves on to discuss the *effects* of the covenant, he switches to a third sense of right, the most usual sense in which one man's right implies other men's duty. This is the sense that makes it possible for Hobbes to speak of the sovereign as his subjects' 'representative' and of subjects as the 'authors' of all the sovereign's public acts.

Hobbes makes great play with this notion that the sovereign is his subjects' representative. 'A multitude of men', he says, 'are made *one* person, when they are by one man, or one person, represented. . . . For it is the *unity* of the representer, not the *unity* of the represented, that maketh the person *one*'.[1] That is to say, a multitude are made one people, distinct from other peoples, by being represented by one man or body of men. We are also told that 'the essence of the commonwealth . . . is one person, of whose acts a great multitude, by mutual covenants one with another, have made themselves everyone the author'.[2] The multitude make no covenant with the sovereign, but by their agreements one with another give him the right to speak and decide for them all, authorizing his every public action as if it were their own.

From this argument, that the sovereign, though no party to the covenant, becomes in virtue of it his subjects' representative and they the authors of his sovereign acts, Hobbes draws his two most important practical conclusions: *firstly*, that subjects never have the right to change the form of their government, because they have bound themselves to obey a particular sovereign and acknowledge all his public acts for their own, and have thereby abandoned the right to put themselves, without his permission, under a similar obligation to anyone else; and, *secondly*, that subjects, because they make the covenant with one another and not with the sovereign, can never 'by any pretence of forfeiture' on his part 'be freed from his subjection'. The sovereign cannot injure though he can hurt them; for an injury is an injustice, and no man can injure himself. As subjects are authors of all the sovereign's acts, nothing that he does can be an injury and so give them the right to throw off his authority. Now, all this makes no sense if natural right is complete absence of obligation; it begins to make sense only if natural right is something that can be

---

[1] *Leviathan*, ch. 16.
[2] Ibid., ch. 17.

granted or transferred, which mere absence of obligation cannot be. The only kind of right that can be granted or transferred is the kind that implies obligation. Only if a house is mine, in the sense that I alone have the right to use it because other people are obliged to keep out of it, can I grant or transfer the right to use it to someone else. But rights, in this sense, cannot be unlimited and universal; if everyone has them, then no one can have a right to all things.

There is really no avoiding the conclusion that Hobbes, in his account of the covenant and its effects, shifts from one sense of natural right to another quite different from it. At one stage of his argument he admits that there can be no actual transfer of natural right, since everyone has a natural right to everything, and yet at all other stages he uses arguments which make no sense unless natural right can be transferred; and this it can be only if it implies obligation, and is therefore not a right to all things. Not content to show that it is always inexpedient or dangerous for subjects to try to change the system of government, or that they have no legal right to do so, Hobbes is eager to prove that they have no natural right to change it. Arguments about legitimacy ought to mean nothing to a man who takes natural right for absence of obligation.[1] But Hobbes is never more insistent than when he tries to prove that every established government, whatever it does, is always legitimate.

When I say that Hobbes's arguments about the effects of the covenant make sense only if natural right can be transferred, I do not mean that they are, on this condition, valid and conclusive. Even if natural right could be transferred, it still would not follow that, when a number of people agree with one another to obey unconditionally some person to whom they make no promise, they would have no right to release each other from the agreement merely because the person to be obeyed was no party to it. However we define right, this argument (which Hobbes makes so much of) is bad. We might as well argue that, if we all agree never to speak to someone whom we all dislike, we are forever bound by the agreement because the object of our dislike was not a party to it. In this trivial case, the argument is clearly defective; and is not the less so when used to settle an important question.

[1] Or, rather, his position ought to be that the legitimacy of a government consists only in its being reasonable for its subjects to obey it because its power is in fact effective. This, too, is a position taken up by Hobbes. But he also, especially when he spoke of the covenant's making the sovereign the 'representative' of his subjects, was trying to prove that government is legitimate in a more usual sense.

Perhaps Hobbes would have done better had he explained political obedience entirely as an effect of self-interest and fear; had he spoken only of maxims of prudence in the state of nature and never of divine laws; and had he always spoken of natural right as complete absence of obligation. The only ground of obedience would then have been the private interest of the person called upon to obey. Covenants made before the sovereign's power was effective could then create neither duty nor right; for duty and right (in the sense of right that implies duty) could exist only where there was a sovereign. If Hobbes had spoken in this way, he would have had to treat the virtually absolute subjection of the subject, not as something entailed by the sovereign's unlimited right, but as the subject's interest; he would have had to say that it is the subject's interest always to obey the sovereign except when the sovereign seeks to destroy him, and that it is never his interest to resist the sovereign whatever he may do to other people. Of course, Hobbes did say this. But he was not content to say *only* this; he also felt the need to use arguments which make no sense unless natural right is more than mere absence of obligation.

If Hobbes has correctly described the subject's interest, then, so long as most subjects see their interest and act upon it, the sovereign's power is as great as it can be or need be. For, in that case, anyone who disobeys the sovereign will find his fellow-subjects arrayed against him as a law-breaker. The more enlightened the community, the greater the sovereign's power.

If Hobbes had reduced his argument to this, he would have been more consistent but perhaps less persuasive. The argument, put in this way, is too naked, too cynical, to appeal to many people at any time. In the seventeenth century, when most people still believed in God, it would have been deeply shocking. Hobbes was as much concerned to prove the legitimacy as the expediency of sovereign power, unrestricted except by the subject's claim to resist attack on his life or person; and we do him less than justice if we fail to recognize this. He tried to prove two things at once, and was probably as sincere in the one endeavour as in the other. Certainly, we have no reason to believe that he himself was convinced only by the arguments for the expediency of absolute government and put the others in because he thought they would be more acceptable. He was probably quite honest with his readers, and marshalled his arguments in good faith.

Therefore we must not treat his arguments for the legitimacy of sovereign power as if they were supplementary to the others; they are just as much a part of Hobbes's political philosophy. But they are, as I have tried to show, unusually confused – much more so, I think, than most writers on Hobbes have been inclined to admit. They are also less new and less striking than the arguments for expediency. It is as the man who tried to prove that absolute government is always expedient that Hobbes stands out among political thinkers. He spent as much time discussing right as expediency, but it is what he said about expediency that is best remembered. Indeed, he has often been accused of reducing right to expediency. Though the accusation is scarcely just, it is true that Hobbes came nearer to doing this than any other political writer of his importance.

It is worthwhile isolating Hobbes's arguments for the expediency of absolute power from the rest of his doctrine in order to see what they amount to and how far they hold.

VI. HOBBES'S ARGUMENT FOR ABSOLUTE GOVERNMENT

Suppose we eliminate from Hobbes's theory all mention of natural right, and all talk of the sovereign being his subjects' representative and they the authors of his acts. What then remains of his argument for absolute government? And government absolute in just what sense? For power, as Hobbes knew, is never unlimited. No man or body has ever stood, or could in the real world stand, to other men in such a relation that whatever he or it commanded they would do.

Hobbes insists that men in fact obey only from hope of benefit or fear of hurt to themselves, only while it is their interest to do so; and he admits that it is not always their interest. A subject may defend himself against a sovereign who seeks to destroy or imprison him. As Hobbes puts it, he has 'a natural right' to resist his sovereign; but we, having for the moment agreed to make no mention of natural right, must say that the subject is well advised to resist whenever it is his interest to do so, which it clearly is when the sovereign seeks to destroy or imprison him.

There is a sense, as obvious as it is important, in which every man is always a judge in his own case; for he alone can decide whether or not to submit quietly to another's judgement. Far from denying this, Hobbes often insists upon it. It is a fact that necessarily limits sovereign power. It is inevitable and not to be regretted because it is a product of the same instinct of self-preservation which ordinarily disposes men to obedience. Creatures so indifferent to life that they would not even defend themselves from someone seeking to destroy them would care so little for security that we cannot imagine them setting up government in the hope of getting it. The sovereign has power only because his subjects obey him, and they obey him for the sake of security; but the sovereign's power also depends on his invading the security of the law-breaker, who therefore resists the sovereign from the same motive that causes other people to obey him.

What then, this being admitted, can Hobbes mean by arguing that authority must be absolute? He can only, as I see it, mean that it is never men's interest that there should be rules or conventions limiting their obedience to government, and also never their interest that supreme governmental authority should be divided. They must never undertake to obey the sovereign only on condition that he governs according to such and such principles, and must never have more than one centre of supreme authority. To assert moral or customary or legal limits to the ruler's authority is to give notice that you will not obey him if he transgresses those limits, and it is also to encourage disobedience in others. It is to do much more than just defend yourself against him when he seeks to destroy or imprison you; it is to put forward the claim to judge between him and anyone who defies him. If the sovereign's power is limited, not merely by the inevitable fact that (human nature being what it is) anyone he seeks to destroy will resist him, but on grounds of principle, then it is possible for anyone to appeal to principle against the sovereign. There is then a law which the sovereign may break and which others may claim the right to enforce. There are then two kinds of law, and the sovereign makes only one of them. But Hobbes's position is that, if there is more than one maker and enforcer of law, there cannot be real security.

Security is threatened, not by everyone's inevitably resisting who-ever would destroy him, but by the claim made on general grounds that the sovereign shall be resisted or disobeyed when he does not respect conditions supposedly laid down for the benefit of all his subjects. When subjects obey conditionally, disputes must arise about precisely what actions of the sovereign infringe the conditions laid down. If the sovereign is the final judge in such disputes, conditions might as well not be laid down, for he will interpret them to suit himself. If another authority is set up to decide the dispute, there is danger of civil strife. If the people generally set themselves up for judges, there must be anarchy. There must therefore be no resisting the sovereign on general grounds, as a matter of principle, or for the sake of justice. Resist him, by all means, when he seeks to destroy you, but do not offer to resist him when he seeks to destroy others.

The chances are that he is seeking to destroy them in order to maintain his authority, and it is your interest that he should maintain it. Never seek to impose for the general good any conventional or legal limit to the sovereign's power, for it is not your interest to do so. That, I think, is the real substance of Hobbes's argument for absolute government, if all talk of natural right is shorn away from it.

The argument is certainly plausible. The merely selfish law-breaker who resists arrest is not particularly dangerous to society. The police will probably catch him in the end, and almost everyone will consider him a public enemy. It is the man who, like John Hampden, defies the sovereign in the name of justice, resisting him as a matter of principle, who threatens the foundations of social peace. The thief often has property which he wants to hold in security; he is therefore anxious that other people should keep the law which he, from time to time, for his own profit, breaks. And in any case, all who know him for a thief are against him. But a John Hampden wants other people to follow his example, and they may well do so; for what encourages him to take his stand is the expectation or hope that others will do as he does. He is not a furtive criminal but a defier of authority. He asserts everyone's right against the sovereign. He makes a challenge which the sovereign must take up even at the price of war.

Hobbes seems to have believed that all agreement about principles or rules to limit authority is at bottom illusory, lasting only as long as the rules are not applied. As soon as the need is felt to apply them, they are variously interpreted. Unless it is agreed whose interpretation is final, there is always danger to peace. But if there is this agreement, then the final interpreter, whoever he may be, can make what he likes of the rules; he is the true sovereign. There was therefore no need to make the rules in the first place, for in practice they must be whatever the final interpreter says they are. His authority is unlimited, and the rules have failed of their purpose. On the other hand, if there is no final interpreter, the rules are a source of contention between all the parties that interpret them differently to suit their different interests. The rules are either useless or else are occasions of strife and even of war. It is impossible that a large number of persons should always agree about the application of general principles to particular cases. But, fortunately, it is easy enough for them to understand that it is their interest that all disputes should be quickly, peacefully and finally decided; and experience must in the end teach them that this can be so only if the final decision of them is left to one person or one body of persons.

Hobbes's argument for absolute government therefore rests on the assumption that, unless supreme authority is undivided, there cannot be a final and generally accepted arbiter in all cases, including disputes about the limits of authority. Now, this assumption is just not true. It is possible so to divide authority between different bodies and persons that none is sovereign in Hobbes's sense and yet no dispute can arise which somebody has not the right to settle finally. In the United States, for example, ultimate authority of different kinds is vested in the President, in Congress, in the Supreme Court and in each of fifty states. Of these fifty-three centres of authority, none is subordinate to any of the others. They all limit one another, but none has the authority which is properly its own by permission of the others. They have it because their authority is in fact generally recognized as long as they use it according to the principles laid down in the Constitution. They have it for precisely the same reason as Hobbes's sovereign has his authority; they are in fact obeyed because it is admitted that they should be. If the limits of their authority were set by the people, in the sense that private citizens could properly refuse obedience whenever they decided that those limits were overstepped, there would soon be anarchy. But the Constitution (both the written part of it and the conventions that have gathered round it) provides methods for settling all disputes peacefully, even disputes about the Constitution. Since all who have authority have it under the Constitution, they all have a general interest that the Constitution should be obeyed. They have exactly the same interest in relation to it as the subordinates of a Hobbesian sovereign have in relation to him. Their power depends on the Constitution's being respected, and its being respected limits their power. Nor can we say that the Constitution is sovereign, for if there is a sense in which a constitution can be sovereign, it is clearly not the Hobbesian sense.[1]

Whether there is a sovereign or not, there is always, where government is stable, a constitution; there are always rules governing the use of power which are in fact obeyed by those who exercise power. Louis XIV was absolute ruler of France only because all persons having authority in France observed a highly complicated set of rules whose general observance made Louis absolute. His authority was absolute but his power was not unlimited, for he – like all other rulers – was even more dependent on his subordinates than they on him. Power is always in fact divided, for the very simple reason that government is always a form of collaboration. Those who have

---

[1] Nor are the bodies which, between them, have the right to amend the Constitution sovereign, for the only authority they share is the right to amend the Constitution.

power in the State must observe some rules in their dealings with one another; for unless they do so, they cannot govern. Government, of its very nature, is a regular activity – a system of behaviour determined by rules.

Hobbes's argument for the expediency of absolute government or sovereign power therefore comes down to this: the rules governing the use of power are more likely to be respected when they place the final right of decision in all spheres of government (in other words, supreme authority) in the hands of one man or assembly than when they divide it between several. If the argument is put in this way, which seems to me a fair way of putting it, it does not look convincing. No doubt, if there is to be domestic peace, the rules governing the use of power must be understood by the persons required to obey them; and no doubt also, whenever disputes arise about what the rules are, there must always be an agreed method for settling them. In Hobbes's England these conditions did not hold: there was great confusion about what the fundamental laws were, there were disputes about them, and there was no agreed method for settling the disputes. As Hobbes saw it, the disputes could only be settled by war, and in fact the victors exercised what could fairly be called absolute authority. But though these conditions did not hold in England in Hobbes's day, it is not true that they hold only where there is a sovereign in the Hobbesian sense. Supreme authority can either all be placed in the same hands, or it can be divided between several persons and bodies and rules laid down for settling disputes between them. Which is the better method depends on circumstances.

Hobbes argued that the body whose function is to decide disputes between other bodies must in fact be sovereign. But clearly this is not true – not if we take his sense of sovereignty. If the United States Supreme Court, as the guardian of the Constitution, has the last word in settling disputes about the limits of executive and legislative authority, that is not enough to make it sovereign in Hobbes's sense. It cannot itself exercise the powers of the President or of Congress, and if it tried to do so would not be obeyed. To settle disputes about the limits of other people's authority is clearly not to do what they do; it is to do something else which is quite different; it is to exercise another kind of authority. Congress and the President are no more subordinate to the Supreme Court than that Court is to them, merely because it has the last word in interpreting a constitution under which all three hold their powers.

Whether or not there is a sovereign, the common interest of all persons taking part in government is ordinarily that the rules, which make the structure of government what it is, should be respected; because it is on this structure that their power depends. If, for any reason, some of them want to increase their share of power at the expense of others, and try to break or to change the rules, they are not the less likely to do so merely because there is a sovereign. So long as the rules are coherent and so long as they are obeyed, the system works well enough. People may want to change the rules for all kinds of reasons: because they want to get more power for themselves, because they believe that thereby the efficiency of government will be improved, or because they want to increase or decrease the influence on government of some part or other of the people. Whatever their reasons or motives, they are as likely to be strong where there is a sovereign as where there is not.

In early Tudor times the House of Commons accepted a body of customs governing the use of power which gave the king greater authority than Charles I had when Parliament went to war with him. The Tudor constitution was unwritten and some of its conventions were vague; it was, like all constitutions, in process of change. There was nothing about it, if we look at it merely as a body of customary rules governing the use of power, that explains why it was more acceptable than the system (which was in fact largely the same) challenged by the Long Parliament. Apart from the specific interests and motives of the defenders and challengers of a political system, we cannot explain why it should be acceptable at one time and not at another. But Hobbes would have us believe that the system which provides a sole final authority in all spheres of government is always the most suitable, whatever men's interests. He took it for granted that, where there is no such authority, there will inevitably arise disputes that cannot be settled except by war. He could not see that, where there are several final authorities, each in a different field, there may yet be a settled procedure for deciding any dispute that may arise; nor yet that, where there is such a procedure, men have precisely the same interest in accepting it as they have in accepting the authority of the sovereign.

VII. CONCLUSION

Many of the weaknesses of Hobbes's political philosophy derive from his too narrow assumptions and definitions. He treats law as primarily command, not taking sufficient notice of the fact that the power to command derives from the habit of obedience. Before there can be political power, there must be rules that men follow, not from fear of government, but from other motives. Law in the broadest sense is prior to government, which is impossible without it. Hobbes does, of course, speak of a law of nature, which is the command of God, prior to government. But he speaks of it equivocally. Though God's power is irresistible, He does not provide His creatures with adequate motives for keeping His law until there is a human sovereign to enforce it. And if obligation is what Hobbes says it is, there is really no need, given his account of the state of nature and the covenant, to assert a prior obligation to obey God in order to explain the duty of obedience to the sovereign. Hobbes does not discard the old tradition of a law of nature which is also the will of God, but he makes such an odd use of it that in his hands it can no longer serve the old purposes. God is very much present in his scheme of things, but is also, at bottom, superfluous.

Again, Hobbes begins by giving such an account of natural right as reduces it to mere power or else, more plausibly, to complete absence of obligation. Then, having defined the covenant setting up the sovereign as a laying down of natural right by the parties to it, he tries to use it to prove the legitimacy of sovereign power. But this he cannot do if natural right is only the absence of obligation; and so he passes, without noticing it, to a more adequate and ordinary conception of right, but a conception not in keeping with his own account of the state of nature. Hobbes, I suggest, was a more confused thinker than he is usually taken to be.

Yet his merits are greater than his faults. He understood that men are not born but are made sociable, that there is no justice without law, and no law without discipline, and no discipline without sanctions. It is under the pressure of authority that man becomes a creature who learns to respect in others the claims he makes for himself. But Hobbes made the mistake of supposing that all authority is at bottom political, and so he could not see that even human law (as custom) is prior to government. And yet, in spite of his calling the law of nature the command of God, and his speaking of obligation *in foro interno* even in the unsocial state of nature, I think that Hobbes came close to believing that morality is something that appears only in society. He spoke, as I have said, in two voices; he used the old conception of a law of nature valid even outside society, and yet made a lame and halting use of it. Perhaps the dissatisfaction sprang from a half-formed belief that it is only as a social creature, as a creature subject to a discipline externally imposed, that man becomes moral.

If Hobbes had seen clearly what this belief implied, he might have rejected altogether the conception of a law of nature prior to all forms of social discipline; he might have done, in the seventeenth century, what Hume was to do in the eighteenth. As it is, *Leviathan*, much more powerfully than anything written before it, brings to our notice what man might be like if he were subject to no discipline, if he were included in no social order. *Leviathan*, more than any political treatise before it, compels us to reflect on what is involved in man's being a social and a moral creature.

Hobbes was mistaken in supposing that all social discipline outside the family is political. But this mistake was not peculiar to him; it was almost universal among political thinkers in his day. It was not corrected until the next century, in France by Montesquieu and in England by Hume.

CHAPTER 6

Divine Right, Absolute Monarchy and Early Theories of the Social Contract

I. CONTRACT THEORY BEFORE HOBBES AND LOCKE

The theory of the social contract was first used in the sixteenth century in the interest of religious minorities.[1] It does not place customary limits on temporal authority, nor assert a merely customary right of resistance; it asserts, as mediaeval political thinkers (despite their insistence that all human authority is limited) did not do, that the people, having agreed to set up rulers over them for certain purposes, therefore have the right to resist or remove them if they persist in courses which defeat those purposes. A contract is essentially a voluntary and deliberate agreement; the parties to it are presumed to be free not to make it, and also to understand what they are doing when they make it. It is odd to speak of great multitudes making contracts; it looks like fantasy or, if the contract is assumed to be tacit, like an abuse of language. The mediaeval idea that popular consent to temporal authority is implied by the general acceptance of what is customary seems much closer to the truth. Yet the language of contract, which seems so obviously out of place when it is a question of explaining the origins of government, was deliberately chosen. Those who used it wanted to suggest that political authority rests on the deliberate consent of the governed. The suggestion is so wide of the mark that, as one difficulty after another faced them, they hedged or took back at later stages of their argument what they had

---

[1] There are references to a social contract in theories earlier than the sixteenth century, but it was then that the idea of such a contract first became popular and, as it were, *central* to political theory.

216

said before. That is why, of all political theories, theirs is perhaps the most equivocal and vacillating. Yet the theory was inspired by the need to make, on behalf of minorities, claims of a kind not made before.

The idea of contract implies free and deliberate choice, and the use of this legal concept in explaining the origins of government, absurd though it may be, is none the less significant. As an assertion of individual and minority rights, it was in practice often effective, though as a theory it was riddled with ambiguities and inconsistencies. The individualism latent in the theory indeed became much more prominent in later than in earlier versions. The early Huguenot contractualists were as much mediaeval as modern in their ideas. It would be absurd to suggest that they were individualists in the same sense as Locke, but the germ of individualism is already present in their theories. They were wonderfully confused and used all kinds of incompatible and unconnected arguments. They relied on Biblical texts and bad history as much as on *a priori* principles and deductions from them. Their philosophy shows little of the sophistication we find in Locke. Yet they did feel the need to speak of government as if it were deliberately set up by all the members of society for the defence of common interests and rights superior even to custom, and they made claims upon government based on those rights. In that sense, they were individualists.

The people with the strongest inclination to use the notion of a social contract were of course those most likely to suffer from the attentions of government, that is, the religious minorities, and the most ardent contractualists among such minorities were the Huguenots and the Jesuits. Of these, the more lucid, acute and rigorous in their contentions were the Jesuits; for they were concerned, not with the affairs of one country, but with all Europe, and so could base their arguments more firmly on general principles. The Huguenots, when Henry of Navarre, their leader, became the legitimate claimant to the French throne, promptly abandoned a theory which they had needed only in order to challenge the authority of kings who were too easily led by an aggressive Catholic League. The Jesuits, as universal champions of militant Catholicism, had a more permanent interest in a doctrine which justified resistance to heretical princes everywhere, and which reminded even Catholic rulers that their authority was conditional.

Admittedly, the main purpose of the contractualists was not to assert a popular right of resistance to misgovernment. They were primarily concerned to defend one particular right, the right of free worship, and even this one right was not the right to adhere to any religion; it was the right to adhere to the sole religion which those who claimed the right believed to be true. The Huguenots did not believe that Catholics should be allowed to practise their religion freely in Protestant countries, nor the Jesuits that Protestants should be allowed to do so in Catholic countries. But theories often have implications wider than the particular concerns of the men who produce them. In practice, it was scarcely possible to use the contract theory to assert man's inalienable right to practise the true religion without admitting that men have other rights which they may need to defend against their rulers. Moreover, the right which both Huguenots and Jesuits wanted above all to assert was not a right of the Church against the State; it was the right of every man to worship God in the only way acceptable to God. It was an individual right: it was the right, not of an order or corporation, but of man. It was not put forward as a customary right.

The contract theory, as we find it in the sixteenth and early seventeenth centuries, is a logically (and historically) indefensible but rhetorically effective way of insisting that the authority of rulers rests, not only on the will of God or on mere custom, but on its being used to defend the interests and rights of the people – their supreme interest and right being to have and to practise the true religion. It also asserts, though ambiguously and hesitantly, that rulers are answerable to their subjects for the use they make of their authority. The Jesuits were less ambiguous and less hesitant than the Huguenots, perhaps because they were a religious order to which the authority of the Church mattered greatly but the authority of princes much less, whereas the Huguenots had more peculiar and less stable needs, and were strong only in parts of France.

1. The Huguenots

The Protestants in France were too few to aspire seriously to the Genevan ideal of the relations between Church and State; they could not hope to subordinate the Temporal to the Spiritual Power, as Calvin had done in Geneva and as other Calvinists were later to do in New England. They could not even hope, in the second half of the sixteenth century, to make their religion preponderant in France. The most they could seriously hope for was tolerance in a country likely to remain overwhelmingly Catholic for a long time to come.

The two most famous Huguenot works justifying resistance to royal power are François Hotman's *Francogallia*, published in

Geneva in 1573, and the *Vindiciae contra tyrannos* of Philippe du Plessis Mornay (perhaps with the collaboration of Hubert Languet), published in Basel in 1579.[1] Hotman's book is not a version of social contract theory. It is, however, worth noting here because its inadequacy to Huguenot needs helps to explain why such a theory was attractive to them. Hotman argued that in France supreme authority in temporal matters belonged by tradition to the Estates-General, the body which alone represented the entire French people. Before Caesar conquered Gaul, supreme authority had always belonged to the people and had been exercised in their name by a representative body. The Romans had for a time destroyed the traditional liberties of the Gauls, but the Franks had afterwards restored them, and thereafter, until the end of the fifteenth century, the right of the people's representatives to make laws, appoint magistrates, and confirm and depose kings had always been admitted.

Hotman's argument is also of interest for what it has in common with claims used in England some two generations later by Parliamentary leaders. Just as Eliot and Pym appealed to the historic rights of Englishmen and of Parliament, so Hotman appealed to the historic rights of Frenchmen and of the Estates-General. But Hotman's argument was not as well suited to the circumstances of his country or the needs of his party. The Estates-General never became the formidable and effective body that Parliament had already become in late Tudor and early Stuart times; it met less frequently, its procedure was extraordinarily cumbersome, it was socially more divided, and the Third Estate in particular was less solid and self-reliant than the House of Commons. The assembly whose supremacy Hotman proclaimed, besides being less efficient and less responsible by far than the English Parliament, was also quite unsuited to serve Huguenot needs. There had been a time when the Estates-General was anxious to avert a religious war; but the war had come and had inflamed religious passions. It was perhaps inevitable, in a predominantly Catholic country, that the body which came nearest to being a popular assembly should prefer the old religion to the new. Whereas the opponents of Charles I's religious policy were for a time powerful in the House of Commons, the Huguenots soon found that they could achieve nothing through the Estates-General.

[1] To this list of the principal Huguenot texts of the period many commentators would now add the *De jure magistratuum* (dating from 1573) of Theodore Beza. Authorship of the *Vindiciae contra tyrannos* has never been resolved. It has sometimes been attributed to Languet and, more recently, to Johan Junius de Jonge.

Too few in number, they could not hope to use that assembly to resist the King of France, and they found it more difficult than it proved in England to make a persuasive case for resistance to the Crown on mainly historical grounds (even by using bad history, as both Hotman and Pym did). When the Estates-General still seemed bent on averting civil war, a Huguenot writer such as Hotman could argue that supreme authority in France belongs by custom to that body which alone represents the entire French people. But as soon as it was clear that the Estates-General would support the Catholic cause, they found it in their interest to set history aside and use a more abstract form of argument. Hence the appearance in 1579 of one of the earliest versions of the contract theory: Mornay's *Vindiciae contra tyrannos.*

The argument of the *Vindiciae*, however confused, is certainly in large part abstract. By no means is it entirely so, for it makes free use of Biblical precedents, but it is far more abstract than the argument of the *Francogallia*. If Hotman's book is bad history, the *Vindiciae* might be called indifferent political theory, and yet political theory it most evidently is, for its arguments, if they are valid, apply to all countries and not only to France.

In the *Vindiciae*, there are two covenants. The first is a kind of double treaty (*duplex foedus*) to which God, the prince and the people are parties. The prince and the people make separate promises, to serve God according to His Word and to see that the people do so too, while the people promise to worship God aright before all other things. Though, by the treaty, prince and people make no promises to one another, they are both answerable to God for their own and each other's conduct. The prince must see to it that the people serve God according to His Word, and the people must worship God aright even if that means offering resistance to the prince.

The second covenant, which is called a contract and not a treaty (*pactum* and not *foedus*), is between the prince and the people. Under it the prince promises to rule the people justly, and the people promise to obey the prince as long as he does indeed rule justly, or, in other words, respects their rights. This second covenant need not be historical; it need not have been made in so many words at some definite time. It may be tacit, a mutual obligation arising from the nature of man and society, and also from the will of God. It is immutable.

Some commentators have argued that the first covenant of the *Vindiciae*, the double treaty, is not really a covenant at all. For the essence of a covenant is that it lays obligations on all the parties to it. But God can hardly be said to put Himself under an obligation by this covenant. It is presumably His will from all eternity that those who serve Him according to His Word shall be saved. And He requires their service; they need make no promise in order to have a duty to serve Him, for they ought to do so because they are His creatures. Their duty of service can depend only on their understanding of what God is in relation to them, and what He requires of them. The double treaty of the *Vindiciae* is merely an idea suggested by the Old Testament account of God's covenant with the Israelites; it does not accord with Christian conceptions of God and His relations with men. There is, moreover, no need to assume it to explain the right of resistance to rulers who persecute the true religion – which is the right that the author of the *Vindiciae* was most eager to assert.

It has also been argued that the second covenant of the *Vindiciae*, the pact between prince and people, is not a true covenant. It is immutable because its character is determined by men's nature, so that it always holds, whether or not it is expressed, and because it conforms with the will of God, which never changes. Therefore – so goes the argument – there is nothing voluntary about it, and it is not properly a covenant. Yet while the objection to the first covenant seems to me well founded, the objection to the second is not. Or at least, if it is well founded, it holds not oₙₗy against the *Vindiciae* but against most versions of the contract theory. The covenant of Hobbes's *Leviathan*, for instance, is also determined by the nature of man and society; it is the only conceivable covenant, for it alone – so Hobbes thinks – can explain rights and duties under government. The same is true of Rousseau's social contract. Neither Hobbes nor Rousseau seriously believes that there actually was a contract, which is, rather, implicit in the nature of every political society, and, for Rousseau, in the nature of every legitimate state.

No doubt, an excellent case can be made for saying that the notion of contract is out of place in any account of the origins of political society – that whatever it is designed to explain can be better explained without it. It can be argued, quite plausibly, that all the contracts of society and of government imagined by political philosophers are not true contracts, and that to call them contracts is apt to create unnecessary and insoluble theoretical problems. For my part, I believe this is true. Contract, as the word is ordinarily used, suggests a voluntary and deliberate agreement which creates obligations that would not exist without it, and is therefore out of place in an account of either the origins or the nature of society and government. It is not, however, any more out of place in the *Vindiciae* than in Hobbes, Locke or Rousseau. The second covenant of the *Vindiciae* does lay obligations on the parties to it, for it explains the authority of princes and the allegiance of subjects. Mornay wished to show that the ruler owed it to his people, and not only to God, to rule in accordance with the *people's* sense of justice, and also that they have the right to call him to account if he does not do so. He wanted to make clear – just as Locke did after him – that the authority of the prince derives from the people, not in the sense that it is a customary right which they do not contest, but in that he is somehow responsible to them for the use he makes of it. The *Vindiciae*, in its second covenant though not its first, uses (or, perhaps, misuses) the notion of contract for much the same purpose as most of the later versions of the contract theory. It is therefore an authentic example of that theory. It is, however, an unusually confused and defective example. It does not make clear the status of the people as parties to the second covenant, which is the only one of the two that deserves the name of covenant; and it leaves it uncertain in whom the right of resistance resides when that covenant is broken.

Government, according to the *Vindiciae*, was set up to protect property and to defend the people against external enemies. The parties to the second covenant are the prince and the people. But who are the people? How are they constituted? What makes them one people over and against other peoples from whose attacks they need to be defended? The *Vindiciae* speaks of them as a people, a single community, even before there is a government over them. For unless they were a community, they could not be collectively one party to a covenant. The agreement made by this community binds all its members. The *Vindiciae* takes it for granted that this is so and makes no attempt to explain it. If, however, the prince's authority over the people requires a covenant to explain it, why is there no need to explain the authority of the people taken collectively over each of the persons who together make up the people? The second covenant, the only true contract of the *Vindiciae*, is a contract of government. There is no contract of society.

According to the author of the *Vindiciae*, the people have the right to resist the prince if he breaks the covenant made with them, and this right of resistance belongs to the people collectively, and not to *any* subject who believes that the prince has abused his authority. But how are the people to exercise their collective right? The people, says the *Vindiciae*, act through their representatives. If the people, taken collectively, are one party to the covenant, it would seem that their representatives, whoever they are, must speak for the entire community – that they must be national and not merely local. But this is not how the *Vindiciae* describes them; for the magistrates to whom it grants the right of resistance are leaders in their local communities, city magistrates, noblemen, officers of the Crown, provincial courts of law, deputies elected by whatever section of the people happen to have the vote. These 'representatives', most of them holding office by hereditary right and not by election, have the right to resist the prince in the people's name, but apparently the people have no right to resist them! So whereas the people who are a party to the original covenant with the prince are the entire community governed by him, the right of resistance is confined to the spokesmen of small communities within the great community that made the contract, and is forbidden to the people against these spokesmen. Now, the idea that the privileged, though only a small part of the community, have the right to speak for the whole of it had long been widely accepted. Indeed, it was not seriously challenged, except by the Levellers, until the rise of radicalism towards the end of the eighteenth century. Locke, for instance, took it for granted that in 1689 Parliament spoke for the people of England, even though he knew that the great majority of Englishmen had no vote; for those who did have the vote were supposed to give expression to the will of the entire nation. Parliament was always thought of as a national assembly.

The peculiarity of the *Vindiciae* is not that it confines to a part of the community – to a privileged order – the right to speak and to act for the whole of it, but that it does not confine it to that order throughout the community. It allows a minority of the privileged to defy, in the name of the people, a ruler whose authority is not contested by the majority of their order. The Huguenots, strong in some parts of France and weak in others, and stronger everywhere among the upper than the lower classes, needed a theory to justify a resistance which was neither nation-wide nor truly popular, and they could not invoke customary rights. Hence the crabbed and peculiar argument of the *Vindiciae*, which aims at justifying the resistance of a scattered minority among the privileged, and yet makes use of an abstract doctrine better suited to justify a resistance which is nation-wide, either because all classes support it or because it is supported in all parts of the community by classes whose claim to speak for the entire community has not yet been seriously challenged. Were the Huguenots in 1579 so much smaller a minority than the Whigs for whom Locke spoke a century later? Perhaps not. But they were not, in the same sense, a *national* minority; they controlled no great national institution, and they were also widely hated and feared. Their resistance to the Crown threatened their country's unity as the resistance of the Whigs apparently did not, at least within the mainland territory of England.

In asserting local and provincial (not to say feudal) rights against a centralizing monarchy, the theory of the *Vindiciae* is peculiarly constructed to suit the specific needs of the Huguenots. It is not merely illogical, for all versions of the contract theory are that. It is also disruptive and anarchic. A minority that pervades the whole nation can claim to speak for the whole nation. The claim may be extravagant, but need not be disruptive if the active minority can dominate the passive majority. We may doubt whether the anxieties and ambitions of the Long Parliament were shared by the bulk of the English people. Yet Parliament had in England a traditional right to speak for the whole people. When Parliament challenged the royal power, there was civil war. But the national unity destroyed by the war was restored by Parliament's victory, precisely because Parliament was by tradition a national body. If, however, the claims put forward in the *Vindiciae* had been realized, the unity of France would have been destroyed, not only temporarily, while the struggle lasted, but also as a result of a Huguenot victory. The pretensions of the *Vindiciae* were dangerous to France just as those of the South were dangerous to the United States.

Fortunately for France and for the Huguenots, when Henry III was murdered in 1589, his legitimate successor was the Huguenot leader, Henry of Navarre. The Huguenots soon forgot about contract theories and local rights of resistance, and became, at least for a time, the most ardent royalists, eager to make good their leader's authority over the whole of France.

2. *The Jesuits*

The Jesuits produced versions of social contract theory which were largely concerned to justify Catholic resistance and conspiracy in countries where not only princes, but parliaments and estates as well, favoured one or other of the reformed religions. Their principles were put forward as having universal significance, and they were accordingly more general than those of the Huguenots. Particularly in the treatises of Mariana and Suárez, published some twenty and thirty years after the *Vindiciae*, we find a much clearer and more plausible use of the notion of contract to explain the origins both of society and government.

Mariana's *De rege et regis institutione*, which appeared in 1599, contains a fuller and more vivid account of the state of nature than any treatise before it. According to Mariana, the peculiarity of man, as compared with other animals, is that his natural strength is not sufficient for his needs. He is a weak animal whose wants are exceptionally great. Fear and need drive him to form groups with other men for mutual comfort and protection, but this coming together only increases human greed and rapacity. From being merely brutish and innocent, men become cheats and liars, dangerous to their own kind. Fear of other animals and the sense of their own weakness first drove men to live together, and then afterwards fear of one another moved them to set up government over them. The family is natural and can exist without law; and it is also natural that families should congregate. But government, which arises from men's needs after the coming together of families, is not natural. It is deliberately created by men for their own convenience.

Mariana contends that civil or temporal authority is granted to whoever possesses it by those who thereby become subject to it, and is always granted conditionally. It does not matter whether the grant is formal or not. Of its very nature, temporal authority cannot be absolute, nor can any person or assembly have an indefeasible right to it; for what is set up by the people for their convenience may be put down or altered by them from the same motive. The authority of temporal rulers depends on the *continuing* will of their subjects, and is limited by the purpose which moved their ancestors to establish it and for whose sake they now recognize it. He suggests that the first governments, created by men without political experience, were probably monarchies with no precise limits set to them. Primitive men could not be expected to foresee dangers still unknown to them, and were concerned only to put an end to the dangers they knew. Later on, taught by experience, as they take on the collective identity of a people, they begin to look for ways of putting their rulers under the restraint of law. To avoid tyranny, the people must reserve to themselves the right to legislate and to vote taxes, a right which they must exercise through a representative assembly, for otherwise they have no means of giving expression to their will. Though Mariana admits that it is for this assembly, and not for individuals, to resist the ruler when he misrules his subjects, he does not suggest (as, for instance, Aquinas does) that where there is no such body with a customary right to speak for the people, active resistance is not permissible. He implies that the people have a right to be represented by some such body, and even allows tyrannicide when the prince defies the assembly or prevents its meeting. The form of religion in the State, he claims, is unalterable, and the prince, if he tries to alter it, is guilty of tyranny. But what if the people wish to alter it? Must the prince, whose authority derives from the people, suppress the attempt? Mariana wisely ignored this question, which can scarcely be answered by a Jesuit who also happens to be a champion of popular rights.

Though there are points of resemblance between Mariana's argument and the argument of the *Vindiciae*, its superiority is striking. It is more imaginative, better developed and more practical. God is not made a party to any covenant; the State is in no sense a theocracy. Government is established by men for their own purposes, and its authority is limited by those purposes, of which the people alone are final judges. To give permanent expression to the people's will, a representative assembly is required. There is a plausible and vivid account of the 'state of nature', of the condition of man before he enters society and of the needs that drive him to establish government. The right of resistance is not merely asserted; it is made clear where it resides, and is attributed to a body that can have no interest in disrupting the nation.

In the *Tractatus de legibus ac Deo legislatore* of Francisco Suárez, published in 1612, we are told that civil authority belongs to the whole community, and is created by the free consent of all its members. It is this consent which makes a community out of a mere collection of men, and which gives to that community the authority it possesses over each of its members. Both community and authority are effects of the same act, for a group having no authority over its members is not properly a community. Suárez calls the community a *corpus mysticum*, a mystical body, and attributes moral unity to it.

A collection of people who have by common consent formed themselves into a community with authority over each of its members has still to make provision for mutual protection and for defence against external danger. The people have created a *corpus mysticum* but have not yet established effective government. Suárez makes a sharp distinction between the contract that sets up government and the act of common consent that creates the community. He claims that a State is created when an already established community goes on to make a covenant binding on whoever is granted the right to rule and on his legitimate successors. While the ruler and his successors govern according to this covenant, their subjects are obliged to obey, and have no right to alter its terms, for they are as much bound by the covenant as their rulers, and may not set it aside on the ground that they would prefer another. But should any ruler break the covenant, they have the right to resist him. Though Suárez does not make it clear how a people are to determine that their ruler has broken the covenant or how they are to resist him, he does assert a right of popular resistance.

He was concerned, as Mariana was, to show that a representative assembly is required to keep the prince's authority within the limits set by the covenant; he was much less inclined to assert popular rights. But Suárez did make a clear and vigorous use of the notion of contract, and also introduced into political theory the distinction between the unanimous agreement that creates a community having a power to make decisions binding on all its members, and the contract that sets up a government. If one assumes that all authority of man over man rests on consent, then it is useful to make this distinction between the 'contract of government' and the 'contract of society'.

3. Hooker

So far, I have discussed the contract theories of Huguenots and Jesuits – of people whose prime motive was to assert the right of every man to follow the true faith. The superiority of the Jesuits, in point of lucidity and logical consistency, is striking, since the position of the Huguenots is peculiar, and they had to devise peculiar arguments to meet their needs. Besides, they made use of the contract theory only for a time. The Jesuits, interested in the fate of Catholic minorities all over Europe, could develop simpler and more abstract theories of more general application. The argument of the *Vindiciae* compared with the arguments of Mariana and Suárez is like the fitful light of a candle against the steady brightness of a lamp.

I have confined myself to the historically most important examples of the contract theory in the sixteenth century, but there is one other that I ought not to neglect, partly because it is interesting in itself and even more so because Locke owed a great deal to it. Hooker is by no means so bold a thinker as Mariana or so clear and precise as Suárez, but there is about him a breadth of mind and a discernment greater than can be found in Mornay.

The first four books of Hooker's *Laws of Ecclesiastical Polity* were published in 1593, and the fifth in 1597, but the sixth, seventh and eighth books not until many years after his death, mutilated and altered by other hands. Hooker's main purpose was to prove that the Puritans, merely as Englishmen, were in duty bound to accept the law of the English Church, because, in England, Church and State were indissolubly united, being but two sides of one society. Our concern is not with Hooker's quite traditional account of how

Church and State were related in England, but with his conception of political society.

There is, he says, a law that men must obey even before they are under human government. This is the Law of Reason or human nature 'which men by discourse of natural Reason have rightly found out themselves to be all for ever bound unto in their actions'.[1] It is a general and perpetual law that men carry written in their hearts, 'the sentence of God himself. For that which all men have at all times learned, Nature herself must needs have taught'.[2] This is the traditional conception of the law of nature, as we find it in Aquinas and in Locke.

Men are by nature sociable and unable, in isolation, to provide for their needs. It is therefore natural that they should congregate together. The mere recognition of the Law of Reason is not, however, enough to keep the peace between them. To be secure from each other's wrong-doing, they need an authority over them all. 'Strifes and troubles would be endless, except they gave their common consent all to be ordered by some whom they should agree upon: without which consent there were no reason that one man should take upon him to be lord or judge over another.' All government arises from 'deliberate advice, consultation, and composition between men'.[3]

To say that without consent there is no reason why one man should be lord over another would seem to imply that no man has a duty of obedience to government unless he has consented to obey it. This was the position adopted by Locke, citing Hooker's authority. But it is by no means clear that it was the position of Hooker, even though what he said implies it. For he also said that every 'independent multitude' – by which he meant, presumably, every group of men living a communal life together – has, even before government is established, 'full dominion over itself'. Its authority over its members does not therefore rest upon their consent. The only authority established by consent is the authority of government, and the consent it rests on is the consent of the community. We have, therefore, two lines of thought in Hooker which are never reconciled: he sometimes implies that all human authority requires the consent of everyone subject to it; and at other times he speaks as if the consent were communal rather than individual, with the majority binding everyone. While

[1] Hooker, *Of the Laws of Ecclesiastical Polity*, ed. A. S. McGrade and B. Vickers (London 1975), I.viii.8, p. 131.
[2] Ibid., I.viii.3, p. 127.
[3] Ibid., I.x.4, p. 138.

Hooker speaks of 'deliberate advice' and 'consultation', moreover, which implies explicit consent, he says that consent may be given 'secretly', by which he means 'tacitly'.

If an 'independent multitude' is a community without government, what makes it a community separate from other communities? What gives it its identity? It is manifestly not a family or a clan, but a collection of people who live together to enjoy each other's company and to provide more effectively for their wants. What is it that gives them, collectively, authority over each member? According to Hooker, it is the Law of Reason, or of Nature, which is also the will of God. God wills the good of His creatures and therefore gives them collectively the right to do whatever is necessary for their security.

There are at least two difficulties with this conception of the 'independent multitude' and its collective authority. If one disregards government and merely looks at men in all their unpolitical relations, one finds that individuals may belong to many communities. Which is the community that has authority over them to put them under government? The only community we know of which claims this kind of authority is the State, but the purpose of Hooker's theory is precisely to account for the State's establishment. He must not assume what he has to explain. And yet this is just what he seems to do when he says that every independent multitude has 'full dominion' over all its members. If there is no reason why one man should take it upon himself to dominate another without his consent, there is surely no reason why a multitude of men should do so.

The second difficulty is this. According to Hooker, the authority of government is limited by the Law of Reason and also by what he calls the 'articles of compact' – the agreement whereby the people first set up their government. But what about later generations? Does their duty of obedience also rest on consent? Hooker says that it does. 'To be commanded we do consent, when that society whereof we are part hath at any time before consented, without revoking the same by the like universal agreement. Wherefore as any man's deed past is good as long as himself continueth; so the act of a public society of men done five hundred years sithence standeth as theirs who presently are of the same societies, because corporations are immortal.'[1] That is to say, we are bound by the consent of our ancestors because we belong to the same society as they once belonged to, and that society survives indefinitely. There is therefore no need for individual consent. Society can undo what it has done, but so long as it does not choose to do so,

[1] Ibid., I.x.8, p. 141.

everyone is bound by the original agreement. Each man consents to it merely by being a member of the society.

Unfortunately, Hooker does not explain how society sets about undoing what it has once done. He sees no need for providing legal means for changing the form of government, or even for replacing rulers who abuse the people's trust. In this respect his theory is less satisfactory than Mariana's. He admits that the authority of many kings rests on conquest, and regards it as no less legitimate on that account. He also says that, where kings were set up by agreement, the terms of the agreement are now, as he puts it, 'clean worn out of knowledge'. He admits that what in fact limits royal authority is either custom or positive law.

Hooker does not even use the notion of consent to justify resistance to authority. He allows that the subject may disobey commands contrary to the Law of Reason but does not admit that he may resist authority with force. The right of disobedience, where it exists, derives not from consent or from any universal agreement, but from the obligation laid on all men to obey God rather than man. Though Hooker sometimes speaks as if society's original consent could be revoked by a 'like universal agreement', he also suggests that it could not – as if it were impossible legally to withdraw authority from the person or persons who first received it or from their legal successors. He admits that there has been misgovernment in the past, and also that there have been changes in government, which he does not condemn. Yet, when he considers whether a body politic may withdraw, if it thinks fit to do so, all or part of the authority it has granted from those persons who in fact exercise it, he answers, 'I do not see how the body should be able by any means to help itself'.

The source of Hooker's equivocation is not hard to find. Though he treats his public society or corporation as if it were prior to government and its creator, he also sees that in practice society has no organ but government. How, then, if it seeks to dispose of the government, can it do so, since it is only through government that it can act? The individual who actively resists government is a rebel; the right of resistance belongs only to society as a whole. But what is society as a whole? How does it stand to government? If we speak of society and government as Hooker does, we are caught in an insoluble dilemma. Government is the agent or representative of society, and yet government is not truly responsible to society, for society cannot act except through government. There is a right of resistance, but it cannot be exercised.

Hooker's theory leaves as many loose ends as the *Vindiciae*, and yet, to my mind, is far superior. Theories that are equally confused are not in consequence equally inadequate. The inconsistencies of Hooker's case arise, not from special pleading on behalf of a minority peculiarly placed, but from the difficult questions he puts. He rightly takes it for granted that men are born into society and do not join it by consent, and yet is also eager to establish that all legitimate government stems from the consent of the governed. Government is the agent of society. If, however, government is removed, what makes society a single whole, with authority over each of its members? Suárez gave a clear answer to this question by identifying the community's authority in terms of the free consent of its members; but his answer is unrealistic. Hobbes also gave a clear answer, denying that society could exist apart from government. I think it unlikely that either Suárez's answer or Hobbes's would have satisfied Hooker, and, if that is so, it is to his credit. Hooker's strength is not logical consistency, but breadth of mind and philosophical temper. His theory is not fashioned to serve the temporary needs of a warlike minority, but is of more general application. There is an attractive largeness of design about it, and it is never harsh or pedantic. Hooker brings to the fore, as the author of the *Vindiciae* does not, the notions of consent and community, and raises problems which are not the less important for being left unresolved.

With the passage of time, the theory of the social contract was refined and made more simple. Its earlier versions, as for instance the *Vindiciae*, postulate only a contract of government, making both people and prince parties to it without explaining how the people acquired the capacity to act collectively as a public person. Its later versions either distinguish between a contract of society and a contract of government, as with Suárez, or else, as with Hobbes, Locke and Rousseau, provide for only one true contract, that of society. For Hobbes, the universal agreement to set up a sovereign is the covenant that creates society, and the sovereign of necessity can be no party to it. For Rousseau, the contract of its very nature places sovereignty collectively in the hands of all the parties who subscribe to it, that is, the people, and the government is merely their agent. For Locke, there is first a universal agreement or contract to establish a community having authority over all its members, and then a simple majority decision to set up a particular form of government. The majority decision is merely an act of the community; it is not a contract between subjects and rulers. Governments, in the theory of Locke, are trustees for the community, and are no more parties to a contract than is Hobbes's sovereign. Pufendorf, with true German thoroughness, uses both contracts and interpolates a decree between them. There is first an agreement of each with all to form a political society together; there is then a decision or decree of the society so formed to confer authority on certain persons; and finally these persons promise to act for the public good and receive in turn from their subjects a promise of obedience. Later on, other German jurists treated Pufendorf's decree as also a contract; they spoke of three contracts, a contract of union, a contract of ordination, and a contract of subjection or government. But this scheme is not an improvement on Pufendorf: it is better to treat a grant of authority as an act of the community than as a contract.

The contract of society was invented after the contract of government and to solve a different problem. It might therefore seem more in keeping with the moral and political assumptions made by the contract theorists to use both contracts rather than only one. It is certainly better to use both than to use the contract of government alone; for if we begin by saying that men are by nature free, in the sense that none can have authority over others without their consent, we put it upon ourselves to explain how they can come together to form a community whose decisions are binding on its members. It seems less obvious that we cannot do with a contract of society alone, such as Hobbes, Locke and Rousseau portrayed it. Hobbes's covenant and Rousseau's contract establish society and a sovereign by one and the same act, while Locke makes do with Pufendorf's first contract and his decree. The contract of society can be used equally well to give unlimited or conditional authority to government. It is perfectly good logic to deny that the ruler is a party to a contract and yet to insist that his authority is limited by contract. It needed the ingenuity and rhetoric of Hobbes to make obscure this quite simple point; for Hobbes wanted to suggest what is logically absurd – that because the ruler has made no promise to his subjects, they are bound to obey him whatever he may do. The contract of government, though the first to· be invented by people anxious to put a check on their rulers, creates insuperable logical difficulties, even if we accept the conventions of thought on which it rests. If ruler and subjects are parties to a contract, who is to judge between them? The people are just as much bound by the contract as their ruler. It is no more for them than for him to decide when it has been broken. Or if it is for them to decide, then the ruler is rather their subordinate than a person whose rights and duties flow from a covenant made by him with others.

There is, however, a much more serious objection to the contract theory than the logical difficulties which can be neither avoided nor solved on the assumptions which underlie it. The essential weakness of the theory is that it seeks to explain the social order as an effect of transactions impossible outside that order. It treats men as if they were already, quite independently of society, what they can become only in society: bearers of rights and duties, capable of making contracts. But if men already possess rights and duties, they ought to accept whatever is needed to make them good, whether or not they have agreed to do so. If we need government to make good our rights, then, if it in fact makes them good, we have a duty of obedience, no matter how government first arose.

The contract theory was meant to justify resistance to tyrannical government. But as it became more fashionable, it was put to other uses. Hobbes used it to prove that there is no such right, and Pufendorf argued that all authority rests on consent, while still accepting absolute monarchy. Such is the usual fate of a theory that comes to be widely accepted. The purpose the social contract was invented to serve was forgotten – not by all who accepted it, but by many. Locke still used it to justify resistance, and he had several imitators. Yet the theory was popular in the eighteenth century all over the Continent among political writers, many of them jurists who were not in the least concerned to make a case for popular resistance. Absolute monarchy and the contract theory flourished together. It was easy enough, by using the notion of tacit consent, to render the theory harmless. But though it could be so tamed, and often was, it was always liable to be used against established authority. All that a writer had to do to revivify the theory was to insist that consent should be taken seriously. This is what Rousseau did in the *Social Contract*.

Even in its harmless form, the theory drew attention to personal rights. The contract might be relegated to the remote past and the present tacit consent of the citizen be taken for granted, but it was still supposed that the contract was an agreement between individuals and that the consent was a personal commitment. The theory might pay only lip service to freedom, but lip service is better than no service at all. What lingers on the tongue cannot be put wholly out of the mind.

II. THE DOCTRINE OF ABSOLUTE MONARCHY BY DIVINE RIGHT

1. Its origins

Perhaps no important doctrine has flourished for so short a time as the doctrine that the authority of kings is absolute because it comes to them from God. Yet the doctrine is more than an historical curiosity; it is one among several answers to the everlasting problem of European political philosophy, the problem of political obligation. If this particular answer was found attractive for only a few generations, it was not because, in itself, it was inferior to the others. It is no more far-fetched than the theory that government was established by a contract defining the rights and obligations of rulers and ruled; it puts no greater strain on credulity, and is perhaps simpler and less confused. It was short-lived, not because the arguments used to support it were unusually weak, but because the circumstances which made it attractive did not long endure. The doctrine flourished in the seventeenth century, and its ablest exponents were English or French, or were Scotsmen settled in France; it flourished in two out of the three most powerful monarchies of the West at a time when they were either in the throes of civil war or had lately emerged from it. 'In the censure of kingdoms', says Filmer, 'the King of Spain is said to be the King of men, because of his subjects' willing obedience; the King of France, King of asses, because of their infinite taxes and impositions; but the King of England is said to be the King of devils, because of his subjects' often insurrections against, and depositions of, their Princes'.[1] But when Andrew Blackwood, a gallicized Scot, and Pierre de Belloy were claiming absolute power by divine right for the King of France, he too was a king of devils. Not that the devils of France had turned into asses by Filmer's time, for in the late sixteenth and early seventeenth century, the king's rebellious subjects, in both France and England, were the well-to-do and the privileged, who weighed as heavily on the asses as ever the king did.

If it did not, in each case, originate in such conflict, the argument of absolute monarchy by divine right, in France and in England, was most fully developed as a product of civil war; it was an argument attractive to men who sought an absolute and unquestionable authority at a time when it seemed easiest to find it in the king. The theory of the social contract, as elaborated by Huguenots and Jesuits, was a challenge to a type of authority unknown in the high Middle Ages, a central and extensive authority making all other authorities subordinate to itself; it was a challenge made on behalf of subjects whose religion differed from that of their prince. To such subjects as these, the growing power of the monarchy, in an age when religious uniformity was everywhere thought desirable, naturally seemed dangerous. But then, to others, their challenge to it also seemed dangerous; and the doctrine

---

[1] Filmer, *Patriarcha*, ch. XXI, in *Patriarcha and Other Political Works*, ed. Peter Laslett (Oxford 1949), p. 95.

of absolute monarchy by divine right was an answer to that challenge. This doctrine is therefore as unmediaeval as the doctrine it answers; and yet, like the contract theory, it has roots which go back into the Middle Ages and beyond. It is a new theory containing old ingredients. Like nearly all political doctrines, it has a long ancestry, even though it denies an almost universal belief of the Middle Ages, that all human authority is limited and may, if abused, be justly resisted.

In the Middle Ages it was generally held that all authority of man over man, whether spiritual or temporal, comes from God and is limited. Though there were plentiful disputes about the limits of spiritual and temporal authority, and extravagant claims were sometimes made by champions of the one or the other, it was almost universally admitted that the two were separate, and that neither should encroach on the other. Not even the most extreme champions of the Pope – not even those who ascribed to him the fullness of power, *plenitudo potestatis* – literally claimed for him what Hobbes was to understand by sovereign authority; and the claim which was never made on the Pope's behalf was also never made on behalf of the Emperor or any other temporal prince. Just as the Pope's claims were resisted, and variously understood, both inside the Church and by the Temporal Power, so the claims made by emperors or kings were resisted and variously understood both by their temporal subordinates and by the Spiritual Power.

To say that all human authority comes from God is not to deny that it may come also from the people; it is to deny only that it can come from the people alone. Though in the Middle Ages it was much more usual to speak of temporal than of spiritual authority as coming from both God and men, there were some who were willing to speak in this way of both types of authority. For though everyone believed that the Church having spiritual authority over the faithful was established by Christ, and would have no authority if it had not been so established, the tradition was not entirely lost that the first bishops, the first overseers, had been chosen by their flocks.

God, the Creator, has full authority over His creatures, and therefore no creature can have authority over another unless God has allowed it. But God need not, and ordinarily does not, grant authority directly to those that have it. He has endowed man with reason, and therefore with the capacity to provide for his needs in ways impossible to creatures not endowed with reason. Men need to be governed in this world, and where God does not Himself undertake to govern them or to appoint rulers over them, He allows them to provide for themselves. Communities of men have authority from God to make provision for their government, and thus it is that the authority of man over man, at least in the temporal sphere, can be both divine and popular in origin; it must be from God, and it can be, and ordinarily is, from the people also.

Those who held that temporal authority comes from the people as well as from God usually had little to say about its origin. For the most part, they were content to argue that whoever has temporal power has a customary right to it, and that what rests on custom has the people's consent; or later, as Roman Law came to be studied more widely, they spoke more often of a grant of authority made long ago by the people to their rulers just as the Roman jurists had spoken of a grant by the Roman people to the Emperor. Some held that the grant was irrevocable, and others that it could be revoked.

The authority of the prince or supreme temporal ruler was thought to be limited in a variety of ways. Every man was held obliged to prefer divine to human law, and must therefore disobey anyone, layman or priest, who commanded what God forbade or who forbade what God commanded. Secondly, there was the acknowledged duty of obedience to the Spiritual as well as to the Temporal Power. Lastly, there were other magistrates besides the Emperor or King – that is, besides the prince – whose authority rested on custom and whose right to defend their authority, even against the prince, was widely recognized. In the feudal hierarchy, lesser magistrates were not the mere agents of their superiors; they were not related, either in theory or in practice, to the suzerain, to the lord paramount, as all having authority under the sovereign are related to him according to either Bodin or Hobbes.

Thus the authority of the supreme temporal ruler was limited in several ways, and could be effectively resisted; for he was supreme only in the sense that there was no one above him in the hierarchy. Indeed, we may say that, in the Middle Ages, all authority, temporal and spiritual, was severely but not precisely circumscribed; it was loosely defined and subject, within uncertain limits, to considerable fluctuations. There were rights in plenty to invoke against anyone having authority. But this does not mean that the right of subjects to resist authority was widely asserted in the sense that Locke or Bentham asserted it. The Spiritual Power had rights against the Temporal Power, and the Temporal against the Spiritual; the Church had rights against the Pope, and a variety of privileged orders and corporations had rights against the king. Men might differ widely about the extent of these rights, but few, if any, denied them altogether. Yet these rights, in so far as they were effective, were the rights of the privileged against one another. In the Middle Ages the right of resistance to authority was confined, more or less, to persons having authority, and so we can say that, while all authority was limited, the right of the mere individual against those in authority was hardly asserted.

However little asserted, it was, nevertheless, seldom denied as explicitly and fervently as it came to be in later centuries. It was neglected rather than denied. True, even the always moderate Aquinas taught that there is no duty of obedience to a usurper nor yet to a legitimate ruler when he commands what is unjust – what is contrary to divine or natural law, or even to human law (which he thought of as mostly custom) where the ruler has no authority to alter it or set it aside. Aquinas preferred a system in which there are customary methods of restraining the supreme holder of temporal power, but he admitted that, where there are no such methods or they are ineffective, it may be necessary to resort to other methods, not sanctioned by custom, against a ruler who persists in tyranny – that is to say, who claims and attempts to exert an authority which is not his. Yet the admission is not evidence against what I have said, for Aquinas believed that these other methods, when the common good requires their use, should be used by established orders and corporations. Thus we may say that, though Aquinas allows any man a right to disobey, he confines the right of active resistance to holders of authority. But, as we shall see, the right merely to disobey was never denied even by the most extreme champion of the much later doctrine that the authority of princes is absolute and comes to them from God alone and not also from the people.

By early mediaeval custom, the Emperor or King was not even above the law, *legibus solutus*, in the sense of not having to answer for his actions; there was a court to decide between him and those who complained against him, and if he refused to accept its decisions, they might be enforced against him by a withdrawal of allegiance or even by force of arms. But these methods were difficult and dangerous, and so attempts were made to put the king under more effective control – as, for example, by the barons of England in 1258 who imposed the Provisions of Oxford on Henry III. Later, as kings felt a greater need to consult the people (or, rather, the privileged orders and corporations) through their representatives in order to explain royal intentions and needs to them, and to get subsidies from them, Parliaments and Estates served both to make the royal power more effective and to limit it. The Roman conception of the Emperor as above the law, as *legibus solutus*, was applied more and more generally to all princes, to all who, in the temporal hierarchy, had no superior. So, too, from the thirteenth to the fifteenth century, the idea of human law as an expression of conscious will steadily gained ground at the expense of the idea of it as primarily custom. Mediaeval writers repeated more and more frequently the sentence of the Roman lawyers, that what pleases the prince has the force of law. But this sentence, as they uttered it, was still not a claim that the prince was sovereign as Bodin or Hobbes understood sovereignty; for they did not go on to assert that the prince had the right to declare or make law without consulting the people, nor yet that, when he acted against natural or divine law, he might not be resisted. As late as the fifteenth century, Nicholas of Cusa was teaching that human law is the law of the entire community, and that the prince is bound by it; and this was also the doctrine of Gerson in France and of Fortescue in England. The sentences which the champions of absolute monarchy by divine right were to rely on so much were already in wide circulation, but were seldom understood in the sense later ascribed to them by those champions.

In both France and England it was widely admitted in the fifteenth century that 'what concerns all should be approved by all' – that is to say, by the body supposed to speak for the entire community. Parliament in England was already consulted more often and about more matters than the Estates-General in France, but the provincial Estates in France met quite frequently. In both countries the king often made decisions (which we should call laws) by ordinance or by order-in-council, without consulting Parliament or the Estates, for no clear distinction was made between the executive and legislative functions. Yet what was widely admitted was not so much that the king could not make laws without consulting his people as that he ought not to take important decisions without doing so. And those who declared that what concerns all should be approved by all did not feel committed thereby to deny that what pleases the prince has the force of law. These two assertions, as they understood them, were not contradictory.

In the early Middle Ages, when both the Spiritual and the Temporal Power were loosely and weakly organized, each interfered in the sphere of the other with very little friction; or, rather, no serious attempt was made to define the two spheres. Later, as the two Powers came to be better organized, each resented the 'interference' of the other; and each defined and redefined its authority in the endeavour to enlarge it. For a variety of reasons, the Church set itself in order more quickly than the State, and the Pope acquired greater authority inside it than the temporal princes in their kingdoms. Until the fourteenth century it was the Spiritual rather than the Temporal Power which took the offensive. To support its pretensions, the Church pointed partly to its superior dignity, and partly to what it took to be history. The function of the Church, as churchmen saw it, was to give men the instruction and guidance they needed to find God – which they claimed was a higher function than that of temporal rulers, which was merely to maintain the peace. The Church, which helps men to achieve their highest end, is necessarily superior to the Temporal Power, which looks after their lesser ends. Thus, though both Powers are divinely instituted, the lesser power is subordinate to the higher in the sense that, though the Church does not itself exercise temporal power, it has a duty to see that those who exercise it do so worthily; and its most powerful instrument in carrying out this duty is excommunication, for when a prince is excommunicated his subjects no longer owe him obedience. These conclusions were supported by other arguments: it was alleged that, by the donation of Constantine, the empire of the West was given to the Papacy, which later made it over to the Germans; that the authority of temporal rulers is not properly theirs until they have been anointed by the Church; that Christ, being God, had *de jure* both temporal and spiritual authority while He was on earth and had granted both to St Peter and his successors.[1]

The claim of the Church that temporal power, though divinely instituted, comes to its actual possessors through the Church was firmly rejected by the Emperor and the other princes. They and their apologists asserted that the authority of princes comes to them as directly from God as the authority of the Pope and the Church. But this assertion, at that time, was not a denial that authority also comes to them from the people; it was merely a refusal to admit that the divine origin of temporal authority implied any subordination of the Temporal to the Spiritual Power. The Emperor, on whose behalf papal and ecclesiastical pretensions were most vigorously contested, was not even an hereditary but an elected prince; there was no question but that his authority was limited. The other prince whose quarrel with the Pope was the fiercest, the King of France, did rule by hereditary right and was already, by the time that the boldest claims were made on the Pope's behalf, much more powerful

---

[1] The text most often quoted to support this argument was from the Gospel of St Matthew, 16.19, where Christ says to Peter, 'I will give unto thee the keys of the kingdom of heaven: and whatsoever thou shalt bind on earth shall be bound in heaven: and whatsoever thou shalt loose on earth shall be loosed in heaven'. See also ch. 1, pp. 28–32 above.

in France than the Emperor in the empire; but his authority also was far from absolute.

In the early Middle Ages it was not admitted that a king came to his throne by mere hereditary right, on no other ground than that he was his predecessor's closest descendant according to some fixed rule; though the king was usually closely related to his predecessor, the claim of an elder son or of the person whose right would have been undoubted, if the rule of succession had been what it later became, was not infrequently set aside in favour of a younger brother or someone else deemed more worthy. The coronation was then no mere formal ceremony; it was an act of investiture, a bestowal of authority. In England it was not till the fourteenth century that succession by mere hereditary right was firmly established. As the power vested in the king grew, it came to seem more important that there should be no disputes as to who had the right to be king; and so it came to be held that whoever succeeds by hereditary right is truly and fully king from the moment that his predecessor dies. Yet this assertion did not imply that temporal authority was not of popular origin; for the rule of succession was customary, and custom was held to imply popular consent.

It was yet another step from asserting succession by hereditary right to saying that that right is indefeasible, that whoever has it cannot lose it whatever he does. This particular doctrine, though sometimes widely held, was never generally accepted in England. It was popular among Yorkists but was denied by Lancastrians. Even as late as Elizabeth's reign, while Mary Stuart was still alive and there were people willing to argue that she had a better title to the English throne than Elizabeth, an act was passed making it high treason for anyone to question Parliament's right to alter the succession to the throne. After Mary's execution, Elizabeth's title was less questionable, and the doctrine of indefeasible right was for a time widely popular, largely because it was denied by the Jesuits, who hoped to see a Catholic prince on Elizabeth's throne. In France the doctrine first became popular during the Hundred Years' War, and was used to contest English claims. Though the English might by force make themselves masters of France – though a French king might be bullied into recognizing Henry of England as his heir – the law of succession remained unchanged. No English victories, no concessions extorted from defeated Frenchmen, could make a difference; there was only one rightful heir to the throne of France. Henry of England could never be King of France; no power on earth – not even the French king, not even the Estates-General – could give him that title. This

French assertion of indefeasible right was originally a declaration of independence; to those who asserted it, it was a doctrine standing for domestic peace, for the unity of France, for resistance to the invader. It did not imply that the power of the rightful king was absolute, nor even that it was not derived originally from the people; but it did imply that what the people had once bestowed, they could no longer take away.

Before the sixteenth century, neither the doctrine that the authority of kings comes from God nor the doctrine that a legitimate king is so by indefeasible hereditary right was used to resist claims made on behalf of the people; these doctrines came to be used for this purpose only after the Reformation. For the reformers, though their defiance of the Church could hardly have succeeded had they not been supported by princes and kings, started a movement which eventually produced a new type of resistance to princely and royal power. Hitherto the authority of princes had been challenged only by the Church or by the feudal lords; it was soon to be challenged by, or on behalf of, religious minorities, of groups unknown to mediaeval society. These groups often could not assert traditional rights or use traditional methods. They often could not, as the mediaeval Church had been able to do, use rights long recognized and doctrines long familiar to resist the Temporal Power or to attempt encroachments upon it; they often could not, as the feudal lords had long been able to do, use an assembly like the Estates-General or Parliament, an assembly dominated by their order, to restrain the king. They could not appeal to customary rights to justify resistance. At least, they could nowhere do so effectively until in England by the seventeenth century they had acquired a considerable influence in the lower House of Parliament, the House which in mediaeval times had been much the less important of the two, but which had recently gained greatly in power and prestige, largely owing to the use made of it by Tudor monarchs.

2. *Its popularity and significance*

Just as some writers were moved to put forward a new type of argument to justify resistance to temporal rulers, so others, who were not concerned with the fate of minorities but with dangers to the peace, were moved to make exceptional claims for those rulers, or for the most highly placed among them. There were others before Bodin who had said that the King of France had sovereign power, but they had not defined sovereignty as he was to do. They did not argue, as he did, that all others having temporal authority in France were mere officers of the king, having only as much authority as he was pleased to grant them, and which he could take away from them whenever he saw fit to do so; they had not claimed for him the sole right of making or declaring law, saying that he consulted the people's representatives, not because he was obliged to do so, but only because he found it useful; they had not insisted that the king was responsible to God alone for how he used his authority, and that no one, no matter what his official capacity, could rightfully refuse to obey him except when what he commanded was contrary to the command of God. It had long been held that the mere subject must not refuse obedience to his prince except when to obey him would involve disobedience to God; but this prohibition had not been understood to apply to every person or body having temporal authority within his dominions. Bodin's conception of sovereignty was as new as the arguments of the contract theorists.

But Bodin was not an exponent of the doctrine that kings have absolute power by divine right. Though he believed, in the sense of the mediaeval writers, that all authority of man over man comes ultimately from God, he did not make a special case for kings. He thought that, in every well-ordered state, there must be a sovereign, but he did not hold that the sovereign must be a king. He preferred monarchy to other types of government, and thought it best suited to a country like France. Further than that he did not go; he did not say that God had blessed monarchy above other forms of government, nor did he forbid resistance to the King of France on the express ground that he was God's deputy in a certain part of the world. He thought it enough to produce what he supposed was good historical evidence that in France sovereignty belonged by tradition to the king, and he rejoiced that it should be so.

Yet Bodin's idea of sovereignty was taken over by the first exponents in France of the doctrine of absolute monarchy by divine right. They claimed, not only for the King of France, but for all kings, that they are God's deputies on earth and therefore have absolute authority over their subjects; they claimed for them, and for them alone, what Bodin understood by sovereignty. The theory of the divine right of kings, as we find it first in France and then very soon afterwards in England, puts forward these propositions: that temporal authority comes to princes from God alone and not also from the people; that it belongs entirely to them and to such persons as they appoint to exercise it and from whom they can withdraw it when they please; that they acquire it by indefeasible hereditary right, and are accountable only to God for how they use it and not to their subjects or to any man or body of men holding authority, of whatever kind, spiritual or temporal. Exponents of the theory, though they do not exactly deny that forms of government other than monarchy are legitimate, usually neglect them, and are at pains to show that monarchy is divinely instituted in some special sense. They appeal to Holy Scripture to show that it was monarchy, and not some other form of government, which God gave to His chosen people; and they also argue that monarchy is a form or extension of paternal authority, which was the first to exist among men and is the most natural, and may therefore be presumed to enjoy the peculiar favour of God, who is the Father of mankind. As the king is the father of his people, so is he to that extent Godlike.

The doctrine became popular because it met a need which was peculiarly strong in countries in the throes of, or threatened by, civil war. It was in many ways better suited to meet that need than the theories of either Bodin or Hobbes. It was simpler, cruder and less elaborately argued than Bodin's defence of the French monarchy; it appealed in a religious age to some of the most deeply and widely held beliefs. Bodin was interested in forms of government other than monarchy; he believed that different forms are suited to different peoples; he was aware that institutions change and are adapted to circumstances, and he adduced precedents often not easy to interpret. If he was not always a clear thinker, he was certainly a subtle one. His argument for absolute monarchy in France rested partly on an appeal to tradition and partly on an appeal to the common interest; it was an intricate and difficult argument, best appreciated by the learned and by men experienced in government. The argument of, say, Pierre de Belloy was, by contrast, bold and simple: the king must be obeyed unconditionally because his authority comes from God, who has made him answerable to Himself alone for how he uses it. The king's authority is absolute and legitimate, not by long tradition or because its being so is ultimately for the people's good, but because Almighty God, in His wisdom and mercy, has made it so.

To the man who appreciates clear thinking and well-constructed argument, Hobbes's account of sovereignty and his apology for it appear more admirable even than Bodin's. Hobbes will always be a favourite among intellectuals. He is a robust, bold, resourceful and at times close reasoner; he uses his arguments with the assurance of a fully prepared general winning a complete victory in a large and intricate battle; he is the most pungent of political philosophers, and has a sharp wit, though he is not bitter or waspish. He is a remedy for dullness; to read him is to be put in a better humour. From a certain point of view, he made the best of all cases for absolute authority. But he did not make a case likely to attract the unsophisticated. He has had, no doubt, a great and long influence; he has had a distinguished intellectual posterity. Many have borrowed from him, including the two most famous among the champions of absolute monarchy by divine right, Filmer and Bossuet. Yet he has been more admired than persuasive; those best able to appreciate his merits, the intellectuals, have also been the best equipped to take from him what they needed without swallowing his arguments whole. To others he has seemed perverse or cynical, and even when they have liked his conclusions, they have wanted to reach them by other paths than he took. He ascribed to the sovereign as much authority as any believer in absolute monarchy by divine right claimed for the king, but he allowed that men had by common agreement set up government for their own benefit. He allowed that the people, when they made this agreement, might place sovereignty where they pleased, and merely expressed, on grounds of convenience, a preference for monarchy over other forms of government. He did not believe in indefeasible right, for he argued that the possessor of sovereignty loses it altogether as soon as he can no longer enforce obedience. Though he argued for absolute authority, and elucidated the idea of it as no one before him had done, he used arguments which offended the prejudices of those who most craved for that authority; his doctrine, to the extent that they took notice of it, was distasteful and disturbing to them. Neither Bodin nor Hobbes, the two ablest apologists of absolute authority, produced a doctrine satisfying to the many who feared civil war and anarchy above all things and looked for a sure refuge against them. The doctrine which came closest to satisfying them, though it owed much, first to Bodin and later to Hobbes, was different. It was simpler and looser, resting on familiar and widely received assumptions and calling for no great intellectual effort from those to whom it was addressed. It also relied heavily on Holy Scripture, on texts and examples which were familiar and venerable; it rested, much more obviously than the theories of Bodin and Hobbes, on a religious foundation. If it was a simple doctrine, it was not bare or bleak; it was profusely illustrated from the Bible; it made ample use of ideas and stories which Christians had not yet learnt to question or to treat as allegory or parable.

Yet it needed years of civil war or the threat of anarchy to bring this doctrine to birth. For, though it made use of the familiar and the venerable, it also denied what had been asserted or implied by the great majority of political writers in the Middle Ages: that the authority of temporal rulers, though divinely instituted, also comes to them from the people and is always limited. At first, even the most fervent champions of royal power and legitimacy in France, though they insisted that the king's authority is 'absolute', took care to explain that it is also limited. When they called it absolute, they meant that there is no authority on earth superior to it, that the king is answerable to no court when he breaks the law, that it is always wrong to take up arms against him; but they did not claim for him what Bodin understood by sovereignty; they did not claim for him that no one can make or declare law in France except the king or whoever has authority from him to do so, and they did not forbid all resistance to his will other than passive disobedience when he commands what is contrary to the command of God. So much reluctance, so much beating about the bush of sovereignty, bears strong witness to the hold over men's minds of the old mediaeval idea that human authority is limited by the purpose it serves. The royalists in France were driven to more extreme opinions only by the extremity of their country's need.

The doctrine of absolute monarchy by divine right flourished earlier in France than in England because domestic war came first to France; and the doctrine was more widely accepted there for a longer time, partly no doubt because the wars of religion brought France much nearer to anarchy than the civil war brought England, but above all because the royalists in England were defeated. The defeat and eventual execution of the English king, far from producing anarchy, gave England the strongest government she had ever had, whereas in France, though royal authority was repeatedly challenged and brought to nothing in several provinces, the rebels were never able to set up an effective government in any part of the country. Besides, the parties to the war, the Catholic League and the Huguenots, were not fighting, as both Royalists and Parliamentarians were in England, for some idea of how their country should be governed. They challenged or supported the royal power according to circumstances; they defended it when they thought they could use it for their own purposes, and challenged it when they feared that their enemies might use it. Though they were engaged in a struggle which was not merely religious, though they were fighting for power and influence and not only to preserve or extend the faith, they were not engaged, as were the parties to the English Civil War, in a constitutional struggle. The civil war in England was won by one of the parties to it – the party that wanted still further to limit the royal power – whereas the religious wars in France were won by neither party to them. They merely served to strengthen the royal power, which both parties had sought in vain to control or to emasculate. Hence the earlier and wider and more enduring popularity in France, embracing a period of more than two centuries, of the doctrine of absolute monarchy by divine right.

Indeed, the doctrine proved respectable in England for just a few generations. Even the Royalists were not much attracted to it during the Civil War, for they were not fighting for absolute monarchy. They were fighting, as also were the Parliamentarians, for constitutional monarchy, though they had a different conception of what it should be. If England ceased for a time to be a monarchy, it was certainly not because Parliament had challenged the royal power in order to destroy it; it was because the victors found that they could not come to a satisfactory settlement with Charles I, and there was no one to put in his place. Filmer's *Patriarcha*, the most famous English version of the doctrine of absolute monarchy by divine right, though inspired by the quarrel which led to civil war, and perhaps written long before the war started, was not published until 1680, twenty-seven years after its author's death. So the doctrine, in English history, achieved its fullest expression in the period of the restored monarchy, during a renewed and bitter struggle between Charles II and Parliament; it owed its popularity in that period, not to actual civil war, but to a fear that the country might again be plunged into civil war. It seemed to many people that the country could avoid a repetition of the troubles it had lived through only if the king's authority were recognized to be absolute. Much the same causes account for the doctrine's appeal in England as in France, but in France they were more urgent and more lasting.

It has been suggested that the theory of absolute monarchy by divine right, though not less widely popular in Catholic than in Protestant countries, found fuller or less qualified expression in Protestant countries.[1] For in Catholic countries it was impossible to deny that the Church was independent of the royal power. The King of France could not aspire to be what the King of England was, supreme head of the Church as well as of the State; nor could it even be claimed on behalf of Catholic princes that, although they had no authority to decide what men should believe in matters of religion, it was for them to see to it that the Church was properly organized, to appoint to benefices inside it, and to maintain ecclesiastical discipline. It was impossible for a Catholic to claim for his king the authority within the Church attributed by Luther to princes, not to speak of

---

[1] See J. N. Figgis, *The Divine Right of Kings*, first published in 1896, ch. VI.

the supremacy accorded to the English king. As early as Henry VIII's reign, it had been argued (for instance, by Christopher St Germain[1]), that, though the Church alone can expound the Scriptures and declare the truth concerning faith, the Church in England must be taken to be the professing Christians of England, whose head and representative is the king. This was to unite spiritual and temporal authority in one person just as clearly as Hobbes united it, and it was something that no Catholic prince could allow anyone to do on his behalf.

Yet the Catholic apologists of absolute monarchy by divine right, in their zeal against the champions of limited monarchy and the right of resistance, by no means forgot the old quarrel of the Temporal with the Spiritual Power. Both Pierre de Belloy and William Barclay, two of the earlier exponents of the doctrine,[2] denied that the Pope, by excommunicating a prince, could release his subjects from allegiance to him. No act of the Pope, said Belloy, could touch Henry of Navarre's right to the French throne, for he was heir to it by virtue of a rule established by God. The Pope, said Barclay, has the right to excommunicate anyone, even a king; but his action can have no political effects. The end of temporal authority is men's security and felicity in this world, whereas the end of spiritual authority is to bring men to God in the next world. Therefore it can never be true that the Pope can help save the souls of the king's subjects by destroying the king's authority over them, and so he cannot have the right to destroy it; he cannot depose a king by putting an end to his subjects' allegiance. Barclay assumed that men's spiritual and temporal needs can be precisely distinguished and quite separately provided for, so that the Pope, whose duty is to care for the first, must never interfere with the king, whose duty is to care for the second; he implies that it can never be necessary, for the good of men's souls, to interfere with the exercise of temporal authority. This assumption and that implication are both doubtful, if not false; but a Catholic had to make them if he was to hold fast to the doctrine of absolute monarchy by divine right. Barclay could not assert that all authority of man over man, no matter what its kind, belongs only to the king, and so he was moved to argue that the temporal sphere is completely separate, so that no exercise of temporal authority can prevent the Church performing its mission.

---

[1] See J. W. Allen, *A History of Political Thought in the Sixteenth Century* (London 1928), pp. 165–8.

[2] Belloy in his *Apologie catholique* of 1585 and Barclay in *De potestate papae* of 1609.

In France, as in England, the kings were faced with two kinds of opposition on religious grounds. In England there were the Catholics, on the one hand, and the Protestant sects on the other. There were many in England who, even though they did not believe in absolute monarchy, sympathized strongly with the king while he resisted the ambitions and demands of both Catholics and sectaries. So, too, in France, there were many who sympathized with the king in his resistance both to the Catholic League and to the Huguenots, and who deplored his falling under the sway of either. To many in both England and France it seemed that the royal power was a moderating influence, that what the king stood for, in Church and State, was more truly popular and more for the common good than what he resisted. To them, not only in theory but in practice, the king came closer than anyone to being the 'representative' of his people. This feeling was to be found among both the laity and the clergy, in France as well as in England. Just as in England the Established Church was ardently loyal to the king, so too in France were the Gallicans. Though the French Church never broke with Rome, there were bishops and lesser priests in it eager to assert its 'liberties' against the Pope; and, like the Established Church across the water, they looked to the king to support them against enemies on both their flanks, against both papal and Calvinist pretensions. The motives and quality of Gallican and Anglican devotion to the throne were not dissimilar. Bossuet, the most vigorous champion of Gallican liberties, was also the most eloquent of all exponents of the theory of the divine right of kings. Of course, most English royalists devoted to the Established Church did not believe in absolute monarchy by divine right, and this is true also of some French royalists who were strong Gallicans; but those who did believe in it were not markedly less moderate and tolerant in matters of religion than those who did not.

In the sixteenth and seventeenth centuries two questions which are now acknowledged to be very different from one another were not clearly distinguished: How does political authority arise?, and What makes it legitimate? The contract theorists argued that political authority was, or must be supposed to have been, set up by agreement between those who became subject to it, and is therefore limited by the purpose which the agreement was intended to achieve. The idea of contract was used to explain the origin of government mostly by persons who wanted to justify resistance to government. But Hobbes used it for the opposite purpose; he sought to show that only an agreement to give unconditional obedience to some person or body of persons could provide the parties to the agreement with the security they wanted. Bodin appealed to tradition, to long establishment, more in the spirit of Burke than of mediaeval political thinkers: time makes authority legitimate, not so much because it offers evidence of popular consent as because it shows that power is exercised for the public good. In France sovereignty belongs properly to the king: it has long been so and therefore ought to be so. But Bodin's account of the French system, as indeed any similar account of any other system, could always be challenged; it is always possible to appeal to tradition, to history, against the use of it made by defenders of any particular interpretation of it. The champions of absolute monarchy by divine right felt the need to rest their claims on what seemed to them more solid foundations. Hence their argument that monarchy is the most *natural* form of government because it arises out of paternal authority, or because it is a copy on earth of God's kingdom in Heaven or of His sole dominion over all things. Hence too their close scrutiny of the history of the Jews, God's chosen people, as recorded in the Old Testament. For where is God's will more clearly manifest than in the history of that people on whose behalf He has intervened directly in human affairs?

The champions of absolute monarchy by divine right, like other political writers engaged in continual controversy, were as much concerned to show up the absurdities of rival doctrines as to state their own persuasively; and it has been suggested that they were more successful in the first aim than in the second.[1] Perhaps they were. At least it is likely to seem so to us, for we now reject both their theory and the theories they criticized, and so we are apt to be more impressed by their reasons for disagreeing with their rivals than by what they had to say in support of their own doctrine. Yet I suspect that this verdict is inspired largely by seeing the doctrine in its English context. In England it was popular only for a brief period, and during that time was vigorously contested. The best English version of it, Filmer's *Patriarcha*, was written long before the doctrine came to be most widely espoused; it was written by someone as much concerned to attack rival (and more popular) doctrines as to put forward his own. Of Filmer, more truly than of any other exponent of the doctrine, we can say that he is more impressive when he attacks others than when he defends himself. The earlier exponents of the doctrine – for example, Belloy and Barclay in France, and Bancroft and Saravia in England –

---

[1] This is the impression created on the reader by Laslett in his introduction to Filmer's *Patriarcha and Other Political Works*, and by Figgis in his *Divine Right of Kings*.

were mere controversialists. If they are important at all, they are so only as early champions of a doctrine more ably stated after their time. Their works are no longer read, except by scholars interested in French and English political controversies arising out of the wars of religion. Filmer, by contrast, is still read and is worth reading; for though he, too, was a controversialist, he was so on a higher level. He was not content to make assertions and to support them with texts; he tried to construct an argument, and got into difficulties in the attempt. Figgis has suggested that Filmer's virtues were the undoing of the doctrine he defended; he drew men's attention to what is the essence of it, and so made it easier for them to detect its flaws. By his method he invited them, not to a war of quotations from Holy Scripture (though he used them freely), but to rational argument; and rational argument (so Figgis implies) was just what the doctrine could not withstand. All unconsciously, Filmer prepared the doctrine of absolute monarchy by divine right to be a fitting sacrifice to Reason (or perhaps I should say, to Common Sense) under the knife of John Locke.

It is a pretty picture and is not altogether untrue; for it was certainly Locke's attack on the doctrine which ruined it in educated circles, first in England and later in France (where no other English political philosopher enjoyed anything like Locke's reputation); and it was Filmer's version of it that Locke attacked. But we ought not to take the measure of a doctrine in the version of it which has remained famous precisely because it was attacked by a man greater than its author. Not that Filmer is worth reading only because Locke attacked him; he would still be worth reading even if Locke had never mentioned his work. Yet the fact remains that he lives on in our memories because he was Locke's victim. Indeed, there are many who have read Locke's attack without reading what he attacked. Those who have argued that Filmer is intellectually much more respectable than Locke's treatment of him might lead one to expect have not been concerned to defend his doctrine; they have been closer to accepting Locke's political philosophy than Filmer's, and so have been more impressed by Filmer's criticisms of others than by his positive beliefs.

No political theory is more completely dead than the doctrine of absolute monarchy by divine right. But it was once very much alive; and, if we want to see what it meant to those who accepted it, we had better look at it, not only in Filmer's version, but in Bossuet's as well. For in France the doctrine was triumphant as it never was in England. In seventeenth-century France it was as widely accepted as was the political philosophy of Locke during the eighteenth century in England. Bossuet expounded it with an assurance, a serenity and a moderation which lent dignity to it; he expounded it even more than he argued for it. He, too, no doubt, was a controversialist, but he was more than just inwardly convinced that he possessed the truth; he also spoke like a man sure of his audience. Bossuet's *Politique tirée des propres paroles de l'Écriture Sainte,* though it preaches a doctrine in many ways similar to Filmer's *Patriarcha,* is altogether different in tone and effect. Not that Bossuet preached to the converted, for his purpose was to instruct and persuade; it is rather that he preached what he believed must persuade if his listeners have not closed their minds to reason. What makes Bossuet impressive is that his confidence in the truth of what he teaches is free of arrogance; it is the confidence of the man who both has faith and has never doubted that faith and reason can be perfectly reconciled. His version of the doctrine is not more impressive than Filmer's merely because, being more moderate, it is less open to some of the attacks that Locke made on Filmer. Nor is it more impressive merely for being the work of one of the greatest of French writers. It is more impressive because it brings home to us, whose beliefs about political authority differ so greatly from his, what the doctrine of divine right meant to those who accepted it wholeheartedly. Bossuet speaks, as no one else does, for a now defunct but once important political order; he speaks for it with the authority that Aquinas spoke with for the social and political order of the thirteenth century.

The earlier and cruder versions of the doctrine were produced in the late sixteenth century, the later and more sophisticated versions, by Filmer and by Bossuet, in the course of the seventeenth. The influence of Bodin and of Hobbes is apparent in all their writings. For Filmer, though he wrote his best-known work, *Patriarcha,* before Hobbes had published any of his reflections on government, came afterwards to read both *De cive* and *Leviathan,* finding them much to his taste. The first sentences of Filmer's preface to his *Observations Concerning the Originall of Government* make it clear what he accepted and rejected in Hobbes:

> With no small content I read Mr. Hobbes's book *De Cive,* and his *Leviathan,* about the rights of sovereignty, which no man, that I know, hath so amply and judiciously handled: I consent with him about the rights of exercising government, but I cannot agree to his means of acquiring it. It may seem strange that I should praise his building, and yet mislike his foundation; but so it is, his *Jus Naturae,* and his *Regnum Institutivum,* will not down with me: they appear full of contradiction and impossibilities; a few short notes about them, I here offer, wishing he would consider whether his building would not stand firmer upon

the principles of *Regnum Patrimoniale* (as he calls it) both according to scripture and reason.[1]

To put the building constructed by Bodin and perfected by Hobbes on a firmer foundation – this is the purpose common to Filmer and to Bossuet. 'According to scripture and reason', says Filmer, believing that the two are perfectly in keeping with each other, 'I cannot but reverence that form of government which was allowed and made use of for God's own people, and for all other nations. It were impiety to think that God who was careful to appoint judicial laws for his chosen people, would not furnish them with the best form of government: or to imagine that the rules given in divers places in the gospel, by our blessed Saviour and his Apostles for obedience to Kings should now, like almanacs out of date, be of no use to us'.[2] The assumption of Filmer and Bossuet is that the political teaching of Holy Scripture is clear and unequivocal. As we look back on the political controversies of the sixteenth and seventeenth centuries, when the Scriptures were quoted to such diverse and even bizarre effect, this may seem to us an assumption reckless to the point of absurdity. But is it more absurd than Burke's faith in tradition, in what he called 'the general bank and capital of nations and of ages'? It is only another example of the perennial need felt for a store of wisdom, a body of doctrine on which all men may rely as a sure guide for action. If even the most important matters are never to be regarded as settled, if everything is always to be open to question, how are men ever to have security and peace of mind? Unfortunately, however, the store of wisdom does not consist of hard coins which keep their shape as they pass from hand to hand; it consists of ideas and doctrines whose meanings change with the minds that entertain them.

III. FILMER

Before we consider the doctrine which Filmer offers his readers for true, let us look at what he has to say against the opinions which he is most concerned to demolish: that, men being free by nature and at liberty to choose what government they please, the right to govern was granted to those who first had it by those who thereby became subject to it; and that the authority of kings is limited by the

[1] Filmer, *Patriarcha and Other Political Works*, p. 239.
[2] Filmer, preface to *The Anarchy of a Limited or Mixed Monarchy*, ibid., p. 278.

terms of that grant. Against these opinions he advances two kinds of arguments, historical and abstract. In the second chapter of *Patriarcha*, for example, he accuses Bellarmine of contradicting his own assertion, that men are by nature equal, when he admits that the patriarchs of the Old Testament were 'endowed with kingly power'. In the Bible we can read how the first man was created, how he acquired a wife and children, and what happened to his posterity; and the account we find there is proof conclusive that in the beginning men were not equal. It was, so Filmer thought, above all the Jesuits and 'some zealous favourers of the Geneva discipline' who were putting about this doctrine of the natural freedom and equality of men. But the Jesuits and followers of Calvin were presumably as certain as was Filmer that the Bible is authentic history. He was producing against the doctrine of natural equality facts which those who asserted it were bound to accept as true. Again, in *The Freeholder's Grand Inquest Touching our Sovereign Lord the King and His Parliament*,[1] Filmer appeals to history to show that the legislative power in England belongs only to the king and is not shared by him with the two Houses of Parliament, though by custom he consults with them when he exercises that power. This is a different kind of appeal to history, for Filmer cites many precedents and quotes amply from documents; but still it is an appeal to history. Filmer here makes the same claims for the King of England as Bodin made for the King of France. If we neglect this part of his argument, it is not because it is in itself bad, for Filmer's use (or abuse) of history is not unusually one-sided or superficial by the standards of his day; it is because it raises no issues of much concern to the political theorist.

To those who say that men are by nature free, Filmer objects that they are in fact born dependent. In his 'Observations on Mr. Hobbes's *Leviathan*', he says, 'I cannot understand how this right of nature can be conceived without imagining a company of men at the very first to have been all created together without any dependency one of another, or as mushrooms (*fungorum more*) they all on a sudden were sprung out of the earth without any obligation one to another'.[2] But men are born of women and into families, whose members have obligations towards one another; and children owe obedience to their parents. Nor can it be said that children become free by nature when they cease to be under age, for 'in nature there is no *nonage*; if a man be not born free, she doth not assign him any other time when he shall attain his freedom'.[3]

---

[1] See Filmer's *Political Works*, pp. 133–84.
[2] Ibid., p. 241.
[3] *The Anarchy of a Limited or Mixed Monarchy*, ibid., p. 287.

It would be unjust to Filmer to say that this argument misses the essential point because those who hold that man is by nature free are not to be taken literally, the essence of their doctrine being, not that men were once free and then voluntarily placed themselves under obligations, but rather that men are born to freedom, in the sense that, given their nature – that they are rational and can make choices – the obligations which they recognize, when they attain the age of reason, are related to ends they pursue, to what they desire or find desirable. Only creatures capable of freedom can have obligations. We must remember that, in Filmer's time, those who spoke of man's being naturally free meant to convey more than what we may choose to call the 'essence' of their doctrine because it seems to us the most valuable part of it. No doubt, the more prudent of them did not mean to be taken quite literally. As Filmer himself recognized, Hobbes did not believe that, as a matter of fact, men had once lived in a state of nature. But he did mean to convey that all authority of man over man rests on consent. He meant, as did all the others who spoke of man's being naturally free, to convey something that is not true, and which Filmer could see was not true. Admittedly, there is something valuable in the doctrine that he attacked which Filmer failed to see. There is a point which he missed. But, we may ask, how clearly did the upholders of the doctrine themselves see the point? They certainly failed to state it, for it is only implicit in what they said. The doctrine that man is naturally free, as it was expounded in the seventeenth century, has some implications which are acceptable and others which are not. At least it can be said for Filmer that he saw the defects of the doctrine more clearly than its exponents saw what was valuable in it.

The idea that men's primary obligations – the obligations on which the social and political order rests – derive from consent seemed absurd to Filmer. He was not hard put to it to demolish the arguments of those who, like Hobbes, contended that even the right of the conqueror is established by covenant because the conquered must be supposed to agree to obey him on condition that he allows them life and liberty. If the conqueror, when he makes his conquest, is in what Hobbes calls a state of nature, he has (as Hobbes admits) the right to subject others to his will, provided he has the power, and so has no need of their consent; and if he is not in the state of nature, he is subject to some sovereign, and so has no right to conquer others and force them into subjection. To another assertion of Hobbes, that even paternal authority rests on 'the child's consent, either express or by other sufficient arguments declared', Filmer merely objects that it is not to be understood how a child can express consent or 'by other sufficient arguments' declare it before it has reached the age of discretion.[1] Those who held that political authority rests on the consent of the governed did not deny that many governments were in fact established by conquest or arose gradually out of paternal rule; they were concerned rather to assert that, no matter how they were established or arose, their authority rests on the consent of the persons subject to them. But it seemed to them that they could not reach this conclusion unless they could show that even conquerors and parents rule by consent. They laid themselves open to such criticisms as Filmer's, partly because they failed to distinguish questions of origin from questions of right, and partly because they persisted in speaking of consent as if it implied some kind of contract.

According to the contract theorists, it is the *people* who have the right to provide for their own security, and therefore the right to set up government to give them security. But who, asks Filmer, are to be reckoned as the people? Who, in the absence of all government, of all authority of man over man, are the people? Are they the whole of mankind? If they are not, how did this come about? If there are several or many peoples in the world, each with the right to set up a separate government, how did they acquire this right? Did all mankind divest themselves of a right which belonged to them collectively in favour of separate multitudes?[2] Do the writers who claim this right for the people understand the nature of their claim? Do they know on whose behalf they are making it? 'Literally, and in the largest sense, the word people signifies the whole of mankind; but figuratively . . . it notes many times the major part of a multitude, or sometimes the better, or the richer, or the wiser, or some other part; and oftentimes a very small part of the people, if there be no other apparent opposite party, hath the name of the people by presumption.'[3] When we use the word *people* in the senses which Filmer calls figurative, we are not speaking of men in the state of nature, for 'by nature all mankind in the world makes but one people, who they [i.e. those against whom Filmer is arguing] suppose to be born alike to an equal freedom from subjection; and where such freedom is, there all things must of necessity be common: and therefore without a joint consent of the whole people of the world, no one thing can be made proper to any one man, but it will be an injury, and a usurpation upon the common

---

[1] Filmer, 'Observations on Mr. Hobbes's *Leviathan*', ibid., p. 245.
[2] See *Patriarcha*, ch. XIII, pp. 81–2.
[3] *The Anarchy of a Limited or Mixed Monarchy*, ibid., p. 285.

right of all others. From whence it follows that natural freedom being once granted, there cannot be any one man chosen a King without the universal consent of all the people of the world at one instant, *nemine contradicente.*'[1]

Filmer's point is simple enough. What makes one part of mankind distinct from the others – what makes them collectively one people – is that they are under one government. Community is not prior to authority. Just as a family consists of all who are subject to the same father, so a people consists of all who are subject to the same government. They are a distinct community because there is an authority to which they are all in fact subject. If we assume the contrary, if we assume that they are a community who by agreement establish an authority over themselves, we have to explain how they came to be a community. And this, says Filmer, we cannot do. For, if by nature all men are equal and free, and all things belong to them in common, no section of mankind can set up a government in any part of the world without injury to the rest of mankind, without curtailing their natural freedom. If all things are by nature common to all men, and all men are by nature free, how can any number of men, short of the whole number, lay it down that there shall be among them (in the part of the world where they happen to be) either government or private property? For by their action they claim to exclude all other men from that part of the world which they have appropriated, and that is a clear invasion of natural freedom. Must we then suppose that mankind unanimously divided themselves into separate multitudes, giving to each a right to set up a government? The supposition is not only fantastic; it is also inadequate. 'Mankind is like the sea, ever ebbing or flowing, every minute one is born another dies; those that are the people this minute, are not the people the next minute, in every instant and point of time there is a variation.'[2] And we cannot say the acts of parents bind their children, for 'then farewell the doctrine of the natural freedom of mankind'.[3] Nor yet can we say that the decision of the majority binds the rest, 'for the major part never binds, but where men at first either agree to be so bound, or where a higher power so commands',[4] and in the case supposed, in the state of nature, no higher power does so command. 'No one man, nor a multitude, can give away the natural right of another.

[1] Ibid.
[2] Ibid., p. 287.
[3] Ibid.
[4] Ibid., p. 286.

The law of nature is unchangeable, and howsoever one man may hinder another in the use or exercise of his natural right, yet thereby no man loseth the right itself. . . . Therefore, unless it can be proved by some law of nature that the major, or some other part, have power to overrule the rest of the multitude, it must follow that the acts of multitudes not entire are not binding to all, but only to such as consent unto them.'[1]

Just as those who seek to derive the obligation to obey rulers from the consent of their subjects are inclined to use the word *consent* broadly and loosely, so those who contest their doctrine are inclined to use it strictly. Filmer attacks the notion of tacit consent which Locke was to employ so freely:

> If the silent acceptation of a governor by part of the people be an
> argument of their concurring in the election of him, by the same
> reason the tacit assent of the whole commonwealth may be maintained.
> From whence it follows that every Prince that comes to a crown, either
> by succession, conquest or usurpation, may be said to be elected by the
> people. Which inference is too ridiculous, for in such cases the people
> are so far from the liberty of *specification* that they want even that of
> *contradiction*.[2]

That is to say, in such cases, the people, far from being able to choose who shall rule over them, cannot even refuse to accept the ruler who puts himself upon them.

No government, says Filmer, ever was set up by the people subject to it. To this it may be objected that in some countries kings come to the throne by election and not by hereditary right. But even in these countries they are elected by only a small part of the people, by nobles or by 'great men' or by princes of the blood. Wherever we look, we never see rulers chosen by even the major part of their subjects, let alone by all of them. And the bodies which claim to represent the entire people are very far indeed from doing so. In England the Commons are no doubt reputed to represent the people, but in fact represent only 'a part of the lower or inferior part of the body of the people, which are the freeholders worth 40s. by the year, and the Commons or freemen of cities and boroughs, or the major part of them. All which are not one-quarter, nay, not a tenth part of the Commons of the kingdom'.[3] This is a kind of turning of the tables on those who wished to limit the authority of kings by an appeal to popular rights. Why should a body representing only a tenth part of

[1] *Patriarcha*, ch. XIII, p. 82.
[2] Ibid.
[3] *The Anarchy of a Limited or Mixed Monarchy*, ibid., p. 290.

the people think themselves entitled to challenge the king in the name of the whole people? Locke, when he comes to 'demolish' Filmer, never troubles to answer that question. It is not taken seriously, except by the Levellers, until the second half of the eighteenth century.[1] To see a champion of divine right using arguments later used by radicals is interesting.

Filmer wins many neat victories over the men who affect to make the people's cause their own. It is not he but Grotius who says that by nature men are free, and yet it is Grotius and not he who speaks of a right to rule established by conquest. True, Grotius speaks of a just war; but how can a man who wages a just war acquire by victory a right to rule the vanquished, if he did not have that right before the war began? For a war of conquest to be just, it must be waged in order to enforce a title which is good independently of the outcome of the war:

> For if a King come in by conquest, he must either conquer them
> that have a governor, or those people that have none; if they have no
> governor, then they are a free people, and so the war will be unjust
> to conquer those that are free, especially if the freedom of the people
> be by the primary law of nature as Grotius teacheth: but if the people
> conquered have a governor, that governor hath either a title or not; if
> he hath a title, it is an unjust war that takes the kingdom from him: if
> he hath no title, but only the possession of a kingdom, yet it is unjust
> for any other man that wants a title also, to conquer him that is but in
> possession, for it is a just rule, that where the cases are alike, he that is
> in possession is in the better condition.[2]

Filmer, when he argues that political authority does not rest on consent, is often forceful and ingenious; he is much less so when he denies that the authority of kings is limited. I have in mind, not his arguments from history to show that the authority of the King of England is unlimited – for they need not concern the political theorist – but rather only the general arguments which apply to royal authority everywhere. The best of them are to be found in *The Anarchy of a Limited or Mixed Monarchy*, which appeared in 1648, and is for the most part a criticism of Philip Hunton's *Treatise of Monarchy* of 1643. They amount to little more than was better said by Hobbes.

Filmer asks who is to judge between the king and any of his subjects in a limited monarchy:

---

[1] And even the Levellers did not seek manhood suffrage. They did not want *servants* to have the vote, and half the adult males in England *were* servants, as the word was then understood.

[2] Filmer, 'Observations upon H. Grotius', in *Political Works*, p. 270.

For instance, the King commands me, or gives judgment against me:
I reply, his commands are illegal, and his judgment not according to
law; who must judge? If the monarch himself judge, then you destroy
the frame of the state, and make it absolute, saith our author [i.e.
Hunton]; and he gives his reason: for, to define a monarch to a law,
and then to make him judge of his own deviations from that law,
is to absolve him from all law. On the other side, if any, or all the
people may judge, then you put the sovereignty in the whole body,
or part of it, and destroy the being of monarchy. Thus our author has
caught himself in a plain dilemma: if the King be judge, then he is no
limited monarch; if the people be judge, then he is no monarch at all.
So farewell limited monarchy, nay farewell all government, if there be
no judge.[1]

That is to say, if there is to be effective government, there must be a
final judge of what the law is, and the final judge is the only true maker
of the law, the sovereign whose precept, in the words of Hobbes,
'contains in it the reason of obedience'. Government affords security
only because it provides those subject to it with a common judge.
If, then, subjects challenge the decisions of the common judge, they
destroy or threaten this security. For then 'every man must oppose
or not oppose the monarch according to his own conscience. Thus at
the last, every man is brought, by this doctrine of our authors, to be
his own judge. And I also appeal to the consciences of all mankind,
whether the end of this be not utter confusion, and anarchy'.[2] The
argument against limited monarchy is more forcefully put in this later
treatise than in the twentieth chapter of *Patriarcha*, no doubt because
Filmer in the meantime had read Hobbes.

Of Filmer's views about what makes government legitimate we
need not take long notice. They are simple, and they are less ingenious
and persuasive than his criticisms of the doctrines he disliked. God
gave Adam complete authority over his children and therefore over
his children's children, which authority, when Adam died, passed
to his successor by a fixed rule of succession. As Filmer puts it,
'civil power, not only in general is by Divine institution, but even
the assigning of it specifically to the eldest parent'.[3] It would seem
to follow, on the assumption that all men are the posterity of
Adam, that there is always only one man in the world having
absolute authority over all other men, one king of men, one heir
of Adam. Filmer does not deny this, but he has to explain how
it comes about that there are many independent kingdoms in the

---

[1] *The Anarchy of a Limited or Mixed Monarchy*, ibid., p. 295.
[2] Ibid., p. 297.
[3] *Patriarcha*, ch. III, p. 57.

world. He tells us that Noah, after the Flood, divided the world up among his three sons, and that after the confusion of Babel some seventy-two separate nations were established, each a distinct family with one man in it having paternal and absolute authority over the whole family. We may ask by what authority did Noah deprive his eldest son of the monarchy of the world to which he was entitled by a rule established by God. Presumably, in the confusion of Babel, the thread of legitimacy was lost. Men no longer knew who was the sole heir of Adam, or (if we suppose that Noah had authority from God to divide the world into three kingdoms) who were the three heirs of Noah's sons. There were presumably seventy-two men each with a clearer title than any other man to paternal authority over a part of mankind, and the seventy-two parts made up the whole of mankind. There was no longer one undoubted king of men, but there were seventy-two kings, to one or other of whom all who were not kings owed obedience, and there was no doubt who owed obedience to whom. All this by the providence of God!

Filmer does not claim anything so absurd as that the hereditary kings of his day are the heirs of the seventy-two who emerged from the confusion of Babel. Nor does he even claim for every king of his day that he is the father of his people, in the sense of being the heir by primogeniture of the parental authority of their common ancestor. 'It is true, all Kings be not the natural parents of their subjects, yet they all either are, *or are to be reputed*, as the next heirs of those progenitors who were at first the natural parents of the whole people, and in their right succeed to the exercise of supreme jurisdiction.'[1] Does this mean that, in Filmer's opinion, every separate people have a common ancestor, even though they have lost all memory of him and their actual king is not his heir by the rule of succession established by God? How far is this unwarranted presumption of a monarchical line of descent to go? Are a people under one king to be reputed to have a common ancestor, even when they have not? Or is the king to be reputed the heir of a common ancestor only where there really was such an ancestor? Filmer does not explain.

Where it is not known who is the legitimate heir, then the independent heads of families 'have power to consent in the uniting or conferring of their fatherly right of sovereign authority on whom they please. And he that is so elected claims not his power as a donative from the people, but as being substituted properly by God, from whom he receives his royal charter of an universal Father,

---

[1] Ibid., ch. V, p. 60, my italics.

though testified by the ministry of the heads of the people'.[1] At this point Filmer has not chosen his words carefully. If the heads of families *are conferring their own fatherly right* on whom they please, they are performing an act of the same kind as the covenant whereby, according to Hobbes or Locke, men in the state of nature put themselves under an obligation to obey a common superior; they are renouncing a right which is theirs in favour of somebody else. In this case, of course, the right is different; it is paternal authority and not what either Hobbes or Locke would regard as a natural right whose renunciation could create political authority. But though the right is different, the transaction, if it is a conferring of their own fatherly authority, is similar; it is a setting up of authority by covenant. Filmer would have done better to have said that, there being no claimant known to be legitimate to an authority to which the whole people are undoubtedly subject, it devolves on the heads of families to find a substitute for the legitimate heir. In other words, where it is not known who is the king by the rule of succession established by God, it becomes the duty of those whose authority in its own sphere is undoubted (i.e. the heads of families) to choose a king. But, in that case, it must be certain that the people really are one people, that they have a common ancestor, that there is someone whose title to rule would be undoubted if the line of descent from that ancestor were certainly known. For otherwise the heads of families would not be providing a substitute for the true though undiscoverable king; they would be creating a king by transferring or renouncing their own rights. They would be setting up authority by covenant, in the manner described by the men whose doctrine *Patriarcha* was intended to refute.

What if the actual ruler is a usurper? What if he is neither the legitimate heir, nor a substitute for him provided in the manner which Filmer describes? This is a question unanswered in *Patriarcha*, whereas in *The Anarchy of a Limited or Mixed Monarchy* Filmer says only this: 'Many times by the act either of a usurper himself, or of those that set him up, the true heir of a crown is dispossessed, God using the ministry of the wickedest men for the removing and setting up of Kings: in such cases the subjects' obedience to the fatherly power must go along and wait upon God's providence, who only hath right to give and take away kingdoms.'[2] This means, presumably, that where an usurper makes his power effective, those whom he compels

---

[1] Ibid., ch. VI, p. 62.
[2] Filmer, *Political Works*, p. 289.

to obedience ought to obey him because his success is evidence that God is using him for some purpose of His own. But what if the dispossessors of a legitimate king change the form of government? What if they abolish monarchy? The authority they set up in the place of what they have brought down is not paternal. They are not usurpers of royal authority (which in Filmer's opinion is merely paternal authority exercised over a large number of people), but creators of another kind of authority, which, so Filmer tells us, is not divinely instituted. Yet their action is as much allowed by God as a successful usurpation of kingly power. About this Filmer has nothing to say, for he remarks only that 'if those who live under a monarchy can justify the form they live under to be God's ordinance, they are not bound to forbear their own justification, because others cannot do the like for the form they live under; let others look to the defence of their own government'.[1] It would appear then that monarchy is like the Jews; it is God's chosen form of government, though every now and again God allows what He has not chosen to prevail over it.

Large claims have been made on Filmer's behalf. Allen thought him more profound and more original than Locke, while Figgis praised him and those who shared his views for conceiving of society as *organic* and not *artificial*, which was how Locke and others thought of it. But these commendations are misplaced. Filmer's views about the origins of society are neither more nor less adequate than Locke's; and the important difference between them is, in any case, not about the origins of society, but about the ground of political obligation. Locke had not neglected to read Aristotle's *Politics*; and he probably did not disagree with Aristotle that villages arose out of families and states out of villages. He was not concerned to challenge the contention that political authority, as a matter of history, often arises out of paternal authority; he was concerned only to argue that it is different in kind and rests, as paternal authority does not, on the *consent* of the persons subject to it. No doubt, he did not properly explain the nature of this *consent*; nor did he succeed in making it clear just what rights he was conceding to subjects and what obligations he was laying upon them. But that is another matter. If he did not see that the problem of political obligation cannot be settled by an enquiry into the origins of government, he was no more blind in this respect than Filmer. Whenever Locke's immediate object was to show that the authority of rulers rested on the consent of the ruled, he was inclined to speak

[1] Ibid., p. 284.

as if men had, some time in the past, deliberately set up government; but when he reflected on the probable origins of government, as he did in the sixth chapter of the *Second Treatise*, he was willing to admit that it may often have happened that 'the natural fathers of families, by an insensible change, became the politic monarchs of them too'.[1]

Filmer comes no closer than Locke to seeing that the obligations on which the social order rests are themselves the product of men's living together in society. To have a deeper sense than Locke had of what is involved in man's being a social creature, it is not enough to deny, with Filmer, that the primary obligations arise from consent. Locke himself admits (and indeed insists) that men have obligations which do not arise from consent; for he says that in the state of nature there is a law of nature which men are obliged to obey. If there were not obligations which do not arise from consent, consent could create no obligations. This is as much admitted by Locke as by Filmer. What Locke does not admit, or rather does not notice, is that man is made moral by education, in the widest sense of that word – that he comes to conceive of himself as a bearer of rights and obligations by being involved in social relations with other creatures of his own kind. There is nothing in *Patriarcha* or in Filmer's other writings to suggest that he takes serious account of what Locke does not notice.

Figgis fails to make it clear just what he is claiming for Filmer when he says that he conceives of society as *organic*. Where Figgis speaks of the *organic*, others speak of the *natural*. Locke explains the political order, the State, as if men had created it for their own convenience, whereas Filmer (so it is said on his behalf) speaks of it as if it had *grown naturally* out of the family; and this is accounted a merit in Filmer. I must confess that I fail to see that the advantage would lie with Filmer, even if what is claimed for him were true. No doubt, it is always misleading to speak of a system of government (or of the social order generally) as if men had deliberately established it for certain ends. Even the boldest reformers change only a part of the existing social and political order, and are in any case themselves born into a social environment which they have not reformed and which profoundly affects their modes of thought and feeling. But then it is no less misleading to speak of the State as if it grew 'naturally' out of the family. Social evolution is no more like growth, or the maturation of an embryo, than it is like contrivance, or the deliberate adaptation of means to ends. A social and political order is partly the unintended and partly the intended product of human activities. It may be, except

[1] Locke, *Second Treatise of Government*, ch. VI, § 76.

very rarely, much more the first than the second; but, whichever it is, the activities which bring it about are activities of rational creatures capable of deliberate choice. To speak of the change which results from such activities, even when it is unforeseen and unintended, as *natural* or *organic* is surely just as misleading as to speak of it as if it were contrivance.

But it is doubtful whether the claim made for Filmer is true; it is doubtful whether he conceived of the process whereby kingdoms arise out of families as being *organic* or *natural* in the sense that those words are understood by those who ascribe to him, in this respect, a deeper insight than Locke's. Though Filmer was a shrewd critic of doctrines he disliked, he was not a deep thinker. Long before Hume (though less neatly) he demolished the theory that political authority derives from a social contract, but he put nothing satisfactory in the place of what he demolished.

IV. BOSSUET

Neither is Bossuet a deep political thinker, although he has certain advantages over Filmer. He does not attempt to reduce all authority of man over man to one type; he does not argue that to be truly legitimate authority must be paternal. Filmer, like the contract theorists whom he belabours, rests everything on a single principle; just as they insist that all legitimate human authority arises from consent, so he insists that it is always paternal. And just as they are reduced to some odd shifts to show that there is consent where to the man without a theoretical axe to grind it would seem obvious that there is not, so he is reduced to others no less odd to show that authority is paternal though the possessor of it is not the natural heir of a common ancestor. Bossuet is reduced to no such shifts. Monarchy is, he thinks, the best form of government, and is the only form which God has established among men by open intervention in their affairs. Yet he does not hold that monarchy is the only legitimate form. All established rulers are legitimate, having their authority from God, provided they are not recent usurpers. Thus Bossuet does not agree with Hobbes that any ruler, from the moment he has made his power effective, has legitimate authority. It is long continuance which makes effective power legitimate, converting it into authority, no matter how it was first acquired, not because its survival is evidence of its being popular but because it is a mark that it comes from God. No doubt, its survival is some evidence of its being popular, and also of its being exercised for the common good, but what makes it legitimate is its coming from God.

It cannot be said for Bossuet that he is even as original as Filmer. He is altogether a borrower; but, given his purpose, he is a discriminating, intelligent borrower. His largest debt is to Hobbes and his next largest to Bodin, but where Aristotle suits his purpose better, he borrows from him. Moreover, he fits his borrowings together into a more or less consistent whole, and is therefore less open to criticism than is Filmer. Or perhaps I should say that he is seriously vulnerable only when his assumptions are questioned, whereas Filmer, like Locke, is open to criticism even when they are not. Bossuet's apology for absolute monarchy is magnificent and compelling, as Filmer's is not, for two reasons: because it is eloquent, dignified and well presented, and because it is simple and full of good sense. There is no need to expatiate on the first reason. The gifts which make Bossuet the greatest of French orators do not desert him when he turns from the pulpit to politics.

To us, until we have translated ourselves in imagination into another age, the doctrine of absolute monarchy by divine right seems extravagant. The repeated appeals to Holy Scripture strike us as irrelevant. We are no longer impressed by an immense display of Biblical and patristic texts, and we see no divinity in kings. There is hardly any political doctrine less congenial to us; and so when we come to read the works of a writer of small talents, a Filmer, we are impressed, not by the doctrine he teaches, but by his shrewd attacks on rival creeds. His exposition of his own beliefs is the price we pay for what we really value, his criticisms of others; we feel about him what someone who preferred his prefaces to his plays felt about Bernard Shaw. But with Bossuet the play's the thing. He can, while we read him, take us out of ourselves; he can show us what monarchy meant to Frenchmen in an age not less respectful of reason and not less discriminating than our own. Bossuet has as strong a preference as Descartes for clarity and order, which is a preference as much aesthetic as intellectual.

In the next century, which Frenchmen sometimes call 'the century of Voltaire', the Church of Bossuet was attacked by the intellectuals, and the monarchy lost prestige; so that Bossuet, the ablest champion of Church and monarchy in France, came to be regarded as an enemy by the *philosophes*. The very title of his *Politique tirée des propres paroles de l'Écriture Sainte* came to seem ridiculous. Who, in an age which prided itself on its enlightenment, would turn to the Bible for his political theory? But, as Gustave Lanson has pointed out, Bossuet did not really get his political theory from that source; he merely made a show of doing so. He whole-heartedly accepted the established order in France, the monarchy called 'absolute', and he found in Hobbes (also well versed in the Scriptures), in Bodin and in Aristotle all his strongest arguments for it. In the Bible he found texts to support those arguments and stories to illustrate them. Lanson quotes a sentence from Bossuet which he says is the key to his book: 'Aristotle has said it, but the Holy Ghost has uttered it with greater force.'[1] Bossuet's texts and illustrations are always well chosen; they add colour and charm to his argument.

The *Politique tirée de l'Écriture Sainte* was written by Bossuet for the dauphin; it is a work of instruction and not of controversy. It is admirably clear; it proceeds carefully, step by step, and each step is simple, though the whole argument is elaborate. It is not in the *Politique*, but in the fifth of his *Avertissements aux protestants sur les Lettres du Ministre Jurieu*, that Bossuet engages in controversy with those who hold that the authority of rulers rests on the consent of their subjects. Jurieu, a Protestant pastor, in the course of a general attack on Bossuet's *Histoire des variations des Églises protestantes*, had put forward this particular doctrine, and Bossuet devotes the fifth *Avertissement* to demolishing it. He is formidable in controversy, and this work is as good an example as any of his method and style; but it offers little that is new to the political theorist. It is as an exponent of political 'orthodoxy' rather than as a critic of political 'heresy' that Bossuet is incomparable. It is the Bossuet of the *Politique* and, to a lesser extent, of the *Panegyric on St Thomas of Canterbury* who is our present business.

Since Bossuet admits that the authority of all established governments stems from God, he need not deny that governments have sometimes been set up by consent of the persons subject to them. He is content to say that, in the beginning, the authority of man over man was paternal. Abraham, he says, has been called a king, but his life was pastoral and he ruled only his family; his 'empire' was domestic. It was only later that true kings arose, either with the consent of their subjects or without it. Thus for Bossuet, as for Hobbes and Locke, political authority differs in kind from paternal, and is no mere extension of it. But, whether it is established by consent or by force of arms, it is equally legitimate; it is legitimate because God allows it to endure and

---

[1] Bossuet, *Politique tirée de l'Écriture Sainte*, Book III. article 3, proposition v. The translations from the French are my own.

requires obedience to it. All authority, paternal and political, comes equally from God; and yet political authority differs from paternal, not because it rests on consent, but because it arises among men in a different way and serves different ends.

There have been forms of government other than monarchy, yet monarchy is the commonest, oldest and most natural form. It is the most natural because, though established by consent or by force of arms, it most closely resembles paternal rule. Bossuet goes so far as to say that the *foundation* and *model* of monarchy is paternal rule.[1] But this does not mean that he agrees with Filmer. He does not say that whoever possesses royal power is (or is to be reputed as being) the heir of the common ancestor of his people, exercising over them the same kind of authority as the ancestor exercised over his family; he says rather that monarchy was the first form of political authority because at the time that it arose among men they were familiar only with paternal rule. He says that the very first governments were established gently, not by conquest but by consent; and the examples he gives suggest that the earliest political rulers, who were kings, were often chosen by their peoples. The earliest kings were the 'fathers' of their people, though in a sense different from Filmer's; they were 'fathers' because their feelings for their subjects were paternal and their subjects' feelings for them were filial. The idea that, where there is a common ancestor, one of his descendants, his heir by the rule of primogeniture, possesses over his entire posterity the same authority as he had over his wife and children is quite foreign to Bossuet. So far is Bossuet from thinking that royal and paternal authority are in principle the same that he claims only for the first and not the second that it is absolute. He says that, since Abraham was not truly a king, Adam was not one either; and therefore the authority of kings does not come to them from Adam, and is not to be assimilated to the authority which God gave to Adam over his wife and children.

Hereditary monarchy has three principal advantages. It is 'self-perpetuating' – that is to say, there is no need to find a new king to take the place of the old one when he dies, for the king has only one heir by the rule of succession. That form of government is best which avoids contests for supreme power and disputes about who is the rightful possessor of it. That government is best which is the furthest removed from anarchy, where it is certain who has supreme authority and who is entitled to succeed to it. A second advantage of hereditary monarchy is that, more than any other form of government, it makes

[1] Ibid., Bk. II, art. 1, prop. vii.

the conservation of the State the interest of the persons who govern it. A prince who works for his State works for his children, and in him love of country and of family run together. A third advantage is that it provides the people with men who are born to authority, who are the descendants of kings, who are invested thereby with a dignity which belongs to a family which has been great for generations. They are heirs of the past as no man raised from obscurity can be; they are the sons and grandsons of men whose achievements are part of the history of their country.

'Government', says Bossuet, 'ought to be mild';[1] and 'princes are made to be loved'.[2] He means that, because they are born to greatness, their subjects are well disposed to them. They have only to behave well to get ready obedience. It is those who come by authority with difficulty, those whose title is most apt to be questioned, who must resort to harsh measures to maintain it. And who better than a hereditary prince can take advice without loss of dignity? The king should be more ready to listen than to speak, for he has the last word. Not for him to argue but to weigh the arguments put before him. He competes with nobody and nobody competes with him. Who is better placed to benefit from the ability and wisdom of others than the man who need fear no comparison with them? Yet Bossuet, who is ready to see all the advantages of an hereditary monarch, sees also the temptations to arrogance and obstinacy which beset him. Absolute power, however it is come by, has a tendency to corrupt; but (so thinks Bossuet) there must be such power if government is to be effective, if it is to provide men with security. He asserts without troubling to argue the matter that disputes about power are more harmful to the people generally than the abuses of power to which absolute rulers are tempted. Perhaps he is impressed by the testimony of Hobbes and by the example of what had recently happened in Hobbes's native land.

Disputes about power can be of two kinds: they can be about the extent of authority or they can be about who is the rightful possessor of an authority whose extent is not questioned. To a patriotic Frenchman of Bossuet's time, well read in history and well versed in contemporary affairs, it might seem that hereditary monarchy, as France then knew it, was best placed to avoid both kinds of disputes: the kind which brought civil war to England and

---

[1] Ibid., Bk. III, art. 3, prop. xii.
[2] Ibid., Bk. III, art. 3, prop. xiii.

the kind which so often brought insecurity to Rome at the death of an emperor.

To the sceptics of the next century, Bossuet, as a writer on politics, appeared little more than a flatterer of kings. 'Majesty is the image of the greatness of God in the prince. God is infinite, God is everything. The prince . . . is a public personage, the whole State is in him; the will of the entire people is enclosed in his will. As all perfection and every virtue are united in God, so all the power of particular persons is united in the person of the prince.' 'See an immense people united in only one person; see this sacred, paternal and absolute power; see reason enclosed in only one head secretly governing the body of the State: and you see the image of God in kings; you have the idea of royal majesty.'[1] 'The title of Christ is given to kings; and so everywhere we see them called Christ the anointed of the Lord.'[2] 'It is so great, this majesty, that it cannot be in the prince as in its source; it is borrowed from God, who gives it to him for the good of the people, for it is good that they should be contained by a higher power.'[3] To later philosophers, who found Louis XV insignificant or even contemptible, it seemed absurd that in the reign of his predecessor a bishop could use such language of a king.

But Bossuet was no flatterer. His attitude to kings is the same as his attitude to priests. Kings are in themselves no better than other men; they are merely instruments of God. They are not set apart from other men, or raised above them, by their merits; and we respect in them, not what they are in themselves, but only their character as agents of God. Those whom God calls to His service are not an aristocracy in the Aristotelian sense; they are not the natural superiors of other men. And yet, because God works through them as He does not work through others, He sets them apart from others; He lends them a dignity which is not theirs by nature. The majesty of kings is borrowed, bestowed upon them for their people's good. Authority should come easily to those that have it, and obedience to those that owe it; and therefore it is good that the ruler should be raised high above his subjects. But the ruler is a man like other men, just as the priest is; and if he is to be raised above them, it must be by virtue of some excellence which is not part of his nature. It must be by virtue of a borrowed excellence, of a majesty which is not in him as in its source but comes to him from God. 'For it is good that [the people] should be contained by a higher power.' Not by sheer power, but by a *higher* power: that is to

[1] Ibid., Bk. V, art. 4, prop. i.
[2] Ibid., Bk. III, art. 2, prop. ii.
[3] Ibid., Bk. V, art. 4, prop. i.

say, by a power which to those subject to it seems of a higher nature than anything they see in themselves.

And the reason 'enclosed in only one head secretly governing the body of the State' is not the unaided intelligence of one man; it is a borrowed wisdom, though borrowed, this time, not from God but from the king's advisers. Bossuet, like Bodin, knows that, whether the king is absolute or not, many heads go to the making of policy. There are many men taking part in the government of an absolute monarchy, and it can rarely happen that the wisest of them is the absolute monarch. And yet, for the good of the people, there must be one man whose decision is final, and that man must from the beginning be set apart from the others; he is the listener, the taker of advice, the supreme governor, who is not answerable to man but only to God for how he rules. Others give their reasons to him, but he need not give his to them: this is the sense in which he governs 'secretly'.

Both Hobbes and Filmer play down the dangers of tyranny. Tyranny, says Hobbes, is merely monarchy 'misliked'; it is a word which men use to express their feelings. Filmer denies that any King of England since the Conquest has been a tyrant. More people, he says, were put to death for political reasons in the last hundred years of the Roman Republic than under all of the worst emperors put together, and he concludes that 'there is no tyranny to be compared to the tyranny of a multitude'.[1] Bossuet has greater misgivings. There is, he thinks, no truth better attested by the Holy Ghost (that is to say, by the Bible) than that wealth and power expose their possessors to great temptations. Some have sought a remedy by placing obstacles in the way of royal power, and Bossuet does not speak of them as if they had acted unreasonably. Without going into detail, he seems to conclude that all governments have grave defects, and that absolute monarchy is merely the least defective. God first established an absolute monarch in the person of Saul. 'We have not forgotten', he says at the end of the second book of the *Politique*, 'that there appear in antiquity other forms of government, about which God has prescribed nothing to mankind: so that every people must accept, as a divine order, the government established in their country, because God is a God of peace, who desires tranquillity in human affairs'.

Bossuet makes a distinction between absolute and arbitrary government which is not unlike the distinction later made by Montesquieu between monarchy and despotism. Where there is absolute govern-

[1] Filmer, *Patriarcha*, ch. XIX, p. 93.

ment, there is a sovereign who cannot be legally compelled, who is free of all human authority, who is under no law except the law of God, and is responsible to God alone for his actions. And yet in practice there are laws such that 'whatever is done contrary to them is legally invalid (*nul de droit*)'. Bossuet is here unusually obscure. He probably means that, where government is absolute but not arbitrary, the sovereign (whom he thinks of as a king), though he is not responsible in law for what he does, actually respects the law in his dealings with his subjects. He rules a people accustomed to impartial justice. Therefore, though his authority to alter the law is uncontested, though no one has authority to declare any public act of his invalid, though he cannot be sued or punished for his private acts, he is expected to act justly; he is expected, in his dealings with all men, to respect the laws which are enforced in his name. If he does not respect them, he is held to have acted unjustly, and there is a wrong to be redressed. His subjects are acknowledged possessors of rights which it is the sovereign's acknowledged duty to define and to enforce. Hence the idea that the sovereign, though his authority is absolute, may act unjustly and even illegally; hence the readiness of subjects to seek redress from the sovereign against himself. The sovereign is sovereign, not because he can do no wrong, but because he alone can redress the wrong he does. The prince who, like the King of France, recognizes that his own laws bind him and who is expected by his subjects to respect them, is an absolute but not an arbitrary sovereign.

Bossuet is less apt than either Hobbes or Filmer to treat the law as the command of the sovereign. He even says that all who have spoken well about law have regarded it as a treaty or pact between men, who are agreed about what is needed for the good of their society. This, he hastens to add, does not mean 'that the authority of the laws depends on the consent and acquiescence of the peoples, but only that the prince . . . is assisted by the wisest heads in the nation, and is borne by the experience of past centuries'.[1] 'There are fundamental laws which cannot be changed.'[2] Only the prince has authority to declare what the law is; only he may alter it, and there is no one with authority to deny that the law is what he says it is. And yet the prince, whose legislative authority is supreme, is in practice only to a small extent a maker of law. There are laws which he could not change without destroying the social order on which his

[1] Bossuet, *Politique*, Bk. I, art. 4, prop. vi.
[2] Ibid., Bk. I, art. 4, prop. viii.

own power rests. Law serves the needs of men, which is why it is
obeyed; and every ruler's power, even when his authority is absolute,
is limited by the character of the social order in which he exercises it,
by the needs of his subjects, by the structure of law. Thus the power
of the absolute sovereign is in practice greatly limited, even when he
happens not to fear God.

Lanson, who takes every opportunity he can to praise Bossuet,
says that the force of his argument depends very much on the fear of
God being a powerful motive with both rulers and ruled. No doubt,
Bossuet everywhere takes it for granted that this motive is strong,
or can be made strong by education. Yet he claims no more for the
sovereign than Hobbes claimed for him, and we may wonder how
much importance Hobbes attached to this motive. Is there no case for
absolute monarchy except among men whose faith in God is strong?
No less of a case, surely, than for absolute government which is not
monarchy, of which we have had several examples in the twentieth
century. If absolute government is more dangerous now than it was
in Bossuet's time, it is not because, as Lanson suggests, belief in God
is now much weaker; it is more dangerous because the power of all
governments is enormously greater.

'The mighty', says Bossuet, 'will be mightily tormented', while the
humble will be treated gently. Yet he appeals to utility as much as to
the fear of God. In the fifth *Avertissement*, in reply to Jurieu, who has
said that rulers have no right to misgovern, he answers that what is
at issue 'is not whether the prince has the right to do wrong, which
nobody has dreamed of [asserting], but whether, if he does do it . . . it
is reasonable for private persons to take up arms against him, and
whether it is not more useful to mankind that no one should retain
a right against the public power'.[1] The true interest of subjects is
not that there should be set limits to supreme authority but that the
holder of that authority should have powerful motives for exercising
it for their good, which he is most likely to have if he is an hereditary
monarch.

The duty of subjects to a heretic or infidel ruler is as great as to
a Catholic prince. Bossuet says of St Thomas of Canterbury that he
never forgot that he was a subject, that he never treated his king
disdainfully nor sought in any way to make him odious to his
people, to stir up disaffection against him. To explain the nature
and limits of the archbishop's defiance, he quotes Tertullian's words

---

[1] *Cinquième Avertissement aux Protestants, Oeuvres complètes de Bossuet* (Besançon 1836),
vol. 8, p. 335(1).

to a magistrate: *Non te terremus, qui nec timemus.* '*Non te terremus*; there speaks the subject, submissive and respectful always; *Qui nec timemus*; there speaks the bishop, firm and unshakeable always. *Non te terremus*; I meditate nothing against the State; *Qui nec timemus*; I am ready to suffer all for the Church.'[1] If the clergy have privileges, it is in order that religion may be honoured; if they possess goods, it is in order to carry on their sacred ministry; if they have authority, it is to use it as a curb on the licentious and a support to discipline. A Catholic prince should be jealous for the privileges of the Church, having nothing to fear and much to gain from its influence on the faithful.

Bossuet, whose life was spent largely in the fight against heresy, took it for granted that the Church, to carry out its sacred mission, needs no authority which can be a threat to the authority of princes. If the prince is not of the true faith, the Church cannot release his subjects from their allegiance to him, and nothing in its doctrine (for the false claims made on its behalf by enthusiasts are no part of that doctrine) serves to weaken his authority; and if he is of the true faith, the Church is a pillar of his authority. Though the Church is not subordinate to the State, its independence cannot be a threat to the temporal ruler, whatever his faith; for he need never attack its independence to assert his legitimate authority. If he does attack it, the Church must defend itself, not by setting his subjects against him, but by refusing to admit that he has authority in the sphere reserved to it. The resistance of the priest, like that of the humblest layman, is passive; he prefers God's law to man's; he refuses to obey the prince when he cannot do so without disobeying God. Since God requires more of the priest than of the layman, there are likely to be more occasions when it is his duty to disobey his prince; but the disobedience is essentially the same. Not only must it never be active resistance; it must also never be an attempt to subvert the authority which belongs properly to the prince.

In matters of religion Bossuet was intolerant, but not conspicuously so in an intolerant age. More so than Henry IV and his English grandson Charles II, but less so than the Jesuits or the Catholic League, and not more so than the Huguenots in France or the Long Parliament in England; not more so than the groups eager, at one time or another, to set limits to royal power. The prince, he says, must use his authority to destroy 'false religions' in his State, but must use severe methods only in the last resort. Christian princes have banished the authors of heresies but have dealt gently with their followers in the

---

[1] *Panegyric on St Thomas of Canterbury*, ibid., vol. 2, p. 557(2).

endeavour to bring them back to the faith. Bossuet, when he speaks of princes, sometimes attributes to them qualities which he would wish them to have; and, no doubt, he does so here.[1] But at least he makes it plain what he takes those qualities to be. He does not deny that Christian princes have put heretics to death, but says not a word in their defence. The early Church, he tells us, always begged the Christian Roman emperors not to apply the extreme penalty to heretics, unless they were guilty of treachery or sedition.[2]

The doctrine which Bossuet and Filmer contested – the doctrine that the authority of rulers rests on the consent of the ruled – is so much more congenial to us than is their doctrine that it is difficult for us to realize that in the sixteenth and seventeenth centuries most advocates of government by consent were no more liberal than the champions of absolute monarchy. The advocacy which we now remember best is, of course, that of Locke, who was certainly more liberal than either Bossuet or Filmer; but the earlier exponents of the doctrine that legitimate authority rests on consent[3] were not much concerned for liberty of conscience or for other rights of the mere individual, as distinct from the rights of parliaments or their own co-religionists. Both among the advocates of absolute and of limited monarchy we can find wide divergences of opinion; we can find bigots intent on forcing others to share their beliefs and we can find men of larger views. Indeed, Bodin, perhaps the earliest champion of absolute monarchy as the seventeenth century was to understand it, was every bit as tolerant as John Locke.

This is not to deny that the idea of a social contract has implications which its first users failed to see. The idea was first used to make,

---

[1] *Politique*, Bk. VII, art. 3, prop. x.

[2] That Bossuet should have welcomed the Revocation of the Edict of Nantes is not surprising, for the privileges granted to the Huguenots by that edict amounted to much more than toleration of their faith. The edict gave them a large measure of autonomy in over a hundred towns; it put them virtually out of reach of the sort of influences to which Bossuet wanted to expose them; it insulated them from the faith which alone in his opinion was true. If Bossuet did not openly condemn the *dragonnades* and other cruel methods used against the Huguenots, he never said a word in approval of them. Bossuet was never really powerful at court, and certainly was not so at the time of the worst excesses against the Protestants; though to later generations, this great champion of absolute monarchy has seemed guilty of the atrocities permitted by the absolute monarch whose subject he was.

[3] Hobbes also argued that the authority of rulers rests on the consent of the ruled, and used the model of a social contract to explain his views about political obligation; but his purpose was quite the opposite of Locke's and of his Jesuit and Huguenot precursors. He wanted to establish that the authority of rulers is unlimited.

on behalf of religious minorities, claims of a kind not made before. Neither the Jesuits nor the Huguenots were greatly concerned that government should be carried on with the consent of the governed, or that the individual should be able to live as seemed good to him provided he did no harm to his neighbours: they cared, not for the freedom of the individual, but for the freedom of worship of those who shared their faith. In a Europe no longer united in one faith, in a Europe where there were minorities claiming to have the one true faith which their rulers did not share, they found it expedient to make bold and elaborate use of an idea which, if not new to their age, had been little used before it. That idea had larger implications than they realized. But it was not until the second half of the seventeenth century that these implications came to be seen more clearly, by Locke and by others. The earlier users of the idea of a social contract, the men whom Filmer and Bossuet attacked, cared no more for the freedom of the individual than did the advocates of absolute monarchy.

Bossuet says that, if there is to be security, there must be nothing in the State, no body and no person, able to challenge what he calls the 'public power'. The State being one, there can be only one public power inside it; that is to say, though there may be many persons and bodies of persons taking part in government, they constitute one public power because there is one person whose subordinates all the others are. Unless all persons except one exercising public authority are the subordinates of that one person, there is no cohesive, no united, public power, and men lack the security which government exists to provide.

Bossuet and Hobbes both speak as if the unity of the State consisted in its having only one sovereign, only one person in whom all political authority ultimately resides. The difference between them is merely that, whereas Bossuet more or less takes it for granted that the sovereign is a single man, a natural person, Hobbes allows that he may be an 'artificial' person, a body of men. Two conceptions are absent from their thinking: the idea of a system of government in which there is no sovereign, no person (natural or artificial) whose right to make law is legally unlimited, but in which, none the less, authority is so distributed among its possessors that there is always some person (or body) competent to give a final decision in any matter, not excluding disputes about how authority is distributed; and, secondly, the idea of a system in which there is a sovereign, in the sense of a legally unlimited legislator, and at the same time a separation of powers. These two conceptions are foreign to the political thought of the sixteenth and seventeenth centuries. Political authority in Hobbes's England was so distributed that there was no recognized way of settling disputes about its distribution, and so it seemed obvious to Hobbes that, if these disputes were not to lead to civil war, supreme authority must all be concentrated in the hands of one person, natural or artificial; and Bossuet agreed with Hobbes. Of course, what was true of political authority in Hobbes's England had also been true of it not long before in France; indeed such dispersion of political authority had been characteristic of all Europe in the Middle Ages. But, then, in the Middle Ages, there had not been felt the same need for a strong central government. In the Middle Ages there had been neither absolute monarchy as France knew it in the seventeenth century, nor constitutional government, as first England and then America came to know it in the eighteenth. The two ideas which I said are absent from the political thought of Bossuet and Hobbes are both ideas of constitutional government.

The first is realized, more or less, in the United States, where political authority is so distributed that there is no sovereign and yet there is always some person or body competent to give a final decision in all important matters, including disputes about how authority is distributed. The second is realized, more or less, in Britain, where there is a sovereign, a legally unlimited legislature, and also a separation of powers. That there is a sovereign in Britain is widely accepted, but not that there is a separation of powers. And yet there is one, at least of the kind forbidden by Hobbes and Bossuet, if not of the kind described by Montesquieu.[1] The absolute king, according to Bossuet, is both the supreme lawmaker and the supreme executive, while Hobbes takes it for granted that whoever has the legally unlimited power to make law stands to all others who take part in government as a superior to a subordinate. The supreme executive power belongs in Britain, in fact if not in name, to the Cabinet, which is not a body subordinate to the supreme legislature, though nearly all its members are also in fact members of that legislature. Now that the royal assent to bills is a mere formality and the House of Lords can hold them up for no more than a year (a residual power which the lower House, if it were determined to do so, could abolish), the House of Commons is virtually a sovereign legislature. But the Cabinet is not a committee of the House of Commons; nor yet, despite the Cabinet's control of a parliamentary majority, is the House of Commons its mere agent. Neither the sense

---

[1] Montesquieu's position has, I believe, been seriously misunderstood, as I try to argue in the chapter devoted to his political theory, in the second volume of this work.

in which the executive is responsible to the House of Commons, nor the sense in which the work of that House is directed by the executive, allows us to call either body subordinate to the other. Nor are the two bodies identical, even though nearly all the members of one are also members of the other. We have in Britain a sovereign legislature and a separation of powers; we have something unimagined by either the champions of absolute or of limited monarchy in the days of Hobbes and Bossuet.

The assembly supposedly representative of the people, which in England alone in the seventeenth and eighteenth centuries came to be regarded as an integral part of the machinery of government, was not so regarded in earlier ages, even in England. The king from time to time 'met his people' assembled in Parliament or the Estates-General, and it was thought good that he should do so, but there was no question of his governing his people through ministers responsible to these bodies, which were not thought of as partaking in government. In an age when men were coming to feel a much stronger need for effective central government, these bodies, which privileged orders and corporations had long used to defend their interests against the royal power, were apt to be regarded as hindrances rather than helps to good government. This was especially so in France.

Bossuet, speaking of the public power, had in mind only the king's government; it never occurred to him to think of the Estates-General (which had not met since 1614) nor yet of the provincial estates (which were still meeting in his day) as parts of the public power. The idea of Montesquieu, the idea of the public power as a system whose parts check one another, did not occur to him; and the idea of Locke, of mere subjects setting themselves up as judges to decide when the public power has overstepped its bounds, seemed to him (as to Hobbes) an invitation to anarchy.

V. PASCAL

Pascal wrote no treatise on politics; he produced no theory of political obligation. He was indifferent to the two questions which excited the political philosophers of his day: How does government first arise among men?, and What makes it legitimate? In the *Pensées*, which contain nearly all his reflections on man in society, on law and on government, he barely hints at an answer to the first question and takes no notice of the second. He says not a word to suggest that the authority of kings comes to them from God or from the people; he is certainly not a champion of absolute monarchy by divine right. Yet the pages of the *Pensées* which treat of matters interesting to the political theorist are not the least moving, the least original, in that incomparable book. Pascal lived under an absolute monarchy and saw nothing to prefer to it.

He has affinities with Hobbes and with Hume. Like Hobbes he sees in government a curb for the unbridled passions and pride of men, and like Hume he sees men governed by habit and imagination more than by reason. But, unlike both Hobbes and Hume, he is interested much more in man than in government; he is interested in how man feels and thinks about law and government rather than in what they are in themselves.

Hobbes takes man as he finds him or thinks he finds him; he affects to speak of him as he might of some species to which he did not himself belong. He expresses no sense of either man's pathos or dignity. Man has appetites which he seeks to satisfy, and comes to desire power as a means to satisfying them; his pride arises from his concupiscence. He must compete with other men to satisfy his desires, and so comes to put a value on whatever gives him an advantage over them: on power in all its forms, as command, wealth and reputation. He strives for superiority and is moved by pride. If he were without government his situation would be intolerable, for, as other men have the same passions as he has, he would be their enemy and they his; but, fortunately for himself and others, he is under government, and can pursue felicity (or the satisfaction of his desires) in conditions which promise success. There is nothing wrong with human nature, as Hobbes sees it. If there were no government, that nature would make life intolerable to the creature afflicted with it, but in fact there is government; for man's nature includes the capacity (reason) which enables him to avert the sufferings that his unbridled passions would bring upon him.

Pascal has different, and perhaps deeper, ideas about the passions which afflict man. He does not see pride arising because, in the endeavour to get the means of satisfying his natural desires, in the struggle for power, man seeks to dominate other men. 'The self', he says, 'has two qualities: it is inherently unjust, in that it makes itself the centre of everything; it is irksome to others, in that it wishes to enslave them: for every self is the enemy of all the others and aspires to tyranny over them'.[1] But this yearning of the self to be the centre of

---

[1] Pascal, *Pensées*, in *L'Oeuvre de Pascal*, Pléiade edition (Paris 1936), p. 863, § 136.

all things does not arise from a striving for power, for the means to the easier and fuller satisfaction of the natural appetites; it is of the essence of the self. It arises from an attitude of the self to itself possible only to a being which thinks. 'Everyone is a universe (*un tout*) to himself, for, when he is dead, everything is dead to him. Hence it is that everyone believes that he is everything to everyone else.'[1] This is true only of man, who alone knows himself. When Pascal says that man knows himself he does not mean that he has true opinions about himself; he means rather that he is an object of thought to himself, that he is aware of himself. He is aware of himself and of others; he appraises himself and others. 'The beasts do not admire one another. The horse does not admire his companion; not that there is no emulation between them when they race, but it is of no consequence.'[2] Other animals are sometimes drawn into conflict by their appetites, but man alone is truly the rival and enemy of his companions. He is so, not because, being rational, he can compete with them for the means of satisfying desire in ways impossible to the beasts, but because, being by nature a creature that thinks and is therefore self-centred, he is everything to himself and aspires to be everything to others.

Hence the inordinate vanity of man, who spends his life in the endeavour to create, preserve and embellish some image of himself in the minds of others; who seeks satisfaction in an imaginary life, in his life as he wishes it to appear to others and not as it really is. Yet this concern for reputation, which is a cause of man's wretchedness, is also a mark of his dignity; it is a tribute to opinion, to the product of thought, to reason, to the peculiar excellence of man: 'He [man] rates human reason so high that, no matter what other advantage he may have on earth, if he is not also placed to his advantage in the reason of man, he is not satisfied. It is the finest place in the world: nothing can divert him from the desire for it.'[3] Even when we despise men, we desire their good opinion, and so belie our own contempt; we desire their good opinion because they are men, because they are creatures who think, who pass judgements, and we recognize in them the dignity of their kind, the dignity of man. We look for happiness and find misery; we look for certainty and find doubt: we look for what only we, being capable of reason, can look for; and so our wretchedness comes of what is most excellent in us.

Man who aspires to be everything has also a sense of his own

[1] Ibid., p. 863, § 139.
[2] Ibid., p. 897, § 277.
[3] Ibid., p. 897, § 276.

insignificance. He cannot bear to be alone with himself, to take stock of himself, to contemplate himself as he really is in the infinity of space and time; and so he seeks to divert himself from himself. Hence his love of noise and movement; he pretends to himself that he is active in the pursuit of what is worth having, of what will satisfy him. But he is active only to escape from himself, to fill the void. Man aspires to be what he cannot be, and yet has reason enough to know that what he aspires to is out of his reach. If he were like other animals, if he had no reason, he would not aspire to be everything, and yet it is also reason in him which makes him aware of his insignificance. Man alone knows that he must die and feels the need to escape the thought of death; man alone can know himself and feel the need to escape from himself. The deliberate pursuit of one object of desire after another which, for Hobbes and the Utilitarians, is the proper business of mankind – an activity which *can* be successful and which brings happiness when it succeeds – becomes, for Pascal, an effect of man's need to hide from himself. Pascal is appalled by the triviality of man, which he ascribes, not to his stupidity, but to his fear of truth.

Man, if he is to escape the wretched condition into which he is driven by vanity and fear of truth, must learn to see himself as he really is; he must accept himself for what he is, despising what is weak in himself and respecting what is excellent, his capacity for thought and knowledge. 'I blame equally those who choose to praise man, those who chose to blame him, and those who look for amusement; and can approve only those who painfully seek the truth (*qui cherchent en gémissant*).'[1] The search for truth leads ultimately to God, through whom alone man finds what he is impelled by his nature to seek, a knowledge which satisfies. But we are not, as mere students of social and political theory, concerned with what is most important to Pascal in his own philosophy, his conception of man's relation to God; we are concerned only with what he says about man's condition before he has found God. Man, in that condition, is afflicted by vanity and by the need to escape from himself in the pursuit of pleasure and ambition. This is the condition of man for which the social order and government are remedies. In this condition, for Pascal as for Hobbes, man is the enemy of man; and he is so by nature, though this is not the whole truth about his nature. Nor is the remedy remedial in the same sense as it is for Hobbes; it is not the only remedy, and is far indeed from being sufficient. It merely protects men from one another but does not enable them to find happiness. The sufficient remedy

[1] Ibid., p. 909, § 333.

is not the order maintained by government; it is the discovery of truth and of God. For Hobbes, who thinks of 'felicity' as merely the successful pursuit of objects of desire, all that is needed to deliver man from wretchedness and put him in the way of happiness is that his environment should be changed. For Pascal, men are not only by nature one another's enemies; they are also their own. Government can save them only from the consequences of the first enmity; from the consequences of the second, which is the worse and in which the other is rooted, they must save themselves by the grace of God.

Pascal says that at one time he believed that human justice was essentially just; but he has now learnt better. Theft, incest, infanticide and parricide have all been counted among virtuous actions. Justice has been defined in several ways, and the definition which pleases Pascal best is that the just is the customary, the commonly received. Nothing, according to mere reason, is in itself just; there are no rules discoverable by reason which we can use to appraise the rules actually accepted and enforced.[1] Montaigne is held to be wrong when he says that custom must not be followed merely because it is custom but because it is reasonable or just. Yet Pascal admits that people follow custom because they believe it to be just. They wish to be subject only to reason or justice; and custom, if it were not thought reasonable or just, would be deemed tyrannical. That what is customary is just, in some sense of justice which does not make *just* and *customary* mere synonyms, is apparently a belief that men cannot do without. At least Pascal suggests that it is so, though he does not attempt to explain why it should be. No doubt he believes that there is after all an 'essential justice', to which men aspire though they cannot discover it; so that they must have something which can pass for justice among them, something which they believe is other than it is without really knowing what they take it for. In the social philosophy of Pascal, the rôle of justice is not unlike that of the *thing-in-itself* in Kant's theory of knowledge; it is something of which nothing can be known except that it exists, and so men take what they can know (justice as it appears to them) to be justice as it really is.

In a work which is not a finished treatise, which consists only of materials brought together for a book and never built into one, Pascal does not trouble to explain how men come to have the customs they

---

[1] Pascal does not hold consistently to this position. Sometimes he speaks as if he believed that rules of conduct are merely accepted or rejected, so that it is absurd to enquire whether they are true or valid in themselves; while at other times he speaks as if there were an essential justice, though men cannot discover it.

do have. He does not anticipate Hume (who even more completely abandons the notion of an essential justice discoverable by reason) in suggesting that, men's capacities and needs being broadly similar all over the world, they come everywhere to accept certain rules which experience teaches them are in everyone's interest, rules without which no society could subsist. He produces no universal rules as substitutes for the law of nature such as it is traditionally conceived. Nor does he suggest that government first arose because it was found generally convenient. He says merely that there must be inequality among men, since they all wish to dominate, though only some can do so. He imagines a struggle between men which ends with the stronger bending the weaker to their wills, the masters deciding how 'force' shall pass from their hands into those of their successors. It is then that 'imagination' begins to take the place of 'force', presumably because men come to believe that what is established is as it ought to be. But Pascal is so little interested in the origins of the social and political order that he gives little thought to the matter.[1]

In his opinion, what laws and forms of government there are matters much less than that they should go unquestioned. What, he asks, appears more unreasonable than to choose the eldest son of a queen to govern a State? If the traveller of noblest birth were chosen to captain a ship, it would be thought ridiculous. And yet, given the perversity, the unruliness of man, the unreasonable becomes reasonable. Should the most virtuous man and the most able govern the State? But anyone may claim to be that. Therefore let the rule be that he is to govern who has something about him that cannot be disputed: let him govern who is the eldest son of the king, of the man who ruled before him. What rule is less hurtful to vanity than one which accords superiority without pretence of merit? The other advantages of hereditary monarchy, so conspicuous to Bodin and Bossuet, count for nothing with Pascal, who does not mention them. If Pascal is right, it is a waste of time to look for the form of government which provides the best rulers. Hereditary monarchy is not to be preferred because those who come to power under it are

---

[1] He is so much struck by the diversity of customs that it never occurs to him to enquire whether there are not some to be found everywhere, men's condition being in some respects everywhere the same. Nor does he ask how it is that some men can come to dominate others where there is not already a social order, where there are not already established conventions. It does not occur to him, as it does to Hume and to Rousseau, that rules must be prior to dominion – that men must already be respecters of customary rules before some among them can acquire power over others.

likely to rule better than those who come to it in some other way, but only because, human nature being what it is, it is easier to contrive that the title to supreme authority is uncontested than that the authority is wisely exercised.

Pascal's scepticism goes further even than Hume's. Hume not only supposes that there are some very general rules accepted by men everywhere because they are everywhere found convenient (the rules which men call, to mark their importance, *laws of nature* – rules which experience has shown to be well adapted to the needs of a creature having the nature of man in the world as it actually is); he also prefers some systems of government (for instance, limited monarchy of the English kind) to others (democracy and absolute monarchy) on the ground that they are the most likely to provide security without being oppressive. Hume is more inclined to believe that customs and forms of government differ from country to country because men's needs differ. In general, he is less given than Pascal to suggesting that it matters almost not at all what custom or authority is established providing that whoever is required to obey it does so willingly. Yet he too is more concerned to advise men to accept what is established than to argue for one system in preference to another; he too wishes to leave men undisturbed in their submission to what they are used to and what has long been received – to custom and prejudice. Pascal asks, 'Why do men follow old laws and old opinions? Is it because they are the soundest? No, but they are unique, and so remove from us the root of diversity.'[1] Hume would perhaps qualify Pascal's answer thus: Old laws and old opinions are likely to be the soundest, but most men are unable to show that they are, and never dream of making the attempt. They accept them unquestioningly as standards of what is right; and it is good that they should do so because the stability of the social order depends on most people's accepting without question what is commonly received, and what they are not competent to question.

Pascal and Hume come closest to complete agreement about the laws of property; they both suggest that, though it is necessary that there should be some rules, it is indifferent what they are. In the first of the *Trois Discours sur la condition des Grands*, which Pascal prepared for the instruction of the eldest son of the Duc de Luynes, he tells his pupil that he is not to imagine that there is a law of nature requiring that he should inherit the property of his ancestors. If the rule were that

---

[1] *Pensées*, op. cit., p. 889, § 240. The diversity Pascal has in mind consists in differences of opinion about what is just or right, which he thinks must arise if the appeal is to reason and not to custom.

a man's estate must revert, after his death, to the republic, it would not be a whit less just than the rule which secures his estate to his eldest son. God allows communities to make what rules of property they please, and no matter what the rules are, they ought to be respected. The heir to great wealth owes his wealth to mere chance: to his being born the son of his parents in a community happening to have a certain rule of inheritance. He is raised above his fellows because the social order is what it is, and it might, no less justly, no less reasonably, be entirely different. There is not a word in Pascal, so far as I know, to suggest that some rules of property are better adapted than others to the needs or feelings of the generality of men.[1]

In the second of the *Trois Discours*[2] Pascal distinguishes two kinds of greatness: greatness by convention (*d'établissement*) and greatness grounded in nature. Dignities and noble rank are of the first kind, and are achieved in one place in one way and in another place in another. It has pleased men that it should be so; and that is all that Pascal has to say about it. Greatness of the second kind consists of such things as intelligence, virtue, health and strength; it belongs *by nature* to whoever possesses it, presumably because it consists of qualities of mind or body, developed by exercise and education. We have obligations to both kinds of greatness. To the first we owe only outward respect or deference. We owe it, not because it is our interest to show it, but because it is right that we should do so; it is right that we should accept what is established. To greatness of the second kind we owe esteem. It is foolish to refuse outward respect to the first kind on the ground that it is not the second, or to expect for the second what is owing only to the first. The superiorities recognized by the world have nothing to do with merit; and it is as simple-minded to suppose that they could rest on merit as that they do. Men are so made that

---

[1] No doubt, Pascal would admit that whatever rules of property do arise in a community do not do so by mere chance. There are reasons why just those rules and not others did arise. But he says nothing to suggest *either* that there are some rules which arise everywhere because they are everywhere found convenient, *or* that the rules which arise in some particular community do so because they are found to be generally convenient in that community. On the other hand, he does suggest in one place (*Pensées*, p. 900, § 289) that organized society results from the victory of the strong over the weak, so that what is first established by force, presumably for the benefit of the strong, comes to be generally accepted as *imagination* underpins what *force* has set up.

[2] Jacques Chevalier, the editor of the Pléiade edition of Pascal's *Oeuvres*, says that Nicole, 'who has preserved the memory' of the *Trois Discours* in his *Éducation d'un Prince* (1670), assures his readers that, though they may not consist of Pascal's actual words, they are true to his thoughts and sentiments. The *Trois Discours* make up only six pages (pp. 387–92) of the text.

they cannot have peace except in a society of unequals; and therefore, since inequality has nothing to do with merit, the wise man does not refuse to high rank the deference it expects. Pascal invites the heir of the Duc de Luynes to think of himself as of a man wrecked in a storm on an unknown island whose people have lost their king. The stranger looks like the king and the people take him for the king; and the stranger, though at first with reluctance, assumes the rôle which chance has thrust upon him. He acts as if he were a king and yet knows that he is not one; he allows himself to be elevated in the eyes of the people, though in his own he remains what he truly is, no better than they are. Their illusion is salutary and he need not destroy it; but he ought not to share it, for if he does, he will abuse the position which has come to him by accident.

The people, Pascal tells us in the *Pensées*, have some very sound opinions: for example, that pursuit is better than capture, or that men are to be honoured for such external qualities as noble birth and wealth, or that a blow is to be deeply resented. The pursuit of what we think we want diverts us from ourselves while its capture proves that it is not worth having; honouring men for external qualities preserves the social order; and to receive a blow without resentment is to lose reputation on which solid advantages depend. Yet these sound opinions rest on illusion, for those who hold them usually do not know why they are sound. They thus honour persons of noble birth, believing in the superiority of the nobly born. The generality of men honour the nobly born, the half intelligent despise them on the ground that the advantages of birth come by chance and not by merit, while the truly intelligent honour them, though not for the reason that the others do. 'True Christians bow to folly notwithstanding; not because they respect it, but because of the order of God, who, to punish men, has subjected them to this folly: '*Omnis creatura subjecta est vanitati. Liberabitur.*'[1] But they are never to become quite free in this world, where the man who has overcome vanity in himself still belongs to a social order which magnifies it in others!

There are questions left unanswered by Pascal. How, in a world where essential justice is unknown, are even the wise to distinguish between the two kinds of greatness? How do they recognize virtue? In what does it consist? Is it no more than obedience to custom? And what makes intelligence or health or strength estimable? True, they are not qualities *external* to their possessors; but then neither are stupidity, ill-health and weakness. What causes men to esteem one

---

[1] *Pensées*, op. cit., p. 905, § 313. The citation is drawn from Romans 8.20–21.

another for having these qualities? Hume, who would no doubt agree with Pascal that the value of what is valuable to man is not determined by his reason but his passions and his will, attempts to answer these questions; but Pascal does not do so. It is not to be expected that he should in a work which is not a book but the raw materials for a book, and which treats of man in society only in passing to other (and in the author's eyes) higher matters. Man, until he finds God, is a creature intolerable to himself, and society provides no remedy for the worst evils which afflict him; it merely preserves him from some of the outward manifestations of these evils, provided he accepts established authority unquestioningly.

In the next century men came to believe in progress; they came to believe that men could discover (and indeed, to a great extent, already had discovered) in their environment and in themselves the causes of unhappiness, and could remove them. Either, like the Utilitarians, they conceived of happiness as the successful pursuit of pleasure, or they thought of it as a way of life suited to what is enduring in man's nature. In either case, it was something which men might hope to achieve in this world, something which they could get for themselves from one another without troubling their heads over much about their relations with God or their fate after death. The greater men's knowledge, the better they could adapt their means to their ends. Whether these believers in progress took the single Utilitarian view, which likens the pursuit of worldly happiness to the accumulation of wealth, or whether they preferred a more subtle conception of it, they took it for granted that this pursuit is the proper business of man. To them, Pascal seemed merely perverse. To his 'the last act is bloody, no matter how fine the comedy in all the rest', they might have answered that the last act appears bloody only to those who have not known how to enjoy the comedy.

It may be that, on this last point, they were right. At least we must hope so, for today, when so few can find consolation where Pascal looked for it, it is good that faith in the possibility of worldly happiness should be strong. And, in any case, we do not get from Pascal a balanced account of man's condition in society; we get only a deeper insight into some aspects of it.

Pascal, who differs so greatly from the believers in progress of the next century, differs also from Bossuet. He is altogether without reverence for kings or for the established order; they are, to him, objects of neither esteem nor contempt. He looks at worldly society with the eyes of St Augustine, without hatred and without pleasure. The established social order accords with the will of God, and yet it is a part of creation in which the Creator apparently takes no delight. It is a remedy for sin but not a means to the good life; it protects man from some of the effects of evil but contributes nothing to his perfection. It is not educative in any important sense. Bossuet, by contrast, following Aquinas and Aristotle, sees the social order as essentially a moral order. Man has a nature which is improved by life in society; his reason and affections find an outlet in it. Man grows into manhood as a member of society. He cannot become all that he ought to be as a mere partaker in social life, for his relations with God are more important than his relations with other men; but he is brought nearer even to his ultimate goal by being a partaker in it. Not merely because the Temporal Power maintains the peace needed to make possible the ministrations of the Church, but also because man learns what it is to need and to love God through his need and love for creatures like himself. Thus, for Bossuet as for Aquinas, worldly institutions are the handiwork of God in a larger and more hopeful sense than they are for Pascal. There are lesser and higher ends for man, and the way to the higher is through the lesser. The hand of God in every part of his universe is a loving hand.

The common motive of all the champions of absolute monarchy, whether – like Filmer and Bossuet – they make kings in a special sense the agents of God or – like Bodin and Hobbes – they do not, is fear of anarchy. This fear takes different forms, and in no one is more acute and all-pervasive than in Pascal. But what he fears most is not the 'war of all against all', the absence of government among men; what he fears above all is a spiritual anarchy, which needs more than government to cure it. Man who aspires to be everything, who wishes to be God, feels the emptiness in himself, the anarchy at the heart of his being, and therefore dare not face himself. His worldly ambitions occupy his mind without satisfying him, and hierarchy and government are needed to impose an external discipline on a creature full of vanity and incapable of happiness, and therefore dangerous to himself and his neighbours. This is the condition into which man's nature necessarily impels him, and the only cure for it is that he should find God. The established social order protects him from the effects of his own and other men's passions, and it also provides the external peace he needs if he is to have the courage and strength to face his predicament, if he is to undertake the painful search which, if it succeeds, leads him to God. The established order is an order proper to a madhouse, because man, until he has found God, does not know himself or what to do with himself; he is either appalled by the senselessness of life or takes refuge in illusion.

This condition of man, which Pascal imputes to his nature before he has found God, was later imputed to society by Rousseau; and thereafter sociology began to take the place of theology. The maladies to be accounted for remain largely the same, but the causes ascribed to them are widely different. Man is so situated that he cannot or dare not become what he must be to come to terms with himself and thereby find happiness: this is the theme common to Pascal and Rousseau.

CHAPTER 7

English Political Theory from the Breach with Rome until the Restoration

I. INTRODUCTORY

The English were the first people to establish free or responsible government on a large scale; until their success, which was perhaps the greatest political achievement of modern times, such government had existed only in city-states. If the ideals of Pericles can still inspire communities many times as populous as the Athens of his day, it is because the English, in their own country and in North America, have produced institutions and philosophies enabling governments to acquire really enormous power and yet be more sensitive to criticism and public opinion than ever before. Though it was not the English, but the Americans, who first created a wide democracy, they did so by adapting institutions and theories inherited from their English ancestors. Free government on a large scale – by which I mean government truly responsible to a considerable section of a numerous people and freely criticized by them – was originally aristocratic, very much so in England and to some extent also in English-speaking America; but in both countries it became democratic with the consent and assistance of the upper classes. The English revolution of the seventeenth century was a victory of those classes against the monarchy; and the American revolution of the eighteenth century was the victory of still far from completely democratic English colonies against an aristocratic mother country. Both these revolutions gave birth to democratic movements, and so made the eventual coming of democracy easier, but the revolutionary leaders were aristocrats suspicious of democracy. In neither country did democracy come as a result of revolution, of force successfully used by the unprivileged against the privileged. When at last it came, it drew the upper classes along with it, making full use of their experience and the political machinery produced by them. The English and American revolutions are remarkable for the moderation and discipline of the men who led them, and also for the strength of the institutions created or transformed by them. They gave to the world parliamentary government and federalism, the two devices which, above all others, have made free government possible on a vastly greater scale than ever before.

The principal philosopher of free government, the apologist of the English and one of the great mentors of the American revolution, is John Locke. Yet Locke is not more than Hobbes the philosopher of the large modern state – of the state that the English-speaking peoples have done so much to create. For that state is above all a deliberate maker of law; it is powerful and controls all lesser associations; it deals primarily, not with classes and corporations, but with individuals; it keeps the peace and promotes welfare at every level of society and is limited only by its own will. The English-speaking democratic state is as forceful as even Hobbes could have wished to see it; it is indeed Leviathan. Yet, in spite of its immense power, it is remarkably scrupulous and more attentive to individual rights than any state before it. It is the state that reconciles the aspirations of Hobbes and Locke. Hobbes was deeply convinced that only the strong can afford to be just, to enforce impartially the rules that give each man as great an opportunity as possible of getting what he wants at the least cost to others. He believed that the greater the power of the ruler the larger the freedom of the ruled. He was right, provided certain qualifications are made, though unfortunately he did not make them. It does not follow, because only the strong can afford to be just, that they will in fact be so. All power is exercised according to rules; it is never entirely, or even predominantly, arbitrary; and so it always affords security of a kind, and without security there is no freedom. These truths were very apparent to Hobbes. He believed that, provided the rules form a coherent whole, or (what to him appeared in practice much the same) provided the machinery of government works smoothly and efficiently, there is as much security, and therefore as much freedom, as it is humanly possible to attain. It is this latter belief that democrats do not accept; strength and efficiency are, they admit, necessary but not sufficient conditions of freedom. It would, however, be wrong to set down Hobbes's political philosophy as a mere apology for absolute government, of no concern to democracy. Hobbes is in many ways more modern, more pertinent to our times, even than Locke, as he is also more profound and original. Both of their theories emerged out of controversies raging in England during the most creative century of her political history.

Those controversies turned on two principal matters: the organization of the Church, and the relations between Parliament and King. The older controversy concerned the Church, because Henry VIII's breach with Rome rendered it necessary to make new provisions for ecclesiastical government. Parliament's challenge of the royal power did not become serious until the latter part of Elizabeth's reign. Nevertheless, the two controversies were intimately connected. The Puritans who disliked Elizabeth's church settlement, and who later denounced the High Church party, were the allies of the Parliament men who attacked the royal prerogative. The enemies of the bishops joined forces with the enemies of the king and won a common victory over monarchy and episcopacy.

II. CHURCH AND STATE IN ENGLAND

At the beginning of the sixteenth century, the wealth of the Church was coveted, the lax morals of the clergy condemned and the supremacy of the Pope resented. But the English were not heretics; the Lollard movement was dead and traditional doctrines were left unchallenged. The idea of a national church was nowhere discussed; it would have appeared absurd and even wicked. God's truth was one and His Church necessarily universal; this still seemed so obvious that it was uncontested, and therefore no one needed to defend it. That Christendom should consist of many churches, each worshipping God in its own way, was something so remote from European experience that it was not even imagined, still less suggested, in that period.

When Henry VIII broke with Rome, it was not at first supposed that England had seceded from the Universal Church. She had merely, so the King's apologists said, rejected papal usurpations, and this only made good claims that had long been put forward. The King remained true to all the old doctrines, and his becoming supreme head of the Church in England was not thought of as separating England from the rest of the Church. Secular rulers had nearly always in the Middle Ages had a large say in appointments to benefices in their own dominions, and they had also often helped the Church to reform itself. Papal pretensions had long been resisted. The Church had been powerful but had never, within the territories of any prince, been completely autonomous; it had always been subject to a variety of secular influences, sanctions and prohibitions. Church and State in the Middle Ages had been closely connected with one another. The break with Rome was popular; it was the consummation of desires and resentments that had been strong in England for at least two centuries. Almost no one understood the implications of that break for either Church or State.

Sir Thomas More did understand them. He understood that, if kings became rulers of the Church, then, since no king ruled more than a part of Christendom, the unity of the Church is destroyed. The bishops and other clergy who supported the King found it difficult to make an effective reply. For them, the Universal Church, the Church Catholic, still remained, though the Pope's authority inside it, being (they thought) a usurpation, was rightfully denied; the Church was still united in all essentials of doctrine and ritual; it was still one Church, though it no longer had one head. While Henry VIII, who disliked the reformers, was alive to maintain the old doctrines, this argument might pass muster, but it quite ignored the real point of More's case against supremacy. Community of doctrine must always be artificially maintained, for men do not all think alike just by chance; and it cannot be so maintained unless the Church has only one supreme government. Christian doctrine is not self-evident, but requires interpretation. Reject the Pope's supremacy over the entire Church, and there is no reason to believe that Christian doctrine will be similarly interpreted in all parts of Christendom. This must be so, whether or not kings and other lay rulers set themselves up for interpreters of doctrine. A universal church existing in the territories of several princes must, if it is to remain universal, be independent of those princes.

Christopher St Germain, a lawyer famous for his controversy with Thomas More, first put forward, unequivocally and forcefully, the English doctrine of royal supremacy over the Church. He argued that the Act of Supremacy gave the King no power he had not had before; all that happened was that the clergy had been deprived of certain privileges, on the sufficient ground that the power which had originally granted those privileges now found them detrimental. St Germain admitted that it is for the Church to declare the truth concerning faith; and yet the Church is not the clergy but the whole body of professing Christians. Since the Church thus conceived has no common organization or head, it is for every part of it to act for the whole in that province of Christendom where it can act. The Church in England consists of the mass of English Christians, whose natural head and representative is the King. The English people are a State and a Church, and in both capacities have the same supreme representative, the King-in-Parliament. St Germain was a lawyer, and he probably came to these views less because he cared for the spiritual unity of Christendom than because he wished to promote the unity of the English State.

The English were Catholics while Henry remained supreme Head of their Church, but by Elizabeth's time they were already deeply divided about religion. Ordinary folk, no doubt, were still mostly attached to the old faith, whose doctrines they had never understood but whose ceremonies were familiar and dear to them. The reformers made most of their converts among the wealthier and more articulate classes, who, of course, counted for more than ordinary people. Elizabeth's church settlement was more 'protestant' than Henry VIII's had been, and no doubt more also than the sentiments of the people as a whole; she went a long way towards placating the wealthy and powerful, for it is always more expedient to make concessions to these classes than to the illiterate and unorganized. By 1571, the mass was officially declared blasphemous and deceitful, and the doctrine of transubstantiation condemned as 'repugnant to the plain words of Scripture'. On the whole, however, there were few official pronouncements about matters of doctrine. Clergymen, on their own authority, taught pretty much what they pleased and, within limits, made what innovations they liked. Doctrine was vague and discipline lax. That was how the Queen preferred it. She wanted only one church, but one so accommodating that the vast majority of her subjects could belong to it without doing violence to their consciences. It was a matter of policy with her to leave the Church fairly loosely organized and doctrine not too precisely defined, for she wanted the Church to be acceptable to as many of her subjects as possible.

Elizabeth's bishops, as might be expected, had rather more definite opinions about religion than she had. They were mostly inclined to Calvinism, though more so in matters of doctrine than in their views about church government. They accepted the royal supremacy and at times even seemed reconciled to the view that the Queen could pronounce finally upon matters of doctrine. Many of them did not at first regard their offices as essential to the proper government of the Church, still less as established by divine right. There were bishops, they held, in the English Church only because the Queen, who was competent to settle such matters, had decided that there should be. Under this lax and comfortable regime, the mass of Englishmen were gradually weaned away from the old religion, not through the concerted efforts of the Church, but because many fervent and reforming clergymen, left to their own devices by the bishops, abandoned the old ceremonies and preached the new doctrines.

It was the persistence and bitterness of Puritan attacks on episcopacy that at last caused some of the bishops and their friends to argue that Scripture, inasmuch as it prescribes any form of church government (which, in their opinion, it does only to a slight extent), favours episcopacy. Later still, the bishops took an even firmer stand, declaring that episcopal authority derived from Christ himself. This was the position adopted, for instance, by Bancroft and Bilson, among the bishops, and by the theologian, Saravia.

At the beginning of Elizabeth's reign, the Puritans had entertained few grievances against the State. They had suffered under Mary Tudor and could feel nothing but relief when Elizabeth succeeded her. They had been few in number and not at all popular. As their numbers increased greatly, especially among the commercial and professional classes, they became more critical and vociferous. They were always a minority; but they were active, enterprising and belligerent. When they declared that the faith is contained entire in Holy Scripture, most of Elizabeth's bishops, themselves inclined to Calvinism, found it easy to sympathize with them; but when they went on to assert that the Bible prescribes how the Church must be organized, and does not allow for episcopacy, the bishops could no longer agree. The Puritans assumed that God must have provided for the spiritual and moral welfare of His people, and that He could not be taken to have done so unless He had determined how His Church should be governed. Since the Bible contains the whole Word of God, it must prescribe not only what men shall believe but also how they shall worship. The Puritans wanted a church governed by elected ministers and elders forming consistories, and they also wanted final authority in matters of faith and discipline vested in a national synod; so they set about interpreting Scripture to suit their wishes. Their ideas about church government may appear democratic, but most historians have doubted their sincere attachment to democracy. The Puritans were always a minority, and they must have known that free election of ministers and elders in the England of Elizabeth and the first two Stuarts would have produced something very unlike the godly discipline for which they yearned. They would almost certainly, when it came to the point, have wanted the ungodly deprived of all say in church government. Their prescriptions were no doubt vague, but their real purpose was clear enough. What they sought was the predominance of the godly in the Church, and there was nothing more evident to them than that the great majority of their countrymen were not godly. Most of the Puritans looked to the State to establish the true Church in the form that they desired, but not thereafter to govern it. Far from wishing the Church subordinate to the State, they wanted the State to be the Church's instrument for the maintenance of true religion and morals. At bottom, they rejected royal supremacy as thoroughly as they rejected episcopacy. But in Elizabeth's time they dared not set themselves against that supremacy openly, for it was much more dangerous to attack the Queen than to attack the bishops.

These were the sentiments of most of the Puritans, but not of all. The Congregationalists or Brownists denied that it was the duty of the State to establish the true Church. In their judgement, it was for the faithful themselves to establish it, the State having no duties except to suppress idolatry and blasphemy; its office is merely negative – not to establish true religion but to forbid the obviously false. The Baptists, who broke away from the Congregationalists early in the seventeenth century and who formed their first church in England in 1611, were more tolerant than the other Puritans. Their *Confession of Faith*, issued that year, declared that all men should have liberty of conscience in religious matters. Their pamphleteers argued that religious tolerance is always and everywhere expedient and that persecution, which is contrary to the Gospel, serves only to multiply the number of hypocrites and nearly always bears most heavily on true believers. As if they had never heard of Luther and Calvin, they spoke of persecution as a specifically Roman practice, which the English bishops had now taken to imitating. But the Baptists, though their ideas come nearer to our modern conception of the proper relations between Church and State, were not really as tolerant as they seemed. Let all men, they said, Christian and Jew, dispute freely about religious matters, each man following his own conscience; but they added that no one should be allowed to appeal to any authority except the Bible. Toleration thus limited would have been cold comfort to the Roman Catholics. The Baptists, the most tolerant of Puritans, and the rather less tolerant Congregationalists, were small and unimportant sects, at least until the formation of the New Model Army. The bulk of the Puritans were less tolerant than the bishops, and much less tolerant than the Queen.

Neither the Queen nor the bishops could like the Puritans: the Queen, because she could not admit their claim to impose their kind of religious discipline on the easy-going majority of her subjects; and the bishops, partly for the same reason as the Queen, and partly because the Puritans thought that the true Church cannot have bishops. The purpose of Hooker's *Laws of Ecclesiastical Polity* was to argue against the Puritans that, since there was nothing about the English church establishment that was contrary to the Law of Reason (by which he meant what was more often called the Law of Nature), or to Revelation, it was the duty of Puritans, merely as Englishmen, to accept that establishment, which was made by the Queen-in-Parliament, whose authority under God was admittedly supreme in England. It seemed to him clearly untrue that Holy Scripture prescribed for the Church a constitution incompatible with that established by Queen and Parliament. The people of England, he said, are both a commonwealth and a church, and their government rests ultimately on consent. The authority of the government is limited only by the Law of Reason and the revealed law of God. Since the church settlement of Elizabeth contravenes neither of those laws, it is the duty of the Puritans, merely as Englishmen subject in all things not required or forbidden by reason or God, to accept the legitimate government of their country. Not disputing the legitimacy of that government, the Puritans had no good reason to believe that the established church violated any of God's precepts; they therefore had no reasonable alternative but to submit to it. Hooker, the wisest and gentlest of men, had great respect for tender consciences. There was, as he saw it, no question of requiring the Puritans to accept doctrines that to them seemed manifestly false; the matter at issue between them and the established church related only to church government. The Puritans appealed to the Scriptures and so also did he; and to him it appeared incontestable that the Scriptures required nothing which the English Church did not fully accept. Perhaps he was right, but the Puritans were unpersuadable. Reading the same Holy Book as he did, they claimed to see written in it what, to him, was invisible.

Elizabeth, when she died, left the Church loosely disciplined and in matters of doctrine equivocal and incoherent. The Puritans had annoyed and the Catholics disturbed her. She had taken measures against them both, but had still done nothing to bring order and doctrinal unity to the Church. This looseness and ambiguity might suit a queen whose chief concern with religion was that it should not divide and weaken but unite and strengthen her country; the bishops and their supporters, however, were more inclined to care for the dogmas of religion. They felt the need for proper discipline, and also for doctrine and ritual to be more exactly defined. The Puritan attack on them had caused them to set a greater value on episcopacy as such. At the beginning of Elizabeth's reign, the bishops had been inclined to regard themselves as overseers, appointed by a sovereign, who, if she had decided not to appoint them, would have been quite within her rights; but towards the end of her reign, they were already seeing themselves as priests whose authority came down in unbroken succession from Christ Himself. Episcopacy was not merely convenient; it was necessary to the Church. Some bishops went so far as to say that the right to determine doctrine and to control ritual belongs, even in a national church, principally to the clergy; to the Queen-in-Convocation rather than to the Queen-in-Parliament. These bishops and their supporters were the beginnings of what was later known as the High Church Party.

Elizabeth's dislike of the Puritans did not cause her to adopt High Church principles. James I, however, was much drawn to system and discipline, and looked with favour on those tendencies. The purpose of the Hampton Court Conference, which met in 1604, was precisely to introduce such virtues to the Church. The Puritans at first sympathized with that aim. They too wanted system and discipline, and being powerfully represented in the Church, they were present in force at the Conference. But King James soon revealed his dislike of them; he broke up the Conference, which had failed to reconcile the dissentients, and he afterwards resolutely took the bishops' part. The Puritans had hoped to reform the Church, but they were now to find it hardening against them. The new canons issued in 1604 were not, when taken separately, serious innovations; precedents for every one of them could be found among earlier laws and formularies. But, taken as a whole, these canons changed the whole character of the Church; they brought order where there had been chaos, making from among earlier ordinances a selection unacceptable to the Puritans. Hitherto, from the point of view of Puritans, the Church had certainly left very much to be desired; they had wanted to reform it but had nevertheless been able to remain inside it without doing violence to their consciences. There had been many Puritans among beneficed clergymen. To them the Church had seemed a house badly needing to be put in order, and they had thought it wise to remain inside that house to help bring order to it. But now it was being put into an order intolerable to them; it was becoming the kind of Church they would soon feel it their duty to leave and to destroy.

Though there were a number of Puritans in Parliament, especially in the House of Commons, they were only a minority. Parliament was offended by the canons of 1604, not so much out of sympathy for the Puritans, as out of resentment of an action which challenged its authority. Henry VIII had used Parliament to make good his breach with Rome, and Elizabeth had used it to make her church settlement. The royal supremacy, according to Parliament, must be exercised, by the King-in-Parliament, at least in the legislative sphere. No doubt there were precedents to justify this disregard of Parliament. In Elizabeth's reign, canons had twice been issued without reference to Parliament, and other kinds of prescripts yet more frequently. But they had not been made so much of and had passed almost unnoticed, whereas the canons of 1604 followed hard upon a much publicized conference at which the King had failed to reconcile the Puritans with the bishops, and had then made clear his preference for the bishops. The canons of 1604 looked therefore like a deliberate attempt to reform the Church against the Puritans and in contempt of Parliament. Convocation even went so far as to pass a resolution that Parliament had no right to meddle in ecclesiastical matters. The bishops and their supporters did not wish to offend the House of Commons; they wanted merely to bring order to the Church and were convinced that Parliament would not help them to do so; and they therefore asserted their right to act without Parliament. It was natural they should make the claim, and as natural that Parliament should resist it – not so much from love of the Puritans as in defence of its own legislative supremacy. The canons of 1604 were a first victory for the High Church party. As that party grew stronger, it was inevitable that the two groups most offended by it, the Puritans in the country generally and the lawyers in London and in Parliament, should become allies. The lawyers objected in particular to the Court of High Commission; and the judges, led by Edward Coke, issued numerous prohibitions against the ordinary ecclesiastical courts, though these, now that the King was supreme governor of the Church, were, as much as any other, royal courts.

The Puritans disliked the High Church party, because the Church, as that party wished to make it, was abhorrent to them; whereas Parliament objected chiefly to the claim that the Church was alone competent to decide matters of doctrine and ritual. The Puritans came to find that they could not bear episcopacy, but Parliament did not object to it in principle. It learnt to distrust the bishops, and even to sympathize with Puritan attacks upon them, but mostly because the bishops were making claims for the Church that Parliament could not accept. Any strong assertion of the Church's independence was suspect to Parliament, and savoured of Romanism – all the more so, no doubt, because James, to placate the Spaniards whose alliance he was seeking, and Charles, on his wife's account, were more inclined to deal leniently with Catholics than with Puritans. Hence the increasing willingness of the House of Commons to lend a friendly ear to Puritan attacks on the abuses of the bishops. Most members of Parliament, though no doubt good enough Christians in their way, were not much concerned with doctrine and ritual for their own sake and did not much care how the Church was organized, provided it was duly subordinate to the State. Political prejudice apart, many of them might have been as much edified by High Church ritual as by Puritan sermons; but, seeing that that ritual went with ecclesiastical pretensions which challenged the supremacy of Parliament, they soon learnt to abhor it. They took it for another symptom of a wholesale and disguised movement back to the Roman faith and an insidious return to Roman practices. For its part, Parliament was half-inclined to believe the Puritans, because the bishops and clergy who introduced that ritual were too often champions of ecclesiastical independence. They were also, of course, champions of the royal power because they needed the King's protection. James was friendly to them and Charles even more so. Hence the alliance, against the King and against the bishops, of the House of Commons and the Puritans – an alliance in many ways unsatisfying to both parties to it, yet strong enough to make one of the great revolutions of modern history.

III. PARLIAMENT AGAINST THE KING

Until the last years of the sixteenth century, English political writers were preoccupied with matters of religion, with the Church and with the State's relations to it. The only important exception was Sir Thomas Smith, author of *De republica anglorum*, which was probably written in the 1560s. Smith did for England what Claude de Seyssel, in *The Great Monarchy of France*, had done for his country; he described the system of government just before the period when it was destined to undergo a revolutionary change. Parliament, he said, may abrogate old laws and make new ones; it has the power to do all that the people may do, for every Englishman is assumed to be present in it in the person of his representative. Parliament's consent may therefore be taken as that of every man. Smith thus asserted the supremacy of Parliament, and no one thought of contesting the assertion. Was he already putting forward, in the sixteenth century, the principle for which Parliament was to go to war with the King in 1642? Was Charles really a political aggressor? Were Pym and his friends defenders of the constitution? Judging by Smith's unchallenged account of the matter, it might indeed seem so.

Nevertheless, in this case, the appearances deceive. Smith was not the champion of any new claims made at the Queen's expense, and he was not anticipating the Parliamentary leaders of the next century; his book was published in 1583, before the defeat of the Armada and at a time when it was still taken for granted that only strong royal government could save England from the dangers threatening her. He was, like Seyssel, moderate and impartial, more concerned to describe the facts as he saw them than to plead for any interested party. When he wrote his book, there was as yet no serious dispute about the constitution, and he certainly did not contest the authority of the Queen. There was nothing about the doctrine of Parliamentary supremacy offensive to such a loyal servant of the Tudor monarchy. Yet, when Pym claimed, some sixty years later, that Parliament was supreme, he made that assertion in a different sense from the meaning of Sir Thomas Smith. He was not, though he might think otherwise, defending the constitution against the king. On the contrary, he was making unprecedented claims at the royal expense and interpreting the supremacy of Parliament as it had never been understood before.

Sir Thomas Smith, when he asserted the supremacy of the English Parliament, and Claude de Seyssel, when, half a century earlier, he made the same claim for the French king, were not attributing to them anything of what Hobbes or even Bodin understood by sovereignty. There is no evidence that Smith supposed that the English Parliament had unlimited legislative power, any more than Seyssel believed that the French king had it. We must not read back into the sixteenth century ideas and distinctions first made clear in the seventeenth century. Neither writer distinguished as clearly as we do now between the legislative and judicial functions of government. Smith believed that there could be no appeal from Parliament's decision on the law's significance, for Parliament was, in Elizabeth's time, the highest court in the realm and its pronouncements were final. It was the supreme interpreter of law, and it also made new laws when they had to be made. But Smith did not claim for Parliament an unlimited right to make what laws it pleased. Since it was Parliament (which included the Queen) that was supreme, the Queen outside Parliament could neither interpret nor make the law, except in a subordinate capacity. The position in France, as Seyssel described it, was different, because, though it was held that the king ought normally to consult his people (that is, the Estates-General) when making important new laws, it was not established that he must do so. Whatever laws he did make, whether with or without the concurrence of the Estates-General, had to be registered with the *parlements*, the highest courts of law, which could delay registration and make remonstrances. Some writers held that the *parlements* must in the end register the king's edicts, if he insisted upon it; others, that they need not do so. This was not yet a settled question. Nevertheless, the king's legislative supremacy was, before the religious wars, generally asserted and seldom contested – though asserted, not in the sense that his command, duly promulgated, was for that reason alone good law, but in the sense that, even when he acted alone, his authority as an interpreter and as a maker of law was greater than anyone else's. The king's legislative supremacy was not quite as firmly established in France as Parliament's was in England; but supremacy in neither country meant sovereignty in the modern sense. The modern conception of sovereignty, which is French and English in origin, was the product of civil war. When Bodin wrote his *Republic*, France was no longer the France of Claude de Seyssel, just as when Hobbes wrote *Leviathan*, England was no longer the England of Sir Thomas Smith.

Neither James I nor Charles I made claims on behalf of the English monarchy seriously inconsistent with the supremacy of Parliament as Smith had conceived it. James's *True Law of Free Monarchies*, in which he claimed absolute power for kings, was a Scottish exercise in philosophy, written before he came to the English throne. In 1610, James admitted to the two Houses of Parliament that he had no power to make laws or to exact subsidies except with their consent. He did, however, make claims distasteful to the two Houses. He asserted, at various times, his right to legislate for the Church with the consent of Convocation alone, to limit freedom of debate in Parliament, to imprison his subjects without showing cause, to impose customs duties by royal proclamation, and to punish members of Parliament for words spoken in Parliament. None of these claims, not even the first, contested the supremacy of Parliament as Smith understood it; for James never denied that Parliament could legislate for the Church, nor claimed that Convocation could disregard the Act of Supremacy or set aside any other statute relating to the Church made by Parliament. He was saying merely that he and Convocation could, when the need arose, legislate for the Church without the assistance of the Lords and Commons. There were precedents in Elizabeth's time to support, not only this claim, but almost every claim made by James and Charles. Elizabeth had often interfered with the freedom of Parliamentary debate, had raised forced loans, had imposed customs duties by royal proclamation without the consent of Parliament, had arrested members of the House of Commons for acts done in the

House, and had also imprisoned quite a number of her subjects without showing cause. She had thought it her business and not Parliament's – as Sir Thomas Smith would no doubt have agreed – to govern England; and she had not been responsible to Parliament for how she governed. Parliament had, of course, the right to present petitions and to ask for the redress of grievances; but she alone made policy, and the two Houses – so she said – had no right to discuss how she made it. She could not make law without their assistance and could not impose taxes without their consent. That much she admitted, but it seemed to her not in the least to follow that she was in any way responsible to them for the manner of her government. If Parliament did more than debate bills, vote subsidies and present petitions; if it presumed to discuss and criticize policy, it was meddling with what was not, and had never been in the past, its concern, and it was liable to punishment for doing so. While she could not make laws without its assistance, moreover, she could issue Orders-in-Council and various other regulations; and though she could not in general levy taxes which had not been voted by Parliament, she could dispose as she pleased of ordinary Crown revenues and even impose certain duties without Parliament's consent. She resisted, sharply and at once, every Parliamentary encroachment on her prerogatives, and yet her attitude was perfectly consistent with what Sir Thomas Smith and other experienced and moderate men looked upon as the traditional and proper system of government in England. With the Queen's interpretation of her rights, Smith would probably have agreed.

Government was necessarily more arbitrary in Tudor and early Stuart times than it is now. The need for prompt action regardless of law had long been admitted, in practice if not in theory, and even Locke, in the *Second Treatise of Civil Government*, acknowledged that the monarch might temporarily set a law aside, provided he did so for the public good. The Tudor monarchy had given the English stronger government than they had known before, and on the whole they liked it. The purpose of government was to provide security and maintain the law, and that this purpose might be fulfilled, the monarch had on occasion to be allowed to act arbitrarily. Most of the expedients that James and Charles employed, and to which the two Houses objected, had in Tudor times been accepted as necessary to good government. It was admitted that Parliamentary and legal processes were slow, and that the monarch might sometimes have to act more quickly than they would allow him to do. He might, in an emergency, need to raise money immediately without waiting for Parliament to vote him a subsidy; he might, to preserve the state from dangerous plotters, need to arrest suspected persons without bringing them to trial; he might, in his often delicate and precarious relations with foreign Powers, be harassed and impeded by the ignorant meddling of Members of Parliament. Responsible for good government and for the country's security, he needed all the powers exercised by his Tudor predecessors. And yet from 1603 to 1629 every claim made on behalf of the Crown to extra-legal powers was denied by the Commons, which also made frequent attempts to impose its wishes on the king in matters of foreign policy. Why did the Commons deny to James and Charles prerogatives so frequently exercised by Elizabeth and her father?

Until the defeat of the Armada, the Catholic and Spanish danger united the country in loyalty to the Queen, who was nothing if not a patriot. When that danger was past, she had already reigned for thirty years; her power and popularity were well established. She kept the Church's doctrine vague and its discipline loose and so made it as little exasperating as possible in an age when the most bitter disputes and resentments were religious. She had trouble, both with the Puritans and the House of Commons, who, against her successors – but more boldly and obstinately – continued their quarrels with her. Historians are largely agreed that she was firmer and more tactful than either James or Charles, but probably not even her virtues could have preserved for very much longer the English monarchy as the Tudors had made it. The political crisis that culminated in the Civil War began in the latter part of Elizabeth's reign; she had to deal only with the first and mildest phase of it. The English monarchy, as the Tudors had established it, lasted until 1640, and then collapsed like a pack of cards. It was strong while it was popular with the dominant and locally ruling classes, but it could not long survive that popularity. It was, in itself, a light structure; the number of its servants was small, for it was not a bureaucratic or a police or a military state. It could be strong only while the upper classes believed in it and allowed themselves to be guided by it; if it lost their confidence, it was almost helpless before them.

Neither James nor Charles understood that, though the monarchy was strong *with* the support of the new upper classes, it could not be strong *against* them. The great mass of Englishmen, attached to the monarchy but indifferent to politics, could be neither a source of danger nor an effective support to the royal power; everything depended on the loyalties and preferences of the nobility and gentry, the merchants and the lawyers, the rich, the educated, the articulate and the locally prominent. These classes, strongly represented in

Parliament, were on the whole united against the King until 1641; and if the union had continued, there would have been no Civil War. There was war only because the more moderate of the King's opponents, satisfied with the concessions extorted from him during the first months of the Long Parliament, were appalled by the new claims pressed by the more extreme party. It has been said that the Royalists fought the Civil War in defence of principles first asserted, not by Charles, but by Parliament itself in 1628, in the Petition of Right. Charles, no doubt, would have liked to rule England as Elizabeth had done or even more absolutely, but when he first took up arms against Parliament he was careful not to revive any of the pretensions abandoned in 1641. Of course, as nearly always happens, as the fighting continued, both sides became more demanding and obstinate. The war strengthened prejudices for monarchy as well as prejudices against it; and there at last appeared in England, on the one hand, champions of absolute monarchy, and, on the other, staunch republicans. But these sentiments rather grew out of the Civil War than gave rise to it.

By expropriating Church lands and redistributing them among laymen, by breaking the power of the old nobility, by keeping England internally at peace for several generations, by encouraging agriculture, trade and industry, by avoiding expensive foreign wars, and by using Parliament to help reform both State and Church, the Tudor monarchy had enriched the country and had made it possible for new classes to emerge and dominate society – classes more patriotic, responsible and law-abiding than the feudal nobility. In Parliament, so often used by the Tudor monarchs and thus improved and strengthened as a national legislature, these classes found a forum for their ideas and an instrument of their ambitions. The House of Commons, subordinate and usually docile to the Lords in the late Middle Ages, had in Tudor times become an assembly altogether more articulate and resolute; it had grown in stature, acquiring a settled procedure and a corporate will. Nowhere else in Europe was there a national instrument like it – one that could be used so effectively to resist the royal power without endangering the unity of the State. Huguenot resistance to the French kings, because it was provincial and used local magistrates against a national monarchy, threatened to disrupt France; but Parliamentary resistance in England did not do so. Parliament was no longer dominated by an assembly of semi-independent feudal lords; it was as national as the King, and, if it challenged his power, might hope to rule the country in his stead. The King could not rule without it. All the expedients he was driven to, all the claims he could maintain with any show of reason in the law courts, could not provide him for long with the resources he needed to govern England. When the Scots and the Irish made trouble for him, he had to convoke Parliament and beg for subsidies; and he could only get them by making the concessions demanded of him. By September 1641, the Long Parliament had already made good all the claims against the King put forward in 1628. An Act was passed requiring Parliament to meet at least once every three years, the prerogative courts were abolished, and it was declared illegal to raise ship money or customs duties without the consent of Parliament.

If Pym and his friends had been content with these victories, the King could have done nothing against them. He would have had, perforce, to suit his manner of government to the new conditions imposed on him. He would no doubt have found it difficult to do so; the powers taken away from him had been used by all his predecessors and by them deemed necessary to the good and effective government of the country. What would have happened to the royal power had there been no Civil War, no one can say. It would, no doubt, have continued to diminish, for the concessions made by Charles to the Long Parliament up to September 1641 would have made it impossible for him to pursue policies to which the two Houses were strongly opposed. The King had not abdicated all real power – far from it; but he had, though neither he nor Parliament might know it, deprived himself of the means of governing England as he and his predecessors had done. By its reforms, the Long Parliament stripped him of all the powers denounced in the Petition of Right. It left him powerful, though not enough to maintain his independent authority to govern England. The moderates in the Long Parliament by no means denied Charles that authority; their intention was only to make it impossible for him to misgovern. Even Pym and the extreme party did not deny his right to govern. They put themselves forward as defenders of the constitution, and not as revolutionaries. Everyone knew that in England it was the King and not Parliament that governed. While the King's power was limited, and he could not make laws or levy taxes except with the consent of Parliament, no one supposed that he was responsible to Parliament for the direction of policy.

But Pym and his friends did not trust the King. They were afraid of his going back on his word. Above all, they were afraid of Strafford, whose vigorous use of the royal power – a use that was completely justified by the need to bring order to the North and to Ireland – seemed to them dangerous. They hated Strafford because, until 1628, he had been a champion of Parliament against the King and had afterwards changed his allegiance. Yet Strafford's behaviour in the King's service had not been a denial of his earlier career in Parliament. He did not want to make the King's power absolute but only to make his government effective; and there is no real evidence that he wanted an army – which had been raised ostensibly to put down the rebels in Ireland – used in England to coerce Parliament. Nevertheless, to Pym, who seems not to have been aware how far he himself had moved from the position taken up by the House of Commons in 1628, Strafford appeared a traitor – not to the King, of course, but to the constitution. The political murder of Strafford (for it was really nothing less) made it impossible for the King and Parliament to be sincerely reconciled; it mortally offended and humiliated Charles, who had been obliged to betray the most able of his servants.

Pym and his friends never said, in so many words, that they meant to take over the direction of policy from the King. Perhaps they never even intended doing so, for at that time almost no one thought Parliament a body fit to control the government. Nevertheless, because they distrusted the King and his ministers and because they feared the use of armed force against them, the Parliamentary leaders soon took actions that were greater and more obvious usurpations than any of which the King had been guilty. After several unsuccessful attempts to persuade the King to put the fortresses and militia under the control of their own nominees, the Houses adopted the Militia Ordinance in March 1642 and proclaimed it law, though the King had not consented to it. They could not cite a single precedent to justify their action; they claimed the right, when the kingdom, in their judgment, was in imminent danger, to take control of the armed forces. When Charles sent a message to them declaring that no one could be obliged to obey an Act or order to which the King had not consented, the Houses passed a resolution that whatever the Lords and Commons declare to be law is law. The Houses, feeling perhaps that they had been too bold, later retreated a little from this position; they could not, they admitted, make law without the King's assent, but they declared that the King, though not legally obliged to do so, was bound 'in conscience and in justice' to assent to bills put before him by both Houses for the good of the entire kingdom. Pym and his party equivocated; they wanted to make large demands and yet not to seem to be making them. They were not self-confessed revolutionaries consciously making unprecedented claims in the name of eternal principles violated by the established system. They put themselves forward as – and no doubt honestly believed themselves to be – defenders of the constitution. And yet, albeit hesitatingly and without quite realizing what they were doing, they were making a revolutionary demand; they were asking the King to admit their right, as representatives of the nation, to control his government. They did not do so because they believed in what a later age was to call parliamentary government, but because they mistrusted the King and feared reprisals. Wishing to put it out of the King's power to hurt them or to take back the concessions he had already made, they asked to be allowed to control the executive. On June 2nd, 1642, in the Nineteen Propositions, they asked that all Privy Councillors, Ministers of State and high officers of the realm be appointed only with their approval. The King refused, and on July 12th the Houses resolved 'that an army be forthwith raised'. For his part, the King, advised by Hyde, Falkland and other prominent members of the moderate party, took his stand on the principles proclaimed by Parliament in 1628. No mention was made in any royal proclamation of the prerogatives abandoned in 1641, although English kings had enjoyed them for centuries. Charles accepted the position created for him by the Acts passed in 1641, because he had appended his signature to them; but the new claims made by the Houses he was determined to resist, if necessary by force of arms. In rejecting the Nineteen Propositions he had caused Pym to make an even greater breach in the constitution, for without the King the two Houses just could not be Parliament; they had no right to make laws or levy taxes, let alone raise an army.

IV. PARLIAMENTARY AND ROYALIST THEORIES

Perhaps the ablest exponent of Parliament's case, on the eve of the Civil War and when it was still hoped that a settlement might be reached, was Henry Parker. In his *Observations upon some of His Majesty's late Answers and Expresses* of July 1642, he attempted a philosophical defence of the position taken up by the two Houses. Power belongs, he said, in the first place to the people, and all authority rests on popular recognition. There was probably a time when laws were made by common consent, with nobody specially deputed to enforce them. When this was found inconvenient, magistrates were set up; and then afterwards, when magistrates began to abuse their authority, there were established representative bodies to watch over them. Parliament, said Parker, is 'the very people itself artificially congregated';[1] and he implied that ultimate authority therefore rests with it. The King acts for the people only for some purposes, and is always bound by the law and by the nature of his office. He must do what he was set up to do and no more. But Parliament, being virtually the people itself, is not so limited. From these premises Parker did not exactly conclude that the Houses might, if they found it necessary, make law without the King. That would still have been too shocking a proposition to advance before hostilities had actually started. He thought it enough to say that the King is bound to assent to all bills that the Houses deem necessary for the people's good, they alone being judges of the necessity. Parker, like most of the Parliamentary champions in the early stages of the war, was a little hesitant; he did not want to appear a revolutionary. But his real position is clear enough. That all authority comes ultimately from the people had for centuries been a commonplace of European political philosophy. The Roman lawyers had admitted it and yet had claimed absolute power for the Emperor; mediaeval philosophers had accepted it but had also denied that either princes or parliaments could make law except within narrow limits; whereas Parker and those who thought like him contended that, because all authority comes from the people, the Lords and Commons may, if necessary with only the King's formal consent, make what laws they please in the people's name. His argument implies that, when the King fails in his duty, it is for the two Houses of Parliament to take what measures they think right, because the ultimate authority of the people is vested in them. He was not perhaps attributing to the Lords and Commons sovereignty in the Hobbesian sense, for he made no claim to the effect that they are unregulated by the laws of nature. But he was attributing to them at least the same legislative supremacy as Bodin had attributed to the King of France. Parker's argument, in all essentials, was already very like Locke's.

Taken abstractly and without regard to English precedents, the Royalist case was no stronger than the Parliamentary. Parker's assumptions once accepted, his conclusions are reasonable enough. There are several senses in which authority can be said to come from the people, and they do not all imply the legislative supremacy of Parliament; but Parker was at liberty to choose a sense that did imply it. Though Parliament was in fact far from truly representative of the people, it was nearer being so than any other institution. It might be an effective argument against Parker that, on his own assumptions,

---

[1] Parker, *Jus populi* (1644), p. 18, cited in J. W. Allen, *English Political Thought 1603–1660*, vol. I (1603–1644) (all published), (London 1938), p. 430.

Parliament's right to speak for the people was much weaker than it could be – in other words, that Parliament should be reformed. That kind of argument was used later, after Parliament's victory over the King, by the victorious army; but in the early 1640s it appealed to no one. The weakness of the case for Parliament was a consequence, not of the abstract assumptions on which it rested, but of the Parliamentary leaders' respect for tradition and their consequent endeavours to justify rebellion as a defence of the English constitution. It was here that the Royalists had an advantage over them; they, at least, could afford to be lucid and consistent. They, too, used abstract arguments, but at first only to defend the English monarchy as it actually was at the time when the Civil War began. So long as it lasted, they seldom argued in favour of absolute monarchy. Neither Hobbes nor Filmer spoke for the Royalists. Hobbes's sympathies were no doubt with the King, but his fundamental argument was really no more favourable to one side than the other; whereas Filmer's *Patriarcha* was not published until 1680, twenty-seven years after its author's death. It was the gospel, not of the Royalists who fought the Civil War, but of the extreme neo-Royalists after the Restoration. It has been suggested[1] that the first arguments in favour of absolute monarchy by divine right appeared in England in 1647, when the war had already been lost, although as a matter of fact they were foreshadowed in the 1590s by Bancroft and Saravia.[2] But with the English Royalists of the seventeenth century, no less than with the French Royalists a hundred and fifty years later, we find that they produced their most intransigent theories after the complete victory of their enemies. When the monarchy was restored, in England in 1660 and in France in 1814, it was immensely weaker than it had been before the revolution; and yet it was for the benefit of this restored and weakened monarchy that the Royalists of both countries produced their most uncompromising doctrines. One might suppose that there is nothing like defeat to convince some people of the rightness of their cause.

During the 1640s, the literary champions of the Royalist cause, still hoping for victory and therefore careful and unprovocative, mostly

---

[1] By Allen in *English Political Thought 1603–1660*, vol. I (1603–1644), p. 482. Allen refers to Robert Grosse's *Royalty and Loyalty*, dating from July 1647.

[2] See J. P. Sommerville, *Politics and Ideology in England, 1603–1640* (London 1986), ch. 1. Sommerville traces the doctrine of the divine right of kings, at least in the history of English political thought, to Richard Bancroft's *Dangerous positions and proceedings* and Hadrian Saravia's *De imperandi authoritate* – works in each case intended to oppose Catholic or Calvinist resistance theories – both dating from 1593.

argued that long tenure of power without opposition implies full consent on the part of the governed. Such powers the kings of England undoubtedly possessed. These writers mostly denied that authority is created by a deliberate act of the people; it comes ultimately from God, but is confirmed in those that have it by their always having had it. They easily disproved the claim of the two Houses that whatever they declared to be law was law; and they also refuted the argument that the House of Commons spoke for the people. The ablest of them, John Maxwell, in *Sacro-sancta regum majestas*, published in 1644, even denied that the people can be a source of authority, using the Hobbesian argument that until authority exists they are not a people but a mere collection of individuals. The people can do no more than subject themselves to a ruler and by their obedience make him powerful. But the ruler's authority comes, not from them, but from God, who, seeing that men need government, grants authority to the rulers set over them. This is not an argument for absolute monarchy, for it justifies all established governments, and therefore also England's limited monarchy. Maxwell's purpose was merely to deny the assumptions on which Parker and other Parliamentary writers rested their case. The Royalists neither claimed absolute power for the King nor denied the subject's right to disobey his commands when they are contrary to the Law of Nature or of God; they merely denied the subject's right to offer armed resistance to established authority, whatever its nature.

The constitution defended by these early and moderate Royalists was different both from the monarchy as it had been until 1641 and from what it was to be after 1688; it was the old monarchy shorn of the prerogatives that the Long Parliament had obliged Charles to abandon. It was like the system of government established at the Restoration, which proved unworkable because it gave the King too little power to govern free from Parliamentary interference and yet did not ensure that his ministers were truly responsible to Parliament. In this matter, the Parliamentary theorists were no wiser than the Royalists. They, too, did not understand that the balance of power set up by the reforms of the Long Parliament was inherently unstable. Though Pym demanded that the King's ministers should be nominees of the two Houses, he did so only because he distrusted the King and was afraid of what he might do. Pym did not, any more than Hyde or Falkland or any other of the moderate men who went over to Charles in 1641, understand that the reforms of that year made it impossible for the King to govern effectively except as a parliamentary monarch – except, that is, through ministers responsible to Parliament.

V. THEORIES THAT EMERGED AS A RESULT OF THE KING'S DEFEAT

Quite apart from the claims it made against the King and the theories produced to support those claims, Parliament, when actually at war, had to assume one power after another. It had to take on ultimate responsibility for all public activities, political and military, in the part of England it controlled, and when, after the King's defeat, it proved impossible to come to terms with him, it had to govern the whole country. It had also, if it could, to devise a religious settlement acceptable to the more powerful sections of the community. The Parliaments of James and Charles, even the Long Parliament when it first assembled, had not been Puritan or Presbyterian; most of their members had not understood or cared much about the matters at issue between the bishops and the Puritans. They had merely, in the course of their quarrel with the King, learnt to regard the High Church party and the bishops as obdurate supporters of the royal prerogative. Most of them had espoused some Puritan prejudices; and of course quite a few of them were Puritans. When the moderates went over to the King, the two Houses, and especially the Commons, became even more susceptible to Puritan influences than they had been before. And, later, when, rather than risk losing the war, Parliament was willing to call a Scottish army into England, it found it expedient to press more vigorously than ever for a Presbyterian church settlement. Parliament proved, in the end, as intolerant as the High Church party, and since the bishops were with the King, it rejected episcopacy. It wanted uniformity of doctrine and a severe discipline in the Church. Pym died in 1643, and the Long Parliament produced no other leader of his ability and proven loyalty to the cause.

For reasons that we need not consider, Parliament could neither make a settlement with the defeated Royalists nor placate the New Model Army it had called into being. If it had succeeded in coming to terms with the King and his advisers, it might have been able, at the cost of a few concessions, to disband the army and so disorganize the new radicalism that was emerging inside it. But as Parliament persecuted the Royalists and at the same time annoyed the army by its religious intolerance, and as the King (who had had no real asset except the prestige of monarchy) foolishly tried to play everyone off against everyone else, real political power effectively passed to Cromwell's army. The King, intriguing with the Scots, brought a Scottish army into England, which Cromwell promptly defeated; and when he returned south from his victory, he made up his mind to remove the King, and to deal brusquely with Parliament.

While there were not many Presbyterians in Cromwell's army, and most of his officers may even have been Anglican, none, of course supported the bishops. Many of the soldiers were Congregationalists, Baptists and other kinds of Independents. They would allow no state church either with bishops or without them. They were not for complete liberty of worship; they would not tolerate either Roman Catholicism or even Protestant Episcopacy, but otherwise they left the sects to their own opinions and religious practices. On the religious issue, all the soldiers, officers and men, were pretty much of one mind.

But in political matters it was not so. The officers, with Cromwell and Ireton at their head, having brought the King to the scaffold and frightened Parliament into insignificance, found themselves obliged to govern the country. They kept order admirably, but they could never establish exactly what sort of government they wanted. Naked military government they did not like; they wanted something parliamentary and legitimate, something more like what England had long been used to. Though effective power was theirs from the time they sent Colonel Pride to drive all the members to whom they objected out of Parliament, they kept that diminished and impotent assembly in existence until 1653. The officers were not quite certain how they wanted England governed; they felt their way and experimented, acquiring stable opinions only in the process of resisting the more radical demands of the soldiers under them. They were firmly resolved to defend private property against the poor, and therefore soon declared against democracy. They were determined not to allow Parliament to foist the Presbyterian church on the nation. They did, however, want all important interests represented in Parliament, and favoured a redistribution of sects. Their plan of government, the *Heads of Proposals*, proves that they wanted Parliament to be freely elected, to meet frequently and to control the executive and the army. They were not even in principle against monarchy, though circumstances had recently caused them to have a King put to death. By birth they were mostly gentlemen.

The rank and file were more democratic. Many of them belonged to the lower middle classes, being by origin artisans, yeoman farmers or small traders. They were not typical of those classes, as they formed only a minority within them, but they were well represented in the New Model Army and had the strongest influence on the political opinions of the ordinary soldiers. They dominated the regimental committees; they were avowed enemies of privilege and monopoly.

They were as much in favour of private property as the officers were, but quite unconvinced that democracy would endanger it. These Levellers, as they were called, led by John Lilburne and Richard Overton, were the first English radicals. Every man, they said, must have a voice in the government he lives under, or, as they put it, 'ought first by his own consent to put himself under that government'. For them, as for Locke, consent was individual and deliberate; they did not take it for granted, as almost all European political writers had hitherto done, that those who happen to have the vote are entitled to speak for the voteless. They did not particularly analyse the notion of consent, but they certainly used it a good deal less loosely than Locke was to do. By consent to government, they did at least mean actually taking part in choosing the persons with whom supreme authority rests.

The Levellers also came closer than any Englishmen before them to being liberals. They wanted to protect the individual against all government, whatever its kind; they wanted a written constitution to limit the authority even of the people's representatives, a constitution incorporating rights with which Parliament would not be allowed to interfere. Parliament, though supreme over the other branches of government, must not trespass too far on the individual, whose security and freedom it exists to preserve. It had long been held that the authority of governments is limited, as well as by custom, by the Law of Nature; but that law was unwritten and every philosopher had interpreted it as he liked. The Levellers were the first Englishmen to propose placing precise limits on what governments could legally do.

They could not, of course, get their own way. The Instrument of Government, England's only written constitution, was drafted by Ireton, adopted by the Council of Officers and then imposed on the nation. It provided for a parliament elected on a middle-class franchise, and for a Protector chosen and assisted by a Council of State. The first Protector, Cromwell himself, and the first Councillors, were named in the Instrument, but it was provided that future Councillors should be chosen by the Protector from among persons nominated by Parliament. Parliament was to meet at least once every three years and to sit for not less than five months. The Protector was given a suspensive veto that lasted only twenty days; he was granted a fixed annual revenue to meet ordinary expenses of government; and he was obliged to take all important decisions with the advice of the Council of State. Power was divided between a single person and a one-chamber assembly, with the Council of State keeping the balance between them. The first Protectorate Parliament, as soon as it met in September 1654, began to attack the Instrument of Government, demanding reforms that would make the Protector more dependent on itself. Cromwell dissolved Parliament a few months after it had met, and did not call another till the summer of 1656. This second Parliament, after a hundred members had been prevented from taking their seats in it, was more to his liking; it increased the Protector's powers and created a second chamber. To reward some of its members for their loyalty, Cromwell put them into the new Other House, only to find that that the persons elected to take their places in the lower one were less tractable. The second Protectorate Parliament was dissolved in February 1658. Oliver had proved himself as incapable as Charles of managing parliaments. All his attempts to give England a stable government without obviously setting aside the principles for which the Long Parliament had taken up arms failed miserably.

Cromwell was an efficient ruler, but he had to rule without Parliamentary assistance. In constitutional matters he had a certain respect for traditional forms but no really settled principles. He rejected – perhaps rightly, for it was hardly feasible in the England of his day – the democracy that the Levellers asked for; he wanted to work with Parliament, but every Parliament made demands he would not concede; he knew that his power rested on the army, and yet he wanted it to be constitutional. He thought the army too narrow a base for stable government. He objected to many things for often very sensible reasons, but he did not know quite what institutions would give him the kind of government he did want. Perhaps he did not even know quite what he wanted. He did not want government to be absolute, nor to depend on the army, nor to be controlled by a parliament. He wanted to be a respectable and constitutional ruler, guilty of none of the offences for which Charles Stuart had lost his throne and his life; and yet he also wanted always to get his own way. He and his officers, able, shrewd, patriotic and tolerant in matters of religion, though they were, had nothing that really deserved to be called a political philosophy. In the army, the Levellers alone had one. Yet the Levellers spoke for only a small minority of Englishmen. They would never have become important and articulate if the New Model Army had not been created; and even in that army, the officers were against them.

It was not in England, where the Levellers mostly belonged to the poorer classes, that their ideas took root, but in the English colonies in America. Many of the emigrants to those colonies belonged to the same classes as the Levellers, and had similar religious opinions; they carried over to New England religious and political ideas very like those that the Levellers brought to the fore in Cromwell's army. Civil war in England, moreover, encouraged political democracy and religious independence in the English colonies. There was greater toleration in some of those colonies than there would be in England for generations to come, and also a much wider franchise.

About the Diggers, I shall say little. The spread of socialist opinions in recent times has caused their memory to be revived and their importance to be exaggerated. They were not, like the Levellers, powerful in the army at a time when the army was the most powerful body in England; and their ideas were unheard of in the English colonies. They had almost no following, and are interesting chiefly as a curiosity from the past. They called themselves 'True Levellers', but soon broke away from the larger movement. Winstanley, whose *Law of Freedom* of 1652 expounds their views, declared that property, especially in land, is the root of evil; that land should be owned in common and its produce shared out among the people who cultivate it; that the law exists to protect the rich against the poor; and that the clergy use influence to make the people submissive to their masters. It is interesting to see these commonplaces of a later communism and anarchism already expounded in the seventeenth century. They were not, however, invented in that century, nor did Winstanley construct a new and comprehensive social theory upon them. Such ideas have, in almost all ages, come readily to the minds of the dispossessed and disinherited. The obscure roots of communism and anarchism lie buried in a past much older than the seventeenth century. The Diggers planted no new seed that came to flower later; they merely gave more pointed utterance to beliefs that have slumbered for ages in the minds of the poorer and more inarticulate classes, as the recurrence of these beliefs in times of popular unrest amply proves. They actually came much less to the fore in England in Winstanley's time than they had done among the Anabaptists in Germany.

VI. JAMES HARRINGTON AND *OCEANA*

1. *Introductory*

Harrington's *Oceana* is a work of a kind that is rare in English political literature. It is not a philosophical treatise, like Hobbes's *Leviathan* or Locke's *Second Treatise of Government*, or a plea for or against particular reforms. Nor is it a utopia, an ideal model, describing a society unlike any in the actual world men inhabit, which the author does not hope to see realized but which seems to him better than what exists, because more in keeping with what he takes to be permanent or rational or healthy in human nature. It is a scheme for the reconstruction of English government put forward at the only time in English history when a reconstruction of that kind seemed remotely possible. Harrington really did believe that his scheme might be adopted, at least in some of its essentials; and the belief, though perhaps mistaken, was not absurd. England's political situation was never more fluid nor her rulers more uncertain what to do next than when Harrington wrote his *Oceana*. Already, since the fall of the old monarchy, several schemes of government had been tried and even more had been discussed. The men who at that time had power and influence found themselves in circumstances unique in English history (though other countries have known them more often); they actually found themselves obliged to make up their minds how England should be governed. In the end, as we know, they allowed England to revert to something like the old ways, though the old ways greatly altered in spirit, if less in form. For Charles, after all, had lost the war, and it was no longer possible for a king of England to govern as the Tudors had done and the early Stuarts had tried to continue doing. The Civil War did make some great changes, and the restored monarchy was in certain ways a new kind of monarchy, with great possibilities of growth. It grew in time into one of the strongest, mildest and freest forms of government the world has known.

All this, of course, Harrington and his contemporaries could not see. To them, the Restoration seemed a return to the days before the war. It put an end to all new-fangled schemes, to the regret of some and to the relief of many. It also put an end to a period unlike any other that England has lived through, one of the boldest and most fertile periods in the history of European political thought. There never was a time again when England contributed so much to that thought; it was then that Hobbes's *Leviathan* and Harrington's *Oceana* were written, within a few years of one another. There were also, besides these great works, many others, books and pamphlets, less systematic and original, but often shrewd and sometimes brilliant. Absolute and limited monarchy, democracy, republicanism, religious toleration, religious uniformity, a written constitution, changes in the distribution of property: all these had their advocates, and advocates with wits sharpened by controversy. For freedom of political discussion and variety of political opinions, there are few periods in history to compare with the years from the start of the

Civil War to the Restoration. Much of the vigour and good sense of this discussion (for it is remarkable how much of it was sensible) were perhaps due to its not being utopian in spite of its boldness. The men who put forward these schemes and proposals were not day-dreamers; they had some hope of convincing an unusually receptive public. They had their illusions, no doubt. Much less was possible than they thought possible. Yet the times were unusually propitious to change and minds more than ordinarily open to persuasion.

Harrington was as ingenious and open-minded as any political writer of his day. He was a schemer, a maker of blueprints and a pamphleteer. He was also a student of history, and of social history as much as political. He did not go back to first principles in the manner of Hobbes; he cared nothing for conceptual analysis, for clear definitions and rigorous argument. He was interested in comparing systems of government, and in that respect was like Aristotle. He was also like Plato, or, rather, the Plato of the *Laws*, and not of the *Republic*, the Plato who liked to make comprehensive and detailed schemes for the reform of government. But among modern writers, perhaps the closest to him is Machiavelli, who shared his passion for history and his interest in political institutions, in the structure of government. Machiavelli and Harrington were both republicans; they both took it for granted that free or responsible government is the best, and were not concerned to justify it so much as to discover what makes it secure. They were both untheological and unscholastic; their political theories are purely secular. Machiavelli, who had little hope for Florence and even for Italy, was a pessimist. Harrington, living in what was politically the most vigorous and aspiring age in English history, was an optimist. The two men differed greatly in temperament, but Harrington recognized in Machiavelli a republicanism and love of freedom quite like his own.

Though Harrington's sympathies during the Civil War were with Parliament and not with the King, he was singularly free from strong political passions. He had known Charles I personally and had even been on friendly terms with him. *Oceana*, Harrington's great work, did not appear until 1656, when the Civil War was long since over.

Cromwell disliked the book, because he thought it too far-fetched and perhaps, also, because he found it too secular in tone. Harrington was condemned by many people for being 'atheistical' and 'irreligious', and for advocating what his critics called 'foreign' innovations. The Fifth Monarchists disliked *Oceana* as well; and so too did the people who respected the Long Parliament which Cromwell had forcibly dissolved. Yet Harrington had friends in high places –

not parties or groups so much as individuals attracted by his ideas and arguments. He believed that Cromwell was the great enemy of his schemes, and when Cromwell died, his hopes grew strong that he could win over enough powerful men to have a chance of seeing those schemes put into practice, at least in part. In the Parliament of 1659, which was convened not by Oliver but by his son Richard, there were at least fifty convinced republicans, of whom ten were disciples of Harrington.

Later on, when Fleetwood and other generals hostile to Richard Cromwell reassembled what remained of the Long Parliament, Harrington and his friends, who disliked that assembly and were also opposed to a restoration, printed a whole series of pamphlets in support of their views. The old Parliament was dissolved, convened for a second time, and then again dissolved before the meeting in April 1660 of the Convention Parliament, which brought Charles II back to the throne. Thus, for a period of several months, a fluid situation prevailed, and anything seemed possible in England. Men with recipes to cure their country's ills were more excited, hopeful and busy than ever, Harrington prominent among them. Already in the autumn of 1659, he had formed the Rota Club to discuss and publicize his ideas. Though it met to discuss, not day-to-day politics, but general principles of government, it was not an academic circle; its purpose was to attract and influence men of affairs, men active in government and politics. It was perhaps the first organized attempt in England by social and political theorists to make converts among the actual rulers of the country. In that respect the Rota Club deserves to be compared with the Political Economy Club of the Utilitarians or with the Fabian Society. The Rota Club ceased to meet at the end of March 1660, when it was clear that further meetings would be useless because the return of the Stuarts was imminent and not to be prevented.

After the Restoration, Harrington could no longer hope to influence the powerful. He was a discredited person, a republican known to have been opposed to the return of Charles II. He was even imprisoned for a time on suspicion of plotting to abolish the monarchy, but was never brought to trial and was soon set free. He was too mild and generous a man ever to have made bitter enemies, and he also had family connections to protect him from serious harm.

2. The Political Theory of Harrington

The scheme propounded in *Oceana* is not meant for any country at any time, but for a country socially like England was in his day, though the principles behind it are of broader application. Within that scheme, Harrington's political theory may perhaps be best illuminated in the light of two basic principles: first, that government cannot endure unless it is soundly constructed on the prevailing social order; and, second, that, given the social order of England in the middle of the seventeenth century, there is a form of government better adapted than any other which would establish uncorrupt and efficient rule. To see just what Harrington meant by these two principles is to grasp the essence of his political theory.

a. Government and the Social Order

Harrington claimed that 'As is the proportion or balance of dominion or property of land, such is the nature of the empire'.[1] Where one man owns all or most of the land, the government is likely to be a monarchy; where a limited number own it, but one of them owns much more than the others, the government is likely to be a mixed monarchy; where the people generally own all or most of the land, the government will probably be a democracy.

Harrington believed that there had occurred, in the previous one hundred and fifty years, a vast change in the ownership of land in England. Henry VII had broken up many of the great baronial estates, and Henry VIII had confiscated the monastic lands and had given them to new men. The number of substantial landowners had thus greatly increased, and this, he imagined, had led in the fullness of time to rebellion against the Stuarts and to the Commonwealth. The new landed proprietors wanted more than their lands; they wanted a share in the government. As the number of landowners grew larger, the balance of property was less and less suited to the old form of government. This disharmony made for political instability, which could be remedied either by changing the form of government or by restoring the old balance of property. Harrington thought it, on the whole, easier to make the first change than the second.

He knew that there were countries, like Holland, Genoa and Venice, where other forms of wealth were more important than land, and he admitted that in their case what mattered was less the distribution of land than of other things. If he mentioned only land in putting forward his general principle, it was no doubt because in most parts of Europe land was still very much the most important form of

---

[1] *The Commonwealth of Oceana*, Preliminaries, in the *Political Works of James Harrington*, ed. J. G. A. Pocock (Cambridge 1977), p. 163.

wealth. His principle would have been sounder theoretically if he had spoken of wealth generally and not only of land, but it can easily be amended and made more comprehensive in its scope without doing violence to his thought.

This principle of Harrington's has been very much praised as an original and fruitful hypothesis. Even though it needs considerable qualification to make it true, it certainly deserves praise, and as much praise as had been lavished on it. But, unfortunately, it has been almost as much misinterpreted as praised. Admirers of Marx have seized upon it, and have thought it wonderful in Harrington that he should have almost, though not quite, anticipated one of the profoundest discoveries of the nineteenth century. The people who praise Harrington in this way no doubt mean well by him. Though I yield nothing to them in admiration of his thought, I feel impelled to defend him from their praise. He was never on the brink of becoming an economic determinist; he never almost stumbled on that false brilliant which to so many has seemed a precious stone.

Harrington was interested only in the distribution of property and its political consequences; he had nothing to say about the production of wealth and economic change. But the heart of economic determinism is precisely the belief that how wealth is produced determines the social structure and the form of government, so that change in productive methods is the most important of all causes of social change. Nothing like this belief can be found in Harrington. He did not even say that changes in the distribution of property always precede great political changes. There is nothing in his theory that corresponds to the Marxian distinction between economic substructure and ideological superstructure. According to Harrington, Henry VII increased the royal power by cutting down the great feudal estates, and Henry VIII confiscated the monastic lands. Thus the rise of the class that destroyed the personal rule of the Stuarts was an effect of policies undertaken by the early Tudors to consolidate their power. Political actions had social consequences which in their turn had political effects. To no class of actions, to no social factor, is ascribed a decisive rôle in human affairs.

Harrington does, of course, stand out among the political writers of his time by observing political problems in a social context, and by turning his mind to a matter of capital importance: the connection between the distribution of property and the structure of government. Where there exists a large class of independent landowners, and where there also exists an instrument like the English parliament which they can use to further their ambitions, there is almost bound to be an attempt to oblige the ruler to govern in ways that suit that class and to coerce him if he proves recalcitrant. Men who are wealthy are attracted by power, and will try to get it if they can.

But Harrington's principle is too absolute, and needs to be qualified. There can easily be stable government even though the wealthy have no share of power. The Roman Republic gave way to the Empire, and monarchy took the place of aristocracy, not because an inordinately large share of land (or of other forms of wealth) passed into the hands of one family, but because it was found impossible to govern a state half the size of Europe by methods evolved to suit the needs of a small Italian republic. Property in land was, in Harrington's time, almost as widely distributed in France as in England. If France became an absolute monarchy and England a limited one, there must have been at work other causes than changes in the distribution of landed property. No doubt, the private estates of the Bourbons were much more extensive than those of the Stuarts, and the gentry and merchant classes were larger and more active in England than in France. These differences had important political consequences. But so, too, did the fact that France was larger and less united than England, that provincial autonomies were greater there than on the other side of the Channel, and above all that France lacked what England possessed: a national assembly sufficiently coherent and responsible to make an effective bid for power. Parliament was already, long before the social revolution described by Harrington, more efficient than the Estates-General; and so, when the time came, it could serve, as the Estates-General manifestly could not, as a national centre of class resistance to royal power. Harrington's law, that the form of government varies with the balance or distribution of property in land, put as baldly as he put it, is clearly not true. It needs to be qualified. But it is original and important; it shows that Harrington turned his mind to questions that other political writers of his day neglected.

He wanted to change the balance of property still further; he wanted to make it illegal for anyone to own land to the value of more than £2000 a year in England or Ireland, or £500 in Scotland. He put the annual value of all the land in England and Wales at about ten million pounds; so that, if his proposal were adopted, there could never be less than five thousand landowners, and in all probability there would be many more. Harrington also proposed the abolition of primogeniture, both because he thought it unjust in itself, and because he wanted to ensure that property was more widely diffused. He was against a powerful monarchy, a too narrow oligarchy, and a too complete democracy. He wanted England ruled by the gentry, by a fairly large class of middling landowners, but he also wanted that class to have the support of the people generally.

He believed that stable government could be achieved by two operations: by making laws to secure a certain balance of property, and by setting up a form of government appropriate to that balance. First, make up your mind what sort of country you want England to be, and then set about making England that sort of country. But do not forget that certain things go inevitably together: if you want a particular kind of government, you must see to it that the balance of property is conducive to it; and if you want a particular balance of property, you must see to it that the form of government corresponds with it. Harrington had no conception of an inevitable course of social or political development; he believed that men, by taking thought, could, within fairly broad limits, create the kind of society and government they wanted. But they could not create it on whatever terms they chose; they had to see to it that its institutions, political and non-political, were in keeping with one another.

b. The Constitution of Oceana

The special virtue of Harrington as a political theorist is that he knew what he wanted and devised a comprehensive and detailed scheme for getting it. He was not content, as Hobbes was, to give the same large, simple advice to all nations everywhere: Get yourselves an absolute sovereign and obey him unconditionally. He did not, as the Royalists and Parliamentarians had done, want to tilt the balance of the old system one way or the other without really troubling to enquire what the effects of this shift might be. He did not, as the Levellers did, confine himself to making claims for classes until then without a share of power. Alone among his contemporaries, he tried to explain what had been happening to England in the last four or five generations and to discover what kind of political system might now suit her. He tried to take account of realities, or what he took for such, and to prepare an adequate scheme. It is an intricate scheme, and yet every part of it is seen in relation to the whole. Everything is explained, everything forms an element of a well-thought-out plan put together to suit particular circumstances. If the plan is unrealistic, it is so only to the extent that Harrington mistook England's predicament, or devised institutions not suited to it or to one another, or expected results that were in fact unlikely. It is not unrealistic in the sense of utopian; it is not presented as universally the best scheme or as the one most in keeping with what is enduring in human nature.

Harrington believed that government would be stable and efficient in England if it were responsible to the whole independent part of the nation but recruited only from the propertied and educated classes. The educated and the well-to-do should initiate and propose but should not have the power to impose their will on the people generally. Government must enjoy the confidence of the whole nation and yet not be the mere creature of public opinion. It must also, if it is to retain this confidence, be efficient and pure.

To ensure that government is as it ought to be, Harrington relied chiefly on three devices: indirect elections, the renewal of elected bodies by parts, and a clear division within the legislature between the functions of debate and decision. Every man who is his own master should have the vote, he claimed. Only servants and dependants should not have it, for they will use it as their masters tell them to; so that to give them the vote is merely to give more votes to men with many dependants than to those with few. Harrington proposed to extend the franchise about as widely as the Levellers had wanted to extend it; every man of independent judgement should have it, and a man must be presumed to have independent judgement if he is economically his own master.

All the voters in a parish should elect one-fifth of their number to form an electoral college, comprised of delegates from all the parishes in their district. There should be fifty such districts, which Harrington called 'tribes'. The college of electors of each tribe should elect the tribe's representatives to Parliament. Elections, both to the electoral college and to Parliament, should be by clear majorities and secret voting. Parliament should have two Houses, a Senate of 300 members and a lower House, or 'Prerogative Tribe', of 1050 members. All Senators should be at least thirty years old, should have completed their military service, and should own property to the value of not less than £100 a year; and just under half the members of the lower House should own property of the same annual value. Thus the well-to-do and wealthy would be much more strongly represented in Parliament than men of humbler means, and yet could not be elected at all unless they enjoyed the confidence of all classes. To retain that confidence, they would have to look after the interests of everyone, but being themselves men of property, they would not curry favour with the poor by sacrificing the wealthy to them.

Of course, in the seventeenth century those who believed that there ought to be a parliament also supposed that it should speak for all classes. The peculiarity of the Levellers and of Harrington was not their belief that there ought to be a national parliament but their conviction that it would not be truly national unless all men who were not servants and dependants had the vote. Even in the eighteenth century most political writers took it for granted that Parliament spoke for the whole nation – that the House of Commons was the popular House. Men of nearly all descriptions had the vote in some constituency or other, and this fact, to these writers, seemed enough to make the House of Commons the people's representative. Harrington agreed with the Levellers that the lower House could not really speak for the whole nation unless *all* freemen had the vote. It was not enough for him that the poorer and more numerous classes should have some votes scattered among them here and there, as the peculiarities of the local franchise allowed; he wanted them all to vote provided they were independent enough not to vote to order. Yet his principle was not 'one man, one vote'; for he would have denied the vote to many men, that is, to all whom he put in the class of servants.

But Harrington was not entirely of one mind with the Levellers. He believed that the wealthy and educated are better able to govern than other classes, provided they govern responsibly. They must neither be left to the mercy of demagogues nor be allowed to get power by any and every means. It must be deliberately contrived both that they have power and that they use it responsibly. There must be indirect elections, and suitable provision made to ensure that most of the elected are men of property. Furthermore, one-third of the members of each House must retire each year, so that Parliament is perpetual and yet entirely re-elected within each period of three years. An assembly renewed by parts at short intervals is both more steadily and less violently affected by popular moods than it would be if it were elected entire at longer intervals. For one-third of its members an election is always imminent, but for two-thirds it is always more or less remote.

It was as obvious to Harrington, as it is to us, that the initiative, even in the legislative sphere, must belong to the executive. He did not expect members of Parliament to propose new laws; he left that function to the heads of the executive branch, whom he called the chief magistrates. They would introduce their bills in the first place to the Senate, where they would be fully debated and amendments proposed. If the Senate approved a bill, the magistrates could then refer it to the lower House, the Prerogative Tribe. There the bill would not be debated, but Senators chosen for the purpose by the Senate would explain the arguments for or against it. The duty of the lower House would be to listen to their explanations, and then to vote on the bill without debating it. The lower House would be a kind of jury, to pronounce for or against proposals put to it without discussing them.

Harrington believed that a popular House, though competent to decide an issue clearly presented to it, would lack the ability required to debate it effectively. But the Senate, he thought, would have this ability, and would use it for the common good if it was given the right to discuss and explain bills without the right of final decision. If Senators had to persuade only Senators, they might be tempted to sacrifice the common good to the interests of their own class; but if they have to persuade the popular House, they cannot hope to be listened to unless they take account of the popular interest. Harrington looked upon his Senate as a chamber of ability whose function is to enlighten public opinion, and his lower House as a kind of sample of the nation, an assembly of typical citizens, able to give effect to the people's will but not to educate or form it. In order to drive home his point, Harrington compared his two Houses with two girls sharing a cake: To ensure a fair division of the cake, let the brighter girl cut it in two and let the other choose which piece she will take. The brighter girl will easily see that, unless she divides the cake into two equal parts, she risks getting less than her share.

Harrington wanted the executive elected by the Senate. It should consist, he thought, of the chief magistrates and of four councils, one a council of state responsible for general policy, and the other three dealing respectively with trade, religion and war. He did not think that freedom would be more secure if the executive were kept separate from the legislature, either by being directly elected by the people or in some other way. On the contrary, he wanted the closest relations between them, and did not fear that the magistrates and councils would lack independence of judgement for being chosen by the Senate. He saw that a large initiative must inevitably belong to the persons who carry on the day-to-day business of government, no matter how they are chosen. He wanted, not the separation of the executive and legislative branches, but the separation from them of the judiciary; he favoured the election of judges.

I have discussed here only some of Harrington's proposals, among the many others that he made: he wanted compulsory and free education for all boys in schools inspected by the government; he wanted home rule for the Scots and Irish; he wanted a national militia with elected officers; he recommended a written constitution superior to ordinary law; he had a scheme for local government; he advocated religious toleration, without which he believed there could be no civil liberty. He would not give full rights to Catholics because they owed allegiance to a foreign prince, the Bishop of Rome, and thought it unwise to allow too many Jews into the country because they held aloof from other people; but otherwise he favoured complete toleration. I shall not, however, consider all his proposals; it is enough to take only some of them to show what kind of political theorist he was.

Most of the devices proposed by Harrington were not invented by him. The secret ballot was used in many kinds of elections in different parts of Europe; indirect election was common in the Italian republics; rotation of office (which he also wanted) was known in Greece and Rome and in several smaller modern states; the renewal by parts of elected bodies was a usual practice in guilds and merchant companies; and the Levellers had already asked for a written constitution. Even the device dearest of all to Harrington – that proposals of law should be discussed by one body and voted on without debate by another – had been tried in several city-states.

The originality of Harrington is not that he invented these devices but that he put them together to make a whole scheme of government which he could defend on rational grounds. Such devices had been adopted for all kinds of reasons peculiar to the communities which had adopted them; they had been decisions reached by compromise in one place and then imitated elsewhere on account of their convenience. They had not been defended in principle. Harrington was the first to recommend their use in the national government of a large state, and to find arguments for them based on general principles. True, the elaborate constitution of Oceana was not meant to do service for all states; it was adapted to the needs of a country socially like seventeenth-century England. Yet the arguments used for that constitution rest on principles of more general application. Harrington believed that wherever there are unequal classes, the system of government must take account of the inequality if it is to endure; that everywhere the initiative, even in the making of law, must belong to the executive rather than the legislature; that wherever there is an elected legislature, it ought to be divided into two parts, with one debating the issues which the other decides. Harrington was as much interested in general principles as in particular institutions, and always related the second to the first. He was a political theorist and a close student of the mechanics of government. This combination of gifts is much rarer than it ought to be. Plato and Aristotle had it, and so had Machiavelli, Montesquieu and the younger Mill; but several of the most famous political philosophers have been without it.

Admittedly the system of government that Harrington wanted for

England was very different from the system established soon after his death by the revolution of 1688. Harrington wanted a written constitution, a republic, an indirectly elected legislature, and an executive chosen by part of the legislature. What England had a generation or so after he died, however, was a still powerful monarch with the largest say in choosing his own ministers, a legislature representing only a small part of the nation, a lower House that debated and also voted on bills, and an upper House whose members were content to leave effective power to the lower House because they controlled so many of the elections to it. The English system of government changed profoundly in Harrington's lifetime and shortly after it, not to become what he would have wanted, but something very different. It may well be that what England was shortly to get was better adapted to her social system than what Harrington proposed to give her.

Yet even if we allow that it was, it would still be absurd to dismiss Harrington for an idle dreamer. The fact remains that he alone tried to devise a scheme of government adapted to his country's needs; that he alone was concerned to do more than make good the particular claims of this or that class or faction; that he alone understood that, because England had lived through a profound social revolution, she needed a system of government different from the old one. He did not, like Hobbes or Filmer, offer one overriding rule, saying 'Keep quiet once you have set up an absolute sovereign', or 'Obey in all things the ruler placed over you by God'. He alone among his contemporaries thought about his country's problems philosophically and historically and politically and socially; he alone was as much at home in the concrete as in the abstract.

We must remember that what England was to become within two or three generations of the Civil War was not what either the Royalists or the Parliamentarians had fought to make her. It was of course in large part an effect of their actions, but it was not what they had intended or even imagined. If to be realistic is to know what you want and how to get it, then Charles I and Pym and Cromwell were none of them more realistic than Harrington. On the contrary, they were less so; they never got what they wanted, any more than he did, and they had, as their actions and arguments prove, much less clear ideas than he had, both about how England was governed and about how she should be.

Harrington's scheme for the government of England reveals an understanding of politics unique in his generation. Most of his contemporaries wanted the executive and legislative branches kept separate from one another, but Harrington saw that the executive cannot govern effectively unless it enjoys the confidence of the legislature. He understood, as no one else did, that in a large and complex society the initiative, even in the sphere of legislation, must belong to the executive. He therefore stipulated that all bills should be introduced into Parliament by the magistrates – that they should be, as we now put it, government bills. The Royalists had fought to resist what they called the encroachments of Parliament on the King, and the Parliamentarians had fought to defend what they called their privileges. Pym and his friends, deeply distrustful of the King, had at one time claimed the right to approve his choice of ministers, but they had never claimed it as a matter of principle; they had never conceived of what would one day be termed 'parliamentary monarchy'. The King, though he defended his prerogative powers against Parliament, never denied Parliament's legislative supremacy. There were all kinds of matters in dispute between King and Parliament, and both sides had stubborn and passionate opinions about them. Yet it is, I think, fair to say that, though most of their disputes concerned the relations between the executive and legislature, neither Royalists nor Parliamentarians had anything that deserves to be called a theory or even a coherent set of opinions about what those relations should be. When the war was over, the army leaders and the various parliaments they quarrelled with were no nearer having one than the men who started the war. Harrington, however, did have such a theory, comprehensive and well-considered.

Though he saw the need for close relations between the executive and legislature as clearly as Hobbes did, he saw no need for absolute authority any more than for a rigid separation of powers. He wanted a balance of powers, a systematic interdependence guaranteed by a written constitution. His scheme made provision for a distribution of functions between different bodies, so regulated that none can work without the others and each is disposed to be co-operative. His object was to prevent any part of government gaining power at the expense of the others, and at the same time to avoid deadlock. His system is one of checks and balances, a mass or sum of power carefully distributed on rational principles. The ideal of constitutional government which it depicts is different from Montesquieu's but not, I think, less deeply considered.

★ ★ ★

It has been shown[1] that the early constitutions of the English colonies founded in America in the second half of the seventeenth century owe much to Harrington's principles. The colonies established in that period were of a new type; they did not grow up more or less haphazard, as the earlier colonies had done, starting as corporations and gradually acquiring new powers and privileges until they became virtually self-governing. They were, from the beginning, provided with elaborate written constitutions. The Crown granted to specific persons a charter to found a new colony, and these persons were known as the 'proprietors' of the colony. According to the terms of their charter, they had the right to decide how the colony should be governed and how land should be distributed within it. Carolina, New Jersey and Pennsylvania were colonies of this new type, and their original constitutions embodied several of Harrington's principles.

Yet it was soon discovered that many of his ideas would not work, especially his scheme for a popular House which voted bills but could not initiate or debate them. No legislators were found willing to put up with these restrictions. Others of his ideas, suitably modified, fared better, and found their way into several colonial constitutions besides the ones already mentioned. Later on, when the colonies won their independence and united to form a new kind of state, at least one of Harrington's devices was adopted in the federal Constitution. The American Senate is still a perpetual body, never entirely renewed, for only one-third of its members are elected every two years.

But I risk doing less than justice to Harrington if I insist too much on this or that device of government. Quite apart from details, there is a certain community of spirit between Oceana and the great republic founded one hundred and thirty years later. No doubt, it is only in part due to Harrington's direct influence on American political thought; it is due even more to Harrington's England (the England of Milton and Cromwell), republican, sectarian, less than usually respectful of tradition, much closer in thought and feeling to the English colonies across the Atlantic than was either the England of before 1642 or after 1660. The makers of the federal Constitution had perforce to do for their country in the 1780s what Harrington wanted to do for his in the 1650s; they had to devise a new system of government for it. There could be no question of a restoration. They saw the need, as he did, for a strong executive and a popular legislature, for a wide franchise and

[1] By R. H. F. Smith, in *Harrington and his Oceana* (Cambridge 1914).

for safeguards against democracy, for complete separation between Church and State, and for a carefully contrived balance of powers. They believed, as he did, that the new scheme of government, to be durable, must rest securely on a social order which they could do little to change, and of which, in any case, they mostly approved. They too looked abroad for what might be learnt from foreigners and yet never lost sight of their country's needs. Harrington was as thoroughly English as anyone could be; but if a monument were put up in his honour, it would be more in its place on Capitol Hill than in the Palace of Westminster.

CHAPTER 8
Locke

I. INTRODUCTORY

It has been disputed whether or not John Locke wrote the second *Treatise of Civil Government* to justify the revolution of 1688.[1] The political theorist, primarily interested in the content of the theories he examines rather than in what moved their authors to produce them, will not wish to take sides in this dispute. Whatever moved Locke to write his *Treatise*, there is no doubt that he approved of the revolution and also of the form of government and social order he found in England. That government, in Locke's day, was a mixture of monarchy and aristocracy, and there is no reason to suppose that Locke found fault with it. Wealth was very unequally distributed, and Locke appears to have been satisfied that it should be so. We may take it for granted that, at least in his opinion, the doctrines expounded in the *Treatise* were perfectly consistent with the established social order and form of government.

Yet Locke's *Treatise* is clearly not an apology for a particular form of government or society. It is much too abstract for that. No one who read the *Treatise* could learn from it how England was governed at the time it was written. No one could guess that the revolution of which its author approved was the work of a small and wealthy part of the nation which dominated a legislature consisting of an hereditary House of Lords and another House elected on a very narrow franchise. The argument of the *Treatise* is that government is not legitimate unless it

---

[1] See especially Peter Laslett's introduction to Locke's *Two Treatises of Government*, second edition (Cambridge 1967), and Richard Ashcraft's *Revolutionary Politics & Locke's 'Two Treatises of Government'* (Princeton 1986).

is carried on with the consent of the governed. But the *Treatise* says little indeed about how government should be organized in order to have the consent of the governed. Indeed, as we shall see, if consent can be given in the ways described by Locke, any form of government has the consent of its subjects provided they obey it.

The revolution of 1688 which Locke's second *Treatise* is supposed to justify did not set up a new system of government; it was merely the final victory, in a struggle which had lasted nearly a hundred years, between classes that had grown strong under the wing of the Tudor monarchy against the monarchy that came after it. One great issue was settled; the supremacy of Parliament was established once for all. The king must govern in broad conformity with Parliament's wishes. But how exactly was he to do so? What precise relations must exist between Crown and Parliament to enable the king to govern effectively and yet responsibly? This second issue, no less important than the first, was not settled by the revolution of 1688. That is not surprising. Civil wars and revolutions do not often decide how a country shall be governed; they often do little more than make it impossible to govern it in the old ways. The period of readjustment comes afterwards. Just as the English colonists in America, having won their independence, still had a long way to go before achieving effective self-government, so the classes which asserted Parliament's supremacy by driving James II into exile needed at least a generation to discover how to reconcile royal government with parliamentary supremacy. The complicated system of Crown and aristocratic patronage which enabled eighteenth-century governments to find and maintain parliamentary majorities was not well established until Walpole's time. What a later age was to call parliamentary monarchy, with the king's ministers unable to govern unless they enjoyed the confidence of Parliament, was unknown to Locke just as it was to the parties to the constitutional struggle culminating in the revolution of 1688. It is much less Locke than Montesquieu or Hume or Burke who deserves to be called a champion of that type of government. Chapter 6 of Book XI of *The Spirit of the Laws* is a powerful argument for the English form of monarchy, an argument of a kind that Locke never produced. Locke's *Treatise* is not concerned to justify any form of government; it is concerned rather to assert the right of the people to resist their rulers when they are misruled by them.

But having said this, I immediately feel the need to qualify what I have said. Though Locke allows that any government carrying out its trust is governing with the consent of its subjects, he does say that it is best for the executive and legislative powers to be in separate hands, and that a government cannot rightfully tax its subjects except with their consent given through their representatives. Where he expresses a preference for any particular institution or device, it is almost always clear that he has been strongly influenced by established practice in his own country. Moreover, he puts forward his highly abstract argument in such a way as to avoid coming to conclusions which could be used to condemn the English system of government and social order of his day.

Locke was not a believer in equality, either political or social. Yet the modern reader can scarcely fail to notice that some of the assumptions made in the *Treatise* were also made by Tom Paine at the end of the next century, and were used by him to justify democracy; while others were made by the early socialists, who used them to condemn the existing distribution of property. Paine agreed with Locke that, since man is by nature free, no man can have authority over another except with his consent, and then went on to argue that therefore, if there must be government, it ought to be democratic. Several of the early English socialists agreed with Locke that, since every man owns his own labour, he is entitled to whatever he produces with his labour, and then went on to argue that the existing system of property, which deprives labourers of a great part of what they produce, is unjust. Locke did not come to these conclusions. I have said that he avoided them. I do not suggest that he did so deliberately. Almost nobody in Locke's time believed in equality, political or social, as Paine or the early socialists understood it. I suggest only that Locke's preference for the established order in England had a strong, though negative and unconscious, influence on the way he developed his argument. Though the *Treatise* is not a defence of Whig aristocracy, it would not be what it is if its author had not approved of that dispensation. It may be that many of the ambiguities and false reasonings which spoil the second *Treatise* arise from Locke's unconscious need to avoid unwelcome conclusions.

They spoil the *Treatise* for us, of course, and not for Locke's contemporaries; we are accustomed to seeing conclusions drawn from Locke's premises different from those which he drew, and which seem to us to follow more logically from them. When we come across anyone saying that he believes in government by consent, we expect him to prefer democracy to other forms of government. Locke's contemporaries, having no such expectations, were not struck, as we are, by the looseness of the terms he uses and his passing, without himself noticing it, from one sense of a word to another. All through the *Treatise*, Locke, though he uses the word *consent* in several senses, seems to be unaware that he does so; he uses it as if he believed that he were using it always in the same sense. He begins by using it in the sense of voluntary agreement, and then, later, creates the impression that he is consistently using it in this one sense, though in fact he is not; he unconsciously creates this impression by first insisting that it is only consent, in the sense of voluntary agreement, which makes authority legitimate and then going on to speak of other forms of consent, which he does not distinguish from voluntary agreement, as if they too had the same effect. If our sympathies are with the author, and his methods of argument are traditional and are widely accepted as appropriate to his purpose, we are not on our guard and we follow uncritically where he leads. We are first told that only voluntary agreement makes political authority legitimate, and then afterwards that other actions, also called acts of consent, have this same effect, and so we are disposed to believe that they too are tantamount to voluntary agreement. This was the condition of Locke's contemporaries who found his argument logically sound and were strongly attracted to his conclusions. They had not seen Paine reach quite different conclusions from the same premises, and they had not been taught by Hume and the more conservative Utilitarians that Locke's conclusions could be derived from other premises, less apt to be misused by radicals.

Locke uses a form of argument fashionable in his day. To explain the use of government and also its legitimacy, he first imagines men without government and then enquires what their motives must have been for setting it up. But, because he uses such traditional concepts as natural law and natural right, and also the myth of a social contract, he is not content to say that rulers are entitled to obedience so long as they carry out the essential functions of government, so long as they do what men in an imaginary state of nature may be supposed to have required of their rulers when they first agreed to have any. He feels obliged to say more than this, to say that they are entitled to obedience only if their subjects have actually consented to obey, and so is committed to showing that they have consented, that they have voluntarily agreed, even when it looks as if they have not. Hence the difficulties he gets into, which he slides out of by what to us appear to be mere verbal tricks, though both he and his contemporaries took them for good arguments.

Yet his *Treatise*, despite the inconsistencies and confusions which strike us so forcibly, was very well-suited to the public at whom it was aimed. It was well-suited to them both because it reached conclusions they liked and because it used forms of argument with which they were familiar and which seemed appropriate to them. Locke's *Treatise* was popular because it suited the social aspirations and also the intellectual prejudices of classes growing in importance, classes living on rents and profits and employing wage-labourers. It is a theory made up of old ingredients presented in a more secular and modern, and therefore attractive, form. In the Middle Ages it had usually been held that the authority of princes and magistrates comes ultimately from God and secondarily from the people, and it had also been argued that what is customary and traditional has the people's consent. But the Huguenots and Jesuits had wanted to justify resistance to rulers whose authority clearly rested on custom and tradition, and had used the myth of a social contract to achieve their purpose. By so doing they had given to the notion of popular consent, the consent deemed necessary to make temporal authority legitimate, a rather different content from what it had had in the Middle Ages; they spoke of it as if it were more than mere acquiescence, as if it were something closer to voluntary and deliberate agreement. Or, to speak more accurately, though they continued, when it suited them, to use the term *popular consent* in a mediaeval sense, they also used it in another sense, which they did not clearly distinguish from the older one. They set an example that Locke followed.

The idea that true consent is personal and deliberate (though not necessarily express) was common among seventeenth-century political writers. We find it in Hobbes and Pufendorf. It could be argued that Hobbes's initial assumptions make the social compact redundant; but the fact remains that he thought of it as a covenant of every man with every man, as a voluntary agreement between equals. It is not, like the consent of the mediaeval philosophers, something revealed in the mere prevalence of custom. Pufendorf, born in the same year as Locke, went further than Locke did in using the notions of consent and contract. He tried to explain all human authority as an effect of contract. Even the slave consents to the authority of his master; for either he is a poor man who, in return for subsistence, engages his services in perpetuity, or he is a captive taken in war whose life is forfeit and who buys the right to live at the price of his freedom. Paternal authority also rests on contract, though the contract here is presumed rather than actual. The child needs, in its own interest, to be looked after by its father, and if it were old enough to know this, would agree to be subject to paternal authority. If the notions of contract and consent are pushed as far as Pufendorf (and others) pushed them, we are forced to this conclusion: that anyone capable of knowing that something is his interest or, when he looks

335

back on the past, of recognizing that it was his interest, may be taken to be consenting to what is done in his interest, even where there is no question of his exercising a choice. Locke never went as far as this; he made a more modest use of the notion of consent than some of his contemporaries.

Locke's *Second Treatise of Government* is a restatement of doctrines current for centuries or else put forward since the Reformation in the interest of minorities liable to persecution. It is simple, attractive, untheological and persuasive. It is the sort of book that strengthens people in opinions they already hold or are beginning to hold; it persuades them of the truth of what they are already inclined to believe. It is not, at a first glance, a puzzling or difficult or disquieting book. The author carries his readers along with him, easily and comfortably. That is, of course, provided they wish to be carried. If they insist on probing his meaning, if they refuse to take what he says at its face value, then difficulties arise inevitably; but it is easy enough, at his own level of discussion, to understand and to be persuaded by Locke.

He demands from the acquiescent reader no great effort. This is not an effect of lucidity. Hume was more lucid than Locke, and yet a greater effort is needed to follow his meaning. An exact and consistent writer requires the close attention of his readers; and close attention is never easy. With Locke, the case is rather the opposite. Too often, the more carefully we attend to his arguments, the less intelligible they appear. I speak of him, of course, only as a political writer; it is not my present business to do more.

Locke's political theory has been called superficial. In a sense it is so. He was by no means a strict reasoner, and the frequent weakness of his arguments is not compensated for, as it is with Montesquieu, Rousseau and Burke, by novelty of method, largeness of design or unusual penetration. He confined himself to ordinary problems and reached by easy methods conclusions that many people found attractive. It was his competence and persuasiveness, rather than his opinions, that were out of the ordinary.

Locke was interested primarily in the problem of political obligation. We can learn almost nothing from him about the nature of power, of the State, of law or of government. This is not just an effect of his non-empirical method. Hobbes, whose method was as little empirical as Locke's, does teach us to think in new ways about law and the State. His ideas about them may now seem inadequate, but we still recognize their importance. By defining moral and political terms in his own peculiar and vigorous way, Hobbes obliged his successors to think again about the things those terms were used to describe and helped them to acquire a vocabulary better suited to describe them. His strictly deductive method enabled him to make a contribution of the greatest importance to political and even social theory – though, of course, a contribution of a different kind from those made by men like Hume or Montesquieu, who used different methods.

Locke made no such major contribution. Our understanding of political and social concepts or institutions is not appreciably greater for anything he wrote which is not also to be found elsewhere. He was not much interested in the facts, and he made no new and important assumptions. That does not mean, of course, that there is little to learn from a close study of his political theory. There is a great deal. But that is primarily because it is a good example of a certain type of theory. In examining Locke's theory, we are examining ways of thought common to many philosophers in his day. Locke's abstract and moralizing political philosophy, though neither markedly original nor carefully argued, was so convincing, so much in keeping with feelings and hopes common among the educated classes in Western Europe (and later in North America), that it was for generations widely accepted as substantially true. Locke, more than any other writer on politics, has been the representative, the most acceptable, accomplished and respectable, interpreter of the liberal philosophy of the West. Old ideas, inherited through the Christian Fathers from the Stoics, about natural law and the essential equality of men, together with other ideas, derived from more purely mediaeval sources, about the limited authority of government and the need for popular consent, receive from him the form which made them look convincing to a secular Europe destined to found new nations in other continents and to dominate the world intellectually. Locke used these ideas to justify responsible government and popular resistance to tyranny. That was a use they could be put to more easily in England than elsewhere; for in England, alone among the great European nations, there existed a representative assembly strong enough to produce a national – and not a feudal, ecclesiastical or sectarian – opposition to monarchy. In England, more than anywhere else, it was possible to limit royal power without threatening national unity.

II. A SUMMARY OF LOCKE'S POLITICAL THEORY

In the state of nature all men are free to dispose of themselves and their possessions as they think fit, and their only obligation is to respect

337

the same freedom in others. They are rational creatures and can see that when they deal with other creatures like themselves they ought to treat them as equals. It is in this sense that men, even in the state of nature, are bound by law; they are bound by the law of nature, by rules of conduct which reason teaches them they ought to observe in their dealings with one another.

This right of every man in the state of nature to dispose of himself and his possessions as he thinks fit, Locke calls property. Thus a man's property, in this large sense, is co-extensive with his rights. Every man, says Locke, has a property in his own person – by which he means that he has a natural right, limited only by God's purposes and by the obligation to respect the same right in others, to do as he pleases. He may not destroy himself, for he is God's creature and his property in himself is not independent of God's will; and he is not free to invade the freedom of others. But otherwise there are, in the state of nature, no limits to his freedom or his property. And property, in this larger sense, is the same as freedom.

Locke also uses the word property in the ordinary sense, to mean the right to the exclusive use of external objects. Property in this narrower sense he derives from property in the larger sense. Natural man has the right to do anything he pleases except to destroy himself or to invade the right of others; he therefore has the right to set aside for his own use whatever he has a mind to, provided, of course, that someone else has not already taken it.

The state of nature is not a state of war, for it has, as we have seen, a law of nature to govern it. But law, if there is no one to enforce it, is in vain. Therefore, says Locke, 'the execution of the law of nature is in that state put into every man's hands, whereby everyone has a right to punish the transgressors of that law to such a degree as may hinder its violation'.[1] This is a right of punishment and not merely a right of self-defence. If it were merely a right of self-defence, no one in the state of nature could rightly use force except against persons invading his own rights. But what Locke says is that everyone in the state of nature has a right to punish anyone who offends against the law of nature, whether he is himself the victim of that offence or not. It is only because all men have this right in the beginning that they can afterwards transfer it to magistrates when civil society is established.

Notice how strong a case Locke makes for freedom at the beginning of his treatise. Property in the larger sense, which makes it equivalent

---

[1] *Second Treatise of Government*, ch. II, § 7.

to freedom, is prior to government; it is man's right, under God, to dispose of himself and of what he sets aside for his own use in whatever ways seem best to him. This right is limited only by the obligation to respect the same right in others, and it cannot be further limited except with the consent of its possessors. The law of nature allows interference only with aggressors; it does not allow the generality of men to require more of any man than that he should respect that law, which means only that he should respect in others the freedom he claims for himself. They cannot legislate for him. The only law to which all men are subject, whether they like it or not, is not a law made by men; it is not even the undeliberate product of their living in society with one another. It is not custom or convention but the law of reason, which defines the rights and duties that constitute and sustain freedom. The law of nature is therefore the law of freedom. It is a law that men do not make but only discover. The maker of law requires of others that they should submit to his will, and no man can rightly require this of another man without his consent. In the state of nature, the right of command belongs only to God, who commands only that men deal justly with one another – or, in other words, that they obey the law of nature, which is obligatory independent of God's will.

For Locke, the supreme question in politics is, What makes government legitimate? Nothing, he thinks, can make it so except the consent of the governed; and that consent, to be genuine, must be personal, deliberate and free. 'All men', says Locke, 'are naturally in that state [of nature], and remain so till, by their own consents, they make themselves members of some politic society'.[1] Notice the words 'by their own consents'. Locke would not have put 'consent' into the plural if he had not meant us to understand that every man must consent for himself alone, because only his own act can bind him.

This was Locke's initial position. In later chapters of his work, as, one after another, he came upon the difficulties it led to, he went a long way in modifying it – a much longer way, indeed, than he ever knew. But in the beginning he was bold; he pushed freedom almost to the farthest limit. No grown man owes a duty of obedience to any other man except by his own consent, and that consent must be free. The authority of government arises, not from men's needs, but from their freely given consents. No doubt, men establish government in the first place because they feel a need for it, but it is the consent, and not the need, which makes government legitimate.

[1] Ibid., ch. II, § 15.

To drive his point home, Locke distinguishes between two kinds of authority. He admits that one kind, limited in extent and duration, rests on need alone and not on consent, but he insists that it is not political. Children cannot look after themselves and must therefore be ruled by their parents. They owe a duty of obedience to their parents while they are cherished, fed and educated by them, but this duty ceases as soon as they can fend for themselves. Paternal authority is different from political, arising from other causes and serving other ends. Men, of course, need government just as children need parental care, though the need is less pressing; but it does not follow that, because they need government, they cannot take care of themselves. On the contrary, they take care of themselves by establishing government; they are the only judges of their needs and of what they must do to meet them.

Locke is quite ready to admit that political rule may have arisen from paternal power. 'Thus', he says, 'it was easy and almost natural for children by a tacit and scarce avoidable consent, to make way for the father's authority and government. They had been accustomed in their childhood to follow his direction . . . and when they were men, who [was] fitter to rule them?'[1] Nevertheless, though the first magistrate may have been a father, his political authority differed essentially from his paternal power. For true political authority rests only on consent.

Men put themselves under government to preserve their property – that is, their lives, liberties and estates. In the state of nature they had the law of nature to guide them. But they must, from time to time, have differed about the law or about its application to particular cases. They must therefore have felt a need for 'an established, settled, known law, received and allowed by common consent to be the standard of right and wrong'; and also for 'a known and indifferent judge, with authority to determine all differences according to the established law'; and lastly for a 'power to back and support the sentence when right, and to give it due execution'.[2] By putting themselves under government, men do not give up *all* their rights, but only those which must be surrendered for the common good, which is the preservation of freedom or property in the larger sense. In particular, they give up their right to punish.

No government has absolute authority, but only as much as it needs for the common good. 'Thus the law of nature', says Locke, 'stands

[1] Ibid., ch. VI, § 75.
[2] Ibid., ch. IX, §§ 124–6.

as an eternal rule to all men, legislators as well as others'.[1] It is for the people to decide whether or not the government is exercising power properly 'to the public good of the society'.[2] The legislative power, which for Locke is supreme in every civil society, is 'only a fiduciary power to act for certain ends',[3] so that the people always retain the right to remove or alter the legislature should they find it untrue to the trust reposed in it. How, exactly, are they to exercise this right? Apparently, by revolution; for against the abuse of trust by their rulers 'the people have no other remedy . . . but to appeal to Heaven'[4] – that is to say, to force.

Though the right of revolution is the ultimate sanction against abuse of power, it is possible to take precautions to make such abuse less likely. The legislative and executive powers ought to be placed in separate hands, for 'it may be too great a temptation to human frailty, apt to grasp at power, for the same persons who have the power of making laws to have also in their hands the power to execute them'.[5] But, though Locke thinks it desirable for these two powers to be separate, he does not insist that they must be so, if government is to be by consent of the governed. About the judicial power, which presumably he includes in the executive, he says nothing. The legislative power is unalterable in the hands in which the people have once placed it, for no one not authorized to do so by the people should have the power to make law.

We have seen that Locke, in the early chapters of the *Second Treatise*, conceived of consent as something free, deliberate and personal. This stronger sense of it survives into the eighth chapter, where we find him saying, 'Whatever engagements or promises any one made for himself, he is under the obligation of them, but cannot by any compact whatsoever bind his children or posterity'.[6] Then, suddenly, after this clear and bold statement, we find an abrupt transition to a much weaker sense of consent; we find Locke arguing that a man, when he inherits his father's property, under the same terms as were enjoyed by him, gives consent, by that act alone, to the government owed obedience by his father. 'And thus', he continues, 'the consent of free men, born under government . . . being given separately in their turns, as each comes to be of age, and not in a multitude together,

[1] Ibid., ch. XI, § 135.
[2] Ibid.
[3] Ibid., ch. XIII, § 149.
[4] Ibid., ch. XIV, § 168.
[5] Ibid., ch. XII, § 143.
[6] Ibid., ch. VIII, § 116.

people take no notice of it, and thinking it not done at all, or not necessary, conclude they are naturally subjects as they are men'.[1] It is enough, for the moment, to notice that this argument involves an abrupt retreat from the bold position that Locke first took up; its implications for his general theory of government I shall consider in a moment.

Locke's account of property, in the narrower and more usual sense of external possessions, is almost as important a part of his political theory as his notion of consent. God, he says, gave the world to all men in common to make use of to the best advantage to preserve life and liberty. But what God provides is not often, in its natural form, immediately useful to men; it has to be made useful by their labour. Since man has an original property in his own person, his labour belongs to himself. Therefore, whatever he mixes his labour with, he takes out of the common store and makes his own, so that no one but himself has the right to use it, except with his permission. 'Whatsoever, then, he removes out of the state that Nature hath provided and left it in, he hath mixed his labour with, and joined to it something that is his own, and thereby makes it his property.'[2]

The law of nature, which gives man the right to acquire property by mixing his labour with what God provides for all men's use, also sets limits to what he can acquire. 'As much as anyone can make use of to any advantage of life before it spoils, so much he may by his labour fix a property in.'[3] If he takes more, he 'invades his neighbour's share' – that is to say, he takes what he cannot use, and so prevents someone else taking it who could use it. Included in the notion of spoiling is allowing anything to go to waste; for Locke says that 'as much land as a man tills, plants, improves, cultivates, and can use the product of, so much is his property'.[4] Notice that Locke says that a man can, by his labour, take as much from the common store as he can use 'to any advantage of life'. This would seem to imply that every man is the sole judge of what he can use to advantage. He may not take more than he can use, for God has given the world to all men in common for their use; but so long as he uses it, he is not accountable to other men for the use he makes of it. This is, I think, implied by Locke's answer to the question: how can we know that anyone has taken more than he can use; that he has, to use Locke's own words, 'invaded his neighbour's share'? The only answer given

---

[1] Ibid., ch. VIII, § 117.
[2] Ibid., ch. V, § 27.
[3] Ibid., ch. V, § 31.
[4] Ibid., ch. V, § 32.

is that he has allowed it to spoil or, if it is land, has allowed it to go to waste. Provided you do not allow what you have mixed your labour with to spoil, and provided you go on mixing labour with it, if such mixing is needed to prevent spoiling or waste (e.g. provided you keep cultivable land in cultivation), you are presumably using your property to some advantage. Since your appropriation of the land thus makes it more productive, and does not deprive others of 'enough, and as good'[1] land for themselves, you therefore retain your right to it against all comers.

When what you make your own is perishable, you can usefully take only a small amount; but when it is not perishable and does not require regular cultivation to prevent its going to waste, you can accumulate as much as you like. Locke tells us that men invented money for their mutual convenience, and thereby created something that could be accumulated in any amount without spoiling or going to waste. Money was adopted by a general tacit consent, for its usefulness was soon apparent to everyone. Locke has not a word to say against the vast accumulations of wealth and the inequalities made possible by the invention of money.

III. LOCKE'S CONCEPTION OF SOCIETY AND OF CONSENT

I have deliberately summarized Locke's theory in a way that brings out sharply the two most important parts of it: the doctrine that all legitimate political authority rests on consent, and the account of how property, in the sense of the right to external possessions, arises. These two parts of his theory are closely connected; for Locke, though he thinks it the duty of rulers to protect their subjects' natural rights – their property in the wider sense – also supposes that political authority was established by consent largely for the preservation of property in the narrower sense, and believes that valid consent can often be inferred when property is inherited. The son who inherits his father's estate thereby consents to the government recognized by his father.

Locke, unlike Hobbes, supposes that property, the exclusive right to external possessions, can exist and valid contracts be made even where there is no government to protect or enforce them. This has rightly been taken for an attack on Hobbes, who held that covenants

[1] Ibid., ch. V, § 33.

involving mutual confidence are unreasonable until a power strong enough to enforce them is set up. But it is, I think, more than an attack on Hobbes; it is also a denial that men come to have rights and obligations only as social creatures, as creatures formed and disciplined by society.

It has often been said that Locke, by allowing that there can be genuine rights and obligations between men even in the absence of government, shows that he has a more adequate notion than Hobbes of what society is. Unlike Hobbes, he does not suppose that all society is political. His state of nature is a kind of society. That, indeed, is why his account of the establishment of legitimate government by contract is the more plausible of the two. This is the claim often made for Locke.

The claim, to my mind, is misleading. No doubt, Locke's account of how legitimate government arises from contract is more plausible than Hobbes's. But it does not follow that he has a more adequate conception of society. Admittedly, if human nature and man's condition without government were as Hobbes described them, no agreement could of itself make government legitimate; and admittedly, too, if that nature and that condition were as Locke described them, it does make sense to use the notion of contract to show what makes government legitimate. But to say this is not to admit that Locke had a more adequate conception of society than Hobbes had.

To have an adequate idea of society without government, it is not enough merely to ascribe rights which entail duties to men in the state of nature. Society, even without government, is more than just a number of people who, quite independently of the influence of society on them, come to see themselves as having rights and duties – who owe their morality only to the light of reason in them. Society is essentially a moral order, and men are moral only because they have been disciplined in society. They are made moral in the process of adapting themselves to society, and this always involves some compulsion. But Locke tells us that they are moral merely as men and not as members of society. He does not trouble to enquire how their living together affects them psychologically and morally. Man, as a moral being, as a bearer of duties and rights, is not, for Locke, essentially a creature of society. Locke has, no more than Hobbes, a conception of a social structure, a settled environment, which, even in the absence of government, can form men's minds. Of social institutions prior to government he says not a word. Property, in his account of it, is not really a social institution; it does not exist in virtue of rules and conventions that arise only in society. It is a natural right. Locke's men in the state of nature, no less than Hobbes's, are as nature and not as society makes them. They are rational creatures who are liable to get in each other's way and who set up government to avoid the inconveniences of the state of nature. They may not be by nature enemies, as Hobbes's natural men are, but this is by no means enough to make social beings of them. For Locke, as for Hobbes, natural man is a creature loose from all social discipline; he is autonomous and self-contained, and belongs to no social order, no community. There is no sense at all in Locke that it is the pressure of society on man, his being brought up to conform with established ways, which makes him sociable and moral.

It could, I think, be argued that it was precisely because Hobbes came rather nearer than Locke to having an adequate conception of society that he got himself into greater difficulties. It is sometimes more disturbing to get a glimpse of the truth than to be altogether blind to it. As I pointed out when I discussed his political theory, Hobbes believed that man is not by nature sociable; and by sociable he meant something more than 'inclined to enjoy other men's company'; he meant 'fit for society'. He spoke of man's being made fit for society by education. He understood that it needs social discipline of some kind to teach men to be sociable and law-abiding. Unfortunately, he was too ready to assume either that all effective discipline is political, or perhaps that no other kind of discipline can be effective except where there is government. He also had too narrow and mean a conception of what is involved in being social and law-abiding. But, for all that, he came closer than Locke to understanding that society is a form of discipline, and that a long process of education or adjustment is needed to make anyone sociable.

It was perhaps because he did come closer to this understanding that he was less inclined than Locke to attribute to natural man some of the qualities which are only acquired in society. For instance, he denied what Locke afterwards asserted, that 'keeping of faith belongs to men as men, and not as members of society'.[1] Since Hobbes took it for granted that all society involves government, he had perforce to conclude that it is only under government that men can rely on one another's doing what they agree to do. At the same time, to explain the legitimacy of government, he chose to use the fiction of a social contract. Thus he put himself in a quandary that Locke avoided; he tried to show how the right of the sovereign to obedience derives from an agreement made between persons having no obligation to

[1] Ibid., ch. II, § 14.

obey unless the sovereign is strong enough to enforce obedience.

Locke, of course, had a more usual and more plausible conception of rights and duties than Hobbes had. His rights entail duties, even in the state of nature. His laws of nature impose genuine obligations, not only to God, but also to men; whereas Hobbes's natural right is only absence of obligation, and his laws of nature are the commands of a God who scarcely requires obedience until there is a human power strong enough to enforce it. Locke was more plausible in this respect because he accepted more traditional and perhaps less sophisticated ideas about morality. He believed that men are moral because they are by nature rational, and can therefore discover, merely by reflecting on what is involved in being human, how they ought to behave. Now Hobbes, albeit confusedly, was inclined to deny that men are moral by nature, and therefore felt the need to look more closely at what Locke took for granted. Unfortunately, he did not look closely enough, and instead of explaining morality, explained it away. Yet Locke's more adequate (and also more orthodox) conception of morality does not reveal a better understanding either of what social life involves or of human nature. If Hobbes was wrong in treating morality as obedience to positive law, human or divine, Locke was no less wrong when he said that men are moral merely as men and not as members of society.

Locke, like Suárez, Grotius and Pufendorf, begins by treating consent as something personal and deliberate. It is here that he and they differ from the general run of mediaeval political philosophers, who had justified the supremacy of custom on the ground that it is generally accepted and therefore expresses the permanent will of the community. Custom, according to their view, rests on natural law but, unlike that law, is not universal; it contains the natural law within it but adapted to the circumstances of particular peoples. Men do not decide what custom is; they do not consciously accept it. They scarcely ever call it in question; they merely do what is expected of them, and have a sense that they are acting rightly when they do so. Consent, so conceived, is not deliberate and voluntary. But for the seventeenth-century philosophers of natural law, Locke among them, it is of the essence of consent that it is an act of choice, whereby the chooser lays an obligation on himself. No doubt, this conception of it gets them into all kinds of difficulties, and they resort to all kinds of shifts to get out of the difficulties. They repeatedly go back on their own assumptions, though without themselves noticing that they do so. They speak of 'virtual' or 'tacit' or 'presumed' consent, without ever admitting that consent so qualified is no longer an act of choice.

Some of them, in spite of their belief in natural freedom and the necessity of consent, are apologists of absolute government. Yet the notion of consent they begin with is clear enough, whatever may become of it afterwards as they strive to accommodate their doctrine that all legitimate human authority rests on consent to the actual facts. Consent, for them, is always the act of a person who knows, or may be presumed to know, what he is committing himself to by that act. The mediaeval idea was that the authority of custom rests on its being generally accepted, because this general acceptance shows that custom is adapted to men's needs and conforms to their sense of right. Custom is not arbitrary; it is not imposed by some men on others, and yet its authority does not rest on its being separately accepted by each person bound by it. Whether a man likes it or not, he must in practice accept it, not because he has agreed to do so, but because it is generally accepted – because it is the 'permanent will' of the community he belongs to. Locke's notion of consent, as he expounds it in the early chapters of his work, goes clean contrary to this mediaeval position.

According to Locke, the only natural obligation of an adult man to other men, the only obligation he is under whether he likes it or not, is not to injure them – or, in other words, to respect in them the rights he claims for himself. Every other obligation he must take upon himself voluntarily. He need not marry, but if he does he must support his wife. He need not have children, but if he does he must protect and educate them. He need not enter into civil society, but if he does he must keep his part of the bargain. Becoming a member of society is, indeed, conceived of by Locke as something very much akin to making a bargain.

Locke took this extreme position because it seemed to him to follow from what he said about man's natural freedom. If man has natural rights which are prior to government and has no obligation in the state of nature except to respect the same rights in others (that is to say, to obey the laws of nature), then surely he can owe no duty of obedience to any man unless he has agreed to obey? Government exists to secure our freedom, our natural rights. How, then, can it be legitimate unless its authority rests on our consent? To Locke it seemed obvious that it could not be.

He was, I think, mistaken. It is not obvious, and only seems to be so if we do what Locke did: if we run two quite different questions together without noticing that they are different; if we ask, how could government be rightfully established among creatures without government and having no obligation except to respect each other's natural rights? and then suppose that the answer to this question will tell us what is needed to make *any established government* legitimate. Where there is no government and no one has any obligation to another person except to respect his natural rights, it is difficult to see how anyone could rightfully impose government on anyone else without his consent. Government is then an untried device; it may or may not do what is intended of it, which is to preserve natural rights more effectively than they are preserved in the state of nature. In a situation of that kind, it is difficult to see how those who want government could rightfully impose it on those who do not. But where government already exists, the situation is no longer the same. Where government in fact protects men's rights, they ought to obey it whether or not they have consented to do so.

Locke says that it is everyone's duty to respect the rights of other people, and also that everyone has a natural right to punish offences against the law of nature. This right to punish is, as we have seen, more than a right of self-defence; it implies a right to take action to ensure that the law of nature is respected. Government, if it really does ensure that the law of nature is respected, is a proper exercise of this right. What does it matter how the institutions that protect freedom (i.e. natural right) were first established? If it is my right to preserve my own freedom and my duty to respect the freedom of others, then it is my duty to accept these institutions, even though I never agreed to do so. The right of everyone to be consulted at the imagined first setting up of government does not arise merely from everyone's having natural rights; it arises from those rights and the imagined situation. There is then no government, and it is proposed to set one up. The issue and effects are uncertain. Therefore everyone ought to be consulted.

Even in this imaginary situation, it does not follow that the decision to set up government, to be valid, must be unanimous – that those who want to try the experiment have no right to do so unless everyone agrees that it should be tried. Those who want government have a right against those who do not that they shall make reasonable provision to enable them to get it; and those who do not want it have a right against those who do that they shall make reasonable provision to allow them to escape it. What is reasonable provision must depend on the circumstances. If most people want government and only a few do not, then the few ought to move away from the place where it is proposed to establish it and accept fair compensation for any property they cannot take with them. But if most people do not want it, then those who do must either make up their minds to do without it or else remove themselves and establish it elsewhere. In either case, there is no need for all who are consulted to come to the same decision. Provided that all are consulted, and that reasonable provision is made for the minority to get their way without preventing the majority from getting theirs, everyone's natural right to freedom has been respected. We can then say that the political community is established with the deliberate consent of everyone who joins it. But the need for this consent arises only because there is no government, and a decision has therefore to be taken to set one up. Where there already is a government, where there is no need to set one up, it does not follow, merely because everyone is by nature free (i.e., has certain natural rights), that he cannot be required to obey unless he has agreed to do so.

If Locke had seen this, he would not have argued, as he did, from everyone's having a right not to have government imposed on him against his will when it is first proposed to establish it, to no one's having a duty to obey it unless he has agreed to obey. But, unfortunately, he did not see it, and so was driven to some odd expedients to show that men have agreed to obey even when they appear not to have done so. Just as it is easy, once you have imagined a state of nature, to go on to imagine people freely and deliberately joining together to form a political society, so it is difficult to explain how, once that society is long established, every adult person subject to it consents to the subjection. Locke, to get over the difficulty, argued that consent can be tacit – indeed, so tacit, that the people who give it do not notice that they have done so.

According to Locke, a man consents tacitly to obey the government whenever he inherits property. Let us examine his argument more closely. 'Commonwealths not permitting any part of their dominions to be dismembered, nor to be enjoyed by any but those of their community, the son cannot ordinarily enjoy the possessions of his father but under the same terms his father did, by becoming a member of the society, whereby he puts himself presently under the government he finds there established, as much as any other subject of that commonwealth.'[1] In other words, because governments lay down certain conditions for the enjoyment of property within their dominions, anyone who inherits property consents to the authority of the government within whose dominions that property is situated. He could refuse his inheritance. If he accepts it, he also accepts the conditions laid down by the government for the holding of property

[1] Ibid., ch. VIII, § 117.

within its dominions, and that acceptance is a tacit consent to the government's authority.

Now, this argument does not square with Locke's account of property. Property, he says, is a natural right *prior* to government. What I own is mine by a right not created by government. Suppose I am not under government and then by my own free choice put myself under it. I pledge myself to obey as long as the government protects my natural rights, including my property. It is not, however, from my owning property that my duty of obedience arises but from my consent. The government protects my property because I have promised obedience; but my right to bequeath that property to my son and his right to inherit it were not created by the government. The rights of bequest and inheritance are both natural rights. My consenting to obey the government so long as it protects my property does not of itself lay upon me the obligation not to bequeath my property to my son except on the condition that he too obeys the government.

In support of the argument I have just considered, Locke puts forward another. He says: 'By the same act, therefore, whereby any one unites his person, which was before free, to any commonwealth, by the same he unites his possessions, which were before free, to it also; and they become both of them, person and possession, subject to the government and dominion of that commonwealth, as long as it hath a being.'[1] Notice that Locke says 'as long as *it*' (the commonwealth) and not as long as *he* (the person) 'hath a being'. The person dies, but because his possessions continue in being after his death, they are, for some mysterious reason, still subject to the commonwealth. Just what is meant by saying that possessions are 'subject to the commonwealth'? Being inanimate, they clearly do not owe a duty of obedience. To say they are subject to the commonwealth is only to say that the commonwealth has a right to regulate their use. As they can only be used by persons, this amounts to saying that those persons are subject to the commonwealth. Thus, the first holder of a piece of property, who by his consent makes it 'subject to the commonwealth', by that same consent binds his heirs to subjection if they decide to exercise their right to inherit what is bequeathed to them. But this argument is clearly no better than the first. The right of bequest and the right of inheritance (being rights of property) are natural rights, and therefore a man does not hold them only on conditions which a government chooses to lay down, merely because an ancestor once promised to obey that government while it

[1] Ibid., ch. VIII, § 120.

protected his natural rights. If a government were to say to a man's heirs, 'You cannot take what is bequeathed to you unless you admit that you are as much subject to our authority as your father was', it would be invading a natural right, and therefore breaking its trust. Indeed, this argument of Locke's denies one of his basic assumptions: that a man's consent can never bind his children and posterity. If I promise to obey a government while it protects my property, I do not thereby bind my son to obey it if he inherits that property, for I have a natural right to bequeath my property to him, and he has a natural right to take his inheritance.[1]

Of course, it is true that a man, by inheriting property, does put himself under an obligation to obey government. Government protects property and makes possible its peaceful transference from one person to another, and anyone who benefits from government owes a duty of obedience to it. Locke is right in holding that even a man who takes lodging for a week or who travels freely on the highway has a duty to obey the laws that make safe lodging and travel possible. Everyone admits the duty in such cases. But the duty does not arise from consent, either open or tacit – not at least if consent is taken to be (and Locke so took it) a voluntary act intended by the doer of it to give other people a right they would otherwise not have.

It might be objected that this is pressing Locke too hard. He was sometimes a careless reasoner, and if we take him up whenever he gives us a chance of doing so, we can reckon up against him a long account of confusion and poor logic. The word consent has many meanings; and surely it is sheer pedantry to insist that Locke should have stuck all through his book to the one he began with. But that is not in the least what I wish to do. I want to say no more than this: since it was Locke's purpose to distinguish between legitimate government and tyranny, and since he believed that it is the consent of the governed that makes government legitimate, he ought to have used the word consent in ways which make it possible to distinguish between legitimate government and tyranny. Let him by all means use

---

[1] In ch. VIII, § 116, Locke speaks of a father making it a condition of his son's enjoying the possessions left to him that he should 'be of that community'. In the same chapter, in §§ 121 and 122, he distinguishes between the 'express promise and compact' which make a man a 'perpetual subject' of a commonwealth and the 'tacit consent' which binds him to obey its laws only while he enjoys its protection. Neither of these points really touches my argument. Moreover, the second point, if we take it literally, obliges us to conclude that, while all naturalized citizens are 'perpetual subjects' and members of the commonwealth, the native-born for the most part are not.

the word in more than one sense; let him speak, if he wishes, of open and tacit consent. All that is required of him is that he should so use the word that we can know when government has the consent of the governed and when it has not. After all, his purpose was not to show that no government has this consent, nor yet that every government has it; his purpose was to discriminate between governments that have it and governments that do not have it. He wanted to put consent forward as a criterion of legitimacy.

The case against Locke is that he failed in his own purpose. If a man's consent is his deliberate and voluntary agreement, and if nothing but a man's consent can make it his duty to obey government, then most people at most times and in most places have no duty of obedience. This was a conclusion that Locke rightly wanted to avoid. He therefore felt the need to abandon the position he took up to begin with and to use the word consent in other and weaker senses. Unfortunately, he went to the other extreme, and gave the name consent to almost any action that creates an obligation to obey. It was perhaps inevitable, given the initial bias of his doctrine, that he should do so. If you begin by assuming that only consent creates a duty of obedience, you are only too ready to conclude that whatever creates that duty must be consent.

Whatever a man does which involves his taking advantage of the order maintained by government puts him under an obligation to obey it. The obligation is not, of course, unconditional, but is not the less real for that. Every government, however bad, maintains some kind of order, and everyone living under it benefits, in one way or another, from that order. Everybody is clearly obliged to obey the government in many things, even when he is rightly plotting to overthrow it by force. Therefore, if there really is no duty of obedience except where there has been consent, everyone has always consented to any government in whose dominions he finds himself.

We have seen that Locke, when he elaborated his doctrine that political obligation arises from consent, took not much interest in the actual machinery of government. He never seriously attempted to link up his doctrine of consent with a theory of parliamentary representation. I am not blaming him for the omission, which is typical of political theory in his day in spite of the great play made with man's natural freedom and the popular origins of governmental authority. But I do suggest that if Locke had taken a serious interest in the structure of government by consent, he would not have begun, as he did, with an impossibly stringent and narrow sense of consent and then passed on to a uselessly wide one.

True, Locke thought it best that legislative authority should be vested in 'collective bodies'[1] and also strongly advised the separation of the executive and legislative powers.[2] But he did not insist that an elected legislature is indispensable to government by consent. He was ready to admit that the people may, when they first set up government, place the legislative power, which he calls supreme, wherever they like; they may even, if they are so disposed, place it in the hands of an hereditary monarch.[3] Monarchy, aristocracy and democracy are all, on Locke's assumptions, equally legitimate, equally government by consent, provided they are established in the first place by common agreement and that everyone who afterwards becomes subject to them gives his tacit consent in any of the ways that Locke describes. As we have seen already, since these ways include not only inheriting property, but even taking lodgings or travelling on the roads, this almost comes down to saying that a man gives his tacit consent whenever he does anything he could not safely or conveniently do in the absence of government. If even an hereditary monarch, with no elected parliament to assist him, can have authority to make laws, it follows that no special device, no general election or other method of consulting the people, is needed to make consent possible. Consent is given whenever subjects go about the ordinary lawful business of their lives.

Locke requires more than tacit consent in only one case. In the eleventh chapter of the *Treatise*, he says that the prince or senate 'can never have a power to take to themselves the whole or any part of the subjects' property, without their own consent'.[4] The context makes it clear that consent, in this case, is something more than can be given by merely inheriting property or travelling on the highway. Locke makes a point of distinguishing between the power of the prince or the senate to control and regulate the use subjects may make of their property (which is an ordinary legislative power that need not be exercised by an elected body, unless it was stipulated that it should be when the form of government was decided), and the power to levy taxes. Only the second power, to be legitimate, *always* requires a form of consent which is not given in the mere process of living a law-abiding life. It always requires more than mere tacit consent. The right to tax property must always be expressly granted by the people

---

[1] See ch. VII, § 94.
[2] Ibid., ch. XII, § 144 and ch. XIV, § 159.
[3] Ibid., ch. X, § 132.
[4] Ibid., ch. XI, § 139. See also § 140.

to their rulers. Without troubling to consult you, the government may have your consent to anything it does for the common good, except when it requires you to pay taxes. You need not pay them unless they have been voted by your representatives.

No doubt, a good case can be made, on historical and practical grounds, for holding that people ought not to be taxed without their consent. 'No taxation without representation' is not even a peculiarly English principle; it is rooted in mediaeval conceptions of good government. You will find as ardent a champion of unlimited royal power as Bodin admitting that the King of France, despite his sovereignty, cannot take away his subjects' property without their consent. Clearly, if the king needs his subjects' consent to tax them, he cannot go nearly as far as he otherwise might in imposing his will on them. Bodin understood this as well as Locke. Yet Bodin was far indeed from believing that governmental authority is legitimate only if it is exercised with the people's consent. Locke's views about taxation are quite sensible in themselves and rest on an old and venerable and justifiable tradition, but they do not fit in with the rest of his theory. If the prince can make laws with his subjects' consent without troubling to consult them, why need he consult them to get their consent to taxation? Or, to put the opposite and more pointed question, if he needs to consult them to get their consent to taxation, how can he have their consent in other matters unless he consults them?

If the people's consent can be had without consulting them, the question must arise, How do we know that they *do not* consent? How do we know when authority has ceased to be legitimate and has become oppressive? We can find in Locke's *Treatise* no direct answer to this question. We can, however, venture to give one. We have seen that, if we accept his examples of what constitutes tacit consent, we virtually have to conclude that a man gives his consent to government merely by going lawfully about his business. If this is so, we are left with only one possible answer to our question: we can know that people do not consent only when they cease to obey on the ground that government is oppressive. They withdraw their consent by challenging the authority of the government. What Locke understands by tacit consent is so wide that in practice it leaves the subject with no means of withholding his consent except by civil disobedience or resistance.[1] Locke's purpose is to show that the duty

---

[1] The man who commits a crime from hope of private gain does not withhold consent. He withholds it only if he justifies his disobedience on the ground that the government has abused its authority.

of obedience arises from consent, and yet he stretches the notion of consent so far that in the end he virtually makes obedience imply consent. We consent to obey by obeying. Obedience creates the obligation to obey. But this is absurd.

In saying all this, I have not lost sight of Locke's strong preference for a separation of the legislative and executive powers, nor the passages in the *Treatise* where he speaks of the 'Legislative' as if it were an assembly. In one place, with England clearly in mind, he even suggests that, where the Legislative consists partly of representatives chosen by the people and representation has become grossly unequal as between different parts of the country, the Executive, having the power to convoke the Legislative, might remedy this defect.[1] But the fact remains that Locke nowhere makes it a *condition* of there being government by consent that authority to make laws should belong to an elected assembly. Where, as in chapter VII, § 90, he condemns absolute monarchy as inconsistent with civil society and says that the absolute prince is in a state of nature in relation to his subjects, he is only attacking the doctrine that the prince is above the law and his subjects owe him unconditional obedience; he is not suggesting that, except where legislative power belongs to an elected assembly, there is no government by consent. The argument of the *Treatise* is emphatically not that political power is only legitimate where there is what, since Locke's time, we have learnt to call representative government; it is rather that political power is legitimate only when it is exercised with the consent of the governed. Today it may seem to many that the second argument, if it is to amount to anything definite, must be equivalent to the first; but at the end of the seventeenth century it did not seem so, even to the author of the *Second Treatise*.

Certainly, Locke thought it best that legislative power should be vested in an assembly; and, though he did not say that the assembly (or any part of it) should be elected, he did argue that, where it is elected, it is a breach of trust in the executive to corrupt the representatives or to bribe or intimidate the voters.[2] There are several indications in the *Treatise* that Locke greatly preferred the English system of government of his day to, say, the French. But we must not allow this strong preference to mislead us. Nowhere in the *Treatise*, except when he speaks of taxation, does he attempt to establish a connection

---

[1] *Second Treatise of Government*, chs. XII and XIII, §§ 147–58.
[2] Ibid., ch. XIX, § 222.

between the giving of consent and the choosing of representatives. He does not use the notion of consent to make a case for representative government; he uses it only to argue that political authority is always limited by the ends it ought to serve, so that, where those who have this authority do not serve those ends, their subjects have a right to resist them or to get rid of them.

It has been said – I think rightly – that, when Locke's *Second Treatise* is thoroughly sifted, what we are left with is not so much a doctrine of consent as a doctrine of resistance. The duty of obedience is conditional: government exists, not for the benefit of those who govern, but for the good of their subjects, who have the right to resist their rulers when they are oppressive. Now, there is nothing startling about this doctrine, which to most people today seems both commonplace and true. The doctrine, taken in itself, has no logical connection with the notion of consent. Logically, there is no difficulty about holding that subjects may rightfully resist an oppressive government, whether or not they have consented to its authority. Yet Locke felt the need to derive the conclusion that oppressive government may be rightfully resisted from the premise that it is the consent of the governed that makes government legitimate.

Why did he feel this need? Simply because what now seems obvious to us did not seem so in his day. Everyone agreed, then as now, that government exists for the good of the governed, but not everyone concluded that therefore subjects have a right to overthrow oppressive government. Even Filmer, against whom Locke wrote his first *Treatise*, was ready to admit that the king ought to rule for his subjects' good; but the king, he said, is responsible to God alone for how he rules, because his authority comes from God. Locke's reply is that the king is also responsible to the people, because his authority also comes from them, and is not legitimate unless he rules with their consent. The connection between Locke's doctrine of consent and his doctrine of resistance is less logical than historical. If he had not argued as he did, his argument would probably have carried less weight with his contemporaries. It was only natural that Locke, writing when it was still widely denied that government could be rightfully resisted merely for being oppressive, should have felt the need to argue that allegiance is always conditional, because government holds its power in trust from the people to govern them well. If it breaks its trust, the people may rise against it; and it is for them alone to decide when the trust has been broken. It was not enough for Locke to say bluntly, 'The people, when they are oppressed, have the right to revolt'; he felt impelled to add, 'because they consented to obey only while their rulers governed them well'. Logically an unnecessary addition, but, at the time it was made, a persuasive one – and all the more persuasive for being sincere.

If we take it by itself, apart from his doctrine of consent, Locke's doctrine of resistance is clear, forceful and adequate. In his fourteenth chapter he says: 'And where the body of the people, or any single man, is deprived of their right, or is under the exercise of a power without right, and have no appeal on earth, there they have a liberty to appeal to Heaven, whenever they judge the cause of sufficient moment.'[1] The appeal to Heaven here referred to is, of course, not prayer but resistance. Any man may resist if he judges the cause of sufficient moment, whether the injury complained of is done to himself or to other people; and he may also resist, even though no injury is done to private persons, if the ruler exercises a power he has no right to.

I do not see how it is possible to object to this argument. The right of resistance cannot be confined, as it was by mediaeval writers and by the author of the *Vindiciae*, to parliaments, courts of law or lesser magistrates. For these may themselves be oppressive. Nor can it be restricted to the people generally or to large groups. If I believe that the government is oppressive and yet have no right to resist unless most people share my belief, how can I know whether or not I have that right? If I set about trying to discover how much support I am likely to get, the government may stop me. Have I then the right to resist? But, for all I know, most people may want the government to stop me. The right of resistance is, *ex hypothesi*, not a legal right, and can therefore never be confined to some definite proportion of the people; for any government worth the name will see to it that would-be revolutionaries cannot make sure beforehand just how much support they can count on. Revolutionary leaders get most of the recruits coming to them after they have started operations. Revolution is always something of a leap in the dark, and is apt to be the more so the more oppressive the government.

It has been said that Locke confines the right of active resistance to the people generally and does not allow it to the lone citizen or to a minority, except in self-defence. I must confess that I was once inclined to believe this myself, on the strength of three paragraphs in the eighteenth chapter of the *Second Treatise*.[2] There Locke first

[1] Ibid., ch. XIV, § 168.
[2] Ibid., ch. XVIII, §§ 208–210. See also ch. XIX, §§ 230 and 240.

357

argues that resistance by only a few people is useless, and then goes on to say that he does not see how resistance is to be prevented when misgovernment affects the majority, nor yet when, though it affects only a few, it seems to threaten all, and all are persuaded in their consciences that there is a general danger. Though, taken literally, these are only opinions about the probable consequences of certain actions or about what people are likely to do, it may be that Locke meant them to be more than just this; it may be that he meant to confine the right of resistance to the majority of the people. But, though this is possible, it is unlikely. It is probable that Locke was saying no more than that no one ought to resist government by force, except in self-defence, unless he is persuaded in his conscience that there is widespread oppression or the danger of it. And this is surely a reasonable doctrine.

No doubt, the would-be revolutionary ought, *so far as he can*, to take account of other people's opinions and feelings. He ought to count the cost of his enterprise and to make a sober estimate of his chances of success. The less other people resent what he condemns as oppression, the more he should hesitate about taking drastic action, not only because such action is then less likely to succeed, but also because he ought not to risk other people's security lightly in a cause that means little or nothing to them. For one or more of several reasons, it may be wrong for a man to resist when most other people think there is no cause for resistance. The less others sympathize with him, the more he risks doing a great deal of harm and almost no good. He is liable to error, and is more likely to be misjudging the government when most people disagree with him than when they agree. These are all good reasons, but none implies that a man has no right to resist unless most people agree with him. Though many people before Locke asserted the right of resistance, most of them hedged it about in ways that confined it to particular bodies and officials, making a sort of privilege of it. That is essentially the mediaeval or feudal conception of it. Locke placed it firmly in the hands of every man, requiring only that he should use it conscientiously for the common good and with a decent respect for the opinions of others. His doctrine of resistance is perhaps the most valuable part of his political theory.

It may seem from what I have been saying that I find no virtue at all in Locke's case for government by consent. I hope that is not the impression I have created, for it was not my intention. With Locke's central purpose, I have the strongest sympathy. He was concerned to safeguard freedom, which he conceived of, not as Hobbes had done – as absence of obligation in the state of nature or as the right to do what the law does not forbid in civil society – but as a moral right which it is the duty of governments to protect. Believing in freedom, he concluded that no man can have a right to command another man except with his consent; because if he had that right, the other man's freedom would be abridged as his own freedom was not, which would contravene the basic principle that all men are by nature equal. This argument, which satisfied Rousseau, Paine, Jefferson and countless other radicals, is, as I have tried to show, not convincing. If freedom is not adequately preserved except under government, then everyone ought to obey the government while it preserves freedom, no matter whether he has consented or not.

Locke, having mistakenly decided that freedom, or the exercise of certain rights, which he called natural, requires universal consent to government, found himself obliged first to put forward a strong notion of consent, and then, in order to avoid difficulties, to replace it by a much weaker notion useless for his original purpose – which was to distinguish rightful government from tyranny. If consent is taken in his strong sense, nothing less than universal suffrage will do; and even that is not enough, for it does not ensure that everyone consents all the time. Yet Locke, as we know, was satisfied with the English Parliament of his day; he neither wanted to extend the franchise nor attempted to show how his theory could be used to justify the English system of government or to condemn James II.

Again, though there is much to be said for the principle 'no taxation without representation', it is difficult to see how that principle fits logically into Locke's general argument for government by consent. If all government, to be legitimate, requires the consent of the governed, why *must* that consent be express when it is consent to taxation but not necessarily otherwise? And lastly, acceptable though Locke's thesis is that the subject has a right to resist government if he is convinced in conscience that resistance is for the public good, it is impossible to agree with him that the subject has this right because he has no duty to obey government unless he has consented to do so. Locke did not even put himself to the trouble of showing that government by consent is unlikely to be oppressive, and thus unlikely to give just cause for resistance.

Yet, I would not deny that there is plenty to agree with in Locke's *Second Treatise*; I would say only that this plenty does not add up to a lucid and consistent political philosophy. Inspired by love of freedom and hatred of tyranny, Locke speaks out boldly, and we get his stronger sense of consent and his admirable doctrine of resistance;

but he also accepts the established order and, to avoid conclusions inconsistent with it, quickly withdraws from a difficult position. As so often happens in such cases, he tries to withdraw without appearing to do so, without admitting it even to himself. That is why he ordinarily speaks of consent in his weaker sense as if it were really exactly the same as consent in his stronger sense; as if the difference lay, not in the nature of the consent, but in the manner of giving it; as if, by calling it *tacit*, he were saying only that it is not expressed in words. Just as consent can be given by writing or by word of mouth, so it can be express or tacit; it is always the same consent, however it is given. That is the impression created by Locke during the course of his argument, and it is a false impression. This is not to say that there is no connection between government by consent and the preservation of freedom, understood as the exercise of rights not created by government; it is to say only that this connection is not made clear by Locke's use of the notion of consent.

To see how government by consent and the preservation of freedom are connected, we must bear in mind that men need two kinds of protection. They need protection from one another as individuals; and this protection any effective government, whether or not it has their consent, can give them. Government can define men's rights and defend them adequately, even though it is not responsible to them. If it does this, then its subjects have civil liberty as Hobbes understood it: they know what their rights are, they know what the law is, what it requires and what it forbids, and they can rely on the impartiality of those in authority over them. They then have security, which is the first condition of freedom: they know what they must do and must refrain from doing, and their rulers, who define these limits to their freedom, also protect their freedom inside these limits. Government, to use Hobbes's metaphor, sets hedges about us, not to impede our motion but to direct it, so that we may, as we go about our business, be as little as possible obstacles in one another's way.

There is little evidence that government is more likely to afford security to its subjects when it is responsible to them than when it is not. Its ability to do so ordinarily depends more on other things: on the power at its disposal, on the independence of the judiciary, on the principles generally accepted in governing circles. A weak government, even though it is responsible to its subjects, is likely to be timid or corrupt, or both together, and is therefore unlikely to be a scrupulous protector of rights. The condition of the people may be such that only an irresponsible government can be strong; for the people may be politically immature and not know what standards they and their rulers must respect if rights are to be impartially and effectively protected. Sometimes rights are best protected where government is virtually irresponsible, at other times where it is responsible to the wealthy and educated, and at still other times where it is responsible to the people generally.

But men may want more than the impartial enforcement of legal rights, more than protection from one another as private citizens or as servants of government. They may also want security against their rulers' governing them in ways that do violence to their sense of right, their sense of what is owing to them as rational and moral persons. Clearly, Locke thought that they do want this security also; for he, unlike Hobbes, insisted that men have rights which their rulers do not sufficiently protect merely by making their own authority effective, rights which even a strong government can infringe. If freedom is more than the secure enjoyment of legal rights, if it matters that men should be able to live as seems good to them provided they do no harm to others, then it is wrong for governments, however impartial their enforcement of legal rights, to violate their subjects' sense of justice or of right. If freedom is (as Locke thought it was) the supreme good, then it is wrong, however excellent your motive, to rule people in ways which offend deeply against their moral principles.

Now it is reasonable to suppose that the more rulers are responsible to their subjects, the less likely it is that they will make laws or pursue policies which are offensive in this way. Moreover, the stronger the government, the greater the danger that it may make laws morally repugnant to its subjects. A government which is weak, even though it may be irresponsible, will take care not to offend its subjects, whereas a government which is both strong and irresponsible will be much less concerned not to offend them. Therefore, if subjects are to be secure from this kind of offence, the stronger the government, the more important it is that it should be responsible to the governed. If we understand by freedom under government no more than Hobbes understood by it, we may agree that the stronger the government, the more secure the freedom of its subjects; but if we understand by freedom what Locke understood by it, we need to go further; we need to insist that, the stronger a government, the more it matters that it should be responsible to its subjects if their freedom is to be preserved.

No doubt, the responsibility of rulers to their subjects where government is strong is not a sufficient condition of freedom, for the people may be ignorant and may lack political capacity. We can easily imagine situations in which responsible government would not protect freedom, even in Locke's sense of it, better than irresponsible government. Or, rather – and this, I think, is a better way of putting it – we can easily imagine situations in which the attempt to make government responsible to its subjects must fail because genuine responsibility requires in the people habits and qualities which they do not possess. Nevertheless, while conceding all this, we can still say that, where government is strong, freedom, as Locke conceived of it, is unlikely to be secure except where the rulers are responsible to their subjects.

Now government, all over Western Europe, had been growing stronger for several hundred years before Locke wrote his *Treatise*. The doctrine that government is not legitimate unless it is carried on with the consent of the governed – a doctrine much more prominent in the seventeenth century than it had been in, say, the thirteenth – was itself a product of a greater fear of government, a fear due partly to the growing power of the State and partly to a deeper concern for individual freedom. It was a concern shared by Locke, and it moved him to produce his argument that rulers are answerable to their subjects for how they rule.

But, unfortunately, owing to the way in which Locke uses the notion of consent to establish his conclusion, his doctrine that rulers are responsible to their subjects is reduced to the mere assertion that subjects have the right to resist their rulers when they honestly believe that they are being seriously misgoverned. This assertion is by no means unimportant, and makes much better sense than many older doctrines of resistance; but it is not enough. The stronger government is, the more dangerous it is to resist, and the less likely that resistance will be effective. Therefore, the argument that rulers are answerable to their subjects for how they rule, where it is inspired by concern for a freedom which is more than mere security under the law, is seriously defective if it does not put the case for a form of government which reduces the risk that rulers will tamper with the freedom of their subjects. Locke does suggest that rulers are less likely to do this where there is an elected legislature, but he does not insist that there must be one. He allows that there can be government by consent which is not representative government.

Of course, it is not to be held against Locke that he did not argue for democracy. Indeed, it is probable that, in his England, a legislature representing only a small part of the people was much more likely than a truly popular assembly to protect freedom. Democracy at the end of the seventeenth century, if it had been attempted, might well have proved fatal to liberty. Monarchy tempered by aristocracy may have been, in Locke's day, the form of government most favourable to liberty, the form securing it to as large a section of the people as could effectively enjoy it.

But, though it is not to be held against Locke that he failed to argue for democracy, it is to be held against him that he did not argue for any particular form of government. From his doctrine that government is legitimate when it has the consent of its subjects, we cannot argue for one form of government in preference to another. If we take consent in his stronger sense, democracy alone is legitimate; and if we take it in its weaker sense, any government is legitimate while no one resists it, because resistance is the only sufficient sign that consent is lacking. Indeed, if we take Locke's stronger sense of consent, even democracy is imperfectly justified; for if consent is personal and deliberate, no government has the consent of all its subjects. If it is true that no man can be rightfully governed except with his own freely given consent, then every government, even the most democratic, is almost certain to be to some extent oppressive.

Two things should by now, I hope, be clear: that we cannot follow Locke in holding that the duty to obey government arises from consent alone, except at the cost of reducing the notion of consent to virtually nothing; and that we cannot use his doctrine of consent to distinguish between responsible and irresponsible government. True, Locke did not want to make precisely this distinction, but he did want to make another which he thought was closely allied to it, between legitimate government and tyranny. He believed that when rulers are answerable to their subjects they are less likely to oppress them, or to behave like tyrants. If, then, Locke's account of consent will not do, what account must we substitute for it to enable us to distinguish between responsible and irresponsible government? Let me attempt an answer to this question.

We must retain Locke's stronger sense of consent, admitting that by doing so we abandon all hope of getting universal consent to any government. But in the place of his weaker sense we must put another quite different from it. Locke was not wrong to speak of two kinds of consent, though he mistook the connection between them and made the second kind too broad to serve his purpose. There is a difference between the consent which grants authority or establishes or alters a system of government and the consent which does not; and there is also a close connection between them. The difference does not lie in the manner of expression. The second kind is not the same as the first, though differently conveyed; agreement must not be presumed when silence can be fairly taken to be a mark of agreement. It may or may not involve making a deliberate choice; but what makes it an act of consent is that it is an action or failure to act which is political and creates a duty of obedience. This second kind of consent is, if you like, tacit; but that is not the important respect in which it differs from the first. For the first kind, though usually express, may also be tacit, as when those who favour a proposal which is carried are asked to keep silent. Where there is a definite choice to be made, and the convention is that silence or inaction is to be understood as preference for one alternative, there can be tacit consent, even in the strong sense, to the alternative actually adopted.

To mark the difference between these two kinds of consent, I shall call the first kind *direct* and the second *indirect*. Direct consent can be either express or tacit; whereas indirect consent is always tacit. These two kinds of consent are thus not the same thing differently expressed; they differ in themselves. Yet they are closely related, because only where the first kind exists do we have the conditions making possible the second kind. There is clearly a difference between consent to the government of particular persons, or to a constitution adopted by plebiscite or by an elected assembly, and consent to a political system long established; and yet both deserve to be called consent, as the tacit consent of Locke does not.

The present generation of Englishmen have not been consulted about the system of government they live under; they have inherited it from their ancestors. Yet they can, I think, be said to consent to it. Not because they own property in England or in any other way enjoy the protection of English law; nor because they put up with the system or even like it; but because they can, if they so wish, change it legally and peacefully. It does not follow, of course, that because no one tries to change it, everyone consents to it. There may be people who detest the system but do not try to change it because they despair of success, knowing that the majority are so strongly attached to it that they cannot be persuaded to change it. However democratic a system of government and however large the initiative it leaves to the ordinary citizen, we can never know for certain that everyone subject to it consents indirectly to the subjection. We can, however, assume that most people give this kind of consent. And this consent has a good deal more to it than Locke's tacit consent; it is more than mere acceptance of what you are powerless to reject.

When you vote for a person or a party that wins an election, you directly consent to his or to their authority, and you also consent indirectly to the system of government. Even when your vote is cast for persons who intend to change the system, you consent to it until it is changed. For you make use of the system in order to change it. Furthermore, by taking part in the election you consent indirectly to the authority of the persons that win it, even if you vote against them. This last consent does not depend on your approval of the system, on your thinking it right that whoever gets power under it should have power, whether or not you voted for him. Even if you dislike the system and wish to change it, you put yourself by your vote under an obligation to obey whatever government comes legally to power under the system, and this can properly be called giving consent. For the purpose of an election is to grant authority to the people who win it, and if you vote knowing what you are doing and without being compelled to do it, you voluntarily take part in the process which gives authority to those people. It does not matter what your motive for voting is, any more than it matters what your motive is in making a promise. If you make a promise to someone with the intention of *not* keeping it, you are not the less bound by it because of your intention. If you make your promise voluntarily, and if you know what you are doing when you make it, your promise lays an obligation on you. Just as it is sometimes right to break a promise, so it may sometimes be right to use force against an elected government, even when you have voted for it. But that is merely to say that the obligation created by a promise or an act of consent is not absolute.

Consent, even when it is indirect, is not *any* action or failure to act which creates a duty of obedience. No doubt, whoever benefits from government is, to that extent, obliged to obey it; but this obligation does not arise from consent. Only when an action involves taking part in an election or decision is it a direct or indirect consent: a direct consent to the authority of the person or to the proposal you vote for, and an indirect consent to the system you voluntarily take part in and to the result of the vote when it goes against you. A failure to act is an indirect consent only when it is abstention from voting or from legal opposition to the system when such opposition is safe and easy and might be effective. The abstention must not be enforced: it must be due either to indifference or to a man's freely choosing not to do what he easily could do. Indirect consent is not a granting of authority or permission, as direct consent is, and therefore differs from direct consent in what it is and not only in the way it is given. Yet it deserves to be called political consent because it is a free political action or failure to act which creates a duty of obedience. Admittedly, when I travel on the highway or take lodging for a week or inherit my father's estate, I voluntarily do something that makes it my duty to respect established authority. But that much I do whenever I in any way benefit from the order maintained by government. It is only when the obligation to obey arises from something I freely do or freely abstain from doing – not just *under* government, but *about* government – to help decide who shall govern or what the political system shall be, that it can be said to arise from consent.

The argument against Locke is at bottom simple enough. No government can be said to rule with the people's consent, direct or indirect, express or tacit, unless the people can safely and legally put an end to its authority – that is to say, unless there are devices ensuring that it is in fact responsible to them. There cannot be indirect consent except where there are also direct consent and dissent. I can be said to consent to something indirectly only when I have the right to reject or to try to change it; or when I freely take part in a process of decision knowing that the decision may go against me. There cannot be indirect consent except where direct consent is safe and easy. Therefore, to give substance to the notion of indirect consent, we must relate it to some established process of choosing or getting rid of governments, or of changing the political system; we must take into account the devices that make government responsible or representative.

Political consent, direct or indirect, must not be treated as a kind of contract, express or implied. Even direct political consent is not a conditional promise of obedience; its significance, the rights conferred by it and the duties undertaken, depend on the political system as a whole. Both the forms of political consent and the moral relations arising from it make it a transaction different in kind from a contract or treaty. How can we explain these differences except by taking account of the process of election and the conventions connected with it? How can we explain them except by taking account of what Locke almost completely ignored?

Locke was one of the most abstract of political philosophers, and at the same time one of the most moderate and sensible. He was abstract in his assumptions and moderate in his conclusions. There is nothing wrong with that. Political wisdom, with all deference to Burke, is not the prerogative of people who have no use for abstract reasoning. The fault of Locke's theory is that there seem to be no clear lines of argument leading from the assumptions to the conclusions. There is a great middle region left out of the *Second Treatise*. It may be that the ideas to fill it were in Locke's mind. If they were, he failed to get them down on paper.

IV. LOCKE'S ACCOUNT OF PROPERTY

We have seen that Locke uses the word property in a wider and a narrower sense: to mean the sum of a man's rights to life, liberty and external possessions; and also to mean the right to external possessions alone. It is what he says about property in the second, the narrower, sense that I now want to consider.

Property, as Locke explains it, rests on two natural rights: the right to use what you need to preserve life and liberty, and the right to set aside for your exclusive use whatever you mix your labour with, provided it does not already belong to someone else. These two rights, as Locke defines and elaborates upon them, are not always compatible, and most of the difficulties in his account of property arise from his not having noticed this.

There are three major defects in Locke's theory of property. In the first place, the limit he sets on appropriation, the injunction to let nothing spoil or go to waste, is either irrelevant or inadequate, for it makes sense only under conditions which are in fact rare; secondly, the right of bequest, which Locke tacitly includes in the right of property, does not derive either from the right to preserve life and liberty or from the right to set aside for your own exclusive use what you have mixed your labour with; and, thirdly, it does not follow, even if your mixing your labour with something gives you a right to use it to the exclusion of people who have not mixed their labour with it, that your being the *first* to mix labour with something gives you the right not to share it with anyone who subsequently mixes his labour with it. Let me consider these three points in turn.

(a). The injunction to let nothing spoil or go to waste is either irrelevant or inadequate, except under the most unlikely conditions. If natural resources were unlimited in quantity and fit for immediate use, there would be no need for anyone to mix his labour with anything, and therefore no need for property. Property arises because man has to work on what nature provides to make it fit for his use. If natural resources were unlimited, and yet not fit for immediate use, there would still be a need for rules of property; or otherwise the lazy could exploit the industrious by seizing the fruits of their industry. But, in that case, though there would have to be rules of property, the injunction about letting nothing spoil or waste would be useless. For if natural resources are unlimited, however much I spoil or let go to waste of what I have mixed my labour with, there is always enough for other people to mix their labour with. I cannot, by my waste, 'invade my neighbour's share'.

367

But if what nature provides is exhaustible, why should the right to acquire property through labour be limited *only* by the injunction to let nothing spoil or waste? Why should it not be limited by the duty to leave enough over for other people to make their own? Why assume that, if nobody takes more than he can use without letting it spoil or waste, there will always be 'enough, and as good' left over for everyone to use to his own advantage? To limit the right of appropriation in this peculiar way makes sense only where natural resources are just scarce enough to ensure that, if they are wasted, some people will get less than they can use to advantage, and just abundant enough to ensure that, if they are not wasted, everyone will get as much as he can use to advantage. But this is a most unlikely situation.

As a matter of fact, Locke never troubled to enquire what conditions must hold to make sense of his rule about letting nothing spoil or waste. He probably condemned waste because he did not like it, without looking closely into its social consequences. According to the fashion of his day, he thought he could justify an institution like property by explaining how it arose or why men first needed it. Not unreasonably, he took it for granted that property first arose in sparsely populated countries among men whose needs were not great, where the work any man could do *or get done* was very limited, because he could in practice appropriate little more than the fruits of his own and his family's labour. In such a situation, a man who took too much land would soon find some of it going to waste. And since men are greedy, it might easily happen that, even if land were abundant, there would not be enough for everyone, unless there were a rule that no man might take more land than he could use to some advantage. And yet (and this is the crux of the matter) even in this case, takers of land, if they let it go to waste, would be 'invading their neighbour's share', not because they wasted land, not because they took more than they could use to advantage, but because they took what other people needed more than they did.

In itself, the rule about not taking more than you can use, about not wasting or spoiling, takes into account only your own interest and not other people's. Since you could spoil and waste, even when there was more than enough left over for other people, the true ground of the rule, *Let nothing waste or spoil*, is your own advantage. Why exert yourself to produce more than you need? Why labour in vain?

This rule of Locke's is well enough suited to simple farmers living in a fertile and thinly populated country, where every family works to maintain itself, taking almost nothing to market, and where there is no labour to hire. But in a densely populated country where there are many people without land, a man can easily accumulate a vast estate without letting an acre of it waste or allowing any of its produce to spoil. He can use every part of his estate to some advantage, either his own or other people's. He can hire labour and cultivate his land intensively, using part of the produce to feed the men he hires and exchanging the rest against other products. However luxurious his style of living, however much richer he is than other people, he wastes nothing and lets nothing spoil.

Even in a natural economy, where no money is used, some men can become vastly richer than others – and can do so, not because they work harder, but because they own land and the others do not. All this they can do without wasting anything or letting it spoil. There need be no fertile acre left uncultivated nor anything produced on their estates which is not used to someone's advantage, their own or other people's.

Indeed, even in a sparsely populated and very fertile and rich country, a few men could appropriate all the land and other natural resources and still keep Locke's rule about letting nothing waste or spoil. They could do it provided they had enough capital to attract and hire labour and could find a market for their produce. True, it is in long-settled and densely populated countries that capital first accumulates and large-scale production for the market first appears; but as soon as there is capital and there are markets, rich men can move into fertile and empty lands, and can take possession of immense natural resources without wasting or spoiling anything. It is only in a primitive subsistence economy that the amount of land a man can take is seriously limited by Locke's rule.

(b). It seemed so obvious to Locke that the natural right of property includes the right of bequest that he did not bother to prove his point. But if property arises as he says it does, this is by no means obvious. It clearly does not follow from the mere definition of property as the right of exclusive use. A man's right to use something to the exclusion of other people does not logically include the right to decide who shall use it after he is dead. The right of exclusive use and the right of bequest are different rights. They may both be called rights of property, and it may be usual for whoever has the first to have the second as well; but the second is not included in the first. A man's right of exclusive use is in no way curtailed if he does not also have the right of bequest.

Locke derives the right to appropriate external objects from two other rights: the right of self-preservation, and man's right of property in his own body. This first right includes, for Locke, more than the bare right to keep yourself alive; it includes the right to make provision for living commodiously, or, in other words, for living as it suits you to live, provided you respect the same right in others. If you are to make adequate provision for keeping yourself alive and for living commodiously, you must be able to set things aside for your own future use, and you must be able to rely on their being to hand when you need them. You must have secure possession; you must have the right of exclusive use. This security is also a condition of freedom; for, unless you have it, you cannot live as you please; you cannot organize your life to suit yourself. There is a clear connection between the right to keep yourself alive and to live commodiously, which is the right of self-preservation, as Locke understands it, and the right to acquire things for your own exclusive use. But there is no such clear connection between the right of self-preservation and the right of bequest. It is not in the least obvious that you cannot keep alive and live commodiously and freely unless you can decide who is to have your property after you are dead.

The other source from which Locke derives the right to external possessions is man's property in his own body. His body is his, and therefore whatever he mixes the labour of his body with is his also. This argument is quaint and obscure. A man's body may be said to be his in two quite different senses: it is his as being part of him, and it is his in the same sense as his external possessions are, as something that he alone has the right to use. In whichever of these two senses we consider, it simply does not follow that, because a man's body is his, nobody else has the right to use what he has set aside or transformed with the labour of his body. This is clearly so if we take the first sense. 'His body is a part of him' is a statement of fact, whereas 'nobody else ought to use what he has set aside or transformed with the labour of his body' is a moral rule; and a moral rule cannot be derived in this simple way from a statement of fact. But even if we take the second sense, which is almost certainly what Locke meant us to do, the argument, though it may look more convincing, is not really better grounded. It is by no means obvious that, because a man has the sole right to use his own body, nobody else has the right to use what he has set aside or transformed with the labour of his body. On grounds of expediency, or because a man has the right to make adequate provision for himself, this may be a good rule; but the rule, good or bad, does not follow merely from a man's body being 'his', whether as part of him or as something which he alone has the right to use. 'My body belongs to me, and therefore what

I have made with it belongs to me' is as much a *non sequitur* as 'my body is a part of me, and therefore what I have made with it belongs to me'. And, in any case, even if these arguments were valid – even if we could infer rules of property from a man's body being a part of him or from his having the sole right to use it – these rules of property would not include the right of bequest. If the right of bequest is to be justified, it must be, I think, largely on the ground that, in the long run, it promotes the general interest; but Locke never refers to any such ground. He considers only the advantage or the situation of the man who first acquires the property. It is because he has acquired it to preserve himself or because he has mixed the labour of his body with it that it belongs to him.

The right of exclusive use is only one of the several rights commonly called rights of property; the right of bequest is another, and there are still others. What Locke has done is this: he has derived one of these rights, the right of exclusive use, from the right of self-preservation, and has then taken it for granted that this right carries the others with it. That is a mistake easily made. If you take any society, you will find that certain rights, related to the same things, usually go together, so that whoever has one of them also has the others. These associated rights are all given the same name, and are treated as if they necessarily involved one another. An argument devised to establish one of them is taken to establish them all; and though, in strict logic, it does not do so, it is not the less convincing for that. Often, it is not until a demand arises for altering or abolishing some of these rights, that the argument is subjected to close scrutiny, and is either rejected or seen to have consequences more limited than was at first supposed. The contested rights are then defended, and new arguments are found to support them. The other rights which Locke ran together with the right of exclusive use to constitute the right of property have often been contested since his time by socialists; and none more so than the right of bequest. My purpose has not been to suggest that the right of bequest is or is not less defensible than other property rights, but only to show that Locke failed to explain or justify it, though he was convinced that he had done both.

(c). My third criticism of Locke's theory of property is that he passes, without seeming to notice it, from the position that what a man has mixed his labour with is his own, to the exclusion of other people who have not mixed theirs, to the quite different position, that what a man was the *first* to mix his labour with is his own even to the exclusion of other people who later mix their labour with it. The second position neither follows from the first, nor can be derived separately from the right to self-preservation, not even if we include in that right (as Locke did) more than the mere right to maintain one's life. To keep himself alive and to live commodiously, a man needs external goods for his own exclusive use, and has the right to acquire them by mixing his labour with what nature provides and no one else has appropriated. So far, so good. But, just as the right to self-preservation even thus widely understood does not allow him to appropriate as much as he pleases without caring what is left over for others, whose right to acquire property by their labour is as good as his, so it does not establish his exclusive right to what he was the *first* to appropriate against people who have no choice but to mix their labour with his property because there is nothing else left for them to mix it with. If labour has this power of creating titles to property, why only some labour and not all? Whence the privilege of the first labourers denied to those who come after them?[1]

Consider the case of the owner of a large estate who finds it profitable to use other men's labour on it. Why should not the labourers, by their mere labour, acquire a title to a share in his estate? Unless they worked for him, his land would go to waste; and to let something go to waste, says Locke, is to lose the right to it. The labourers cannot refuse their labour to the landowner, because in this instance there is no virgin land left for them to acquire. Yet they have the right, no less than the landowner, to preserve life and liberty;

---

[1] It might be objected in Locke's favour that, since every man's labour is his own, he has the right to sell it for a wage. This is true but does not affect my argument. His having the right to sell his labour does not deprive him of the right to appropriate what he mixes his labour with; he cannot justly lose this second right merely because others have appropriated all that there is to appropriate, for by so doing they have invaded his (their neighbour's) share. Were he to choose to appropriate what he produces (or were he to claim his share of a joint product), no one could rightfully deny him what he claimed. This must be so, if the right of appropriation by labour is, as Locke says it is, a natural right; for a natural right is a right which everyone possesses, and which government must therefore secure to everyone. Of course, we may insist on the labourer's right to sell his labour because we need to justify a social order where he has no choice but to sell it in order to get a living. The need is plain enough, but the argument is not sound. We cannot justify the loss of one natural right by showing that those who lose it retain another right – not even if this other right is also natural. Nor does Locke strengthen his case by saying that money, which enables men to appropriate much more than they can consume without danger of letting it spoil, came to be used by common consent. It is perfectly consistent with the natural right of appropriation by labour that men should use money if they find it convenient to do so, but it is *not* consistent with that right that they should so use money as to enable the propertied to deprive the propertyless of the right.

and the right to appropriate by labour derives from this right. How, then, can the work of the labourers, while it preserves the landowner's right to his land by preventing its going to waste, create no right of property in them? Can the landowner, merely because he owns the land, maintain his title to it through the work of others, even though he does not work himself? This is an odd conclusion to reach if you hold, as Locke does, that God gave all things in common to all men to use to keep themselves alive and to live commodiously, and that property, the right of exclusive use, originates in the mixing of labour with external goods.

Locke ought not to have said that a man has a right to the exclusive use of what he was the *first* to mix his labour with; he ought to have said, rather, that he has a right to the exclusive use of what he *alone* has mixed his labour with. If there is not enough left over for other people, a man cannot justly forbid them to work on what he has appropriated; for if he does, he violates their right to self-preservation. Nor do I see how he can justly refuse to share his property with them if he allows them to mix their labour with it. For they, no less than he, have a right to acquire property by their labour. No doubt, this second right derives from the right to self-preservation, but it is, none the less, a universal right. Locke calls it a 'natural right', and a natural right, by definition, is a right that everyone has. If the landless say to those who have all the land, 'Let us work on your land and share it with you', they are not by that claim contesting anyone's right to acquire property by labour, but are only asserting that their right is as good as other people's. But suppose the owners of the land say to the landless, 'Everything has been taken, and there is nothing left for you to take; you may, if you like, sell your labour to us for a wage, and so keep yourselves alive, but you may not by your labour acquire property'; then, on Locke's premises, they act unjustly. They act unjustly because they implicitly deny that the right to acquire property by labour is a natural right, a right which belongs to everyone, so that no one can justly assert it in such a way as to deprive another person of it. The landowners could justly refuse to share their land with the landless only if by sharing it they risked starvation; only if there were not enough land to support the entire population.

The right of self-preservation and the right to acquire property by labour do not, of course, exclude all inequalities. Those who labour more have the right to more property, provided they do not by their labour deprive other people of the chance to appropriate. The right of bequest, though it does not follow from these two prior rights, is not excluded by them; it is only limited. People may, on perfectly good grounds not discussed by Locke, bequeath what they have appropriated, as long as they do so without curtailing other people's rights of self-preservation and of acquiring property by their labour. In certain unlikely conditions, it would be possible for all men to have the fundamental rights ascribed to them by Locke, and for some to be rightfully very much richer than others. But just how much inequality is compatible with these rights must depend on circumstances.

Locke's account of property was widely accepted in Europe and America even after Hume had produced a more lucid and consistent alternative to it. For Hume, like Locke, did not criticize the system of property that existed; his purpose was merely to explain it. Though Hume's explanation might be more convincing to people with a taste for abstract reasoning and sound logic, it accorded less with current conceptions. Property, for Hume, is a conventional or customary and not a natural right. But convention and custom change, as natural law and natural right do not; so that what is grounded in them is not as firmly grounded as it might be. Locke's defence of property was more reassuring than Hume's, and therefore, for all its defects, more popular.

The real challenge to Locke's theory of property came with the rise of socialism. Hume rejected Locke's initial assumption that property is a natural right, but accepted the system that assumption was meant to justify; whereas the early socialists mostly did not reject the assumption, but used it to attack what Locke was concerned to defend. They mostly admitted the right of self-preservation, as Locke had described it, and also his rule that whatever a man has applied his labour to ought to belong to him to the exclusion of others; but they demanded that these rights be carried to their logical conclusions. By seeing where Locke's arguments are defective, we can understand how it was that the early socialists could use his assumptions to reach conclusions very different from his own. That is why I have gone rather more minutely into his arguments than I would have done otherwise.

There is one great virtue in what Locke says about property. He does not justify it only as a means to security or happiness, or because it encourages industry; he also sees it as a means to liberty. This is a side of it that meant much more to him than it did, for instance, to most of the Utilitarians. It is not absurd, it is even helpful, to speak of a natural right to property, in the sense of a right that every society ought to secure to its members: a man's right to acquire by his labour an exclusive domain, an area of privacy, a degree of material independence to serve as a cushion against the outside world. Even if we are socialists, we can agree with Locke so far. To have nothing to fall back on when you are at odds with your neighbours or with authority, to have nothing to sell but your labour when it is for other people to decide how you shall labour, is to be curtailed in your freedom, whether your employer is a private person or a public body.

V. CONCLUSION

I have been more critical, perhaps, of Locke's theory than of some others. If that is so, it has not been because, in my opinion, there is less that is true in it, but because so much that is true is supported by bad arguments. For all its weaknesses, Locke's political philosophy is supremely important, not only because it was so influential for a hundred years or more after he produced it, but because so much that seemed valuable to him still seems valuable to us.

Locke was deeply concerned about two things, property and freedom. He believed that they are closely connected with one another. In the wider of the two senses in which he uses the word *property*, it includes freedom, and in the narrower of the two senses, it is a means to freedom. Locke accepted the established social order whole-heartedly, though within that order most men lacked the property which he believed to be a condition of freedom. Presumably he knew this, and yet was not interested in redistributing the wealth so unequally distributed. In practice, therefore, he was concerned only for the freedom of a small part of the community. His desire to make property secure was so strong, and his sympathies for the class which Saint-Simon was later to call the most numerous and the most poor were so slight, that some of his critics have been loath to admit that he cared much for freedom. They see him much more as a champion of property than as a champion of freedom.

They do less than justice to him. There was no question, when he lived, of redistributing property, and he merely took for granted what almost everyone accepted. Whoever, in his day, put a value on freedom put a value on what in practice could be enjoyed fully only by a small part of the community. Locke claimed for all men what he could hardly have denied, had he been seriously challenged, was still within the reach of only a few. Only the well-to-do, only men of property, could hope, in his day, to take effective action against the abuse of authority; only their conception of a moral law superior to civil law could set a limit to the power of governments. Locke was content that it should be so. It seemed natural to him, as it seemed to nearly all his contemporaries, that the right to resist rulers who have abused their authority should in practice be confined to the educated and propertied classes, to those whom he called 'the industrious and rational',[1] to the section of the community alone capable of passing an intelligent and responsible judgement in such a matter. 'Property is a means to freedom, and only those who have property are able or much concerned to defend freedom.' Though Locke never said this, in so many words, he almost certainly believed it. But his believing it at a time when most men had little or no property is no evidence that he cared for property more than for freedom or that he understood by freedom little more than security of external possessions. The man who wrote the *Letter Concerning Toleration* as well as the two *Treatises of Government* understood by freedom something larger than that, something much closer to what we now understand by it, even though we no longer speak, as he did, of natural rights. Locke did not equate freedom, as Hobbes did, with the right to do what the civil laws do not forbid; nor, as Machiavelli did, with the right to participate in government; nor yet, as Bodin did, with security of external possessions and family rights. Freedom, as Locke understood it, is man's right to live as seems good to him provided he respects the same right in others.

Since Locke's time we have become acutely aware of how much the freedom of the propertyless can be curtailed by the unrestricted exercise by the wealthy of their rights of property. We have therefore gone a long way in restricting these rights. We have also transferred many rights of property from private into public hands. Almost the whole business of government, as Locke and his contemporaries saw it, was to make secure private property as a means to personal freedom; but, as we see it, a large part of its business is to administer public property and to restrict the rights of owners of private property. We justify this great extension in the business of government partly on the ground that it makes for a more smooth and efficient production of wealth and partly on the ground that it extends to all classes some of the freedom which used in practice to be confined to the well-to-do. To Locke it seemed obvious that private property is the condition of freedom, just as to us it seems obvious that private property must be greatly restricted if more than a minority are to have freedom. But Locke was no more guilty than

---

[1] *Second Treatise of Government*, ch. V, § 34.

we are of confusing rights of property with personal freedom. He saw the two as closely connected, as indeed they are. Nobody disputes the closeness of the connection. The freedom men have must depend, in any society, very largely on how property is distributed. We have sought to extend freedom less by ensuring that all men have private property than by transferring rights of property from private to public persons; and now it is being brought home to us that property rights vested in the community can sometimes be as much a threat to the freedom of all classes as the wealth of the rich was to the freedom of the poor.

Locke, at a time when only the wealthy could have much freedom, made a bolder and larger claim for the individual against public authority than anyone, except a few of the extremer sects whose doctrines seemed to threaten the social order, had done before him. He made freedom, conceived more broadly than it had been in the past, seem desirable to a minority strong enough to get it for themselves; he made it seem desirable without making it seem dangerous. Had he foreseen the conclusions to be drawn from his premises by later critics of the political and social order which he cherished, he might have made different assumptions and have aimed at producing a political doctrine justifying aristocracy and condemning democracy. But he did not foresee them, and therefore was not afraid of claiming for all mankind what only a small number could then enjoy.

His political philosophy is, if I may so put it, the soul of liberalism, still confused and inadequate, still far from self-knowledge, strong in its faith and yet ignorant of much that that faith implies. More emphatically than anyone before him, Locke makes freedom a supreme end of government. It is a man's right, he tells us, merely because he is a man, to be allowed to make the best of his life according to his own notion of what is good. Government has nothing better to do than to help him achieve his end, not by giving him what he wants, but by making it possible for him to get it by his own efforts. Coercion is justified, not as a means to national greatness, nor for the sake of Heaven, nor to enable men to attain virtue, nor to increase happiness, nor in the service of a common good transcending individual rights; but only because freedom is not to be had in this world without it. Power held on trust to secure freedom: this, since Locke's time, has been the most persistent of European political doctrines, especially in the liberal West. It was the doctrine of Montesquieu and of several of the French rationalist philosophers, of Kant and even (in some moods) of Hegel, of both the Whigs and the radicals in England, and of the founders of the American republic.

Though Locke, if we take account only of his political philosophy, was not a profound or subtle thinker, that philosophy was and still is strongly attractive. Much more so, indeed, than many others which are logically sounder. Though Locke does not tell us how power should be organized to preserve freedom, his is the first of the great political philosophies to make freedom, conceived in a larger sense than the ability to do what the law allows or what God commands, its central theme. It is freedom which is precious above all things, and not security or salvation or virtue or happiness or national greatness.

The system of government which he preferred to all others was not mere aristocracy; it was liberal aristocracy. His ideal was at bottom much the same as that of Burke and Alexander Hamilton, but he felt no need to condemn democracy since no one was asking for it when he wrote. Thus, though he was certainly no democrat, the principles which he proclaimed in an era of aristocratic resistance to absolute monarchy are still used in the West to justify liberal democracy. We may find many of Locke's arguments inconclusive; we may think him too often careless and superficial. But his heart, we feel, is in the right place; for that place is pretty much where our heart in the West is today. Locke was the first of the great liberals of our era, the first to speak the political language still the most familiar to us. It is a secular, an untheological, language, without being materialist and without excluding God. It is, on the contrary, on easy terms with religion. Yet it explains government, not as an instrument of divine will, but as a device of human wisdom to meet the needs of men taken as rational and moral beings.

Further Readings

A list prepared by Robert Wokler

CHAPTER 1 THE POLITICAL THOUGHT OF THE MIDDLE AGES

R. R. Bolgar, *The Classical Heritage and its Beneficiaries* (first published 1954, Cambridge 1973). A vast, erudite and elegant study of the fortunes of the Graeco-Roman tradition to the end of the sixteenth century, showing how modern civilization drew sustenance from its predecessor by assimilating it, until innovation and discovery came to supplant imitation as the measure of its progress.

J. H. Burns, (ed.), *The Cambridge History of Medieval Political Thought c. 350–c.1450* (Cambridge 1988). A comprehensive study of the development of political ideas and movements in the Middle Ages from their Christian, Greek and Roman sources to the Council of Basel and the conciliarists of the fifteenth century, by twenty leading scholars.

R. W. Carlyle and **A. J. Carlyle,** *A History of Medieval Political Theory in the West* (first published 1903–36, Edinburgh 1950). Completed over a period of forty years, a richly documented, perambulating study of the main currents of political thought from the Roman lawyers of the second century A.D. to doctrines of popular representation in late sixteenth-century France, with particular emphasis upon theories of the supremacy of law.

Otto von Gierke, *Political Theories of the Middle Age,* trans. and intro. F. W. Maitland (first published 1900, Cambridge 1987). A conspicuously learned history of the unity of Church and State, as well as of the tensions between them, in mediaeval political thought, with special reference to ideas of corporate representation and sovereignty which shaped the emergence of the modern State.

Charles H. McIlwain, *The Growth of Political Thought in the West* (New York 1932). A notable history of political theory to the end of the Middle Ages, encapsulating a variety of formulations of the Stoic proposition that authority belongs to kings, and property to persons.

D. J. O'Connor, *Aquinas and Natural Law* (London 1967). A philosophical analysis of the ethics of Aquinas, dealing with the connections between reason and morality, the doctrine of the freedom of the will, and the nature of this theologian's debt to his pre-eminent philosophical precursor, Aristotle.

Alexander Passerin d'Entrèves, *The Medieval Contribution to Political Thought: Thomas Aquinas, Marsilius of Padua, Richard Hooker* (Oxford 1939). An introduction to late mediaeval and early modern Christian doctrines of political obligation, conceived largely as commentaries on Romans 13.1–6, that is, around the proposition that the powers that be are ordained by God.

Brian Tierney, *Religion, law and the growth of constitutional thought, 1150–1650* (Cambridge 1982). A subtle and closely reasoned examination of mediaeval notions of spiritual authority around a variety of concepts such as sovereignty, consent and federalism, in an attempt to show how the juridicial culture of the twelfth century blossomed into early modern constitutional thought.

Walter Ullmann, *Medieval Political Thought* (Harmondsworth 1975). A masterly introduction to theocratic, feudal, imperial and populist doctrines of law and government in the Middle Ages, by way of the multifarious conflicts between the principles and exercise of communal power and rights of resistance, on the one hand, and divinely appointed secular power, on the other.

CHAPTER 2   MACHIAVELLI

Hans Baron, *In Search of Florentine Civic Humanism,* 2 vols. (Princeton 1988). A luxuriantly authoritative collection of essays, produced over a period of fifty years, on the early Italian Renaissance and the vicissitudes of Florentine humanism from the age of Petrarch to that of Machiavelli.

Felix Gilbert, *Machiavelli and Guicciardini: Politics and History in Sixteenth-Century Florence* (Princeton 1965). A richly illuminating study of the intellectual relationship between the foremost political thinker of the Renaissance and its pre-eminent historian, situated at the margins of both Italian politics and humanistic historiography, together undergoing transformations which infused the Florentine spirit of the early sixteenth century with its extraordinary creativity.

J. H. Hexter, *The Vision of Politics on the Eve of the Reformation: More, Machiavelli, and Seysell* (New York 1973). An allusive treatment of three authors and three texts of the same period (above all of More's *Utopia*), each of which exposes the theoretical imperatives of rule to a close scrutiny of concrete circumstances in ways that transformed political perceptions and language.

Friedrich Meinecke, *Machiavellism: The Doctrine of 'Raison d'Etat' and its Place in Modern History,* trans. Douglas Scott (first published in German in 1924, Boulder and London 1984). A still compelling treatment of a central doctrine of political morality, and of its multifarious varieties and critics, most especially in Germany, given its first great formulation by Machiavelli at an extraordinary juncture of European history, when political collapse was confronted by intellectual renaissance.

Hannah Fenichel Pitkin, *Fortune is a Woman: Gender and Politics in the Thought of Niccolò Machiavelli* (Berkeley 1984). A tantalizing study of the sexual conflict between *virtù* and *fortuna* in Machiavelli's thought, around various images of the manliness of independent persons, soldiers and states, whose triumph requires the conquest or seduction of fortune.

J. G. A. Pocock, *The Machiavellian Moment: Political Thought and the Atlantic Republican Tradition* (Princeton 1975). A remarkably broad and compelling discourse on the age of civic humanism, and on the theory and practice of active engagement in political life in the Italian Renaissance, whose influence upon public consciousness is traced through republican doctrines in Stuart and Puritan England, in the work of Harrington, Bolingbroke, the American Federalist Papers and much else besides and between.

Roberto Ridolfi, *The Life of Niccolò Machiavelli,* trans. Cecil Grayson (first published in Italian in 1954, London 1963). The best-informed biography of Machiavelli, full of elegiac admiration for its subject as a brilliant historian, dramatist and correspondent, as well as a uniquely profound and astute political thinker, observer and diplomat.

Quentin Skinner, *The Foundations of Modern Political Thought,* vol. I: *The Renaissance* (Cambridge 1978). A superb commentary on late mediaeval and early modern political thought, addressed to the diverse doctrines of the ideal and rhetoric of liberty, and to the triumph of princely government, in the age of humanism.

Quentin Skinner, *Machiavelli* (Oxford 1981). A fine introduction to the political thought and career of Machiavelli, as counsellor to princes, as philosopher of *virtù,* liberty and glory, and as historian of Florence.

Leo Strauss, *Thoughts on Machiavelli* (first published 1958, Seattle and London 1969). A dazzling interpretation of both *The Prince* and the *Discourses,* pointing in ingenious ways to the irreligious and evil doctrine which Machiavelli taught by insinuation and subterfuge to perceptive readers equally determined to unravel the webbing of his real warp and woof.

CHAPTER 3   THE REFORMATION AND LIBERTY OF CONSCIENCE

J. H. Burns and **Mark Goldie,** (eds.), *The Cambridge History of Political Thought 1450–1700* (Cambridge 1991). A comprehensive study of European political ideas and movements from Florentine civic humanism to Locke's doctrines of toleration and revolution, by twenty-one leading scholars.

A. G. Dickens, *The English Reformation* (first published 1964, 2nd ed. London 1989). A comprehensive, now classic, study of religion and politics in England from the late-fourteenth to the mid-sixteenth century.

A. G. Dickens, *Martin Luther and the Reformation* (first published 1967, London 1977). A compelling biography of Luther, interwoven with a social and intellectual history of his teaching and of the spread of Lutheranism in the early sixteenth century.

Harro Höpfl, *The Christian Polity of John Calvin* (Cambridge 1982). An incisive study of the connections between Calvin's theology and his political career, elaborating the different forms of his commitment to the view that an ecclesiastical polity ruled in accordance with Scripture should co-operate with whatever kind of civil government it happens to find established.

Donald R. Kelley, *The Beginning of Ideology: Consciousness and Society in the French Reformation* (Cambridge 1981). A majestic study of sixteenth-century French political dissent, rebellion, heresy and subversion before the great upheavals of the 1570s.

Elizabeth Labrousse, *Bayle,* trans. Denys Potts (Oxford 1983). A fine bantam intellectual biography, mainly addressed to Bayle's philosophical fideism, not only as a sceptic in a line from Montaigne to Voltaire, but also as a religious thinker in the tradition of Calvin to Rousseau.

Steven E. Ozment, *Mysticism and Dissent: Religious Ideology and Social Protest in the Sixteenth Century* (New Haven and London 1973). A profoundly learned and elegant study of religious dissentients and nonconformists who rejected the authority of the princes, priests and universities of Christendom in favour of spiritual, individualist or communitarian ideals which have come to seem modern but were in fact largely inspired by late mediaeval mysticism.

Quentin Skinner, *The Foundations of Modern Political Thought,* vol. II: *The Age of Reformation* (Cambridge 1978). A richly detailed and pellucid account of the conceptualization of the State in its modern sense as a legal power responsible for government and the sole object of citizens' allegiance, addressed to the Lutheran Reformation, the constitutionalism of the Counter-Reformation, and Calvinist doctrines of resistance.

W. D. James Cargill Thompson, *The Political Thought of Martin Luther,* ed. Philip Broadhead, intro. A. G. Dickens (Brighton 1984). A study of Luther's complex theology of government and society, as informed by a fervent moral radicalism that prompted his critiques of the failings of rulers and subjects alike, and an equally intense political conservatism which excluded reform and resistance, in each case imbued by an Augustinian doctrine of two kingdoms and two callings.

Michael Walzer, *The Revolution of the Saints: A Study in the Origins of Radical Politics* (first published 1965, London 1966). A provocative historical and sociological study of Calvinist politics in the hundred years preceding the English Revolution, showing how discipline and duty inspired neither capitalism nor liberalism but a revolution of saints along lines which would later be adopted by revolutionary citizens.

CHAPTER 4   BODIN

Roger Chauviré, *Jean Bodin, auteur de la 'République'* (Paris 1914). An elegiac intellectual biography of dated style, comprehensively researched, which contends that Bodin's scientific system of politics, in its rejection of utopian principles and embrace of universal in preference to ancient history, surpassed even that of Machiavelli in importance.

Horst Denzer, (ed.) *Jean Bodin* (Munich 1975). The most notable collection of essays ever assembled, in English, French and German, by contemporary authorities, on Bodin's historical, jurisprudential and political writings.

A. London Fell, *Origins of Legislative Sovereignty and the Legislative State,* vol. 3, *Bodin's Humanistic Legal System and Rejection of 'Medieval Political Theology'* (Boston 1987). An erudite discourse on the notion of a legislative state as the most central feature of sovereignty in early modern political thought, addressed to the whole corpus of Bodin's legal and political philosophy, embracing much material on his intellectual world in Toulouse and his opposition to Corasius.

Julian H. Franklin, *Jean Bodin and the Rise of Absolutist Theory* (Cambridge 1973). An interpretation of the shift in Bodin's theory of sovereignty from a doctrine of limited supremacy to one of absolutism, occasioned by his unwillingness to acknowledge legitimate resistance in response to the threat of revolution sparked by the St Bartholomew's Day Massacre.

Julian H. Franklin, *Jean Bodin and the Sixteenth-Century Revolution in the Methodology of Law and History* (New York 1963). A commentary on the humanistic and comparative approach to the study of law of Bodin and other sixteenth-century French jurists, in their move from the method of exegetical authority to that of historical empiricism, anticipating Montesquieu.

Nannerl O. Keohane, *Philosophy and the State in France: The Renaissance to the Enlightenment* (Princeton 1980). A comprehensive study of French absolutist and constitutionalist theory in a period throughout which the monarchy was consolidating its control over a territory of divided peoples, including a commentary on Bodin's theory of sovereignty, which was destined to achieve canonical status in the subsequent history of jurisprudence in France.

Preston King, *The Ideology of Order: A Comparative Analysis of Jean Bodin and Thomas Hobbes* (London 1974). Stresses that sovereignty, for Bodin, refers not to a state's power but to its highest office, conceivably held by an aristocracy or even the populace but generally a king, whose power to command, however, must always be indivisible.

CHAPTER 5   HOBBES

Deborah Baumgold, *Hobbes's political theory* (Cambridge 1988). A thoughtful commentary on specifically political themes in the *Leviathan* (rather than its account of human nature), pointing to Hobbes's concern with the institutionalization of authority and his view of obligation as tied to rôles connected with the performance of civic duties.

Keith Brown, (ed.), *Hobbes Studies* (Oxford 1965). A collection of trenchant and some outstanding essays on themes in Hobbes's moral and political philosophy, pursuing major differences of interpretation by leading scholars of the day.

Maurice Cranston and **Richard S. Peters,** (eds.), *Hobbes and Rousseau: A Collection of Critical Essays* (New York 1972). A notable collection of essays on the central political doctrines of each author, by leading modern experts, mainly gathered from other writings.

David P. Gauthier, *The Logic of Leviathan* (Oxford 1969). Distinguishes Hobbes's masterpiece from his other political works which preceded it and argues that the account of authorization of absolute sovereign power which it sets out forms his most striking and durable contribution to political theory.

F. C. Hood, *The Divine Politics of Thomas Hobbes* (Oxford 1964). An analysis of Hobbes's philosophy which contrasts the *Leviathan* from his other writings on important points of detail but concludes that the whole of his political doctrine remains compatible with Christian ethics, notwithstanding the assumptions of generations of his readers and interpreters who have thought otherwise.

C. B. Macpherson, *The Political Theory of Possessive Individualism: Hobbes to Locke* (first published 1962, Oxford 1979). The most imaginative and provocative study ever published of seventeenth-century English political thought, addressed to apparently bourgeois social assumptions implicit in its leading doctrines.

F. S. McNeilly, *The Anatomy of Leviathan* (London 1968). A closely reasoned account of the profoundest contribution to English political thought, following the formal structure of a system of rational deliberation about the principles of association deduced from definitions of human nature.

Michael Oakeshott, *Hobbes on Civil Association* (Oxford 1975). A collection of pieces led by the author's majestically buoyant introduction to the *Leviathan*, first published in 1946, which elaborates his contention that the political philosophy of Hobbes is the image of the civil order reflected in the mirror of reason.

D. D. Raphael, *Hobbes: Morals and Politics* (first published 1977, London 1982). A fine and discriminating study mainly of Hobbes's moral philosophy, which finds fault with both his metaphysics and psychology, and embraces a useful commentary on recent interpretations.

Leo Strauss, *Natural Right and History* (first published 1953, Chicago 1968). A highly influential account of the transformation of ancient natural law into modern natural right around the pivotal influence of Hobbes, whose conception of man was addressed to the problem of self-preservation in a state of nature and not to the noble prospect of perfection in civil society.

Richard Tuck, *Hobbes* (Oxford 1989). A brisk but comprehensive introduction to the intellectual career of a deeply philosophical sceptic, whose mistrust of the ethics of ancient and humanist precursors, and his dislike of ecclesiastical government, kindled his attraction to the more comforting verities of modern natural science.

Howard Warrender, *The Political Philosophy of Hobbes: His Theory of Obligation* (first published 1957, Oxford 1970). The most closely argued and compelling of the interpretations which identify the natural laws of Hobbes as commands of God that remain obligatory even when unenforceable, thereby explaining how the State may be established by agreements which lack the compulsory character of civil laws.

J. W. N. Watkins, *Hobbes's System of Ideas* (first published 1965, London 1973). An analysis of the political theory of Hobbes designed to show how it is implied by his philosophical ideas, particularly the resolutive-compositive method of mid-seventeenth century Paduan science.

CHAPTER 6   DIVINE RIGHT, ABSOLUTE MONARCHY AND EARLY THEORIES OF THE SOCIAL CONTRACT

J. W. Allen, *A History of Political Thought in the Sixteenth Century* (first published 1928, London 1961). Lively, learned and profound, still a reliable and engaging commentary on the ordeals and principles of Reformation and Renaissance political thinkers.

James Daly, *Sir Robert Filmer and English Political Thought* (Toronto 1979). A close study of Filmer's intellectual milieu, his critics, sources, reputation and relationship to other royalist thinkers of his day, embracing discussions of his doctrines of sovereignty and patriarchalism and his objections to the idea of government by consent.

John Neville Figgis, *The Divine Right of Kings* (first published 1896, New York and London 1965). A work of dated style and gently fading significance, but still notable for its treatment of divinely appointed monarchy, formulated or endorsed by divines, as an anti-clerical weapon of independence from papal control.

J. W. Gough, *The Social Contract: A Critical Study of its Development,* 2nd ed. (first published 1936, Oxford 1957). A patchwork study of contractualist theories of the origin of society and of the establishment of government, from ancient Athens to the American Civil War, including reflections on sixteenth-century *Monarchomachs*, Puritanism and early eighteenth-century German thought.

Bernice Hamilton, *Political Thought in Sixteenth-Century Spain: A study of the political ideas of Vitoria, De Soto, Suárez, and Molina* (Oxford 1963). A commentary on the leading Jesuit and Dominican political thinkers of Spain in an essentially mediaeval world which witnessed a great Thomist revival, mainly devoted to principles of natural law and doctrines of political community.

Donald R. Kelley, *François Hotman: A Revolutionary's Ordeal* (Princeton 1973). A highly engaging biography of the author of *Francogallia*, protégé of Calvin, professor of law, scholar, Huguenot, diplomat and political conspirator during one of the most turbulent periods of European history, perhaps unrivalled in the richness of its major contributions to Western political thought.

Patrick Riley, *The General Will before Rousseau: The Transformation of the Divine into the Civic* (Princeton 1986). An illuminating study, by way of commentaries on Pascal, Malebranche, Bossuet, Fénelon, Bayle, Montesquieu and Rousseau, of the transformation of a theological notion, originally designed by God for the salvation of the soul, into political idea, conceived by citizens to promote the public interest of ᵗate.

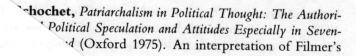

ᵗhochet, *Patriarchalism in Political Thought: The Authori-*
Political Speculation and Attitudes Especially in Seven-
(Oxford 1975). An interpretation of Filmer's

patriarchal justifications of absolutism on the grounds that familial authority is natural, divinely sanctioned and unlimited, and that political power is identical to paternal rule, set in a wider context of predominantly English political thought.

W. J. Stankiewicz, *Politics and Religion in Seventeenth-Century France* (Berkeley and Los Angeles 1960). A study of the fate of the Huguenots and of the politically expedient forms of toleration under autocratic governments in France from the Edict of Nantes of 1598 to its Revocation a century later.

Richard Tuck, *Natural Rights Theories: Their Origin and Development* (first published 1979, Cambridge 1981). An intricately subtle account of the early history of natural rights theory, addressed mainly to the periods 1350–1450 and 1590–1670, when doctrines of rights of dominion and self-ownership, and principles of state authority built upon their contractual exchange, flourished as never before or since in European political thought.

CHAPTER 7 ENGLISH POLITICAL THEORY FROM THE BREACH WITH ROME UNTIL THE RESTORATION

J. W. Allen, *English Political Thought 1603–1660*, vol. I (1603–1644) (all published) (London 1938). In its day masterly, and now a still impressive interpretation of the doctrines and controversies which shaped the great political and religious schism that divided Royalists from Parliamentarians and transformed the constitution of government in England.

H. N. Brailsford, *The Levellers and the English Revolution*, ed. Christopher Hill (London 1961). A learned and impressive, if unfinished, assessment of the principles and interests of the Levellers, as well as of the class, professional and geographical divisions which marked the most exciting chapter in English national history.

G. R. Elton, *The Tudor Revolution in Government: Administrative Changes in the Reign of Henry VIII* (first published 1953, Cambridge 1969). A remarkable study of bureaucracy and public administration under a regime of limited monarchy which sought to provide peace and order without despotism, focused especially on the rôle of the privy council and the reforms of Thomas Cromwell.

Julian H. Franklin, *John Locke and the Theory of Sovereignty: Mixed Monarchy and the Right of Resistance in the Political Thought of the English Revolution* (first published 1978, Cambridge 1981). A study of the doctrine of popular resistance in a mixed monarchy, drawn mainly from George Lawson's *Politica sacra et civilis* of 1660, as adapted later by Locke in his account of the people's right of revolution.

W. H. Greenleaf, *Order, Empiricism and Politics: Two Traditions of English Political Thought 1500–1700* (Hull and Oxford 1964). An expansive and reflective study of two, predominantly English, traditions of political thought, one Christian, associated with royal authority and the divine right of kings, the other Baconian and empiricist, characteristically disposed to mixed government and limited monarchy.

Christopher Hill, *The World Turned Upside Down: Radical Ideas during the English Revolution* (London 1972). A worm's eye view of the popular revolt within the English Civil War, addressed to the doctrines and campaigns of the Levellers, Diggers, Fifth Monarchists, Ranters, Seekers, Muggletonians and, more widely, the fermentation of the common man, longing for self-expression and the millenium.

Joel Hurstfield, *Freedom, Corruption and Government in Elizabethan England* (London 1973). Essentially a collection of essays excavating the mental world of sixteenth-century Englishmen to establish their perceptions of freedom, corruption, patronage and the holding of public office, including comparisons with contemporary affairs in France.

J. G. A. Pocock, *The Ancient Constitution and the Feudal Law: A Study of English Historical Thought in the Seventeenth Century* (first published 1957, revised Cambridge 1987). An exceptionally learned, dazzling study of English constitutional historiography in the seventeenth century, situating the common lawyers' belief in an immemorial constitution against dissentients who pointed instead to its feudal origins, with much sifting of contemporary political debate, foraging into Harrington's account of the history of land tenure, and the rôle of the ancient constitution in the Settlement of 1689 and beyond.

J. P. Sommerville, *Politics and Ideology in England, 1603–1640* (London 1986). An engaging, richly authoritative, often iconoclastic, treatment mainly of the pamphlet literature, sermons and speeches of figures whose doctrines, around the divine right of kings, government by consent, and the ancient constitution and common law of England, were widely representative of informed public opinion in the period from the accession of James I to the advent of the Civil War.

Corinne Comstock Weston and **Janelle Renfrow Greenberg,** *Subjects and Sovereigns: The Grand Controversy over Legal Sovereignty in Stuart England* (Cambridge 1981). A well-researched elaboration of the claim that the radicalization of English political thought following the Restoration was inspired by notions of consent and community, and a principle of co-ordination which bound the King to share legislative authority with Parliament, that had progressively gained ascendancy after 1642.

Perez Zagorin, *A History of Political Thought in the English Revolution* (first published 1954, London 1965). A commendably wide examination of the ferment of predominantly democratic, populist, republican and millenarian, but also communist and royalist, ideas in the most imaginative and incisive period of English political thought, dramatically immediate in its pertinence to the upheavals of contemporary affairs.

CHAPTER 8 LOCKE

Richard Ashcraft, *Revolutionary Politics & Locke's 'Two Treatises of Government'* (Princeton 1986). As comprehensive a study in depth as could ever be hoped for of Locke's place among political and religious dissentients in Restoration England, identifying the *Two Treatises* as a specially radical manifesto unrepresentative even of mainstream Whig opinion in the Glorious Revolution.

John Dunn, *The Political Thought of John Locke: An Historical Account of the Argument of the 'Two Treatises of Government'* (first published 1969, Cambridge 1982). A boldly original contextual reading of Locke's moral and political philosophy around his Calvinist notion of a calling which gives warrant to a popular right of resistance, and explains why labour should be an entitlement granted by God only to the industrious and rational.

Ruth W. Grant, *John Locke's Liberalism* (Chicago 1987). An account of the cautiously liberal implications of Locke's theory of natural equality, which gives rise to a doctrine of consent as the sole foundation for political obligation, and warrants a right of resistance that does not justify anarchy.

W. von Leyden, *Hobbes and Locke: The Politics of Freedom and Obligation* (first published 1981, London 1983). An incisive philosophical reading of the political systems of Hobbes and Locke, particularly notable for its treatments of liberty and determinism in Hobbes's doctrines, and of natural and political powers in Locke's.

Geraint Parry, *John Locke* (London 1978). An elegantly compact treatment of Locke's major writings on politics and religion, embracing his opposition to authoritarianism and to dogmatism, and his attachment to rights protected by the rule of law.

Andrzej Rapaczynski, *Nature and Politics: Liberalism in the Philosophies of Hobbes, Locke and Rousseau* (Ithaca 1987). An incisive and often contentious study of the main contours of the liberal tradition, around Hobbes's, Locke's and Rousseau's divergent but in essence apparently similarly inspired reconstructions of the philosophical foundations of politics, following the birth of modern science and the collapse of both Aristotelian and mediaeval perspectives.

Alan Ryan, *Property and Political Theory* (Oxford 1984). A succinct study of modern political and moral ideas on the relationship between property and work, embracing the philosophies of Locke, Rousseau, Kant, the Utilitarians, Hegel, Mill and Marx.

Nathan Tarcov, *Locke's Education for Liberty* (Chicago 1984). A close reading of Locke's *Thoughts Concerning Education*, showing how his pedagogical ideas, on the education of a gentleman and the cultivation of worldly wisdom, were designed to promote principles of self-reliant and publicly interested citizenship which accord with his political teaching.

James Tully, *A Discourse on Property: John Locke and his adversaries* (first published 1980, Cambridge 1982). A meticulous reading of Locke's theory of property, with reference to the seventeenth-century natural law tradition which forms its most immediate background, showing how Locke adopted many of its conventions while at the same providing a strikingly original account of persons as the proprietors of their own actions or labour.

Jeremy Waldron, *The right to private property* (first published 1988, Oxford 1990). An extraordinarily subtle critique of a variety of arguments purporting to justify an exclusive and unequally distributed right to property, embracing a largely sympathetic treatment of Hegel and a sharply critical account both of Locke's theory and Tully's interpretation of it.

Index